D1281446

The Reading Interests of Young People

THE

Reading Interests

OF

Young People

by

GEORGE W. NORVELL

MICHIGAN STATE UNIVERSITY PRESS

1973

★
★
★
★
★

PREFACE

"Is it not time to revolutionize the teaching of English?" Not until the author has presented analysis of all the data of this forty-year study of literary selections commonly used in junior and senior high school classrooms does he ask this pointed question—the last sentence in the book.

The first edition, published in 1950, *was* revolutionary. It provided statistically reliable data on young people's reactions to seventeen hundred widely used literary selections and was published in the hope that it might accelerate reform and result in the abandonment, so far as class study in common is concerned, of many disliked selections and their replacement by materials of equal quality which young people approve.

Subsequent data, published in this revised edition, more than double the quantity of individual responses and greatly extend the range of the study to include periodicals, newspapers, and comic strips; they confirm a major conclusion of the first edition: that even dedicated teachers in the field of English are poor judges of the reading interests of students.

Teachers searching for solutions to current program problems will sense the author's theme in every chapter and summarizing table. That theme was stated succinctly by Alfred North Whitehead many years ago: "There can be no mental development without *interest*. . . . without *interest* there will be no progress."* Today many more teachers will agree that student interest should be the guiding principle in the choice of literary selections to be read by junior and senior high school students, but they may have only impressionistic information to guide them.

The revised lists provided in this edition should be helpful to the teacher who wishes to base judgment of student interest on a methodologically sound approach. It is especially useful to be reminded that there is a large body of standard literature which has met the tests of scholarly acclaim and of student interest; it is equally useful to recognize the sharp differences in interest of girls and boys. Any teacher can apply the same testing methods in his or her own classes to evaluate interest in more recent literary items not included in this study and to test for changes in interest in older items.

In his Preface to the 1950 edition the author acknowledged his obligation to the thousands of students and hundreds of teachers in

*Alfred North Whitehead in *The Aims of Education*, The Macmillan Company, 1929.

all types of communities and schools who have cooperated in the investigation and especially to Mary P. Eaton, Leah Siegel, Florence Boole, Dr. Kent Pease, and Anthony E. Terino for undertaking independent investigations employing the procedures of the study. For reading all or part of the manuscript and for their valuable suggestions, he expressed appreciation to Dr. Helen M. Walker, Dr. Warren G. Findley, and Mr. Charles M. Armstrong. Quoting the author, "To Dr. William A. McCall, more than to any other individual, the author's indebtedness is deep. His generous guidance during the early stages of the study was invaluable, as were his suggestions for revision of the manuscript." The author further expressed his appreciation to D. J. Kilmade, who tabulated much of the data, and performed innumerable computations, and to Dr. George W. Grill, Grace E. Grill and Jennie Lush for help in the preparation of the manuscript.

At the time of his death in 1970, the author had completed the analysis of all data in the revised edition, the substantial revision of Chapters I through XIII and the writing of new chapters XIV through XIX. In completing the preparation of the final manuscript, I am deeply indebted to Florence C. Eaton for extensive editorial assistance and to Dr. George H. Watson and Elizabeth Grill Watson for critical reading and advice on the manuscript. Mr. Charles M. Armstrong again made a great contribution by reviewing the statistical analysis of data.

ANNABEL NORVELL
Albany, New York

CONTENTS

PART I. *The Investigation*

Part I

The Investigation

CHAPTER I

An Overview of the Problem and Findings

THE DEVELOPMENT OF A READING HABIT BASED ON A LOVE OF reading may well be the most important contribution the school can make to the student's education. Achievement of this purpose would transform the whole program of in-school and after-school education.

Those who have made studies in the field agree almost universally that a habit of voluntary reading will develop only within the limitations set by (1) the reader's ability and interests and (2) the difficulty and attractiveness of the reading materials. It is widely recognized that young people now read below the standards justifiably to be expected for their ages and intelligence. More disconcerting, great numbers of them fail to turn voluntarily to reading for information and recreation.

How best to vitalize reading for young people is a matter of controversy. One group, long dominant in our schools, has insisted that adults should choose from classic and contemporary literature the selections which they are convinced young people should know. This plan has failed to establish the love of reading which had been anticipated. More recently a second approach predicated upon the supposed popularity with boys and girls of lightweight and ephemeral materials has had wide vogue, but it, too, has achieved indifferent results.

Meanwhile there has been increasing recognition of the role played in learning and habit formation by the factor of interest. Granting the dominance of this factor, it seems the high objective— a love of good reading—might be attained through providing young people with an ample supply of literary selections which stand where the lines of student popularity and critical approval converge. The major difficulty in testing this plan has been the lack of knowledge as to which selections pupils genuinely enjoy. It is true that there have been many reading lists issued by experts on reading interests. However, these experts in many instances have been in conflict with each other and with the results of the investigations which have been made in the field. Even the findings of the investigations themselves have been frequently in conflict; and, because the approaches to the problem made by the various studies have been so diverse and so dependent at times upon intricate statistical manipulation, means have been lacking for harmonizing the conflicts.

The current study undertook to establish a procedure for studying the reading interests of adolescents which would incorporate the following specifications:

1. Be sufficiently simple that it could be carried out in any school by a careful teacher without any special training in statistical procedures.
2. Yield results readily incorporable with the results obtained by other independent investigations carried out through the same procedure, thus providing for an accumulation of basic data.
3. Make possible the determination of the number of pupil reports on a literary selection (secured by a given number of teachers in a given number of schools) required to yield a dependable reading interest score for the given selection.
4. Provide a measure of the relative effect upon reading choices caused by the interest factors present in the reader: age, intelligence, sex.
5. Provide a measure of the influence upon reading choices by such interest factors present in the selection itself as adventure, humor, romantic love.
6. Provide a measure of the influence upon reading choices by the

quality of the teaching (superior, average, weak) in the classes where the selections were read.

7. Provide a measure of the change from grade to grade in the enjoyment of literary materials.

The report, it is hoped, may be of interest to two groups: first, to individuals who may wish to make practical application of the findings (teachers, librarians, makers of courses of study, compilers of reading lists, editors of anthologies, and all who are interested in guiding pupils' reading); and second, to students in the field of research who are primarily concerned with the adequacy of the data and the reliability of the methods. Since the technical matter is extensive and may lack interest for the majority of readers, it is proposed at this point to present with chapter references a preliminary summary of the content believed to be of interest to the first group of readers, and to follow that with brief additional references for research students.

The first group may be interested in answers to the following questions:

What is the influence of age, intelligence, and sex upon young people's choices of reading materials? What is the influence of such special characteristics of reading materials as humor, adventure, poetic form, etc.? How well do boys and girls like the individual selections they read or study in school? Which selections are favorites? Which are seriously disliked? How do the various literary types rank in popularity? What are the favorable and the unfavorable interest factors that influence boys' reading? Girls' reading? What evidence is there that boys are discriminated against in the choice of reading materials for school use? Could better materials be substituted? What are the implications of the study for the teaching of reading and literature?

The size of the study (number of titles tested) was nearly tripled, and young people were encouraged to report on selections *read independently* (in contrast to the investigation as first printed, which used only selections studied in class). The final study, using a total of 4,993 selections read independently or studied in class,[1] revealed the following distribution by types:

[1]The total number of selections investigated in this study is 4,993. A limited number are duplications, the same literary selection having been studied in class (as reported in the 1950 edition) and subsequently having been chosen also for independent reading during the latter part of the investigation. In each instance the figures have been given for the teaching method which yielded greater student interest, and no selection appears twice in either of the comprehensive lists.

GRADES	BOOK-LENGTH FICTION	BOOK-LENGTH NON-FICTION	SHORT FIC-TION	SHORT NON-FIC-TION	BIOG-RAPHY	PLAYS	ALL PROSE	ALL POET-RY	TOTAL
10–12	347	107	314	419	99	117	1539	1183	2722
7–9	367	83	364	261	103	30	1327	944	2271

The totals for the prose subdivisions do not include all the titles tested since some do not fall precisely into any of the classifications. In addition to the literary selections tested, scores were obtained for magazines, comic strips, reading topics, and activities. In many instances, the same magazines, comic strips, and reading topics were tested at more than one level. The aggregate of scores from these testings is more than 500.

Based upon an analysis of the data collected, the following suggestions are made in reply to the previously stated questions:

I. Under the plan of grouping young people by grades as now practiced in our public secondary schools, the divergence in ages among pupils of the same grade, so far as the vast majority are concerned, is not a markedly significant factor in selecting reading materials for that grade. The collected data show that in the eighth grade 96 per cent of all pupils were found to be within a four-year span (ages 12–15). Mitigating this divergence in age was the fact that weak pupils average 1.6 years older than superior pupils. Thus, from the standpoint of understanding reading materials, it would seem that the span is considerably reduced. In the eleventh grade, 95 per cent of all pupils were within a four-year span (ages 15–18), while the weak pupils averaged 0.6 year older than superior pupils. Doubtless the smaller spread in age between weak and superior pupils of the eleventh grade as compared with the spread in the eighth grade is accounted for by the withdrawal from school of many overage pupils (Ch. VI).

II. Under the plan of grouping young people by grades as now practiced in our public secondary schools, the divergence in intellectual ability among pupils of the same grade, so far as most are concerned, is not a markedly significant factor in selecting reading materials for that grade. Special consideration should be given to the reading materials selected for those of subnormal ability. For those of superior ability, reading materials should be extensive and widely varied in subject matter (Ch. V).

III. In governing the choice of reading materials of young people in our secondary schools, sex is a universal and highly significant factor (Ch. VIII).

1. If adolescents are to be provided with satisfactory materials, the reading interests of boys and of girls must receive separate consideration.
2. The reading materials commonly used in literature classes are better liked by girls than by boys in a ratio of more than two to one. If boys are to be given a fair chance to develop the reading habit, a major revision must be made in the materials studied in school (Ch. VIII).
3. For reading in common, only materials well liked by both boys and girls should be used.

IV. In choosing reading materials in our secondary schools there are certain special interest factors to be considered: some of these special factors promote interest in reading in both boys and girls; some promote dislike of reading in both boys and girls; others arouse interest in reading in boys only; others arouse interest in reading in girls only (Ch. X.).

The special factors which arouse boys' interest in reading materials, as revealed by the current study, are: adventure (outdoor adventure, war, scouting), outdoor games, school life, mystery (including activities of detectives), obvious humor, animals, patriotism, and male rather than female characters. Unfavorable factors for boys are: love, other soft sentiments, home and family life, didacticism, religion, reflective or philosophical approaches, extended description, "nature" (flowers, trees, birds, bees), form or technique as a dominant factor, female characters.

For girls the favorable special factors are: adventure without grimness (mild outdoor adventure, games, school life, detective and other mysteries), humor, animals, patriotism, love, other gentle sentiments, home and family life, male and female characters. Unfavorable factors: grim adventure (including war), extended description, didacticism, form or technique as a dominant factor, and "nature" (flowers, trees, birds, bees). It should be noted that some factors listed as unfavorable for both boys and girls (form or technique, "nature") are tolerated to a considerably greater degree by girls than by boys. Further, a number of the special factors are not listed as definitely favorable or unfavorable. These factors are regarded as approximately neutral in effect in the majority of selections where they occur (Ch. X).

It should aid in the choice of reading materials to recall that boys give a favorable rating on the average to novels, plays, short stories, and biographies of men; girls rate favorably the same literary types and, further, include biographies of women. It is noteworthy, also, that girls place essays and poems definitely higher than do boys, particularly the ones dominated by the special interest factors found to be favorable for girls (Ch. VIII).

V. The evidence assembled in this study suggests strongly that if teachers generally were to recognize the crucial importance of leading young people to a love of reading, and were to make full use of the means available, the reading program of the schools could be profoundly improved (Ch. XIII; also tables in Chs. XIV–XIX).

Since treatment of the specific procedures used in the study will be found throughout the report, students of research will be directed to particular parts of the discussion through questions and chapter references.

How were the data gathered and processed? (Ch. II.) To what extent are the findings reliable? (Chs. III, IV.) How many pupil reports are required to provide reliable interest scores? (Ch. IV.) How great are the effects exerted on adolescents' choices of reading materials by the influences of the classroom and the community? (Ch. III.) How does good and poor teaching affect reading interests? (Ch. XI.) How do the findings of the current study compare with the findings of other studies? (Chs. VI, XII.)

Is there a need for further investigation in this field? There is general agreement that a wide and detailed knowledge of young people's choices of reading materials and of the factors influencing those choices is of significant concern in the field of education. The extent of the field, embracing both established literature and current writings with respect to which dependable information is urgently needed, makes it obvious that a single investigator can hope to make but a limited contribution.

An examination of the studies made in the field of reading interests makes these factors evident:

1. No two studies have been carried out under the same conditions and by the same methods.
2. There is no means of comparing the results of one study with the results of any other.
3. The conditions and methods have been so involved in many instances that similar investigations on a broad scale would be impracticable.
4. In some studies the data were so scattered that, though large in amount in the aggregate, the usable returns were meager.
5. In some instances the readers' opinions were so obscured by other influences that even after large amounts of data had been summa-

rized there was no way to determine to what degree pupils' views were represented in the results.

6. In certain investigations the procedures employed (e.g., "frequency of mention" in determining the popularity of literary selections) were so distorted by chance factors (e.g., a selection might be on the required reading list of the school reporting, or it might be highly approved by teachers and parents and, consequently, avabilable in every library) that the findings did not represent what they were believed to represent.

7. In some instances dependence was placed by investigators on the number and intricacy of the statistical formulas employed rather than upon adequate data.

8. At times so little of the collected data (e.g., the number of pupils expressing opinions on a particular selection) was published that there is no means available to the prospective user of the results for assessing the reliability of the findings.

An examination of a considerable number of the studies in the field of reading interests seems to indicate that certain fundamental errors in collecting and processing data have been repeated again and again in spite of earlier demonstrations of superior procedures. Every belief, no matter how sanctified by tradition and the support of authorities, should be tested by scientific investigation. Though error in these beliefs be demonstrated but rarely, its discovery will more than justify the search.

In view, then, of the critical need for a continuous supply of dependable data concerning young people's reading interests, and the extent of investigation required, might it not be a justifiable undertaking for a university or educational foundation to establish a permanent research center in this field?

CHAPTER II

Collecting and Tabulating the Data

COLLECTING THE DATA

THE PLAN EMPLOYED FOR COLLECTING THE DATA PROVED TO BE readily understood and easily followed by both teachers and pupils. The instructions which were sent to teachers who agreed to cooperate follow:

PROCEDURE IN FINDING READING INTERESTS OF PUPILS

We greatly desire to find out just how interesting or uninteresting literary selections used in the seventh through the twelfth years are to pupils who read them. This information can be secured from a class in twelve to fifteen minutes, we have found by trial. Would you be willing to secure this information from your classes?

Procedure. The following procedure may be used: announce to the pupils that we desire the frank opinion of each pupil without reference to what any other pupil thinks. This information will make it possible for recommended lists to be prepared which will contain reading materials genuinely interesting to the pupils who are to use

them. BE CAREFUL TO IMPRESS UPON PUPILS THE IMPOR-
TANCE OF GIVING THEIR OWN CANDID OPINIONS. ALSO
PLEASE SEE THAT PUPILS DO NOT CONSULT ABOUT THEIR
REPLIES.

Ask each pupil to take one-half sheet of paper and prepare it to
correspond with the sample enclosed. Half a sheet is suggested because reports will be only half as bulky as would be the case if large
sheets were used. Perhaps the easiest way will be for the teacher to
sketch the heading of the form on the blackboard. (Later, as the study
was continued, mimeographed forms were prepared and furnished
to cooperating schools.)

When the pupils have prepared the forms, except blanks for I.Q.'s
which should be added by the teacher later, read to the class the titles
of selections (poems, essays, short stories, plays, novels, biographies)
studied or read by the class this school year. After writing the title
each pupil should check (x) in column one if the selection was very
interesting to him, in column two if fairly interesting, and in column
three if uninteresting.

NAME OF PUPIL _____ (check one) BOY, GIRL
GRADE _____ AGE _____ I.Q. _____ DATE _____
TEACHER _____ SCHOOL _____

SELECTION AND AUTHOR	VERY INTERESTING	FAIRLY INTERESTING	UN- INTERESTING

We particularly desire to have selections definitely mentioned
by individual titles. For example, if a collection of short stories or
poems was used, list each short story or poem and check separately:

> The Gold Bug—Poe
> The Daffodils—Wordsworth
> Compensation—Emerson

After the reports have been collected, teachers are requested to
add the pupils' I.Q.'s. This information is *very* much desired, if obtainable. *If I.Q.'s are not obtainable please place I, II, or III AFTER
THE NAME OF EACH PUPIL to indicate that the pupil is superior,
average, or slow in his ability to read and understand what he reads.*
The reports should be checked to see that the pupils have properly

filled all blanks. We will summarize the results in Albany. (End of instructions.)[2]

While there was wide variation in the number of literary selections on which individuals reported, pupil questionnaires usually included reports on from 10 to 40 or 50 selections during the school year. In the original investigation, expressions of opinion numbering 1,590,-000, made by more than 50,000 pupils, were tabulated according to the reader's grade in school, sex, and level of intelligence. In more than 200 schools of every size, and representing every type of community and all geographical areas in the state, 625 teachers collected and reported the data.

During the subsequent investigation which was continued through 1963, reports were received from schools in Connecticut, Massachusetts, Illinois, and Ohio, in addition to New York. To the reports on 1700 selections of the first edition, this revision adds 2,556,090 student reports on selections read during the subsequent two decades, yielding a total of 4,993 selections.

A problem in making any investigation based on the approach through questionnaire or report is to eliminate returns that lack genuineness. Often such returns bear evidence of their unsuitability and can thus be readily detected and discarded. With the purpose of providing a further basis for measuring the genuineness of the data received, certain short "key" selections were sent to a considerable number of the cooperating schools with the request that they be read to pupils and the pupils' reactions obtained at the same time that they expressed their reactions to the selections which had been studied as regular classroom assignments. It was hoped that after dependable interest scores had been established for these key selections, they could be used thereafter to measure responses from individual schools or classes, and thus assist in detecting reports that did not represent serious responses. Several thousand reports were secured for each of these key selections and interest scores established for them. An effort was then made to use these key scores as a test of the suitability of returns from schools where the key selections were read to pupils. However, because of the wide distribution of interest scores for a given selection when the groups of pupils reporting are smaller than 150 to 200 each, the plan did not prove as useful an approach to the problem as had been hoped. The tabulated data for these key selections did prove useful in certain other phases of the study, and reference will be made to them at appropriate points in

[2]This procedure was employed throughout the forty-year study, even after George Norvell's retirement.

the report. It is hoped that at a later time a plan may be offered for detecting unreliable data.

Attention is called to that part of the procedure which explains the primary purpose of the study: to improve the level of interest of the reading materials used in English classes. Repeatedly teachers have volunteered the comment that pupils were greatly interested in their part in the investigation and earnest in their efforts to assist in making the study of literature more valuable to future classes. This is not intended to imply that there were no exceptions to this attitude. The evidence appears convincing, however, that most students reported thoughtfully their honest convictions.

The summaries of the pupils' reports were made in Albany for two reasons: (1) summarizing the reports would have required considerable extra work by the local teachers, and thus would have made their cooperation in the study more difficult to secure, and (2) tabulation by trained personnel at a central point would insure, it was believed, more nearly uniform results.

TABULATING THE DATA

Tabulation of the data involved several steps. First, the data from a single class were entered on a first summary sheet. The reports of boys and girls were kept separately. Further, the summaries showed the number of superior (I.Q. above 110) boys and girls who reported a given selection as very interesting, the number reporting it fairly interesting, and the number reporting it uninteresting. Similar data were secured for average (I.Q. 91–110) and below average boys and girls.

The next step was to bring together on a second summary sheet all the data for grades 7 to 9 from various schools which related to a particular literary selection. The data for grades 10 to 12 were kept in another file. Since the records for boys and for girls were kept separate, it was possible to note, for example, on the second summary sheet that 40 superior boys, 60 average boys, and 20 below average boys had found a certain selection very interesting. Likewise, the numbers who found the selection fairly interesting and uninteresting were recorded. These data provided the basis for computing the reading interest scores for the book.

The formula for finding an interest score follows: To the number of pupils reporting a selection "very interesting" add half the number who reported it "fairly interesting." Divide the resulting sum by the total of all pupils reporting. Since there are data throughout for boys and girls separately, scores for boys and for girls are first obtained. These two scores are then averaged to give the interest score for the group.

The possibility of having pupils report on as many as five degrees of liking for a selection instead of three was considered. This procedure would have added greatly to the amount of record keeping and computation. When a statistician pointed out that, with a large number of reports on a given selection, a range of three choices would give, within a negligible fraction for practical purposes, the same scores as a range of five choices, the smaller number was decided upon.

Before applying the formula for interest scores, the reports of superior, average, and below average boys were combined, and a like procedure was followed with girls' reports. Further, all seventh-, eighth-, and ninth-grade reports for boys and girls were combined. A similar plan was followed for reports from students in grades 10 to 12.

After the publication of *The Reading Interests of Young People* in 1950, it was recognized that young people read many selections in addition to those chosen by teachers for class study, and that their reactions might be more favorable to some of these selections. The effect would be to broaden the list of titles satisfactory for class study or for reading by boys and girls in common in their free reading programs. The result was to extend greatly the list of titles fully tested in accord with the approach established for the titles chosen by teachers for class study. As a result the lists found to be suitable for joint study by boys and by girls (or by boys only, or girls only) have been greatly increased and have been given in later chapters: Chapter XIV, fiction; Chapter XV, nonfiction; Chapter XVI, biography; Chapter XVII, poetry and plays.

Each of the selections in Table 41 (for grades 10–12) and in Table 42 (for grades 7–9) includes the following: the total number of boys who reported on it; an interest score for boys in percentage points; similar data for girls; and finally the total number of reports by boys and girls on the selection and a final interest score, the average of the interest scores for boys and girls.

CHAPTER III

What Factors Affect Young People's Reading Preferences?

THE MEMBERS OF A CLASS ARE INFLUENCED IN VARYING DEGREES
by a variety of factors in their enjoyment of the literary selections
they read or study as a class. Among such factors must be considered:
(1) sex; (2) age or maturity; (3) intelligence; (4) special interest factors,
as adventure, humor, etc.; (5) the classroom situation; (6) the teaching
methods used; (7) community influences (including the influence of
the school but not of the particular classroom). The first four of these
factors will each be discussed in an independent, succeeding chapter;
the others will be considered here.

The teacher's influence upon pupils' reactions to their reading will
be discussed under two headings: the classroom situation and teaching methods. The expression "classroom situation," as used here,
means the aggregate resulting from the teacher's personality, his
discipline of the class, and the learning attitude of the pupils. Put
another way, the term designates the factors in the classroom for
which the teacher is primarily responsible, excluding the specific
methods used by the teacher in presenting and developing a particular class assignment. All who are intimately acquainted with the work
of the teacher recognize, I believe, that this "classroom situation,"

with the resulting mind-set of the class, plays a definite part in determining both the amount learned and the satisfactions students derive from their study.

Evidence is available which indicates that the teacher has a definite influence upon the pupils' reactions to the literary selections read or studied in common. This is not the same as saying that the "good" teacher invariably or even usually influences young people to develop a higher than average liking for what they read. This latter point will be dealt with in Chapter XI.

Light is thrown upon the teacher's and the community's influence upon pupils' reading preferences by the data assembled on the key selection "Written in March," which was read to pupils without comment (Ch. II, p. 12). The mean interest score was computed for each of a large number of classes. Classes were paired three different ways, and correlations computed between the mean scores. When the two classes in each pair were taught by the same teacher, the relatively high correlation of 0.67 was obtained; when the two classes in each pair were in the same school but not taught by the same teacher, the correlation was 0.27; when each class was paired at random with a class in a different school, the correlation, expected to be approximately zero, was in fact -0.01. The mean and standard deviation of the differences between paired classes were also computed and are of interest. When the selection was read by the same teacher to two classes in the same school, the mean difference was 8.18 and the standard deviation, 6.03; when it was read by different teachers to two classes in the same school, the mean difference was 10.22 and the standard deviation, 8.55; when it was read by different teachers to two classes in different schools, the mean difference was 13.82 and the standard deviation, 10.49. These data may be summarized as follows:

TABLE 1

CRITERIA FOR PAIRING CLASSES	CORRELATION BETWEEN MEAN SCORES		DIFFERENCE BETWEEN MEAN SCORES		
	N	r	N	MEAN	STANDARD DEVIATION
Same teacher, same school	102	0.67	95	8.18	6.03
Different teachers, same school	116	0.27	116	10.22	8.55
Different teachers, differenent schools	180	−0.01	142	13.82	10.49

For pairs of classes directed by the same teacher, compared with pairs of classes directed by different teachers in the same school, the critical ratio of the mean difference to its standard error is 2.04 (for N of 102 and 116). This difference is in the direction we would expect, and may be said to be reliable at the 2 per cent level of significance. In other words, a difference this large and in this direction would occur fewer than three times in one hundred in such samples if teacher presentation had no tendency to influence pupils' interest in the selection read. We must, therefore, conclude that teacher presentation has an influence on pupil interest.

When results for pairs of classes directed by different teachers in the same school are compared with results for pairs of classes directed by different teachers in different schools, the critical ratio is 3.03 (for N of 116 and 180). This difference is also in the direction to be expected. It is so large that it is reliable at the 1 per cent level of significance. Similarly, when data for pairs of classes directed by the same teachers are compared with data for pairs of classes in different schools directed by different teachers, the critical ratio is 5.24. This difference is highly reliable.

The influence of the teacher and of the community upon reading preferences when the selections were *taught* to students under usual classroom conditions rather than only read to them also was considered. Since no single selection among those studied furnished a sufficient number of cases, random samplings were made from the data available for eight selections totaling 45,260 pupil reports from 39 schools of all sizes and representing all types of communities: *A Tale of Two Cities, The House of the Seven Gables, Julius Caesar, A Christmas Carol, Ivanhoe,* "The Ransom of Red Chief," *The Merchant of Venice,* and "The Freshman Fullback." The following data were obtained:

1. The average of the differences between the scores of 108 pairs of classes when the same selection was taught to both classes of a pair by the same teacher was 6.85, and the standard deviation, 7.67.
2. The average of the differences between 144 pairs of classes when the same selection was taught to each of a pair by different teachers within the same school was 10.50, and the standard deviation, 7.99.
3. The average of the differences between the scores of 99 pairs of classes when the same selection was taught to each of a pair by different teachers in different schools was 12.74, and the standard deviation, 10.75.

These data may be interpreted by the same method employed for results obtained when selections were read to pupils. For pairs of classes when selections were studied under the same teacher, compared with pairs of classes taught by different teachers in the same school, the critical ratio of the mean difference to its standard error is 3.67. So large a difference in the expected direction is reliable at the 1 per cent level of significance. A comparison of results for pairs of classes taught by different teachers in the same school with pairs of classes taught by different teachers in different schools yields a critical ratio of 1.76. The difference is reliable at the 4 per cent level of significance. Finally, when data for pairs of classes taught by the same teachers are compared with data for pairs of classes in different schools taught by different teachers, the critical ratio is 3.87. This difference is reliable at the 1 per cent level.

The data available for the eight selections studied make possible the running of correlations similar to the correlations obtained for "Written in March." The first, comparing the scores of 108 pairs of classes taught by the same teacher, yielded $r = 0.33$. The second, comparing the results for different teachers in the same school (144 pairs of classes) yielded $r = 0.26$. The third correlation, between scores for 99 pairs of classes from different schools, yielded $r = -0.06$. Here, as with "Written in March," the greater relationship is found when the same teacher has charge of both classes of a pair, and little or no relationship is shown when the two classes of a pair are in different schools.

Since we have extensive data on results when reading only was employed, and also extensive data when selections were taught, it might seem desirable to attempt to assess the effect of specific teaching methods as compared with the effect of the "classroom situation" only (p. 15). Unfortunately any conclusions based on a direct comparison of the standard deviations for selections read and selections studied must be regarded as highly tentative because of two factors. First, the selections used in the two procedures were not the same, and the current study provides evidence that the averages and standard deviations of the scores for different selections may vary considerably even when the data are gathered under comparable conditions. Second, it is known that the standard deviations of high percentage scores (e.g., 70 to 100) on the average are smaller than the standard deviations of scores from 40 to 70. This fact can be illustrated by reference to the standard deviations for the key selections used in this study. The average standard deviation for three key selections with high scores (82.3, 92.3, 72.1) is 9.86; for four key selections with lower scores (45.2, 52.4, 54.8, 68.1) is 12.96. The difference between the two averages is 3.1 points.

It may be assumed that a "correction" of some three points in each of the standard deviations obtained for "Written in March" (having the low score 54) is justified in order to permit a more equitable comparison with the standard deviations for selections studied (average interst score, 76.2). These corrected standard deviations would indicate a considerable influence on young people's reading interests through specific classroom methods as distinct from the influence of the "classroom situation." If no correction is made, the evidence for the influence of specific classroom method is negligible.

Taking into consideration the data for "Written in March," which was *read* to pupils, and the data for the eight selections *studied*, the following conclusion appears justified. Assuming an equal number of pupils in each instance, when data relating to the reading preferences of adolescents are gathered from a single school, the resulting interest scores will be closer to the true scores for young people in general if the data are gathered from several teachers' classes rather than from one. Conditions otherwise being equal, scores revealing reading preferences also will be closer to the true scores for young people in general when gathered from several schools rather than from only one school. Further, generally we must expect data on young people's reading preferences secured in a single school or by a single teacher to be skewed by the special influences of the community, the school, and the teacher, regardless of the number of pupil reports assembled.

CHAPTER IV

How Reliable are the Scores for Reading Interests?

A MAJOR RESULT OF THE INVESTIGATION, AS PREVIOUSLY MEN-
tioned, is the provision of interest scores for 4,993 selections read or
studied in grades seven through twelve. (See Part II, Tables 41 and
42, pp. 179–432.) If the data are to be of service to teachers and
curriculum planners, the limits within which they are dependable
should be known.

Studies available at the time this investigation was undertaken had
not determined the number of reports needed to provide a practical
guide for determining the level of popularity of a given selection. In
actual practice a wide divergence was found in the minimum number of reports offered as a basis for an interest score for a given title.
Crow (No. 5) used a minimum of 119 reports; McConn (No. 13) 100
reports; the Winnetka study (No. 23) 25 reports. In Abbott's study
(No. 1) and in the one made by Huber-Bruner-Curry (No. 10), the
number of reports received on individual selections was not stated.
In the absence of reliable information as to the minimum number of
reports required, a decision was made to publish data on a given
selection only when a minimum of 300 pupil reports was available.

The average number of reports for the selections tested in this study is 828.

Believing that such factors as the community, the particular school, and the personality and methods of the teacher were factors that might influence to a significant degree of level of liking pupils might have for a given selection, an additional rule was made. In formulating the following rule the teacher and the school were regarded as representing equal influences in modifying a pupil's reaction. If one teacher from each of two schools obtained pupil reports the teacher-school score would be 4 (two schools, two teachers). If three teachers in the same school obtained reports, the teacher-school score would be 4 (one school, three teachers). A teacher-school score of 16 was required with a minimum of 300 reports.

However, when the number of reports was 350 or more, the rule that there be a minimum of 16 teachers and schools was modified. Since it was known that increasing the number of reports increased the reliability of the findings, it was assumed that, as the number of reports increased, the teacher-school total could be lessened without lessening the reliability of the interest score. Lacking data for determining how great an increase in the number of reports would be equal in influence to one school or one teacher, an arbitrary decision was made that in applying the rule of 16 the factors would be assigned the following values: 1 school equals 1 teacher equals 50 pupil reports. To illustrate: 400 reports from 14 teachers and schools, and 300 reports from 16 teachers and schools, both met the minimum requirements. Admittedly this rule of 16 was an unscientific attempt to safeguard results against influences that at the time were only assumed to exist.

Since for each of the selections reported upon in the current study there are from 300 to more than 8,000 pupil reports, it seemed useful to determine the reliability of interst scores based on widely varying numbers of reports. Because the amount of work involved is great in establishing empirically the standard deviation for one total of reports (e.g., 300), and a minimum of 12 such standard deviations was desired, the plan followed was to compute standard deviations for three totals of reports: 100, 300, and 800. Through the use of the formula $\sigma_\rho = \sqrt{\dfrac{pq}{N}}$, theoretical standard deviations were obtained also for the same three totals as well as for ten additional totals of reports. A comparison of the three empirical standard deviations with the corresponding theoretical standard deviations provided a basis for estimating the empirical standard deviations in the ten additional cases where the theoretical standard deviations only had been obtained. The use of the formula $\sigma_p = \sqrt{\dfrac{pq}{N}}$ will be further

discussed later in this chapter.

In finding an answer to the question "How dependable are the 4,993 interest scores established in this study and reported in Tables 41 and 42?" certain data that had appeared excessive when tabluated proved to be highly useful. The instructions to cooperating teachers requested that reports be secured from pupils on all selections used in a given class during the then current year. Because certain selections are used much more frequently than others in English classes, the numbers of pupils reporting on different titles varied greatly. By the time 300 reports had been tabulated for some of the less frequently used titles, certain others had totals of 4,000 to 7,000. These selections, with thousands of reports each, provided the data used in computing the reliability of interest scores based on varying totals of pupil reports. It was assumed that an interest score based upon 4,000 to 5,000 reports was close to the true score. This assumed true score was used to measure or test scores obtained from samples of 100 or 300 or 800.

The plan followed, though simple, called for extensive tabulation and computation. To determine the reliability of interest scores based on 800 reports, samples of 800 reports (average) were taken from the final summary sheets for *Treasure Island* and other selections having large totals of reports. These samples were taken in such a manner as to satisfy the minimum requirements as to number of teachers and schools. Randomness of sampling was secured through having data taken at uniform intervals on the final summary sheets (e.g., the total number of reports from every third school until approximately 800 had been secured). Sampling was so planned and carried out as to duplicate, so far as possible for each sample, the returns that would have been secured had the 800 reports been collected in a completely independent study. It was realized that only by such a procedure would the figures for reliability represent actual field conditions and procedures. As shown in Table 2, a total of 58 samples of 800 each was secured from 8 titles having total reports from 4,813 ("Sohrab and Rustum") to 6,721 *(Ivanhoe)*.

Since the total number of distinct samples of 800 reports each which could be obtained from the data for any one title was too small, interest scores for all 58 samples of 800 reports from the 8 selections were used. These 8 selections had slightly different averages but similar variability. In order to secure a single distribution representing the characteristic dispersion, the averages of each selection were equated to the averages of the 8 selections. The standard deviation

TABLE 2

EMPIRICAL AND THEORETICAL VALUES FOR σ FOR VARYING NUMBERS OF REPORTS
(Interest Scores, 70 per cent*)

VALUE OF N	NO. OF SAMPLES USES TO FIND THE EMPIRICAL σ	EMPIRICAL σ	THEORETICAL σp IN PERCENTAGE POINTS	RATIO OF EMPIRICAL σ TO THEORETICAL σp	ESTIMATED EMPIRICAL σ	VALUE OF 1.5 σ
25			10.00		12.50	18.75
50			7.07		8.84	13.26
100	79	6.14	5.00	1.23		9.21
200			3.54		4.43	6.65
300	124	3.40	2.89	1.18		5.10
400			2.50		3.13	4.69
500			2.23		2.79	4.19
800	58	2.31	1.77	1.30		3.47
1250			1.41		1.83	2.75
1600			1.25		1.63	2.45
2500			1.00		1.30	1.95
5000			0.71		0.92	1.38
8000			0.56		0.73	1.10

*An interest score of 70 would be produced if 50 per cent marked a selection "very interesting," 40 per cent marked it "fairly interesting" and 10 per cent, "uninteresting." The score of 70 could, of course, arise from many other combinations.

of these 58 interest scores was found to be 2.31. This may be interpreted to mean that when interest scores are based on a minimum of 800 pupil reports, approximately two thirds of such scores will fall within 2.31 points of the theoretical true scores. For example, with an obtained score of 75 the chances are two out of three that the true scores lies between 72.7 and 77.3

Further, we may expect the true score to lie within 1.5 standard deviations (3.47 points) of the obtained score approximately 87 per cent of the time. Since the true score is as likely to be above 75.0 as below it, we may say further that only once in about 15 times may we expect the true score to *lie below* 71.5 (75 − 3.5). For practical purposes our primary concern is that the true interest score shall not be too far *below* the obtained score. That the true score for a particular selection should be higher than the obtained score not only would not weaken the selection's usefulness in the classroom but would enhance it.

In view of the operation of the principle of diminishing returns when the number of pupil reports is increased beyond 300, the next 500 reports reduce the standard deviation by only 1.09 points. Remembering the considerable range within which interest scores are regarded as indicating selections desirable for reading in common in the classroom (80.0 to 100), it is believed that 1.5 standard deviations represent an appropriate limit of error to be added to, or subtracted from, an interest score to indicate the probable range within which the true score will be found. With this in mind the values of 1.5 standard deviations, as well as the values of 1 standard deviation, have been given for the 13 values of N in Table 2. Anyone preferring to use 2 or 3 standard deviations rather than 1.5 standard deviations in this calculation can readily prepare his own table of values.

On pages 21–22 the method employed in determining the empirical standard deviation of interest scores based on 800 reports was described in some detail. By a similar procedure the standard deviations for interest scores based on 100 reports and 300 reports were obtained. In securing the standard deviation for scores based on 100 reports, 79 samples of 100 reports each from 6 selections were used. Since 300 pupil reports is the minimum used in the current study, it seemed advisable to go to considerable effort to determine as nearly as possible the empirical standard deviation for samples of this size. Therefore, 124 samples of 300 reports each from 10 selections having a total of 55,000 pupil reports were used.

Column 3 of Table 2 gives the empirical standard deviations for interest scores based on 100, 300, and 800 pupil reports. It is recognized that such an empirical standard deviation is not the exact sampling standard deviation of interest scores but a very close approximation to what would be found if infinitely many samples of the same size and kind could be taken. The term "empirical" is used to distinguish the standard deviation based on large numbers of samples of reports from the theoretical standard deviation obtained by using the formula $\sigma_p = \sqrt{\dfrac{pq}{N}}$.

In column 4 of Table 2 we have σ_p for scores based on varying totals of reports from 25 to 8000. A comparison was made between the σ_p and the empirical standard deviation, which showed that for scores based on 100 reports the empirical standard deviation was 0.23 greater than the σ_p; for scores based on 800 reports the empirical standard deviation was 0.30 larger. In column 6, then, the estimated standard deviations derived from σ_p are given. For values of N from 25 to 500, the σ_p in each case was increased by 25 per cent, and for values of N from 1,250 to 8,000, the σ_p was increased by 30 per cent. It is believed that the values for the standard deviation given in column 6 represent close approximations to the standard deviations which would have been secured had they been calculated from obtained interest scores rather than by the use of the formula σ_p.

Why should the empirical standard deviation prove to be uniformly greater than the theoretical standard deviation even with large samples (800)? During the collecting and processing of the data, the writer had noted and been puzzled by a greater than expected variation in interest scores for the same selections when these scores were based on pupil groups that represented variations, for example, in social or economic status. A colleague[3] in the State Education Department of New York pointed out that the data of the study manifest the characteristics of a Lexis Series[4] in which the probability of liking a selection varies from group to group (economic, religious, social, ethnic, etc.) instead of remaining constant, as would be expected in a single homogeneous population. Previous investigations of children's reading interests have usually assumed a homogeneous population and applied formulas suitable for a Bernoulli distribution. The current study has been conducted on the same assumption. However, the findings above presented, as well as the evidence of Waples and Tyler's investigation[5] of the reading interests of adults, suggest that future studies should give careful consideration to the influence of group differences in determining reading choices.

[3]Charles M. Armstrong, Associate Statistician, State Education Department, Albany, New York.
[4]Arne Fisher, *The Mathematical Theory of Probabilities*, pp. 117–126, Macmillan, 1923.
[5]Douglas Waples and Ralph H. Tyler, *What People Want to Read About*, pp. 172–186, University of Chicago Press, 1931.

CHAPTER V

Influence of Intelligence on the Reading Interests of Young People

THREE FACTORS INHERENT IN PEOPLE INFLUENCE THEIR READING: intelligence, age, and sex. We may call these the general interest factors. Certain other interest factors residing in the reading materials, which may relate to content (humor, adventure) or to form (poetic, prosaic), will be designated the special interest factors. It is proposed in the following chapters to consider the extent to which each of the general factors, and certain of the more important special factors, influence young people's reading interests.

As noted on page 11, the teachers who secured the reports of young people's reading interests entered upon the blanks either the pupils' intelligence quotients or the teachers' estimates of the pupils' ability in reading. These data made it possible to consider the effect of intelligence upon adolescents' choices of literary selections.

Thirty-six selections ranging from very difficult to easy were chosen for this purpose: the 12 key selections (page 12) which were *read* to pupils and 24 of the selections *studied* in class. Since the proportion of pupils rating below 90 intelligence quotient was known to be low (16.9 per cent of the pupils who reported on the 36 selections and for whom intelligence quotients were available), a prime consideration in the designation of the 36 selections was that they have large totals of reports. This was necessary in order that interest scores derived for weak pupils alone should be based upon sufficient reports. Aside from this requirement the sample was random. The smallest number of pupil reports for any selection read was 5,045; for any selection studied, 1,203. Both the selections read and the selections studied represented a wide range in difficulty and in interest.

Two tabulations were made of interest scores for all 36 selections using only the reports from pupils for whom there were recorded intelligence quotients. For the 36 selections there was a total of 50,745 votes from more than 12,000 pupils with recorded intelligence quotients. For these pupils the average interest scores for the 36 selections were as follows: for superior pupils (I.Q. above 110), 69.14; for average pupils (I.Q. 90–110), 68.88; for weak pupils (I.Q. below 90), 69.06.

It will be observed that the spread between the average interest scores of superior and average pupils is 0.26 point; between the average scores of superior and weak pupils, 0.08 point. It appears that ordinarily superior, average, and weak pupils enjoy equally well the selections commonly studied in secondary school. Further observation of the data tended to strengthen this conclusion. The interest scores of superior, average, and weak pupils for each of the 36 selections were examined to determine whether differences in scores revealed a uniform trend up or down. In other words, did the 3 interest scores for a given selection increase or decrease consistently from superior to weak, or were there cases where the score of weak pupils was closer to the score for superior pupils than was the score of average pupils? A tabulation revealed that for 17 selections there was an increase or decrease in score by regular steps, while for 19 selections the score for weak pupils was nearer the score for superior pupils than was the score for average spupils.

A second tabulation of the interest scores for the 36 selections based on the reports from pupils whose intelligence quotients were furnished provides further evidence as to the part played by reading ability in determining the ratings by young people of literary selections for interest. This time the data for the 12 selections read to pupils and for the 24 selections studied were tabulated in separate sections. For the 12 selections *read* to pupils, the average scores were: for superior pupils, 57.5; for average pupils, 57.5; for weak pupils, 57.2. For the 24 selections *studied*, the average scores were: for superior pupils, 74.9; for average pupils, 74.6; for weak pupils,

74.8. A comparison of the 2 sets of scores indicates that when pupils did no reading but merely listened, the same uniformity of interest was shown by the 3 ability levels as was shown when selections were studied.

NOTE. The fact that for the selections *read* the three scores are much lower than the three scores for the selections *studied* is not evidence pro or con that young readers like the same selections better when studied than when read, since the selections read to pupils were originally chosen to include several which young people strongly dislike.

The question may be asked: Regardless of averages for groups, do superior children like *different* selections than do the weak? An approach to the problem was made by dividing the 36 selections into three groups: very easy selections; selections of medium difficulty; and very difficult selections. Of the 8 classified as very easy, 5 proved to be better liked by superior pupils, 3 by weak. Of the 24 classified as of medium difficulty, 10 were better liked by superior pupils; 14 were better liked by the weak. Of the 4 very difficult selections, 3 were better liked by superior pupils, and 1 was better liked by weak pupils. Obviously, it is not possible to draw the conclusion that easy selections are better liked by weak pupils, and more difficult selections are better liked by the superior. Indeed, the fact is that the three very difficult selections which were less liked by the weak pupils than by the superior, are also disliked by the superior. That is, the use of the criterion of pupil-appeal results in the rejection of the three selections by all groups of pupils. Further, the one very difficult selection liked better by weak than by superior pupils is acceptable to all groups.

An examination of the total list of thirty-six selections demonstrates the same relationship. The selections well liked by the superior are liked also by the weak, and selections rejected by the weak are the ones rejected by the superior.

The writer made an extended investigation of the preferences of superior, average, and slow children in grades 4 to 6 and reported the results in *What Boys and Girls Like to Read* (No. 15). On the basis of reports on 316 selections in 11 reading fields, it was found that 123 of them were better liked by the superior, 187 better liked by all children, and 6 equally liked. The superior rated the 316 titles on average 0.8 point lower than children in general.

A further investigation of the problem was carried out in grades 3 to 12 and published in Chapter 5 of *What Boys and Girls Like to Read* (No. 15). In the elementary grades, the evidence indicates that in the following areas there is no significant difference in interest between I's and all children: adventure, patriotism, wild animals, farm animals and pets, home and mother, myths and legends, and fairy stories. Of 50 selections about nature, 42 were preferred by all pupils compared with 7 preferred by the bright; and of 45 dealing with the didactic and religious, 30 were preferred by all pupils while 15 were preferred by the bright. A summary for 316 titles representing 11 reading areas showed 187 preferred by all chidren; 123 by the superior.

Since educators assume that literary quality is a major factor in reading interest and that bright children are especially moved by it, it was given extended attention. Critically acclaimed selections (72) by more than a dozen great writers were tested for interest with the bright and with all students in junior high school. The average interest scores for the two groups differed by only one-tenth of a point. A similar procedure in senior high school with 26 titles of high literary quality found the two ability groups two-tenths of a point apart. In grades 4 to 6, 40 selections of outstanding quality were better liked by all students compared with the superior by an average of 1.3 points. When 29 high grade poems by children's poets were used in the same grades, similar results were obtained. In the third grade, ratings for 30 poems by great writers supported the findings at the other grade levels.[6] It may be added that selections noteworthy primarily for artistry are ranked among the lowest of the special groupings by children of all intelligence levels.

In the writer's earlier report, it was noted that the study of children's interests in humor had not been carried far enough to permit conclusions as to the relative preferences of students of different ability levels in this field. A careful investigation of the question has since been made.

"Bright Children's Interests in Humor, Grades 10 - 12," which was published as a table on page 47 of *What Boys and Girls Like to Read* (No. 15) presents data for the senior high school. It shows that of 144 titles of subtle and of obvious humor from prose and poetry, more than two thirds (103) are better liked by superior students than by all students by 2.1 points, high enough to be significant. It appears significant also that the superior boys and girls combined gave higher scores than students in general to all four of the divisions of humor. The study revealed further that bright girls enjoy humor definitely better than bright boys. When a comparison is made of the 7.9 points by which all girls like the 144 selections better than all boys with the

[6]For a discussion of possible reasons for the lower ratings by bright children, see pages 45–46 of *What Boys and Girls Like to Read* (No. 15).

score (5.1) by which the same girls rate the 144 selections higher than bright boys only, we note that bright boys in senior high school enjoy humorous selections more than all boys.

In the elementary grades, 59 humorous stories and poems were tested with the bright as well as with all students. Twenty-eight were better liked by the superior and 31 by all children. The average interest score of the superior was 0.4 point lower than the interest score of all. Of ten humorous limericks, all children preferred seven with an average score 1.4 points higher than that given by the bright. The results suggest that with young children in grades 4 to 6 (in contrast to the findings for senior high school students) humor is almost equally favored by children of different levels of intelligence. In grade three, it was found that two thirds of 105 humorous titles were better liked by all pupils compared with the bright by the significant average difference of 1.7 points.

That content rather than literary quality is reponsible for the reading preferences of children of all ability levels is supported by Coy (No. 4), who compared the reactions of a class of gifted children with a control group of average and below average pupils with this conclusion: "In literary value of the books preferred, the two groups are practically equal." Huber's investigation of youngsters' interests in reading (No. 9) states: "A striking similarity exists in the choices of dull, average, and bright children for types of literature, each type representing equally good selections from the available materials of that type."

The extensive evidence examined in grades 3 to 12 supports the view that in *most* reading areas there are no significant differences in the preferences of the bright and of all young people. However, there appear to be minor exceptions. Selections on nature and didacticism and religion appear to be less liked by the bright, and in the senior high school, humor is better liked by the superior compared with students in general.

The question may be asked: What influence, if any, do variations in the ages of children of different ability levels have on their reactions to reading? Thorndike concludes on page 35 of his study (No. 21): *"In their pattern of reported reading interests, bright children (median I.Q. about 123) are most like a group of mentally slower children (median I.Q. about 92) who are two or three years older than they are.* The patterns of interest for bright and slow children of the same age are much alike . . . , but the resemblance is increased when the bright children are two or three years younger than the slow group."

Further evidence is afforded by the writer's study. The ages of

3,583 students in grades 7 to 9 from 16 representative schools were so tabulated as to show separately the data for the three ability groups. The tabulation revealed that weak students in junior high school classes averaged 1.62 years older than superior students. Among 3,326 senior high school students from 16 representative schools, the weak were found to average 0.82 of a year older than the superior students. In view of the finding that superior and weak students on average enjoy equally the literary selections studied in secondary schools, we appear justified in concluding that the spread of approximately two years in average age between the superior and weak students in junior high school classes, and of approximately one year between superior and weak students in senior high school classes, does not affect adversely the reactions of young people toward the literary selections studied in class. Indeed it appears difficult to escape the conclusion that moderate retardation of weak students and moderate acceleration of superior students contribute to the near identity of interest of these groups toward selections studied in common.

CHAPTER VI

How Age Influences Reading Preferences: Major Trends

To WHAT EXTENT DOES AGE INFLUENCE READING PREFERENCES? Before presenting data from the current study which bear on this question, certain limitations restricting the scope of the discussion will be pointed out. First, all evidence collected by previous investigators, as well as general observation, suggests that during the elementary school period children's reading interests undergo a more rapid change than during the subsequent period (covered by this investigation). Second, few of the selections included in this study would be classified as juvenile; yet here, too, the consensus is that young people's tastes change more rapidly in juvenile than in adult reading materials. The data to be presented next relate only to students' reactions to adult literature during their years in junior and senior high school.

At the time of the writer's first investigation of the reading interests of high school students (as published in 1950), a tabulation was made of paired scores for 236 selections: one score at the eighth grade level, the other at the eleventh. The net gain in interest was found to be 0.5 point yearly. The more extensive study revealed that there is little, if any, gain or loss during this period. During the current investigation, paired scores by random sampling for 100 miscellaneous titles tested in both junior and senior high school indicated an average loss of interest of 0.25 point yearly. Lyric poems averaged a gain, while narrative poems registered a loss for the three years. Literary essays showed an average gain; stories of adventure, a loss. An examination of 30 groupings of prose and poetry suggests that young people in junior and senior high school are almost equally interested in general reading.

As already explained on page 14, the data on a given selection for the three years of junior high school were combined to yield a single interest score rather than used to produce a separate score for each year. Data from senior high schools were treated in like manner. As a result the junior high school score for grades 7, 8, 9 is considered as a score for grade 8 and the senior high school score, a score for grade 11. This provides a measure of the change in interest occurring during a three-year high school period.

Two movements of adolescents' reading interests which these data permit us to measure are of value in planning reading programs:

1. the amount of change and the direction of the change of young people's interest in adult literature *taken as a whole;*
2. the average rate of change of young people's interest in individual selections *regardless of whether the interest in a particular selection increases or decreases.*

First, let us attempt to answer the questions implied in the statement of movement 1. Tabulation of the pairs of scores for the 236 selections (one score at the eighth grade level, the other at the eleventh) showed that 137 selections had an average gain of 6.1 points for the 3 years, and 98 selections had an average loss of 4.9 points. (One selection showed no change.) The net gain in interest was 0.5 point yearly for the 236 selections.

The average rate of change in pupils' reading interests in *individual selections* between grade 8 and grade 11 (movement 2, above) was obtained by totaling the changes, *both decreases and increases,* for all selections and dividing by 236. This average rate of change for the three-year period was found to be 5.6 points, or 1.9 points yearly.

It was recognized when the first study was made that this yearly average (1.9 points) would be increased by any reversals of the trend of interest occurring during the three-year period. To illustrate: Suppose selection A rose in interest from a score of 70 in grade 8 to 74 in grade 10, and then declined to 73 in grade 11. The difference in interest scores for grade 8 and grade 11 would be 3 points, an apparent yearly change of one point. However, the actual change would be 5 points (4 points up to 74, and then one point down), or an average yearly change of 1.7 points.

Though the data on reversals were insufficient at the time, a study of the subject was made later in *The Reading of Americans*.[7] Among conclusions were the following: Both individual selections and reading fields are subject to reversals of trends in interest. The ages when reversals of interest in major reading fields as well as in subdivisions of a field (lyric poetry; narrative poetry) may vary. Reversals of interest trends may occur at different ages for boys and girls. During the period from childhood to old age, both boys and girls average approximately one reversal in each reading field. Individual prose titles have reversals of trend in interest oftener, on average, than one from age 10 to age 60, and individual poems average almost two reversals during the same period. The downward trend in interest in reading reaches a nadir in young adulthood.

Though the average change in interest during the three-year period is small, individual changes vary considerably. Based on the data for the 236 selections, only 1 in 6 selections changes in interest level as much as 3 points yearly during the high school period; only 1 in 47 changes 5 points; and only 1 in 236 changes as much as 8 points per year.

Assuming that these rates of change are approximately correct, the teacher has in them an aid for extending the applicability of interest scores established for a particular grade. As noted earlier, results of the current study have been used for many years in many schools for making assignments in literature. Reports indicate that selections with an interest score of 70.0 have proved generally acceptable for class study. It may be noted, too, that the interest level 70.0 is high enough to exclude two out of three of the selections now most widely used in high school literature classes. To illustrate, suppose that the interest score for selection C has been found to be 82.0 in the tenth grade. Without waiting for further testing the teacher could use the selection in classes two grades above and two grades below with high probability that it would prove interesting to the students concerned. Similarly, a selection scoring 75.0 could be used one grade above and one grade below the one for which the score had been established.

Earlier in this chapter the problem of reversals in the trend of interest in young people's reading interests was discussed. An allied

[7]Although the author completed the manuscript of *The Reading of Americans*, reporting his investigations into adult reading interests, it is at this time unpublished.

problem will be discussed here because it has an important bearing on the application of the findings of studies of reading interests. Do children's interests in a particular selection increase over a period of years to a peak and then level off or decline, or is there an erratic zigzagging of interest with a change in direction every year or two? There is wide agreement among investigators that where juvenile fiction is concerned there is a rise extending through a period of years to a peak of interest and then a decline, and that young people do not later return to an interest in juvenile stories. Is the pattern for secondary school pupils with respect to adult literature completely different? Do the reading interests of these older adolescents change direction frequently and erratically, or do their reading interests with respect to a particular kind of material rise or decline, as the case may be, over a period of years? Obviously, if interest in adult adventure stories, for example, were high in the seventh grade, low in the eighth, high again in the ninth, etc., it would be impossible to have any idea with respect to the suitability of adventure stories for any particular grade except through the most extensive testing for that grade, and for every other grade in which it might be proposed to use such stories. On the other hand, if young people's interest in adult adventure reaches a peak in the eighth or ninth grade and the interest remains high throughout the remainder of the high school period, the problem of guiding adolescent reading is considerably simplified. The question is raised here because there is conflict in the evidence furnished by previous investigations. It is proposed to examine the evidence and conclusions of certain studies which have considered this problem, and to present the findings of the current study.

Russell and Bullock (No. 18) asked fifteen hundred pupils to express their preferences as to stories relating to the following: adventure, travel, great men, great women, love, ghosts, detectives, and war. Their data, collected from pupils in grades three to twelve, show that for every one of the interests tested a high point was reached after a period of years and then remained high or gradually receded over a period of years.

Anderson (No. 2), in 1912, made a study in which data with respect to boys' and girls' reading interests were collected in a manner similar to Russell and Bullock's. One of Anderson's instructions submitted to high school pupils in Fort Dodge, Iowa, read as follows: "Underline the kinds of reading that you like: travel, great men, great women, adventure, love stories, ghost stories, detective stories, war stories, how to make things, and science." Reports were received from 588 pupils for grades 9 to 12. In view of the fact that the 588 pupils represented 4 different grades further subdivided into boys and girls (a total of 8 groups), and that pupils checked only the kinds of reading which they *liked*, the results for the subdivisions could hardly be expected to be entirely dependable. However, for grades 9 to 11 the findings accord with those of Russell and Bullock to a fairly high degree.

Thorndike (No. 21), through the use of annotated titles in grades 4 to 12, drew conclusions with respect to trends in reading interests. Pupils were supplied with questionnaires on which they indicated their interest in particular titles by checking one of three levels of interest. Interest scores for the various titles were computed through the use of the formula employed in the current study.

Results obtained by Thorndike correspond with those of Russell and Bullock, and Anderson in finding that there is with most interests a rise to a high point and then a decline rather than a frequent change in direction. Certain differences in Thorndike's approach prevent a *pari passu* comparison with the two studies just discussed. Possibly the difference in Thorndike's approach which interferes most with a satisfactory comparison is the fact that in certain groupings the specific titles employed prevent the pupil's decision from being made solely on the intended specific interest factor. For example, under "Adult Adventure" we find the title "Fortunes of War." The annotation reveals that this is a story having a girl as the leading character and a strong love element. Boys would be prejudiced against this title (as shown later) in spite of the fact that stirring adventure is probably the most favorable single interest factor with boys. On the other hand, girls who are unfavorably affected by "war," are very favorably disposed to both "women characters" and "love."

Under "Mystery and Detective" two of the four titles, "Pieces of Eight" and "The Skeleton Walks," are shown by the annotations to be juvenile stories. These examples, which could be multiplied, are cited to bring out that the high point of interest for a given story might have been found at a different age level had the interest factor concerned been uninfluenced by alloying elements, as was true in the two earlier studies. Russell and Bullock, and Anderson used such general terms as "stories of adventure" and "detective stories," which permitted the pupil to interpret the interest factor without modifying influences.

While it may not be possible, then, to compare fairly the results of Thorndike's study with the other two so far as the time of the high point of interest for various factors is concerned, it does appear significant that in not one of the twenty-two categories under which

Thorndike deals with reading interests, and for each of which he designates a "maximum interest level," does he suggest a second high interest level. On the contrary, he states on page 38 of his monograph: "The changes of interest with age, between 10 and 15, are gradual and, for many titles, small."

Terman and Lima (No. 20), too, found that there was a rise over a period of years to a maximum and then a decline over a period of years.

There is one extensive study, however, which reports marked zigzagging in pupils' reading interests in individual selections. This study will be considered later in this chapter after data on this point, collected for the current study, have been presented, since comparisons will be made between the data afforded by the two studies.

Next, the figures on the effects of increasing age on young people's reading interests obtained in the current study will be compared with the results obtained by Thorndike. On pages 20 to 21 of his report he presents figures showing the changes in interest scores for readers 10 to 15 years of age inclusive. The change for all boys, obtained by combining the medians for superior, average, and weak, for the five-year period is 15; for all girls, 16; for boys and girls, 15.5 points. This is an average change of 3.1 points per year. In view of the fact that the subjects in Thorndike's study averaged some three or four years younger than those in the current study, who reported for grades 8 to 11, and the even more important consideration that Thorndike's scores were obtained in many instances for juvenile selections with respect to which young people's interests change more rapidly than they do toward adult materials, our findings of an average change in interest scores of approximately 2.0 points yearly seem to agree well with Thorndike's results. Pertinent is Thorndike's statement on page 23:

"A study of Tables 9 and 10 suggests that the titles which show large amounts of change are likely to include one or more of the following elements: child characters and heroes; magic; animals, especially humanized animals; remote and unreal adventures. The titles which show stability of appeal at a fairly high level seem more likely to include elements of: adult characters; realistic or historical characters; crime or criminals in the case of boys; romance or a romantic life in the case of girls."

Our findings are again in harmony with Thorndike's conclusion on page 38:

"The changes of interest with age, between 10 and 15, are gradual, and for many titles, small . . . many of the animal, adventure, mystery, sport, travel, science and invention, and other topics show quite small changes even over a span of four or five years."

A comparison of the findings of the current study with those of the Huber-Bruner-Curry study (No. 10) with respect to the effects of increasing age on reading choices may prove of interest also. The authors carried out an exhaustive preliminary investigation to discover which poems were "generally considered as being appropriate for children of the various grades." As a result a list of 573 poems was compiled for use in the experiment. The object of the experiment was to find out which poems were the most interesting "when poetry is taught as it is taught." After their study of the poems the pupils expressed their preferences on printed slips. These preferences were summarized by the teacher and forwarded to the sponsors of the study, who made final summaries. The number of readers voting on individual poems was not stated.

The conclusions of the Huber-Bruner-Curry study are contrary to the findings of Thorndike, Russell and Bullock, Anderson, Terman and Lima, and to the findings of the current study. On page 36 the authors say: ". . . although a few poems seemed to be equally well liked in several grades, most of those selected ranked much higher in the interest of the pupils and teachers in certain grades than in others." Again, on page 66: "There were, also, only 59 poems or 10.3 per cent of the entire list of 573 poems ranking among the upper 50 poems of three or more grades." Finally, on page 71: "In the main the experiment points with convincingness to the fact that most poems are liked much better in certain grades than in any others."

Table II on page 67 of the Huber-Bruner-Curry study lists the 59 poems which showed the *least* variation in interest ratings by "ranking among the upper 50 poems of three or more grades." The 59 poems are listed in such a way as to show the changes in position from grade to grade for each. For example, "America," the first poem listed, is shown to have ranked thirty-second in popularity in the first grade; twenty-second in the second grade; tenth in the third grade; and fortieth in the fourth grade.

There are two features of the tabulation worthy of special note. The first of these is the extent of the shift in interest shown in many cases in the period of one year. For example, "Darius Green" drops from third place in the eighth grade to forty-seventh in the ninth grade (44 steps); "The Courtin' " drops 13.5 steps between grades 6 and 7, rises 15.5 steps between grades 7 and 8, and rises 13 additional steps between grades 8 and 9. Nearly all the 59 selections furnish examples of abrupt changes in interest ratings.

It has been possible to compare these changes in terms of the current study by expressing the amount of change represented by one step in change of position on the Huber-Bruner-Curry lists in terms of change in percentage points as employed by the current study. Based upon the 96 selections of the Huber-Bruner-Curry lists for grades 7, 8, and 9 (arranged in order of popularity) for which the current study affords percentage scores, the average change in points represented by a change of one step in position was found to be 0.85 point. Substituting this value in the examples given above we find that "Darius Green" drops 37.4 percentage points in interest in one year; and that "The Courtin' " drops 11.5 points in interest between grades 6 and 7; rises 13.2 points between grades 7 and 8, and rises 11 additional points between grades 8 and 9. A further examination of the data reveals frequent shifts in interest in a single year of 5 to 8 points even in the 10 per cent of the selections in the Huber-Bruner-Curry study found to be most stable in this regard.

The second feature of the tabulation of Table II of the Huber-Bruner-Curry study referred to above provides an even sharper contrast with results obtained by Thorndike and by the current study. A study of the data shows not only that there are saltatory changes from year to year, but also that these changes zigzag with no apparent explanation, except that the reading tastes of young people as a group presumably suddenly and frequently change direction. For example (again from the 10 per cent of poems showing least changes): "Barbara Frietchie" drops from seventh place in the fourth grade to thirty-third in the fifth (22.1 percentage points), and to thirty-sixth in the sixth (2.6 points additional); rises to twenty-third place (11.1 points) in the seventh, and to twelfth place (9.4 points additional) in the eighth grade; thence falls to twenty-fourth place (9.2 points) in the ninth grade. "John Gilpin's Ride" drops from thirty-fifth place in grade three to below the fiftieth in grade four (12.8 points); rises to thirteenth place in grade five (31.5 points); drops below fiftieth place in grade six (31.5 points); rises to seventeenth place (28.1 points) in grade seven; falls to twenty-eighth place (9.4 points) in grade eight. Similar examples are frequent.

It might be argued that the average change per year in interest, 2.0 points, based on the interest scores of the current study (see page 33), could not be fairly compared with the results shown in the Huber-Bruner-Curry study, since in the current study scores for prose selections as well as for poems are included, while the Huber-Bruner-Curry study deals with poems only. Because this appeared to be a valid objection, additional computations were made. It was found that for a total of 15 of the poems listed in Table II of the Huber-Bruner-Curry study, the current study provided data showing the average yearly change in interest scores. For these 15 poems the

average change shown by the current study (1.3 points) was less than
the average change for the combined total of 236 poems and prose
selections. To determine whether the results would be different
when a number of poems larger than 15 was employed, the average
yearly change in interest score for 145 poems, for which the necessary data were available, was computed. Again the change (1.2
points) was found to be smaller than the change for literary selections
in general.

SUMMARY: The results of five studies (with a sixth study in dissent)
indicate that the year-to-year changes in young people's reading
interests between grades 8 and 11 are usually gradual and small. The
evidence of the current study suggests further that the average
yearly change in interest for the three-year period from grade 8 to
11 is approximately two percentage points, and that a literary selection well liked in a particular grade will usually be liked two or three
grades above or below.

CHAPTER VII

How Age Affects Interest in Various
Reading Materials

OVER A PERIOD OF TIME YOUNG PEOPLE'S INTERESTS IN SOME SE-
lections increase while they decline in others. It is helpful to know
what factors of content and technique account for changes of interest
in literary materials, and the extent of the influence of each. A comparison of the eighth grade and eleventh grade interest scores of
groups of selections strongly influenced by the same factors can assist
in revealing the extent and direction of change.

There are elements limiting the dependability of the conclusions
which may be reached through the proposed comparisons. The restricted number of examples of influence by a particular interest
factor is one such limitation. A more serious obstacle to clear-cut
results is the fact that every literary selection presents a number of
interest factors, some of which may enhance and some of which may
decrease interest. The fact must be recognized that there should be
at hand a considerable number of cases of the presence in important
degree of a given interest factor, so that other factors in the selection
(some increasing, some decreasing interest) may in part, at least,
neutralize each other's effects upon the level of interest. Where only

a few examples are available, the interest factor being studied should be highly dominant.

The first edition of *The Reading Interests of Young People* issued the following warning: "In examining the data (interest scores) it is particularly important to remember that groups of three to six selections are so small that they must be regarded only as providing suggestions for further study, except where the evidence of one group strongly supports the evidence in another." With nearly three times as many interest scores now available, the propriety of this caution becomes evident. In some cases where considerable numbers of titles had been tested in a single field in the first study, the larger numbers of scores now available have modified findings. In 1950 reading materials as a whole were credited with making an average gain in interest of a half point yearly, grade 8 to grade 11. A larger number of titles now suggests that there is little, if any, gain or loss for the period. It is relevant that there are other factors aside from the increased number of selections that might cause variations in results reported by the two sections of the study. For example, the earlier study used selections exclusively chosen by teachers and studied under teacher guidance. The continued study includes a large proportion of selections chosen and read independently by students.

Another factor affecting results, operative in both sections of the study, is found in the field of poetry. Tests show that lyric poetry gains in interest while narrative poetry loses in interest from grade 8 to grade 11. Consequently, the proportion of these two types represented when tests were being made of poems in general would influence both the extent of change and its trend.

To obtain further evidence as to changes in the average interest in reading from the junior high school to the senior high school, the following approach was made. Using the final lists of scores for the junior and senior high schools, and beginning with titles listed under the letter *E*, the scores for all titles tested in common were listed separately until 100 scores were entered on each list. The averages for the two lists were obtained. These average scores indicated that senior high school students rated reading in general 0.9 point higher than the junior high school students, an average yearly gain of 0.3 point.

It is evident that scores for reading fields and changes in interest in these fields with the passage of time should be regarded as approximate only. With this limitation in mind, the data can be helpful. It will be recognized that in choosing specific reading materials, primary reliance must be placed on the interest scores given by boys and by girls to the individual selections.

At the time of the writer's first report on reading interests, the number of titles on which interest scores were available for grades 8 and 11 limited the assessing of changes imposed by age to seven factors. Selections high in the supernatural factor registered a loss on average. Gains were made by groups of selections high in sympathy, didacticism, the religious, the reflective or philosophical, and by selections notable primarily for artistry. Additional testing now permits comments on additional groups.

ADVENTURE. Both girls and boys are less interested in strenuous adventure as they grow older, except the adventure of war in which boys' interest shows little change, and girls' interest increases. Noteworthy is the fact that nonfiction adventure stories are fully as well liked as fiction of adventure. In sports and school games there is a loss of interest, more marked with girls than with boys. The detective story interests girls and boys slightly more in the junior high school than in the senior high school.

ANIMALS. Both the direction of trends of interest and the extent of changes in writings on animals (as well as in other fields) are influenced not only by the reader's growing maturity and sex, but by the literary form used (as fiction, poetry), by restricting the field (as horses, dogs, wild animals), and other factors. When all animals are included, there is a slight loss of interest from grade 8 to grade 11 in fiction and in poetry. Interest in horses and in wild animals decreases. With dogs there is little change. Boys reject poems about birds equally at the two ages; girls definitely lose interest.

CHARACTERS: WOMEN VS MEN. In the senior high school as compared with the junior high school, both girls and boys show greater approval of fiction emphasizing the leadership of men. Boys as they mature are readier to approve the prominence of women.

ESSAYS. While familiar essays except the humorous are not generally enjoyed by young people, there is a moderate advance in interest from the eighth to the eleventh grade. The advance is registered by the following types of essays: humorous, didactic, descriptive, and nature.

FICTION. Considerable fiction decreases in interest during the period under consideration. This is marked with stories of home and family, of games and of horses. Little change is evident for stories of dogs, for humorous stories, and stories combining adventure and love. The novel, when many types are included, shows little change in attraction. The few books of religious fiction for which we have scores at both age levels record, on average, an increase in interest, particularly with girls. Fiction featuring war also gains in interest with girls in the senior high school. While boys as a group are never reconciled to the unalloyed love story, a slightly less hostile attitude develops as they mature. On the other hand, girls, devoted to romantic love throughout adolescence, exhibit some abatement of enthusiasm in the senior high school.

THE JUNIOR NOVEL. The story of school life and romance which ranks near the top with junior high school girls has faded markedly in the senior high school. Boys refuse to read this type. The junior novel of sports and adventure declines in popularity with both boys and girls during adolescence.

MAGAZINES (ADULT). The older boys become less interested in adult magazines, while older girls continue to read them with approximately the same interest they showed in junior high school.

MYTHS, LEGENDS, FAIRY TALES. Myths and legends which appeal to elementary school children are already in marked decline in the junior high school. Rapid loss of interest continues in senior high school. Fairy stories record a similar decline, though girls are more reluctant to abandon them than are boys.

NONFICTION. Miscellaneous nonfiction, on average, is liked approximately as well in junior high school as in senior high school. Letters, accounts of travel, and history score slightly higher with the older pupils; speeches and biographies, slightly lower. Science advances in interest, particularly with boys.

DRAMA. The reading of plays varies little in popularity, grade 8 to grade 11.

SUPERNATURAL. The tale of the supernatural loses interest as readers mature. This change is particularly rapid with the ghost story.

SCIENCE. This field calls for special comment. Because of reader enthusiasm for popular science magazines and for science fiction, some have assumed that science per se is popular with young people. The evidence is clear that, except for a small minority, this is a mistake. At the time of the earlier study, scores were obtained for only eight selections dealing with science, and these, it was noted, probably receive higher ratings than they otherwise would because each is written in popular style, and most of them include elements of the dramatic. The current study includes for the senior high school ten additional titles on science which considerably reduce the average interest score, already low. Forty-six science titles have been tested in the junior high school, most of them prepared for popular reading. Their average scores (boys, 57.6; girls, 52.2) place science near the bottom in reading interest.

To gain further evidence, the writer consulted a prominent educator in the science field. The request was for an article on science that would appeal to junior and senior high school students. The recommendation was "The Speed of Light" by Richard T. Cox. This selection was tested with more than 1000 young people in junior and senior high school. The interest scores were: in grades 7 to 9, boys 36.8 and girls 24.3; in grades 10 to 12, boys 51.4 and girls 27.0.

The few titles on science tested in both junior and senior high schools indicate a gain in interest with advancing age, definitely greater for boys than for girls. When students were asked directly as to their attitude toward reading about science, both boys and girls reported very low interest, with the girls' reaction much the less favorable. Both boys and girls reported a gain in interest in senior high school.

POETRY. The average score for 200 lyrics confirms the earlier finding that there is a gain in interest from grade 8 to grade 11. When 174 narrative poems are used, a loss is registered for the three years. It is clear that a variation in the proportion of lyric and narrative poems may be a determining factor in indicating an average gain or loss for poetry in general. Using at the two age levels 546 poems chosen at random, it is found that there is an average change of less than one point from grade 8 to grade 11.

It would be easy to conclude that the increase in young people's interest in lyric poetry with advancing age is caused primarily by a growing enjoyment of the poetic form. May not the principal influences be that with increasing maturity adolescents (1) *better understand* the content of lyric poetry (certainly much more difficult on the average than narrative poetry), and (2) have developed a greater appreciation of adult ideas and viewpoints?

Poems of different types on average change their trend of interest, junior to senior high school.

Poems of adventure decline moderately.

Poems about animals decline moderately.

Poems notable primarily for artistry gain.

Poems about birds decline moderately.

Didactic poems gain.

Poems of home decline with boys; register little change with girls.

Humorous poems decline moderately.

Love poems show little change.

Nature poems gain.

Patriotic poems register little change.

Religious poems gain strongly.

Requiems and laments gain.

War poems gain.

The fact that gains in interest in some areas of reading almost exactly offset losses from grade 8 to grade 11 does not mean a similar lack of change at lower and higher levels. The extensive changes in interest in juvenile materials during childhood have been mentioned. The average scores for 93 adult poems tested at three levels (elementary grades; junior high school; senior high school) indicate that boys' interest declines markedly between grades 5 and 8 while remaining almost unchanged between grades 8 and 11. The girls' decline in interest between grades 5 and 8 is definitely less than the boys'. However, the girls join the boys in their lack of significant change between grades 8 and 11.

From high school to young adulthood (average age 23), the decline of interest in reading both prose and poetry (with religious poems an exception) is drastic for both men and women. Sufficient titles have been tested with senior high school students and with the middle-aged to permit additional, tentative comments on time's influence on the reading interests of adults. During the 22 years from high school to middle-age, men and women register losses of interest twice as often as gains. Marked declines are shown for Shakespeare's *Plays*, nonfiction prose, general fiction, and strenuous adventure told both in fiction and nonfiction. Moderate declines are recorded for adult poetry as a whole, religious novels, and adult magazines. By contrast, religious poetry makes strong gains in favor, continuing a trend established in the period from junior to senior high school. Significant of the influence of religion is the fact that with adults religous fiction loses interest less than half as rapidly as fiction in general. The decline from childhood to middle age for reading in general is followed by a resurgence of interest in old age.

Were attention given only to the evidence for changes of interest when groups of selections are observed, it would be easy to conclude that time's influence on interest in reading, particularly from junior to senior high school, is of minor consequence. Yet, in reading fields where the average interest is nearly identical at two age levels, individual titles show wide differences. From age 13 to age 16, boys' interest declines 17.5 points for "The Concord Hymn," 17.8 points for *The Boys' Life of Mark Twain*, and 16.5 points for *The Courtship of Miles Standish*. Shelley's "Ozymandias" in the same period gains 20.1 points with boys, and 30.0 points with girls. "Hohenlinden" by Thomas Campbell gains 21.4 points with boys, and 15.4 points with girls. These are illustrative of innumerable similar instances. Often the change degrades a rating, "well liked" in the junior high school to "disliked" in the senior high school. The opposite also occurs. At times interest trends of a selection even in the same field warns of the crucial significance, when choosing reading materials, of scores given by boys and by girls to individual titles.

CHAPTER VIII

The Influence of Sex Differences on Interests in Literary Types

---

EXPERIENCED TEACHERS ARE AWARE OF A WIDE GAP BETWEEN THE reading interests of boys and girls. The data of this study indicate that sex is so dominant and ever-present a force in determining young people's reading choices that it must be carefully considered in planning any reading program for the schools. It will be helpful to consider the influence of sex in relation to a number of the special interest factors.

Since a reader's liking for a literary selection, even the simplest, is compounded of several factors in addition to sex differences—some tending to increase interest, others to decrease it—the question arose: How can these interlacing factors be disentwined to show the influence of each? The use of partial correlations, an approach which has had some vogue in similar investigations, was considered. This method depends for success upon very accurate measurement of the amount of each of several influences entering into the total. Precise measurement cannot be claimed. Even the validity of the technique of partial correlation has been seriously questioned by competent critics who argue that the procedure is incapable of disentangling one and only one factor at a time.

48   THE READING INTERESTS

The plan chosen was to examine the reactions of boys and of girls toward a list of selections, each of which was dominated by a single factor, and to depend upon the minimizing of the potency of other factors through cancellation. Undoubtedly the method has pitfalls, since cancellation may not function as expected. To the writer, however, it seemed the better choice to attempt to winnow selections involving a high degree of a particular interest factor (e.g., humor) and depend upon a favorable degree of cancellation of other factors than to attempt by partial correlation to determine for a particular selection the extent of the influence of each of ten to twenty-five interest factors.

It is proposed, first, to consider the extent of the influence of sex upon reading interests in general through an examination of the data for the 236 selections affording scores in both junior and senior high school. The mean of the differences between boys' and girls' ratings of the 236 selections was determined at the eighth grade level (9.32 points), and also at the eleventh grade level (8.41 points). The difference between these means (0.91 point) suggests that sex may be a slightly less potent factor in influencing young people's reading choices in the senior high school than in the junior high school. Thorndike's (No. 21) "correlation of interest pattern, boys vs. girls," while inconclusive, points toward an increasing community of interest in reading between secondary school boys and girls with increasing age.

A subsequent study (No. 15, p. 36) found that the average differences in interest between boys and girls when prose and poetry both were included were as follows: Grade 5, average difference 5.6 points; Grade 8, average difference 9.3 points; Grade 11, average difference 8.4 points.

The fact that there is not much *change* between junior and senior high school in the influence of sex as shown by average scores must not prevent recognition that sex is a highly influential factor throughout the secondary school period. The mean difference in the reading interests of boys and girls in the secondary school, 8.87 points (the average of 9.32 for junior high school and 8.41 for senior high school), shows this clearly. The high power of sex as a factor in influencing young people's interests is revealed by comparing the differences caused by sex with the differences caused by intelligence and by increasing age. As pointed out earlier (page 27), the differences between the interest scores of superior, average, and weak pupils in the same school grades is so small as to be almost negligible. Increasing age in the secondary school was found to produce an average change of 2.0 points yearly. This means that, on the average, four and one-half years' growth is required to produce in the pupil a change in interest as great as the divergence caused by sex between boys and girls in the same grade. The evidence indicates that among younger children in the elementary school, age is more influential in governing reading choices than it is in the secondary school; while *beyond the secondary school* changes in age have progressively less influence in modifying reading preferences. On the other hand, it appears that at least from the fifth grade to adulthood, sex is a dominating influence which attains its maximum during the junior high school period.

In addition to the measurement of the influence of sex differences on reading interests through the data for the 236 selections, a further approach to the problem was made through the data available in this later study. Scores for hundreds of additional titles which high school students read voluntarily (free reading) were added to the scores found for the original list of titles assigned for study by teachers. This total list of selections (4,993) is used in the current report in the consideration of titles enjoyed by young people. First, the comparative popularity with girls and with boys of a number of important literary types was determined. The ranking of a particular type by boys and by girls was found by tabulating and averaging a large number of scores for titles of that type. The difference in points between the girls' average score and the boys' average score was also recorded. By averaging the boys' score and the girls' score for a particular literary type a composite score was obtained. For example, the popularity of the novel as a literary type was found by averaging the girls' and boys' interest scores for 47 novels.

The data for literary types are presented in Table 3, and are listed in the order of popularity. The data show that girls enjoy almost all literary types better than do boys. The two types represented in this table which are better liked by boys are the speeches and biographies of men, though the difference in the rankings by boys and by girls is not great in the novel and in the short story.

Disregarding the groupings by type it may be noted that of the selections examined in this part of the study, girls like 69.3 percent of them better than do boys. Further, if the 946 selections are representative, the conclusion may be drawn that girls enjoy literary materials of the types usually studied in high school 4.9 percentage points better than do boys.

The data recorded in Table 3 suggest that for all classifications represented, with the exception of biographies and descriptive essays, these differences cannot be considered to be chance differences. Even in biographies of women and in science materials where the numbers of selections were small, the differences are significant.

Attention is called to the fact that the levels of significance of the data in this book which compare boys' and girls' reading interests can be relied upon only to the extent that interest factors, other than the one designated as dominant, cancel. With small numbers of selections the probability of a high degree of cancellation of secondary factors is much smaller than with large numbers of selections.

TABLE 3

LITERARY TYPES AS RATED BY BOYS AND GIRLS

LITERARY TYPE	NUMBER OF SELEC-TIONS	INTEREST SCORES			DIFFERENCE GIRLS-BOYS	NUMBER BETTER LIKED BY BOYS	NUMBER BETTER LIKED BY GIRLS
		BOYS	GIRLS	AVG.			
Novel	47	78.4	79.6	79.0	1.2	22	25
Play	62	71.3	77.2	74.3	5.9	13	49
Short Story	214	72.3	74.0	73.2	1.7	106	108
Biography (men)	41	70.9	68.3	69.6	−2.6		
Biography (women)	9	53.4	73.3	63.4	19.9		
Essay	81	63.1	66.3	64.7	3.2	21	60
Poem	466	60.7	68.3	64.5	7.6	88*	377*
Poem (narrative)	72	68.9	70.7	69.8	1.8		
Poem (lyric)	377	57.1	67.0	62.1	9.9		
Letter	12	60.6	64.9	62.8	4.3	2	10
Speech	13	63.9 .	59.7	61.8	−4.2	11	2
Boys' Books (41 bio-graphies, 65 novels & short stories)	106	75.5	72.3	73.9	−3.2		
Girls' Books (9 bio-graphies, 17 novels & short stories)	26	59.1	76.8	68.0	17.7		
TOTAL	946	65.6	70.5	68.1	4.9	286*	658*

*One poem equally liked by boys and girls.

NOVEL. The results of this study reveal the novel as the favorite literary type with young people. The difference in the popularity ratings accorded by boys and by girls is so small for the novel (1.2 points), and the difference is so unreliable as to suggest that this literary form may be equally enjoyed by boys and by girls.

PLAYS. The closeness of the average scores for plays and for short stories suggests that more extensive testing might reverse the relative popularity of these types. It may be noted also that because plays present unusual reading difficulties, young people usually do not read them voluntarily. As a result the teacher-directed class discussions of the plays included in the tabulation may account in part for their popularity.

SHORT STORY. Taken as a whole, short stories are almost equally well-liked by boys and by girls. It may be a surprise to find that the short story is less popular than the novel and the play. One explanation may be that teachers, because of their desire to illustrate special literary forms and offer only the highest quality, have chosen for class study many tales which are too mature and subtle for high enjoyment by most adolescents. On the basis of the literature studied in our schools, the novel, the play, and the short story are favorite literary types with young people.

BIOGRAPHY. The differences in boys' and girls' interests in biographies of men and of women are so great that the two types are presented separately. Including all of the 50 biographies in a single group would result in a difference between boys' and girls' interests of 1.5 points only. This would fail to reveal the actual situation since boys' preferences for biographies of men tend to offset the girls' preferences for women's biographies. The data show that while boys rate biographies of men at 70.9, they rate biographies of women 53.4.

BOYS' AND GIRLS' BOOKS. The fact that girls enjoy biographies of men almost as much as boys do, and on the average rate them only five points below biographies of women, is one of the evidences that while boys will not tolerate books primarily about women, girls generally read books about men with satisfaction. This point is corroborated in the table by tabulations for boys' books and for girls' books. Girls rate 106 boys' books within 3.2 points of the boys' rating. On the other hand, boys value 26 girls' books 17.7 points lower than do girls.

ESSAY. Table 3 tells us that, in general, essays are not enjoyed by secondary school students. However, humorous essays as a group provide an exception to the rule. It is well to remember that (a) among didactic essays there are a few that are liked, (b) humorous essays often make points as important as those scored by the more serious types, and (c) as a whole, without those of the humorous type, essays would rank in interest below poetry.

POETRY. In contrast to the results for short stories, where boys' and girls' ballots on 214 titles were found to be almost equally favorable, the spread between boys' and girls' scores on 466 poems is 7.6 points. Further, in comparison with novels, biographies, and plays, as well as with short stories, poetry as a whole is not well liked. On the other hand, many individual poems are popular, and, what may seem surprising, there are several subdivisions in which *groups* of poems rank high. Also, while the composite ratings for essays (64.7) and poems (64.5) are close, it should be remembered that there are many more poems than essays which are approved by young people. As a result, poems when chosen for high interest may provide a more favorable field for class study than the familiar (literary) essay.

NARRATIVE VERSUS LYRIC POETRY. A separation of poems into two groups, lyric and narrative, permits some interesting observations. Three hundred thirty-seven lyric poems are found to be liked 10 points better on average by girls than by boys. Of the total, 305 lyric poems are better liked by girls; only 32 are better liked by boys. This time a difference of only 1.8 points separates the boys' and girls' scores. Further, boys like 36 of the narrative poems better than do girls; girls like 37 better than do boys. These figures point strongly to the conclusions that both boys and girls enjoy narrative poetry better than they do lyric poetry; that while girls' approval of lyric poetry approaches their approval of narrative poetry (the difference, 3.6 points), boys on a comparative basis reject lyric poems decisively in favor of narrative poems (the difference, 11.8 points).

To a considerable degree the subdivisions that serve for classifying short stories serve also for classifying narrative poems. As with short stories, narrative poems as a whole are found to be almost equally liked by boys and by girls, though the composite score for boys and girls on narrative poems is 3.4 points lower than the composite score for short stories. A noteworthy point is that this difference is so small.

As soon as a consideration of lyric instead of narrative poetry is undertaken, favorable comparisons with short stories end. Note the following scores: short stories (all types), 73.2; narrative poems, 69.8; lyric poems, 62.1. It will be found that various patriotic poems and humorous poems of the lyric type are popular, and that some lyrics of home life and about animals are approved. With many exceptions we may generalize, however, that poems of nature, sentiment, reflection, religion, philosophy, and didacticism rank low.

What accounts for this low estate of poetry among young people? Is it primarily word choice, meter, rhyme, compression, or other devices that distinguish poetry from prose? No doubt certain poetic usages, such as unusual word order and exotic or subtle vocabulary, at times interfere with their understanding of a poem's meaning. Yet an examination of well-liked as well as disliked poems suggests that basically not form but content is the touchstone of popularity. The vast majority of poems deal with themes and ideas which young people would reject if offered to them in prose.

SUMMARY: When the average scores for boys and for girls for the 946 selections dealt with in Table 3 are obtained, it is found that girls rate them as a group 4.9 points higher than do boys. Of the total, boys prefer 286 (30%) and girls 658 (70%). The data of the table are derived from the titles used in class instruction. (See Chapters XIV-XVII for tables of specific selections approved by young people.)

CHAPTER IX

The Influence of Artistry on Interest

BEWITCHMENT WITH LITERARY ARTISTRY BY TEACHERS IS THE MA-
jor barrier to a love of reading by young people. This conclusion
appears inevitable after 40 years' investigation. The arbiters and
teachers of English in chorus declare "Children must enjoy their
reading" while a major part of their imposed reading program con-
sists of literature which young readers reject. Because fidelity to
enjoyment as the first test of literature for class study would revolutionize America's reading attitudes and reading habits, it is proposed
in this chapter to present sufficient evidence for firm conclusions.

This evidence will demonstrate that youths do not enjoy literature
noteworthy primarily for artistic quality; that those of superior ability
join the average and weak in rejecting such writings; and that readers of all ability levels derive high satisfaction from selections of
appealing content regardless of the absence or presence of literary
style.

Let us begin with young people's reactions to two great poets. Our
files for grades 10 to 12 afford data on a total of nine poems by
Shakespeare and 11 by Keats. Tables 4 and 5 record the scores given
to the 20 poems by all students in contrast to the scores by the

TABLE 4

THE INTEREST OF SENIOR HIGH SCHOOL STUDENTS IN POEMS BY
SHAKESPEARE

POEMS—SHAKESPEARE	SCORE ALL	SCORE I'S
Ariel's Song	29.3	26.2
Hark! Hark! the Lark	42.9	40.2
Orpheus with His Lute	24.3	22.8
Sea Dirge	60.0	62.1
Sonnets	54.9	51.4
Under the Greenwood Tree	56.8	56.1
When Icicles Hang by the Wall	55.1	49.9
When in Disgrace with Fortune and Men's Eyes	52.2	44.7
Who is Sylvia?	58.6	56.0
AVERAGE	48.2	45.5

TABLE 5

THE INTEREST OF SENIOR HIGH SCHOOL STUDENTS IN POEMS BY KEATS

POEMS—KEATS	SCORE ALL	SCORE I'S
Endymion	51.9	53.2
Eve of St. Agnes	62.4	62.6
La Belle Dame Sans Merci	55.9	55.5
Mermaid Tavern	57.4	58.2
Ode on a Grecian Urn	57.4	59.8
Ode to a Nightingale	64.6	67.4
Ode to Autumn	50.9	51.6
On First Looking into Chapman's Homer	49.3	49.2
On the Grasshopper and the Cricket	32.5	32.1
Sweet Peas	52.7	55.6
When I Have Fears	64.0	74.1
AVERAGE	54.5	56.3

superior. To the nine poems by Shakespeare, all students give an average score of 48.2; the superior group, 45.5. (A score of 51.0 places a selection in the lowest 10 per cent of the thousands tested. A score above 80.0 means "very well liked" and designates a selection satisfactory for reading by boys when they give this rating, and by girls when they give it.) Clearly, both groups reject this high art, in most cases, but the superior emphasize their rejection by an average score 2.7 points *lower* than the rating by all senior high school students. Keats's finest poetry is rejected also by these average scores: all students, 54.5; superior students, 56.3. It is of interest to note that the 20 poems on average rank slightly higher with young people in general than with the elite, and that they are unsatisfactory for the great majority of young people of all ability levels when enjoyment is an important aim of literary study.

The examination of the evidence regarding young people's reactions to literature noteworthy primarily for artistry did not end with the poetry of Keats and Shakespeare. Our records for the senior high school include a total of 125 poems by 11 poets acclaimed by critics, each represented by six or more poems (Table 6). The 125 poems on average scored 54.6, a rating which places them as a group in the lowest quartile of the poems commonly used in high school classes. Not one of the 125 is rated by students as "very interesting."

TABLE 6

ELEVEN SUPERIOR POETS WITH THE NUMBER OF POEMS OF EACH, WITH AVERAGES

POET	NO. OF POEMS	AVERAGE SCORE
Emily Dickinson	16	55.6
Edna St. V. Millay	7	58.0
Amy Lowell	11	51.2
Walter de la Mare	13	53.6
John Keats	11	54.5
William Shakespeare	9	47.9
William B. Yeats	7	48.5
Robert Frost	13	59.0
Eleanor Wylie	6	54.4
Percy B. Shelley	9	58.4
Carl Sandburg	23	55.8
TOTAL	125	54.3

Another assessment of the preferences of bright students used 24 selections which are disliked by young people generally (below 65.0), but are above average in quality, and therefore presumably of higher appeal to the superior students (Table 7). The average score of the 24 titles by I's was 55.7—only 0.3 point higher than the score by all students. It will be noted that very high quality as represented by Shakespeare's *Julius Caesar*, Lamb's "Old China", and Thoreau's

TABLE 7

COMPARISON OF THE INTEREST SCORES OF SUPERIOR STUDENTS ON 24
LITERARY SELECTIONS WITH SCORES GIVEN BY ALL STUDENTS
(Grades 10–12)

| | INTEREST SCORES | |
TITLE AND AUTHOR	ALL	I'S ONLY
Alice in Wonderland—Carroll	56.8	57.0
Autobiography—Franklin	51.3	49.0
Benjamin Franklin—Van Doren	63.6	64.2
Compensation—Emerson	56.4	56.6
Fall of the City—MacLeish	39.2	41.9
Fall of the House of Usher—Poe	55.7	61.4
Ides of March—Wilder	54.5	58.7
Importance of Being Earnest—Wilde	64.2	64.6
Julius Caesar—Shakespeare	63.2	61.8
King Midas—Greek Myth	52.2	50.3
Kit Carson—Trail Blazer–Garst	49.3	50.2
Life of Johnson—Boswell	64.2	72.1
Little Britches—Moody	63.6	59.6
Lord Jim—Conrad	63.3	62.6
Madame Curie—Curie	62.9	66.5
Old China—Charles Lamb	52.4	45.6
Old Folks—Daudet	55.2	56.3
Pilgrim's Progress—Bunyan	53.9	48.1
Prologue to the Canterbury Tales— Chaucer	56.4	60.3
Riders to the Sea—Synge	53.9	55.3
Song of Myself—Whitman	38.8	38.0
Strife—Galsworthy	57.0	56.4
Translating Literature into Life— Bennett	43.1	42.7
Walden—Thoreau	57.8	56.7
AVERAGE*	55.4	55.7

*The difference between the average scores given by I's and by All is 0.3 point.

Walden did not receive approval by the best students. Further, not one of these 24 selections was rated "very interesting" by the superior; not one is satisfactory for class reading by the superior if enjoyment is a major aim.

Since an increase in the number of student reports increases the reliability of the interest scores, the following variation in procedure was used. Fifty selections of all types were chosen at random from selections with a minimum of 1500 reports by senior high school students. The superior (I's) on average rated the 50 miscellaneous titles 0.8 point higher than all students.

TABLE 8

COMPARISON OF THE READING INTERESTS OF WEAK READERS (BOYS III) WITH THOSE OF ALL BOYS, GRADES 7 TO 12

Reading Materials	Grades	No. of Books	Boys III's	Boys All	Differ- ence
Well-liked Adult Books	10–12	86	82.2	81.5	0.7
Well-liked Adult Books Read Independently	10–12	25	83.6	84.2	0.6
Well-liked Adult Books Read Independently	7–9	62	83.4	83.4	0.0
Juvenile Books	7–9	36	81.1	78.1	3.0

Table 8 contrasts the reading interests of weak high school boys (III's) with the interests of all high school boys. The average score given by boys (III's) in senior high school for 86 well-liked books was 0.7 point higher than the score by all boys in the same grades. When the results for 25 books read independently by boys in the same grades (10-12) were compared, boys (III's) scored them 0.6 point lower than all boys.

In the junior high school, 62 well-liked books read independently were given equal average scores by III's and all boys. In the same grades, weak boys scored 36 juvenile books 3.0 points higher than all boys. Conclusion: There is little difference in the reading interests of weak boys and all boys in high school, though the weak boys rate juvenile books slightly higher than all boys.

Seventy-two selections of high quality by more than a dozen writers including Coleridge, Milton, Shakespeare, and Hawthorne were used in comparing the reading interests of the superior with the interests of all students in *junior* high school. Thirty-four of the 72 were rated higher, and 38 lower by the superior as compared with the scores by all students. The average score given to the 72 titles by the superior was within less than half a point of the score by all junior high school students. All groups—weak, average, and superior—rated the selections as uninteresting on average.

In the elementary grades (4—6), 40 titles of high quality were used. All children rated 22 higher, 16 lower, and 2 as equally liked when compared with the scores by the superior. Similar results were obtained with 30 poems of high type in grade 3.

What Boys and Girls Like to Read (No. 15) reports the findings in grades 4 to 6 when 316 selections in 11 reading areas were used to compare the interests of bright children (I's) with the interests of all children. Of the 316 titles, 123 were ranked higher by I's; 187 by all children; and 6 were equally liked. Nine of the 11 fields were rated higher by all children. Myths and legends were ranked higher by the bright by 0.2 point, and wild animals higher by the bright, also by 0.2 point. All children ranked the 316 selections higher than the bright by 0.8 point.

Attention is called to the evidence offered in Chapter V: "Influence of Intelligence on the Reading Interests of Young People." Reported are the findings when the interests of more than 12,000 young people with recorded intelligence quotients on 36 selections were tabulated separately for the three ability levels. It was found that literature, whether read to students by their teachers, or studied in class, aroused almost equal interest among superior, average, and weak students.

James R. Squire (No. 19) found, after a careful study of adolescents' responses to literature, that intelligent high school students were able to understand the content of literature, but unable to respond adequately "to form, the connotative meanings of rhyme, to emotional overtones." I.A. Richards tested the responses of students reading for honors in literature at Cambridge University, England, to literature with which they were unacquainted (No. 17). He concluded that they had almost no capacity for distinguishing between the tawdry and the artistic.

The writer made a study[8] of the reading preferences of 450 college students. When the interests of the superior (I's) in 70 literary selections of moderate reading difficulty were compared with the interests of all college students, the superior men and women students rated the 70 selections on average only 0.7 point higher than all college students.

In this study a further comparison was made of the interests of college graduates and all adults in 186 selections of above average quality from 13 reading fields. All men preferred 116 of the selections; men college graduates preferred 67; and 3 were equally liked. All women preferred 91 selections; college graduates preferred 95.

A further examination of the preferences of adult readers was made, using 49 titles of high literary quality which are easy reading. Easy-to-read materials were used to prevent the handicapping of

[8]Although the manuscript is complete, this study has not been published.

readers of moderate education. Of the 49, all men rated 30 higher than college graduates. All women placed 16 higher. When the results for men and women were combined, college graduates on average rated the 49 selections only one-tenth of one point higher than men and women in general.

When the writer directly questioned college graduates as to their preferences in two representative fields of belles-lettres, poetry and essays, they rated both fields very low: poetry, 50.2; essays, 37.8. This low placement by the highly educated is strongly reinforced by evidence presented earlier in this chapter. To summarize: The writer's study of interest in various activities made in the elementary grades, the junior high school, and the senior high school showed the reading of poetry and of essays ranking as least liked. Dr. Helen K. Mackintosh stated in *A Critical Study of Children's Choices in Poetry* (No. 12) "children prefer practically every other type of literature to poetry." Jordan (No. 11) reported that poetry provides fewer than 3 percent of the books best liked by girls and boys. Witty's report (No. 25) in *Education* (October 1961) recorded that high school girls and boys scored essays and poetry lowest among six types of reading (p. 106). Gray and Monroe found that among college graduates 50 percent had *no* interest in poetry, and 71 percent, *no* interest in essays (No. 8).

When eight groups of readers indicated their favorite books, the highest ten on the list by women college graduates were from best seller lists of the not too distant past. Women college students included one classic, *Jane Eyre* (a love story). Of their other choices, seven duplicated the favorites of the women college graduates. It seems ironic that the group of women whose education ended below high school graduation, in contrast to the highly educated and highly intelligent groups, included two classics: *A Christmas Carol* by Dickens, and *Little Women* by Alcott.

The following illustrations among many of similar sort may be cited: Men college graduates prefer *The Winning of Barbara Worth* to *The Education of Henry Adams;* and women college graduates prefer *How to Win Friends and Influence People* to Emerson's *Essays*.

Fourteen poems of high quality were tested with senior high school students in general and with college graduates. The high school students scored these poems 0.3 point higher than the college graduates. Obviously the higher level of intelligence of the college graduates and their four years of additional training in English failed to lead to increased interest in these superior poems. The result carries added significance in view of the fact that adults in general rate poetry slightly higher than senior high school students.

There is ample evidence that content is the major factor in reading choices and that superior, average, and weak readers of the same age levels approve and disapprove of the same kinds of reading materials. All three ability groups are enthusiastic about stories of adventure, wild animals, dogs and horses, detective stories, and humorous stories, to name a few. All three groups give low ratings to letters and speeches, to articles on history and science, to descriptions of nature —no matter how artistically written—to poetry in general and in particular to lyric poetry. It is noteworthy that certain kinds of narrative poetry, such as poems of adventure, and humorous verse are ranked comparatively high by all three ability groups. There are reading areas about which girls and boys disagree, yet here too, the three ability groups, whether of girls or of boys, agree.

As mentioned earlier, there is consensus that a major outcome of the reading and literature program must be enjoyment. The ranking of the four major school subjects provides challenging evidence. An investigation was carried out by the writer in 183 classes in nine representative senior high schools, and in 174 classes in 14 representative junior high schools. The subjects ranked for interest were mathematics, English, science, and social studies. Tabulation of the results was made separately for superior, average, and weak students. In both senior and junior high schools, all three intelligence groups placed English lowest in interest.

These results are supported by a study made by the United States Office of Education and Northwestern University under the direction of Paul Witty (No. 26). When students in grades 7 and 8 were asked to name their favorite school subject, both boys and girls placed English below mathematics, science, and social studies (p. 170).

Shall we still proclaim that young people must enjoy their reading? Are we prepared to face reality: that neither high school students as a group, nor superior students as a group are ready to appreciate the subtleties of belles-lettres? The evidence is convincing that if young people are to enjoy literature, it must be chosen because of its content appeal, not because of artistic finesse. This does not mean, however, that the chosen selections must forego artistry—only that intriguing content is the first requisite.

CRITICAL QUESTION: Is it possible to offer for class reading a broad-gauged, high-quality program which includes *only titles thoroughly enjoyed by students?* The answer is an unequivocal YES. Almost 5,000 selections have been carefully tested in grades 7 to 12 with more than 1200 rating very interesting. Of these 1200, very many are of high literary quality. See Chapters XIV-XVII for titles of high quality for use in class instruction. Replacement of the current, boring, and disheartening program with literature of high appeal would transform English classes. Students would develop a life-long reading habit based on a love of reading.

CHAPTER X

Special Factors Influencing Reading Interests

IN ADDITION TO THE MAJOR INTEREST FACTORS INHERENT IN READ-ers (age, sex, intelligence) which have been discussed in earlier chapters, there are special interest factors relating to content and to form. Of these, which are the most significant? To answer this question an attempt was made to discern the factors which the data suggested, and to employ them tentatively. As a result of this plan, comments will be offered under 20 headings: adventure; animals; artistic quality; characters, male and female; description; didacticism; home and family; humor; love; mood and symbolism; mystery; narration and dramatic action; nature; patriotism; poetic form; the philosophical; religion; science; sentiment; the supernatural.

A serious problem relating to these factors concerns their exact nature, and how to delimit them in such a way as to show their influence. "Adventure" has frequently been designated as one of the special interest factors by writers on young people's reading. However, if it is true, as this study indicates, that grim physical adventure influences girls' choices adversely compared with milder types of adventure, while boys respond favorably to both of these types, a more exact designation than "adventure" would be useful. Further, if obvious humor produces a markedly different reaction than subtle humor, it appears desirable to employ two classifications instead of one. Since every literary selection presents to the reader several interest factors the relative influence of which can only be estimated, the most we can say even for favorable examples is that they are dominated by this or that interest factor.

ADVENTURE. Boys enjoy stories and poems of adventure except when they are alloyed with disliked elements such as love and the supernatural. Even in such cases the story or poem may be ranked high provided the alloying factor is found in moderation and other factors (e.g., humor, animals) support a stirring adventure. Boys favor in particular grim or violent struggle as illustrated by "All Gold Canyon" by Jack London, and "The Most Dangerous Game" by Richard Connell. Twelve stories of physically grim adventure are given a high average rating by boys while the girls' average score is 15.0 points lower.

Poems (21) emphasizing physical struggle are scored 7.4 points higher by boys than by girls. Fifteen war poems are ranked on average 8.1 points higher by boys than by girls.

Girls, especially in the junior high school, enjoy many adventure stories almost as well as boys, provided that the element of grim physical struggle is absent. Noteworthy is girls' approval of the detective story, the mystery, and, indeed, almost all kinds of adventure stories which omit fierce or gory struggle.

ANIMALS. Of all the special factors causing boys and girls to rate reading material high, the factor "animals" ranks at or near the top. The evidence indicates that girls enjoy stories of domestic animals and pets almost as much as boys, and that the lower rating they give to some of the stories of wild animals is a reflection of girls' dislike of grim physical struggle and savagery. When the literary form is verse, girls exceed boys in approval of animals. An extended examination shows that of all animals dogs and horses are the most popular with both boys and girls and that selections about them are enjoyed almost equally by the sexes.

ARTISTIC QUALITY. The evidence is strong that selections which depend upon artistry rather than content seldom attract secondary school readers. This does not mean, of course, that young people are totally unaffected by the beauties of form and technique. Though both girls and boys place this type of writing very low, girls are much more tolerant than boys. The effect of artistry upon interest is discussed in Chapter IX.

CHARACTERS, MALE AND FEMALE. An examination of 106 selections in which male characters predominate (the average difference between boys' and girls' scores, 3.2 points) shows beyond reasonable doubt that girls are almost as ready as boys to read with interest of the doings of boys and men, the principal exception being writings in which violent or deadly physical struggle is a factor. It is just as evident that boys reject most selections in which female characters play the dominant roles (the average difference for 27 titles, 17.7 points). Terman and Lima (No. 20) report: "From the reading records of our children it was found that 18 percent of the girls' reading was in the field of boys' books, but only 2 percent of the boys' reading was the human interest story of home or school life that girls so much enjoy."

DESCRIPTION. That description alone is unattractive to girls and boys in almost equal degree is indicated by the narrowness of difference in the average scores they give to titles of this type and by their low ratings of such titles. An examination of boys' and girls' preferences among descriptive selections strengthens this conclusion by suggesting that such divergencies as exist result from the presence of interest factors recognized as influencing young people's choices. Each of these three descriptions preferred by boys ("Description of Little America," "Jungle Night," "Trees at Timberline") reveals nature in a challenging mood. By contrast, girls prefer "Sunday in London" and "Sunrise in Louisana."

DIDACTICISM. Except when well concealed, didacticism is an unfavorable factor with both boys and girls, though girls are slightly more tolerant. Forty-five didactic essays, for example, averaged among the lowest in interest of all literary types tested, with the boys' score 3.0 points lower than the girls'.

HOME AND FAMILY. The very wide spread between boys' and girls' scores for poems and stories relating to the home emphasizes how popular this theme is with girls. Fourteen short stories of home and family were rated 17.7 points higher by girls and eight poems with this theme were rated 16.4 points higher.

HUMOR. Both boys and girls enjoy humor of the simple, obvious type, though girls rank such selections higher than boys. Both boys and girls reject most examples of subtle humor, though again girls' ratings are the more favorable. In this study "subtle humor" includes not only humor which calls for mental acumen for its understanding, but in addition humor which depends upon allusion, parody, and other devices making a demand (even slight) upon the erudition of the reader. That subtle humor ranks much below obvious humor is revealed by its 9.5 points lower rating, and by its placement by students among the unpopular literary types.

LOVE. The dominance of romantic love in a selection, even a story, places it beyond the pale with the great majority of boys. The opposite is true for girls. Love stories rank 21.9 points lower with boys than with girls, and poems of love average 14.9 points lower. Classifications rivaling love poems in unpopularity with boys are poems and essays of nature, description, didacticism, and compositions relying primarily on artistry. Junior high school girls' avidity for love stories is particularly evident with the junior novel of school life and romance.

MOOD AND SYMBOLISM. Stories of mood and symbolism often lack the dramatic action so appealing to young people.

MYSTERY. Both girls and boys highly approve of detective stories. Usually, both rate other types of mystery stories lower.

NARRATION AND DRAMATIC ACTION. It is clear that narration, especially if it relates dramatic action, is a component of the vast majority of the reading materials approved by young people. Two interest factors may be successful without this aid: humor and patriotism. It is interesting and important that narrative verse is not far below the prose story in popularity.

NATURE. Nature as represented by flowers, birds, bees, and trees has a greater appeal for girls than for boys. (Sixty-five such poems are ranked 12.1 points lower by boys.) Yet even with girls, nature divorced from narrative stirs little enthusiasm.

PATRIOTISM. Patriotism is a distinctly favorable factor with girls and boys in both poetry and fiction.

POETIC FORM. Note was taken earlier that high school readers are less interested in verse than the very young. Many adolescents, both boys and girls, regard the study of poetry with deep aversion though girls are more appreciative than boys. Dr. Helen K. Mackintosh has reported (No. 12) ". . . . children prefer practically every other type of literature to poetry." Dunn (No. 6) and Wissler (No. 24) reached similar conclusions. Jordan (No. 11) made a careful investigation of young readers' choices among books with poetry accounting for fewer than three percent. A majority of the poems which pupils are forced to endure in classes in English are of types shown by the current study to be rejected by high school students. The evidence indicates that this low valuation may be primarily because of content rather than poetic form. The challenge is to revise the program in poetry.

THE PHILOSOPHICAL. Poems featuring the reflective and philosophical point of view rank low with young people. Girls are the more receptive as shown by their ranking of 59 poems of this type 8.5 points higher than boys.

RELIGION. Religious poetry ranks low with adolescents, especially with boys who place it 10.4 points lower than girls. However, it is noteworthy that from junior high school onward religious poetry makes gains with senior high school students, with young adults, with the middle-aged, and with the old. In the "religious novel," religion is often one of several important elements such as history, war, and romantic love.

SCIENCE. It was pointed out in the writer's discussion of science in *The Reading Interests of Young People* (1950) that since a majority of the eight selections tested in science included dramatic elements they were probably rated too high to be representative in interest. Actually, the three without drama, though in popular style, were rated an average of 49.9 points by boys and girls, which was 18.1 points lower than the score for the group of eight. Later a longer list of titles on science was tested in the junior high school, materials written to attract average readers, such as those by Slosson and Beebe. To 28 such selections, boys and girls gave an average score of 51.7 points, a rating which places science among the most unpopular types of reading. A few boys are enthusiastic. Interest in popular science magazines and in science fiction should not be confused with interest in science.

SENTIMENT. Girls are much more favorably moved by the gentler sentiments than boys. Among them are sympathy, self-sacrifice, generosity, charity, and kindliness. Eighty-eight poems of sentiment were placed 10.1 points lower by boys than by girls, and 17 short stories featuring sentiment, exclusive of romantic love, were placed 10.2 points lower by boys. Boys reject physical weakness and lack of aggressiveness in males. They honor physical courage and heroism.

THE SUPERNATURAL. Girls' and boys' choices among stories of the supernatural often depend to a large extent on other interest factors. Boys show a preference for "The Gray Champion" (fighting) and for "The Masque of the Red Death" (bloody death). Girls may be influenced by the element of romantic love in approving "The Specter Bridegroom." When feats of strength or prowess are involved, as frequently occurs in myths, legends, and hero tales, boys usually give a higher rating than girls. Examples: "Adventures of Thor," "Hercules," "King Arthur Stories." Girls vote for love and the other soft emotions: "The Weaver Maiden and the Herdsman," "Persephone," "The Other Wise Man." Toward poems of the supernatural, girls in almost every instance show greater tolerance.

CHOOSING INTERESTING READING MATERIALS FOR YOUNG PEOPLE

Since the differences in the reading interests of boys and girls are marked, the appraisal of the suitability of a selection should be made separately for boys and for girls. Then, if the objective is to determine the suitability of a certain selection for both boys and girls, it is necessary only to answer the question: Does it rank high by both ratings?

In examining a selection for interest factors attractive to boys, we may well look first for action. If the selection fails to tell a story, its chances with boys, except where obvious humor or patriotism is a dominant factor, are poor. A second factor equally to be insisted upon, if human characters are present, is that male rather than female characters be dominant. With these two requisites present, we may then balance the favorable against the unfavorable interest factors. If the narrative is dominated by any one or a combination of the following (assuming certain adverse factors mentioned below to be absent), we may be reasonably confident that the selection will rank well with boys: adventure (including war), animals, obvious humor, and patriotism. Sentiment, except romantic love, and the supernatural may be considered neutral factors if they are not obtrusive. The same may be said of didacticism if the "lesson" is concealed. Factors that lower the ranking of the selection (the degree of lowering depending upon the prominence of the factor) are: romantic love, home and family life, religion, and philosophizing. It should be added that there are certain factors which appear to have no adverse effect when they are minor accompaniments, yet will not be tolerated as major factors: artistry, nature subjects as defined above, and description. Two interest factors are sufficiently powerful to recommend a selection to boys even without narration: obvious humor and patriotism.

As with boys, the first characteristic to look for in appraising selections for girls' reading is action. Girls are a little less insistent on this factor than boys. Characters may be either male or female, though girls rank selections whose chief characters are girls or women higher on average. Several of the special factors that are favorable to popularity with boys influence girls in a similar way. However, some of these favorable factors are more influential with girls; some less. Somewhat more interesting to girls than to boys is humor; less interesting are outdoor adventure and fierce wild animals. Favorable, too, are the benevolent sentiments, romantic love, and home and family. As with boys, there are elements which will not be tolerated by girls as dominant factors that are accepted in moderate amounts: emphasis on artistry, nature, description and didacticism. As a general rule we may say that the neutral and rejected factors are tolerated to a greater degree by girls than by boys.

To repeat what has been said earlier: If a selection is to be satisfactory for reading by girls and boys in common, it must meet the separate standards for girls' and boys' reading materials.

Attention has been called to the fact that the reading materials generally used in literature classes are better liked by girls than by boys in a ratio of more than two to one, and that on the evidence of the data collected in this study most of the literary types are better liked by girls than by boys. The question arises, then, whether these figures are true with respect to boys' and girls' reactions toward literature in general or whether they apply only to the materials chosen by educators for classroom use. Since the question is posed most strongly with respect to poetry (1) because of the marked divergence in the attitudes of boys and girls toward it, and (2) because poetry constitutes such a large part of the literary material offered to high school pupils, an investigation was made. The results suggest a tentative answer.

The plan was to compare the list of several hundred poems afforded by the current study with a standard anthology of poetry prepared for sale to the general public. If this collection included a better proportional representation of poems better liked by boys than by girls than did school classrooms, it might be expected that among the poems common to both the anthology and our list, a somewhat higher proportion would prove to be better liked by boys than the proportion shown by our total list of poems. The results, whatever they showed, should help to determine the relative attitudes of boys and girls toward poetry. This comparison would throw light also on the question as to whether the poems commonly used for class study were better liked, as a whole, than selections found in more representative collections.

To insure that the general anthology of poetry to be compared with our list should not be unconsciously skewed by feminine preferences, it seemed desirable to choose a collection edited by a man. *What I Like in Poetry*, by William Lyon Phelps, was selected. Every poem found in this book and also included on our lists was tabulated. Of the 150 poems thus secured, only 10 per cent were better liked by boys, compared with 19 per cent for our list of 466. Boys gave the 150 poems an interest score of 57.6 (our 466 poems, 60.7); girls rated the 150 poems 67.5 compared with 68.3 for the list of 466. The spread between boys and girls for the 150 poems of Phelps's collection was 9.9 points; for the 466 poems, 7.6 points.

If Phelps's collection is a fair sample of the poetry read by the general public and is representative as to literary quality, the comparisons made tend to confirm certain findings presented elsewhere in this study:

1. Girls like poetry decidedly better than do boys.
2. Girls' tastes in poetry are more literary than boys' tastes. (The assumption is made that the Phelps collection is of good literary quality.)
3. If boys are to enjoy poems in the classroom as much as girls do, teachers and curriculum specialists must make a major revision in the poetry offered as a basis for class instruction.

CHAPTER XI

The Influence of Good and Poor Teaching on Reading Interests

THE ASSUMPTION IS ALMOST UNIVERSAL, AND PROBABLY JUSTIFIED, that pupils learn a great deal more under "superior" teachers than under "average" or "weak" teachers. "To learn," as used here, means to acquire facts, formulas, rules and techniques—the learning which can be imparted by a teacher with a strong personality, using traditional methods, based primarily on specific work assignments. It may be recalled that studying the contents of a literary selection and facts about it is not equivalent to developing a fondness for it.

If, as many are now persuaded, the development of a reading habit based on a love of reading is a primary concern in planning the school's program in literature, it is of high consequence to know to what degree the "good" teacher using "good" methods is a factor in attaining this objective. This question might be answered, it seemed, if we could fairly compare the results secured in the classroom by superior teachers with the results secured by average and weak teachers.

Since the raw data from which classroom results could be computed had already been collected as the basic operation of the investigation, the second major step was to compile lists of superior, average, and weak teachers. To make this possible, forms were sent to a large number of principals whose teachers of English had secured reading reports from their students. The form listed the teachers concerned and asked the principal to rate each teacher on a five-point scale: superior, above average, average, below average, weak. The request was made that each teacher be rated from the standpoint of teachers of English in general, and not by comparison only with the teacher's colleagues in the local school, who might not be a representative group. The further suggestion was made to the principal that since the average teacher was to be found at the midpoint of the scale taken as a whole, as many teachers would be found below this point as above it.

When the data from these blanks were compiled, it was found that more than twice as many teachers had been designated "superior" as were listed as "weak." Without inquiring into the reasons that might lead a principal to rate an undue proportion of his teachers "superior" as compared with "weak," the fact that the many schools and teachers involved assured a reasonably normal representation of English teachers seemed to justify adding the teachers designated "below average" to those designated "weak." A further justification of this procedure is found in the fact that even this combined group totaled a smaller number of teachers than the single group rated "superior" by the principals. In any case, it is clear that the two groups—"superior" as compared with the combined "below average plus weak"—represent, so far as the principals' judgments are concerned, *good* teachers as contrasted with *poor* teachers.

The number of cases available for this phase of the study was reduced by the fact that only those teachers could be considered whose classes (1) were balanced as to the number of boys and girls included, and (2) had reported on several different selections for which scores had been established by the study as a whole. The latter restriction was necessary, since the reactions of a teacher's pupils to a single selection would provide too narrow a basis for assessing the teacher's influence. Further, the classes were so chosen that the classes of good and poor teachers were balanced from the standpoint of their proportions of superior, average, and weak pupils.

The reading reports of the classes of twenty-eight "poor" teachers and sixty "superior" teachers affording data on an average of five selections each were found to be usable.

The data for a single teacher's students were tabulated as follows. Entered after each title were: (1) its interest score as found for the local student group only; (2) its interest score as established by the study as a whole; (3) the difference in points between the local score and the score established by the study as a whole, preceded by a plus or minus sign to show whether the local score was greater than or less than the established score; (4) the quotient of the algebraic sum of differences as obtained in point 3 above divided by the number of selections. This quotient (plus or minus) represented the average number of points by which literary selections were better liked—or less liked—than average under the particular teacher. Scores were obtained in this manner for all 60 superior teachers. The total tabulation revealed that under 33 superior teachers reading materials were better liked, and under 27 superior teachers they were less liked than under teachers generally. Under the 60 superior teachers, students rated reading materials 0.81 point higher than under teachers generally.

A similar plan was followed in dealing with the data for the 28 weak teachers. The results were: (1) in 19 cases selections were less liked than average under weak teachers, and in 9 cases they were better liked than average; (2) under 28 weak teachers, students rated reading materials 2.78 points lower than under teachers generally.

Computation of the standard deviations and the standard deviation of the difference of scores for superior teachers and for weak teachers permitted the finding of the critical ratio 2.19. Since the difference is in the expected direction, it may be said to be reliable at the 5 per cent level of significance.

The 0.81 point by which students rated selections higher under superior teachers than under average teachers is so small as to raise the question as to whether the better results under superior teachers were not caused by chance factors rather than by the teacher's personality and methods.

It might be suggested that (1) since the instructions to principals called for the classification of the teacher with respect to total performance in English teaching, some teachers might have been ranked superior to whom the principal would not have given that ranking had the instructions specifically stated that ability to teach literature only should be considered; (2) principals are likely to designate as "superior" teachers who have strong personalities, who have no trouble with discipline, and whose students absorb enough of the subject matter and skills assigned so that they pass regularly from grade to grade. A skewing of the principals' ratings by these influences may have caused certain teachers to receive ratings as "superior" who were not in fact superior in promoting an interest in literature. Conversely, the same influences may have caused certain other teachers who were actually outstanding in leading their pupils to a greater interest in literary materials to be designated as "average" or "weak." The difference of 0.81 actually found may therefore be accepted as a conservative estimate of teacher influence, which probably would have proved greater if principals' estimates had been based specifically on teacher skill in promoting reading interest.

Early in the tabulation of the data relating to the teacher's influence on young people's interests in the selections studied, it became evident that the results would show that not every teacher designated as superior would have results indicating that his pupils had been led to a greater than average liking for the selections studied in his classes. At that point two special lists were drawn from among the superior teachers: (1) a list of 21 teachers whose teaching of literature the writer had observed and whom he considered "superior" from the standpoint not of teaching content but of providing experiences calculated to promote a reading habit based on a love of reading; (2) a list of 10 teachers from the 21 with whose work he was well acquainted and whom he rated among the upper 2 per cent of English teachers in New York State from the standpoint of inspiring young people with an interest in literature and a love of reading. The results of the tabulation of data for the teachers on the two special lists were surprising.

The reports of the students of the 21 teachers on the first list indicated that, on the average, they liked literary selections 0.3 point better than do children in general. Under 11 of the 21, results were below average.

The pupils of the 10 teachers who had been judged as belonging to the upper 2 per cent in their skill in stimulating a love of reading, were found to like the selections on which they reported 1.54 points better than average and 4.32 points better than the interest scores under weak teachers. Even here, however, only six of the ten teachers secured results better than average.

Deductions: (1) It appears to be strongly indicated that "superior" teachers (whatever the merit of their work in other respects, and presumably this merit is great) have little, if any, greater influence than do average teachers in increasing the pupils' liking for individual selections studied in those teachers' classes. (2) The average of 2.78 points by which selections taught by poor teachers are less liked than average, suggests strongly that the methods and personalities of weak teachers do produce unsatisfactory results from the standpoint of young people's interest in literary selections.

What explanation may be offered of the surprisingly narrow spread (0.81 point) between the results secured under superior teachers and under teachers generally? First, it must be recognized that the teacher who is regarded as "successful" may receive this recognition on the basis of "good discipline" and the success of his students in acquiring a knowledge of content. A little reflection will show that quite possibly the more a pupil learns to parrot about Burke's Speech, the more he may hate it. In the second place, it appears reasonably obvious that young people may develop a marked love of reading without liking many of the selections they read—particularly selections chosen by someone else and with respect to which they are required to perform a variety of distasteful assignments. Third, under the very teacher who greatly stimulates wide, interested, and open-minded reading, the reaction to selections commonly assigned for school study may be comparatively unfavorable, since under this type of experience with literature the student is encouraged to rely upon his own judgment rather than to adopt the high appraisal of critic and teachers.

From the standpoint of instructional procedures and results, it appears that if we wish young people to enjoy classroom reading assignments, the assignment of suitable selections for study is much more influential than the teaching methods employed. This conclusion is based on the data of the current study, which show that there is a difference of more than 20 percentage points between the average popularity scores of the upper one-third and the lower one-third of the selections commonly used in English classrooms, while the average difference in popularity scores under superior and weak teachers when the *same* selections are taught is only 3.59 points.

CHAPTER XII

The Findings of Certain Other Studies

A NUMBER OF PREVIOUS STUDIES OF YOUNG PEOPLE'S READING IN-
terests have been discussed earlier. This chapter will be devoted to
comments on the conclusions of certain other studies in the light of
the findings of the current study.

Although the pupils who contributed to Jordan's study (No. 11)
averaged younger than those of the current study, results of the two
studies agree in the main. Stories of various types (novels, juvenile
fiction, adventure) constitute the major part (91 per cent) of boys'
reading, according to Jordan, with adventure at the top of the list.
For boys ten to thirteen, books dealing with war and scouting, school
sports, boy scouts, and strenuous adventure constitute by far the
larger part of reading materials. Jordan finds also that biography,
history, poetry, science, travel, information, and humor are much
less popular. Jordan's results differ from those of the current study in
showing humor more popular with boys than with girls. However,
this finding is clearly the result of a difference in classification, since
Jordan includes *Tom Sawyer* and *Huckleberry Finn* as humor, while
the current study treats them as books of fiction. Had Jordan ex-
cluded these two books from his classification "humor," this topic

would have received a higher rating by girls than by boys.

Girls, too, are more interested in stories than in other forms of writing. The types of narrative popular with girls are different, Jordan finds, from the types best liked by boys. Home, home and school, school, love, stories with historical background, mild adventure, and fairy stories are the best liked fields. In nonfiction, girls read some poetry and drama.

Comparison between Jordan's results and the findings of the current study is somewhat handicapped because of differences in methods of collecting and organizing the materials. A detailed examination of Jordan's tabulations, however, confirms the major agreement between the two studies.

The study made by Terman and Lima (No. 20) concerned the reading of pupils 6 to 16 years of age. The reference here will be to the study's report upon the reading interests of those aged 11 or older. For the age period 11 to 16 the authors report that boys are interested in adventure, sports, biography, historical narrative, inventions, mechanics, mythology, and science. The current findings agree so far as the interests which Terman and Lima report to be dominant. These authors imply that interest in mythology is declining by the time children are 12 years of age: "They still read mythology." The authors indicate that a strong interest in mechanics and science is confined to smaller groups than is the interest in adventure, sports, and biography. "About 25 per cent of 11-year-old boys express some interest in books on mechanics, electricity, aircraft, or exploration." Their observations are further borne out by the table presented by Terman and Lima on page 73. Under "Percentage of Books Read by Groups" is the information that boys' reading includes the following: history, biography, and travel, 5 percent; science, 3 per cent; adventure or mystery, 56 per cent.

Terman and Lima report that girls 11 to 16 enjoy stories of home and school life, of adventure, of domestic animals, and of love; and biography. They state that eleven-year-old girls "still retain an interest in fairy tales and fantastic stories." This last interest is not mentioned in the authors' statements with respect to the reading of older girls.

Atkinson (No. 3) reports boys' interests as adventure, mystery, invention, combat, humor; and girls' interests as adventure, mystery, love, humor, and kindness.

Mackintosh (No. 12) made a very careful study of children's interests in poetry in the public schools of Grand Rapids, Michigan, because earlier investigations indicated the failure of the current courses of study in literature "to provide poetry within the range of children's interests and experiences." She concluded that "children prefer every other type of literature to poetry," and recommended that a minimum of about 500 pupil reports be used to determine the popularity of each poem at a given grade level.

Thorndike (No. 21) reports that sex is "conspicuously more important" than age or intelligence in influencing children's choices of reading materials. For boys the more favorable special interest factors are: animals, outdoor adventure, mystery, success, sports, travel, exploration, biography, war, occupations. The unfavorable factors are: mild child adventure, child life in other lands, magic and fantasy, romantic love, school life, feminine activities, self-improvement. For girls he found the following factors to be favorable: animals, mild child adventure, child life in other lands, magic and fantasy, romantic love, adult adventure, success, school life, feminine activities, war, self-improvement, occupations. Unfavorable factors: sports, mythology, travel, hobbies, science, biography. In the main, Thorndike's findings and those of the current study are in close agreement.

It seems probable that some, possibly all, of the seeming disagreements result from differences in the ages of the readers contributing the data, or from the differences in the ways the data were collected. Thorndike's data were collected from pupils in grades 4 to 12, with grades 5 to 6 contributing the largest numbers, while the numbers of reports from grades 10 to 12 were small. It appears a safe conclusion that the average age of the readers in Thorndike's investigation was three or more years younger than the average age of those in the current study. It must be noted, too, that it is generally agreed that considerable changes in children's interests occur between grades 4 and 7. This difference in age probably explains the approval of magic and fantasy by the girls of Thorndike's study. Indeed, Thorndike says (page 38): "The interests of earlier childhood in stories of talking animals, magic, dolls, child life, etc., show a sharp decline as the child grows older." It may well be, also, that the girls of Thorndike's investigation gave an unfavorable rating to sports stories because a large proportion of them were too young to have developed an interest in high school sports. Thorndike found that girls rated biography "rather low to moderate" except biographies of women, while the current study shows that girls rate biography moderately high. It may be that the unenthusiastic rating of biography in Thorndike's study is due to the particular titles offered. The evidence of the current study is that girls are less interested in aviation than in most forms of outdoor adventure, yet one of Thorndike's five titles for biography is *Fliers All*. Invention (allied to science) is not a very favorable interest factor for girls, yet *Born an Inventor* is another of

Thorndike's titles under biography. A third title in the group is *King Richard the Lion-Hearted* (life and battles). This title, too, may have received an unfavorable rating by girls because of the emphasis on fighting, a factor shown by the current study to lack appeal for girls. At this point it might be countered that Thorndike found that girls approve of war. In reply, attention is called to the two titles relating to war employed by Thorndike's investigation: *Must America Fight?* and *Japan Loses the War*. The current study reveals that girls approved selections *against* war, while they disapproved the accounts of actual fighting. It is suggested that if Thorndike's technique were used in such a way as to keep two factors, "war" (fighting) and "against war," separate, the reactions of girls would be found to be different in the two cases.

Witty, Coomer, and McBean (No. 27) investigated the book choices of children in ten elementary schools in and near Chicago. The results for pupils in the upper two grades (7 and 8) will be compared with the results of the current study for the same grades. In spite of the fact that the data are not directly comparable because of different methods of assembling (the Witty study asked pupils to list the five books they had read and most enjoyed during the school year, 1944–45) there is a good degree of correspondence in the ranking of well-liked books as determined by the two studies. There is agreement between the Witty and the current study on a number of findings.

1. The list of favorites for grades 7 and 8 is definitely weighted with books of action and adventure.
2. Humor is a favorable factor in young people's choices of reading materials.
3. Interest in fairy stories has waned markedly by the time young people have reached the seventh grade.
4. Many of the favorite books are found to be included on approved lists made by librarians, teachers, and other adult groups interested in young people's reading.
5. Many books written for adults are read with satisfaction by pupils in grades 7 and 8.

SUMMARY: With respect to the interest factors influencing children's reading interests, the findings of Jordan, Terman and Lima, Atkinson, Mackintosh, Thorndike, and Witty, Coomer, and McBean accord in the main with those of the current study.

CHAPTER XIII

A Proposed Approach to the Teaching of Literature

THE HEAVY TEACHING LOAD ALMOST UNIVERSAL TODAY MANDATES the saving of time and labor wherever such can be effected without lowering the efficiency of instruction. If, then, a particular teaching procedure yields greater effectiveness, as well as a saving of effort, that procedure merits careful consideration. It is the almost universal practice in American public high schools for a part, at least, of the program in literature to consist of selections studied in common. Aside from the question of time and labor saving, this approach has the advantages of (a) providing opportunities for helpful oral discussions of a wide variety of human problems, and (b) the establishment of a background of common literary experience useful in leading students to develop an intelligent approach to their independent reading.

This plan (reading in common) has been vigorously assailed, particularly on the grounds that the reading materials actually used (selected by teachers and course-of-study makers) were frequently seriously disliked by a considerable percentage of the pupils. The result, it was pointed out, was a disgust with literature rather than a love for it. That this attack was soundly based receives voluminous support in the current study. The cure, the attackers claim, is to provide an individualized reading program for each child. Were it obligatory to choose between the reading in common of disliked selections and an individualized program, the second, even with the sacrifices it would entail, would be preferable. Such a choice is not necessary.

The alternative plan proposed is this: (a) that part of the class program in literature consist of the reading or study in common by the class or by groups formed within the class of a list of selections *known to be well liked by both boys and girls,* with the retention, consequently, of the advantages of this approach; (b) that a second part of the program consist of wide reading of individually chosen selections carried out under the guidance of the teacher. Considerable, and possibly convincing, evidence that such a program is preferable to either of the other two is provided by a study[9] which was carried out in twenty-four classes in the New York State schools which varied widely in size and type of community represented.

The returns from the 233 students who composed the 12 experimental classes in the study (there were 12 control classes also) revealed that 91.4 per cent answered "Yes" to the following question: "Do you approve the plan of using part of the time for reading one or more selections by all pupils in common and part of the time in reading additional selections chosen by the pupil himself?"

That there might be no doubt that students understood the effect of their replies, the further questions were asked: "Do you approve the plan of using a part of the class time for rather free and informal class discussion of the various materials pupils have been reading according to the plan used this semester (the beginning of each unit in literature with a study of selections in common, and following with a wide reading of materials chosen by pupils individually within wide limits set by the teacher)?" The reply of 90.2 per cent of the pupils was "Yes." "Would you prefer that all class time in literature be spent by pupils in silent reading with no time given to class discussion of the selections read?" "No," replied 96.3 per cent.

The ten teachers whose classes participated in the study also gave their views in a questionnaire. It seems desirable at this point to note that each of the ten teachers taught one class using the experimental

[9]Results of the study were published in *The School Review,* Vol. XLIX, No. 8 (October 1941), pp. 603–13.

plan and a second class using the teacher's own customary plan. Overwhelmingly the teachers voted that the experimental plan, as compared with the teachers' own, developed greater enthusiasm on the part of the students, and that with the necessary materials at hand (primarily, sufficient materials to carry out wide individual reading following the reading in common), the experimental plan would be no more difficult. The teachers further found the experimental plan of teaching the more enjoyable of the two.

If the classroom approach to literature above discussed is an advance over plans customarily used by English teachers, the current study has definite significance in making the approach practicable and effective.

The data of this study show that more than 50 per cent of the selections commonly provided for class study rank low in interest with secondary-school students. Probably no one would deny that this situation is inimical to the development of a reading habit based on a love of reading. On the other hand, this study also presents for junior and for senior high school a sufficient number and variety of well-liked selections to insure genuine satisfaction for young people in that part of the school program devoted to reading and discussing selections in common. Further, the list, because it is more extensive than required to implement the program of common reading, provides guidance for the teacher in helpfully advising pupils as to their individually chosen reading. It may well be that in this area of the reading program the teacher's knowledge of what to *refrain* from recommending is more important than his actual recommendations. Since this study lists a considerable number of selections which have in the past constituted the traditional teacher recommendations, an instrument of some potency is provided in the halting crusade for a more effective teaching of literature.

A corollary of the proposition just discussed relates to the need for unusual care in the choice of reading materials for boys. The current study confirms previous findings that girls enjoy a large part of the reading materials liked by boys, and that boys reject a formidable proportion of reading materials popular with girls. The unfavorable attitude taken by many boys toward the English class doubtless may be traced in part to the fact that two out of every three selections used in the English classroom are better liked by girls than by boys. The data on the differences in the reactions of boys and of girls to the 4,993 testings of selections used in this study in grades 7 to 12 (Tables 41 and 42) provide the means of insuring that materials to be read in common shall be only those which rank high with both boys and girls.

Since there is almost universal agreement that enjoyment must result from the reading of literature, the subsequent six chapters list titles well liked by boys and by girls in grades 10 to 12 and in grades 7 to 9 in the following fields: fiction (novel, short story), general nonfiction, essay, play, biography, and poetry. The teacher wishing to use in mixed classes only selections enjoyed by both boys and girls should check through available materials when making choices. Supplementary lists of titles popular with boys only or with girls only are also provided. In classes of boys *only* (or girls *only*), the teacher will have available for use all of the materials listed for both boys and girls added to the titles popular with boys only (or popular with girls only).

It is crucial that teachers shall not rely on the *average* interest score for boys and girls in choosing a selection for use in classes of both boys and girls. For example, a book may rank high enough on the composite list to appear to be a satisfactory choice for joint study by boys and girls. However, when the apparently satisfactory placement is the result of a very high rating by girls and a low rating by boys (or vice versa), the book would be decidedly unsuitable. Its use with boys would reaffirm their distrust of teacher-chosen reading materials and defeat the major purposes of presenting literature in the classroom. Fortunately, every field affords satisfactory selections as illustrated for the novel by the following examples: *Huckleberry Finn, Arrowsmith, Les Miserables, Typhoon, Call of the Wild.*

Certain observations may be made with respect to the classics. The generation-long opposition by certain leading English teachers to such widely used classics as Burke's "On Conciliation," "L'Allegro,"-"Il Penseroso," *As You Like It, The Vicar of Wakefield,* Webster's "Bunker Hill Oration," *The Odyssey,* and Macaulay's *Life of Johnson* are borne out by students' reactions. On the other hand, some of the classics have met the test: *Macbeth, Hamlet, Silas Marner, David Copperfield, Treasure Island,* "Old Ironsides," "The Barefoot Boy," "Paul Revere's Ride," "The Deacon's Masterpiece," "A Dissertation upon Roast Pig."

It is not necessary, then, for the teacher to throw overboard all classic literature to meet the interests of young people. However, in view of the high standing both artistically and in the favor of young readers of many modern selections, the use of a large proportion of modern literature seems justified.

The English teacher should be aware of the major interest factors in reading, favorable and unfavorable, for boys and for girls. Assistance may be found in Tables 9 and 10, and in the summary of guiding principles which follows.

TABLE 9

IMPORTANT FACTORS IN THE READING INTERESTS OF HIGH SCHOOL BOYS

FAVORABLE	UNFAVORABLE	NEUTRAL
Action: lively or violent	Description	Literary quality
Physical struggle	Didacticism	Brief description
Characters: male, aggressive	Fairies	Women or girls as minor characters
Animals: wild, domestic	Romantic love	
Humor	Sentiments (soft)	
Courage, heroism	Sentimentality	
Mystery (particularly in detective stories)	In male characters: physical weakness, lack of aggressiveness	
Patriotism		

TABLE 10

IMPORTANT FACTORS IN THE READING INTERESTS OF HIGH SCHOOL GIRLS

FAVORABLE	UNFAVORABLE	NEUTRAL
Action: lively	Violent or bloody action	Brief description
Home and school life	Description	Literary quality
Characters of all ages (including babies)	Didacticism (girls are more tolerant than are boys)	
Humor	Dangerous wild animals	
Animals: domestic; wild, except the dangerous or savage	In poetry: subtle or involved rhyme	
Romantic love	Namby-pambyism	
Sentiments (soft)		
Sentimentality		
Mystery		
Supernatural		
Religion		
Patriotism		

A summary of the guiding principles and suggestions developed during 40 years' study of young people's reading is offered below under six headings.

Guidelines for the High School Program in Reading and Literature

I. In General

1. The reading habit based on a love of reading is the most important academic aim of the school, and every activity requiring reading should be appraised in light of this aim.
2. Reading readiness at every age level is vital.
3. Skill in reading should reach the point where the reader is unconscious of effort. Otherwise, the reading habit may not become permanent.
4. Let young people read what they enjoy except the morally objectionable.
5. Make frequent investigations of what young readers enjoy and keep a cumulative record.
6. There are lessons to be learned from comic books and comic strips: the importance of (a) illustrations; (b) continuous action; (c) ease of reading; (d) ease of access.
7. For guidance in understanding pupils' interests in reading, consult Terman, Jordan, Dunn, Lazar, Witty, and other men and women who have made the effort necessary to base advice on information.
8. Beware of advice from guides who are sentimental about children and sentimental about literature.

II. The Significance of Interest

9. Mental development requires interest.
10. It requires stamina to adhere in practice to a rule all writers on young people's literature acclaim: no selection is good for young readers unless they enjoy it.
11. Old poems and old stories are new to youngsters.
12. When making choices among untested poems, favor those that rollick.
13. To attract most adolescent readers, writings on science must include a story.
14. Didactic poems without a story seldom succeed.
15. Poems of patriotism are still moderately popular in junior and senior high school.
16. Humor is one of the most important interest factors.
17. Interest in fairy stories, fables, myths, legends, and folk tales wanes rapidly during adolescence, particularly with boys.

III. The Importance of Sex Differences in Reading Interests

    18. Sex is so powerful a factor in reading interests that any selection considered for use in mixed classes should be checked for interest with boys and with girls, and if rated low by either group, should be rejected in favor of one approved by both groups.

    19. Girls enjoy many boys' books, but boys reject almost all girls' books.

    20. Romantic love is a decidedly unfavorable factor in stories or poems for boys; favorable for girls.

    21. Violent struggle is an unfavorable factor in reading for girls; favorable for boys.

    22. Mystery is favored by both boys and girls.

    23. Stories of dogs and horses are very popular with both boys and girls.

    24. In gereral, adult magazines are more popular with adolescents than children's magazines.

IV. The Influence of Intelligence and Artistic Taste in Reading Choices

    25. Superior, average, and slow students usually enjoy the same kinds of reading materials.

    26. When selecting poems for young people, avoid those whose principal attraction is literary style.

    27. Young people usually reject subtle and "clever" verse.

    28. Don't be afraid of James W. Riley, Eugene Field, T. A. Daly, and Arthur Guiterman because some authoritarian is unimpressed.

    29. An artistic masterpiece is not good literature for boys and girls unless it gives them genuine pleasure.

V. Selecting Reading Materials for Adolescents

    30. Reading materials for young people have an excellent chance for popularity when they combine several of the favorable interest factors—action, humor, animals, mystery, patriotism (with additional factors for boys: courage, physical struggle, aggressive male characters; for girls: romantic love, home or family life, sentiments of helpful kind)—and are free of the unfavorable—long descriptions, didacticism, fairies, subtleties, and namby-pambyism.

    31. Young people approve and disapprove *individual selections* regardless of authorship.

    32. Do not reject a book because it is one of a series. Judge each series by the same standards used for other books.

33. Use only reading lists known to be based upon adequate evidence.
34. Remember that Shakespeare's songs depend for their appeal upon a very high degree of artistic quality, and reserve them for the literary pupil or literary adult.
35. When told as adventure, biography is popular with boys and girls.
36. When assessing new reading material for young people, recall that in the past the authorities have labeled as dangerous or trashy *Tom Sawyer, Huckleberry Finn, Treasure Island,* the Waverly novels, Dickens in toto, and dozens of other startlingly new works of genius—because they did not conform to accepted canons. The same will, of course, happen again.
37. Reject completely the advice: "Consult your own taste," and enjoy the selection through the pleasure of boys and girls.
38. In addition to the reading shared with associates, every student should have his own reading program encouraged by parents, teachers, and librarians.

CONCLUSION: After 40 years of continued, careful research, a conclusion: *Ultimately,* investigation will supersede divination in the field of young people's reading interests.

CHAPTER XIV

Choosing the Titles to Vitalize the Reading Program: Fiction

THE MAJOR PURPOSE OF THIS CHAPTER IS TO ASSIST TEACHERS AND librarians to introduce young people to reading which will first delight and then captivate with the reading habit. The value of the reading lists offered in vitalizing the high school program in English has been developed by this forty-year study. Teachers who recognize the basic function of interest in transforming learning have here the opportunity to make use of it. In this and following chapters the problem will be examined in various important fields of reading. Chapters will deal with the following literary types: fiction (novels and short stories); nonfiction (general) and literary essays; poems and plays; biographies.

In the past the importance of the marked opposition of the interests of girls and of boys has received inadequate attention; in part, probably, through lack of realization of the extent of this variance, and from the practical consideration that very little precise information has been available concerning the differences in the interests in the literary selections assigned for reading. The interest scores for boys and for girls for thousands of widely used titles now make possible the planning of enjoyable courses for mixed classes, and for classes of boys only or girls only.

FICTION. Fiction is the literary type most widely chosen by boys and girls. In view of the ample supply of well-liked novels and short stories, it is appalling that the majority of high school reading programs rely on a large proportion of the disliked. Particularly unfortunate is the use of so many titles which are liked by girls, but seriously disliked by boys. For successful reading in common, every title should be checked for interest by both boys and girls. Otherwise a large number of students are taught to reject reading. The lists in this and the following chapters provide an ample supply of well-liked titles including those of high quality.

From their choices for class reading, it appears that experts as well as teachers are either unaware of or disregard differences in the interests of boys and girls. In many cases, when the *average* interest of boys and girls appears satisfactory, boys' interests are so much lower than girls' interests that a large number of students are bored or disgusted.

It is significant that there are books and other selections that are suitable for class use over several grades (e.g., grades 7 to 12), as shown by the high scores students give. A choice of the grade in which to present a selection, in addition to its high standing with both boys and girls, may depend on a number of factors related to the local situation: its availability, previous use in the school's program, and conformity with special interests of the class. If the class is composed of boys only, the teacher's choices should be expanded for *novels* in grades 10 to 12 (31) by adding the list enjoyed by boys only (22) to the list favored by both boys and girls (a total of 53). For a class of senior high school girls only, the total available list is 63.

The plan for the *novel* in grades 7 to 9 is similar to the plan for grades 10 to 12. The joint list for boys and girls offers 63 titles. There are 19 additional novels enjoyed by boys only (total 82), and 23 endorsed by girls only (total 86).

SHORT STORIES. There are 68 short stories on the joint list for boys and girls in the senior high school with 11 more well-liked by boys (total, 79). Girls only approve of 35 (total, 103). The junior high school list affords 99 popular short stories for mixed classes with 26 favored by boys only (total, 125), while girls give special endorsement to 35 (total, 134).

In view of the hundreds of short stories tested, it may surprise that the lists of the suitable ones are so restricted. It seems probable that the authorities who have designated the short stories for use in high schools have failed to note the subtlety and sophistication of many of them.

Special care should be exercised in making choices among junior novels, particularly those that deal with adolescent problems. Many of them have a high appeal for girls but are rejected by boys. There are also junior novels for boys, usually of adventure. Frequently, these junior books may be recommended for supplementary reading, or used in classes of girls only or boys only.

Among the hundreds of titles of fiction listed in the complete table of tested selections, teachers will find other novels and short stories rated 80.0 or higher by both boys and girls which they may prefer to use in their classes instead of the ones on these special lists.

Another and most important use for the lists of well-liked selections from the literary types is provided when the teacher recommends titles for *individual* reading. *Adequate* advice on the student's personal reading is a service of unsurpassed importance. This service is heightened when the librarian or teacher makes it a point to become acquainted with the student's previous reading, his hobbies, his ambitions. Even more important, perhaps, is enthusiastic, non-patronizing cooperation with the youngster in his search for the interesting book.

Listed first will be novels approved by boys and girls for mixed classes in grades 10 to 12, followed by a supplementary list approved by boys only, and a third list approved by girls only. Next are lists of novels for use in grades 7 to 9. Following the lists of novels, are lists of short stories treated in similar fashion.

TABLE 11–1

Novels for Reading in Mixed Classes of Boys and Girls, Grades 10 to 12 (The lists approved for grades 10 to 12 should be checked with comparable lists for grades 7 to 9 since some of these novels are better liked in the junior high school.)

TITLE AND AUTHOR	Scores	
	BOYS	GIRLS
African Queen—Forester	84.1	78.9
Arrowsmith—Lewis	84.3	86.5
Beau Geste—Wren	90.3	87.7
Call of the Wild—London	91.1	87.4
Captain Blood—Sabatini	91.2	82.5
Catcher in the Rye—Salinger	83.1	84.8

TITLE AND AUTHOR	Scores	
	BOYS	GIRLS
Dr. Jekyll—Stevenson	84.4	82.0
Drums Along the Mohawk—Edmonds	86.5	83.1
Gone with the Wind—Mitchell	82.2	93.8
Grapes of Wrath—Steinbeck	78.1	80.1
Hawaii—Mitchener	88.4	88.7
Huckleberry Finn—Twain	91.2	90.5
Human Comedy—Saroyan	81.1	85.5
Les Miserables—Hugo	83.4	83.3
Let the Hurricane Roar—Lane	83.0	92.5
Mr. Roberts—Heggen	87.0	85.8
1984—Orwell	82.0	80.9
Northwest Passage—Roberts	89.1	81.2
Quo Vadis—Sienkiewicz	81.1	82.5
Seventeen—Tarkington	80.2	85.7
Silas Marner—Eliot	75.0	90.1
Silver Chalice—Costain	80.2	86.6
Song of Bernadette—Werfel	81.8	91.5
Tale of Two Cities—Dickens	77.0	83.2
Thunderhead—O'Hara	87.2	83.1
To Have and to Hold—Johnston	83.9	87.1
Treasure Island—Stevenson	91.1	78.7
Turmoil—Tarkington	80.4	90.0
Typhoon—Conrad	83.1	82.5
Virginian—Wister	82.8	83.3
White Fang—London	90.9	85.5

TABLE 11-2

Novels Approved by Boys Only, Grades 10 to 12

(This list approved for grades 10 to 12 should be checked with the list for boys only in grades 7 to 9 since some of these novels are better liked in the junior high school.)

TITLE AND AUTHOR	SCORES
Animal Farm—Orwell	85.2
Bridges at Toko-Ri—Michener	85.2
Caine Mutiny—Wouk	87.3
Captain Horatio Hornblower—Forester	80.2
Drums—Boyd	84.1
Enemy Below—Rayner	84.0
Goodbye, Mr. Chips—Hilton	80.2
Ivanhoe—Scott	80.1
Jim Davis—Masefield	80.4

TITLE AND AUTHOR	SCORES
King Solomon's Mines—Haggard	80.7
Last of the Mohicans—Cooper	89.5
Men Against the Sea—Nordhoff and Hall	84.0
Mutiny on the Bounty—Nordhoff and Hall	86.6
Old Man and the Sea—Hemingway	81.5
One Million Pound Note—Twain	85.0
Pudd'n Head Wilson—Twain	82.5
Riverman—White	88.6
Robinson Crusoe—Defoe	84.9
Run Silent, Run Deep—Beach	85.8
Sea Wolf—London	80.3
Smoky—James	86.1
War of the Worlds—Wells	81.6

TABLE 11–3

Novels Approved by Girls Only, Grades 10 to 12
(This list approved for grades 10 to 12 should be checked with the list for
girls only in grades 7 to 9 since some of these novels are better liked in the
junior high school.)

TITLE AND AUTHOR	SCORES
Anna Karenina—Tolstoy	82.0
Beloved Vagabond—Locke	88.0
Bent Twig—Fisher	93.3
Christmas Carol—Dickens	85.5
Crisis—Churchill	82.4
David Copperfield—Dickens	88.8
Dragon Seed—Buck	85.5
Ethan Frome—Wharton	83.4
Farewell to Arms—Hemingway	84.4
Fortitude—Walpole	88.7
For Whom the Bell Tolls—Hemingway	84.3
Giant—Ferber	85.2
Giants in the Earth—Rölvaag	84.4
Good Earth—Buck	85.7
Green Mansions—Hudson	80.0
House of the Seven Gables—Hawthorne	81.3
How Green Was My Valley—Llewellyn	84.9
Jane Eyre—Brontë	90.6
Little Women—Alcott	90.4
Mama's Bank Account—Forbes	85.1
National Velvet—Bagnold	87.7
Of Human Bondage—Maugham	82.1

TITLE AND AUTHOR	SCORES
Oliver Twist—Dickens	82.0
Rebecca—Du Maurier	85.9
Return of the Native—Hardy	82.6
Sayonara—Michener	88.6
Seventeenth Summer—Daly	90.8
Show Boat—Ferber	84.8
So Big—Ferber	88.5
Tales of the South Pacific—Michener	84.7
Teahouse of the August Moon—Patrick	80.9
Wuthering Heights—Brontë	85.7

TABLE 12–1

Novels for Reading in Mixed Classes of Boys and Girls, Grades 7 to 9
(This list approved for grades 7 to 9 should be checked with the comparable list for grades 10 to 12 since some of these novels are better liked in the senior high school.)

TITLE AND AUTHOR	SCORES	
	BOYS	GIRLS
Around the World in Eighty Days—Verne	80.9	79.6
Baldy of Nome—Darling	87.1	84.6
Bob, Son of Battle—Ollivant	85.4	86.6
Call of the Wild—London	90.9	89.1
Captains Courageous—Kipling	83.9	73.7
Circular Staircase—Rinehart	85.0	89.2
Connecticut Yankee in King Arthur's Court—Twain	83.3	82.1
Count of Monte Cristo—Dumas	88.4	83.9
Covered Wagon—Hough	86.2	79.5
David Copperfield—Dickens	75.4	86.6
Dog of Flanders—Ouida	81.2	83.9
Dr. Jekyll—Stevenson	82.7	80.0
Gulliver's Travels—Swift	82.9	79.8
Hoosier Schoolboy—Eggleston	80.1	76.8
Hound of the Baskervilles—Doyle	92.9	88.7
Human Comedy—Saroyan	80.6	78.2
Hunchback of Notre Dame—Hugo	79.0	80.9
Johnny Tremain—Forbes	75.9	81.5
Jungle Books—Kipling	90.8	86.7
King of the Golden River—Ruskin	85.2	86.4
Lance of Kanana—French	91.1	81.0
Lassie Come-Home—Knight	93.1	96.5

TITLE AND AUTHOR	SCORES	
	BOYS	GIRLS
Let the Hurricane Roar—Lane	81.7	88.3
Lorna Doone—Blackmore	82.6	85.2
Man Without a Country—Hale	81.7	76.1
Men of Iron—Pyle	86.7	81.3
Merry Adventures of Robin Hood—Pyle	91.4	81.5
Mutiny on the Bounty—Nordhoff and Hall	85.9	82.5
My Friend Flicka—O'Hara	96.2	94.2
Mysterious Island—Verne	89.7	85.3
1984—Orwell	85.3	82.6
Northwest Passage—Roberts	91.2	76.4
No Time for Sergeants—Hyman	89.8	85.6
Old Yeller—Gipson	86.7	87.0
Oliver Twist—Dickens	83.9	91.2
On the Beach—Shute	86.0	85.2
Penrod—Tarkington	84.3	85.8
Penrod and Sam—Tarkington	88.7	88.7
Pinocchio—Lorenzini	82.9	84.8
Prince and the Pauper—Twain	79.8	83.8
Quintus Getting Well—Mitchinson	86.6	85.9
Real David Copperfield—Graves	82.7	88.3
Red Pony—Steinbeck	79.1	83.6
Remarkable Wreck of the Thomas Hyke—		
Stockton	92.2	85.1
Robin Hood, His Book—Tappan	93.1	81.9
Robinson Crusoe—Defoe	89.7	81.3
Seventeen—Tarkington	74.2	84.8
Shaggy, the Horse from Wyoming—Carter	83.8	88.2
Silas Marner—Eliot	76.1	92.5
Silver Chief—O'Brien	93.0	90.1
Smoky—James	87.8	83.3
Song of Bernadette—Werfel	82.7	92.7
Swiss Family Robinson—Wyss	84.4	84.7
Three Musketeers—Dumas	85.4	75.9
Thunderhead—O'Hara	93.2	92.9
Tom Sawyer—Twain	95.3	93.9
Treasure Island—Stevenson	90.3	77.8
Uncle Tom's Cabin—Stowe	85.8	87.2
Virginian—Wister	80.7	83.0
Voyages of Dr. Dolittle—Lofting	84.6	74.3
White Fang—London	93.2	82.8
White Stag—Seredy	81.6	84.2
White Tiger—Scoville	86.4	85.8

TABLE 12–2

Novels Approved by Boys Only, Grades 7 to 9
(This list approved for grades 7 to 9 should be checked with the list for boys
only in grades 10 to 12 since some of these novels are better liked in senior
high school.)

TITLE AND AUTHOR	SCORES
Big Red—Kjelgaard	80.2
Caine Mutiny—Wouk	84.2
Grizzly King—Curwood	90.6
Guns of Bull Run—Altsheler	80.7
Jim Davis—Masefield	80.7
Kazan—Curwood	90.2
King Solomon's Mines—Haggard	82.2
Last of the Mohicans—Cooper	86.4
Log of a Cowboy—Adams	80.9
Lost Worlds—White	82.0
Run Silent, Run Deep—Beach	89.5
Sea Wolf—London	83.3
Shane—Schaefer	82.5
Story of King Arthur and His Knights—Pyle	85.2
Street Rod—Felsen	86.0
T-Model Tommy—Meader	82.6
Twenty Thousand Leagues Under the Sea—Verne	88.0
White Panther—Waldeck	84.7
Yea! Wildcats!—Tunis	80.5

TABLE 12-3

Novels Approved by Girls Only, Grades 7 to 9
(This list approved for grades 7 to 9 should be checked with the list for girls
only in grades 10 to 12 since some of these novels are better liked in senior
high school.)

TITLE AND AUTHOR	Scores
Blind Colt—Rounds	82.2
Boarded-Up House—Seaman	88.0
Dragon Seed—Buck	87.7
Eight Cousins—Alcott	81.4
Gone with the Wind—Mitchell	91.9
Good Master—Seredy	85.3
Green Grass of Wyoming—O'Hara	81.0
Hans Brinker—Dodge	82.1
Heidi—Spyri	93.2
Junior Miss—Benson	87.1

TITLE AND AUTHOR	Scores
King of the Wind—Henry	84.8
Little Lame Prince—Mulock	85.0
Little Men—Alcott	86.1
Little Women—Alcott	96.5
Mama's Bank Account—Forbes	91.0
Misty of Chincoteague—Henry	81.9
Mrs. Mike—Freedman	86.9
Mrs. Wiggs—Rice	80.3
National Velvet—Bagnold	93.3
Old-Fashioned Girl—Alcott	84.6
Seventeenth Summer—Daly	84.2
Witch of Blackbird Pond—Speare	84.0
Yearling—Rawlings	79.5

TABLE 13-1

Short Stories for Reading in Mixed Classes of Boys and Girls, Grades 10 to 12

(This list approved for grades 10 to 12 should be checked with the list for grades 7 to 9 since some of these short stories are better liked in the junior high school.)

TITLE AND AUTHOR	Scores	
	Boys	Girls
Adventure of the Mason—Irving	80.3	78.3
After Twenty Years—Henry	96.8	96.0
Black Cat—Poe	85.3	85.2
Blue Cross—Chesterton	84.7	85.1
Boob—De Leon	82.6	90.0
Boomerang—McNeely	95.2	99.3
Brothers—Björnson	82.9	85.7
Bunker Mouse—Greene	87.4	79.9
Business Is Business—Lardner	78.6	83.0
By Courier—Henry	88.5	96.8
Comforter—Jordan	82.6	95.9
Cop and the Anthem—Henry	85.5	81.4
Dark Brown Dog—Crane	84.6	89.3
Devil and Daniel Webster—Benét	85.9	84.4
Discourager of Hesitancy—Stockton	82.0	87.1
Face in the Window—Pelley	84.3	88.8
Freshman Fullback—Paine	89.3	86.1
Gallegher—Davis	87.9	82.3
Goliath—Aldrich	91.1	95.4
Gulliver the Great—Dyer	88.2	90.9

TITLE AND AUTHOR	Scores	
	Boys	Girls
Haircut—Lardner	83.8	79.1
I'm a Fool—Anderson	89.7	87.1
Killers—Hemingway	79.6	79.7
King of Boyville—White	87.7	94.8
Krambambuli—Ebner-Eschenback	89.0	89.2
Lady or the Tiger—Stockton	80.0	86.1
Last Leaf—Henry	80.3	90.3
Long Pants—Cobb	85.1	84.3
Mammon and the Archer—Henry	82.3	86.8
Miss Hinch—Harrison	79.7	90.3
Monkey's Paw—Jacobs	82.9	82.0
Moti Guj—Mutineer—Kipling	81.8	82.4
Mr. Conley—Van Loan	86.3	81.2
Mysterious Card—Moffet	90.6	89.9
Mystery of Room 513—Markey	85.6	96.2
Night of the Storm—Gale	86.0	96.4
On the Dodge—James	91.9	81.5
Passion in the Desert—Balzac	87.7	82.1
Paul Jesperson's Masquerade—Boyesen	89.0	93.3
Penrod's Busy Day—Tarkington	82.3	91.2
Peter Projects—Brady	85.6	90.6
Priest's Tale—Bikelos	88.4	87.7
Prodigal Son—The Bible	77.4	81.5
Prunier Tells a Story—Longstreth	81.3	83.8
Pusher-in-the-Face—Fitzgerald	91.5	86.2
Ransom of Red Chief—Henry	88.1	83.0
Retrieved Reformation—Henry	93.4	92.7
Rip Van Winkle—Irving	80.8	75.9
Romance of a Busy Broker—Henry	89.3	92.9
Shoes—Henry	83.5	86.8
Seige of Berlin—Daudet	78.4	82.9
Snows of Kilamanjaro—Hemingway	81.4	76.2
Song in France—Henry	89.2	89.8
Speckled Band—Doyle	89.2	87.8
Tell-Tale Heart—Poe	82.9	84.8
Terrible Night—Chekhov	90.4	94.6
Test—Witherow	80.6	82.9
Three Questions—Tolstoy	80.4	80.3
To Build a Fire—London	87.5	80.6
Tol'able David—Hergesheimer	88.1	82.9
Tony Kytes—Hardy	78.9	85.9
Trial in Tom Belcher's Store—Derieux	89.8	87.1
Twenty Cigarettes—Wylie	96.5	95.3
Waltz—Parker	79.0	88.7

TITLE AND AUTHOR	Scores	
	Boys	Girls
Where Love Is—Tolstoy	83.0	91.8
Wolf, the Storm Leader—Caldwell	88.1	86.3
Wuthless Dog—Holt	81.8	90.7
Yellow Cat—Steele	87.4	75.6

TABLE 13-2

Short Stories Approved by Boys Only, Grades 10 to 12
(This list approved for grades 10 to 12 should be checked with the list for grades 7 to 9 since some of these short stories are better liked in the junior high school.)

TITLE AND AUTHOR	Scores
Adventure of the Black Fisherman—Irving	79.3
All Gold Canyon—London	83.2
As a Dog Should—Alexander	80.1
Fathoms Deep—Cohen	80.9
Gold Bug—Poe	81.3
Home Is the Sailor—Adams	82.4
Instrument of the Gods—Colcord	81.1
Little Regiment—Crane	81.7
Specimen Jones—Wister	87.6
When Grandpa Logged for Paul—Watt	84.5
Why Are Women Like That?—Cobb	80.6

TABLE 13-3

Short Stories Approved by Girls Only, Grades 10 to 12
(This list approved for grades 10 to 12 should be checked with the list for grades 7 to 9 since some of these short stories are better liked in the junior high school.)

TITLE AND AUTHOR	Scores
Basquerie—Kelly	88.4
Bedquilt—Fisher	80.9
Bill—Gale	87.0
Birthday—Winslow	80.1
Bred in the Bone—Singmaster	80.0
Clothes Make the Man—Tarkington	84.0
Cop and the Anthem—Henry	81.4
Evening Clothes—Gale	85.3
Fat of the Land—Yezierska	82.6
Friend of Napoleon—Connell	87.1

TITLE AND AUTHOR	Scores
Frill—Buck	82.8
Gift of the Magi—Henry	87.1
Heart of Little Shikara—Marshall	82.9
Her First Ball—Mansfield	87.0
His Mother's Son—Ferber	84.2
"Ice Water, Pl——!"—Hurst	83.9
Jean-ah Poquelin—Cable	80.3
Jury of Her Peers—Glaspell	82.1
Knives from Syria—Riggs	82.5
'Lijah—Smith	84.8
Mary—Mansfield	87.7
Necklace—Maupassant	86.6
Other Wise Man—Van Dyke	80.9
Papa Was Foxy—Milburn	81.4
Paul's Case—Cather	84.2
Quality—Galsworthy	81.6
Revolt of Mother—Freeman	85.9
Sheener—Williams	82.2
Silent Brothers—Bennett	82.7
Sisterly Scheme—Bunner	87.2
Soul of the Great Bell—Hearn	82.1
Stove—Pickthall	83.9
They Grind Exceeding Small—Williams	80.1
Third Ingredient—Henry	87.2
Wee Willie Winkie—Kipling	80.5

TABLE 14-1

Short Stories for Reading in Mixed Classes of Boys and Girls, Grades 7 to 9

(This list approved for grades 7 to 9 should be checked with the list for grades 10 to 12 since some of these short stories are better liked in the senior high school.)

TITLE AND AUTHOR	Scores	
	Boys	Girls
Adventure of the Mason—Irving	85.2	85.9
Adventure of the Norwood Builder—Irving	83.4	81.8
Adventure of the One Penny Black—Queen	89.8	92.2
After Twenty Years—Henry	94.6	93.6
Aladdin and His Wonderful Lamp—Arabian Nights	86.2	93.6
Ali Baba and the Forty Thieves—Arabian Nights	87.3	84.4
American, Sir!—Andrews	80.6	79.2
Baby Sylvester Leaves the Mining Camp—Harte	80.3	82.5

TITLE AND AUTHOR	Scores	
	Boys	Girls
Barbed Wire—Perry	84.3	80.7
Barker's Luck—Harte	80.3	82.1
Billy, the Dog That Made Good—Seton	89.9	86.3
Biography of a Grizzly—Seton	89.9	89.0
Bishop's Silver Candlesticks—Hugo	78.3	85.3
Black Beaver—Scoville	87.6	83.9
Black Eagle—Ford	94.8	89.4
Black Hero of the Ranges—Mills	96.0	84.5
Boomerang—McNeely	83.0	96.3
Boys Will Be Boys—Cobb	86.7	83.4
Christmas Present for a Lady—Kelly	78.0	93.9
Citizenship, the Northfield Ideal—Heyliger	82.9	90.0
Clothes Make the Man—Tarkington	83.9	93.8
C'n I Have a Dog?—McNeely	90.3	93.5
Coaly Bay, the Outlaw Horse—Seton	87.9	81.5
Collie in the Desert—Mills	88.5	84.9
Combat with the Octopus—Hugo	93.3	78.7
C.Q.D.—Lanier	92.7	88.4
Czar and the Angel—Folk Tale	85.2	89.9
Dark Brown Dog—Crane	85.6	91.4
Discourager of Hesitancy—Stockton	82.4	91.0
Dog That Lied—Mitchell	78.2	86.1
Dog That Saved the Bridge—Robbins	93.3	87.9
Face in the Window—Pelley	94.4	95.4
Fawn—Rawlings	85.3	90.1
Fight with a Hawk—Watson	91.3	84.1
Five Thousand Dollars Reward—Post	83.8	80.2
Fools Walk In—Brier	95.2	92.3
Gallegher—Davis	90.0	85.3
Ghitza—Bercovici	88.7	86.7
Great Race—Hawkes	93.9	83.2
Grizzly Mother—Mills	92.4	92.3
Growing Up—Morris	88.6	89.8
Gulliver Among the Giants—Swift	90.6	90.0
Gulliver the Great—Dyer	87.9	86.3
Happy Prince—Wilde	89.9	92.6
Hercules—Sabin	89.0	80.1
How Abe Lincoln Paid for His Stockings— Eggleston	90.5	96.3
How Potts Saved the Night Express—Baker	90.5	85.3
How Thor Found His Hammer—Mabie	80.2	82.1
How Tom Sawyer Whitewashed the Fence—Twain	89.2	89.9
Huck Finn in Disguise—Twain	95.3	92.9
Interlopers—Munro	83.0	83.3

TITLE AND AUTHOR	Scores	
	Boys	Girls
Irish Witch Story—Wilde	81.8	86.9
Israel Drake—Mayo	91.8	86.2
Judas Goose—Van Etten	92.7	93.1
Kiskies—Vontver	84.5	91.0
Lame Duck—Curry	95.7	96.3
Last Lesson—Daudet	81.7	89.4
Leader of the Herd—Cooper	87.0	86.8
Legend of Sleepy Hollow—Irving	82.6	83.7
Legend of the Moor's Legacy—Irving	79.0	82.5
Little Orvie's New Dog Ralph—Tarkington	87.1	92.7
Lone Wolf—Roberts	92.9	89.1
Lost and Found—Cohen	83.9	96.0
Monkey's Paw—Jacobs	80.4	83.6
Mystery in Four-and-One-Half Street—Peattie	93.8	93.8
Night of the Storm—Gale	90.3	97.4
Old Pipes and the Dryad—Stockton	81.3	87.3
On Trial for His Life—Fox	87.8	83.0
Paul Bunyan and His Great Blue Ox—Wadsworth	84.4	79.6
Penrod's Busy Day—Tarkington	81.8	90.2
Perfect Tribute—Andrews	81.9	82.0
Pete of the Steel Mills—Hall	90.8	90.1
Ransom of Red Chief—Henry	89.3	85.7
Retrieved Reformation—Henry	89.5	90.0
Reward of Merit—Tarkington	85.8	87.8
Rider of Loma Escondida—Dobie	90.5	82.4
Rikki-Tikki-Tavi—Kipling	84.8	85.8
Rip Van Winkle—Irving	80.2	81.3
Robin Hood and the Butcher—Tappan	89.8	89.1
Satan the War Dog—Baynes	86.8	79.6
Shipment of Mute Fate—Storm	91.0	87.2
Silver Blaze—Doyle	87.8	81.7
Song in France—Henry	85.3	83.4
Spark Neglected—Tolstoy	87.2	88.9
Spot, the Dog That Broke the Rules—Bailey	98.0	95.8
Story of Aboo Seer and Aboo Keer—Arabian Nights	81.7	80.2
Story of Gareth—Malroy	82.0	78.3
Swimming with a Bear—Miller	81.9	79.6
Tabby's Tablecloth—Alcott	86.0	94.0
Tale of Three Truants—Harte	88.4	87.6
Three-Alarm Dogs—Kearney	94.8	93.1
To Build a Fire—London	88.5	77.6
Too Much Horse—Butler	84.0	93.8
Trial in Tom Belcher's Store—Derieux	89.1	91.7
Water Clock—Kummer	80.1	84.0

TITLE AND AUTHOR	Scores	
	Boys	Girls
Where Love Is—Tolstoy	78.1	87.3
Why Bother with Ladders—Davis	91.6	90.0
Winner Who Did Not Play—Allen	84.6	85.9
Wuthless Dog—Holt	91.2	86.7

TABLE 14–2

Short Stories Approved by Boys Only, Grades 7 to 9
(This list approved for grades 7 to 9 should be checked with the list for grades 10 to 12 since some of these short stories are better liked in the senior high school.)

TITLE AND AUTHOR	Scores
Baker, Manager—Voorhees	84.1
Beowulf (retold)—Gummere	82.2
Bunker Mouse—Greene	85.5
Coming of Arthur—Malory	79.5
Elephant Remembers—Marshall	81.2
Enough Gold to Load a Pack Horse—Dobie	87.4
First Bow and Arrow—Waterloo	86.1
For the Supremacy of the Trail—Darling	82.0
Freshman Fullback—Paine	86.9
Gold Bug—Poe	84.2
Heart of Little Shikara—Marshall	81.9
Horseshoe Captures Five Prisoners—Kennedy	86.8
How Balto Brought the Serum to Nome—Kasson	80.2
Last of the Irish Wolves—Seton	84.4
Law of Club and Fang—London	84.9
Lobo, King of Currampaw—Seton	88.5
Luck of Roaring Camp—Harte	79.9
Paul Bunyan of the Great North Woods—Wadsworth	88.0
Paul Bunyan's Great Flapjack Griddle—Wadsworth	87.5
Raid on the Oyster Pirates—London	88.9
Scrub Quarterback—Williams	86.3
Tamerlane—Neal	84.8
Thundering Herd—Hawkes	81.8
Trail of the Sandhill Stag—Seton	84.0
Ulysses and Polyphemus—Lamb	83.3
Wild Thoroughbred—Mills	88.8

TABLE 14–3

Short Stories Approved by Girls Only, Grades 7 to 9
(This list approved for grades 7 to 9 should be checked with the list for grades
10 to 12 since some of these short stories are better liked in the senior high
school.)

TITLE AND AUTHOR	Scores
Actor and the Pig—Phaedrus	80.5
Adventures of Joe Dobson—Unknown	80.7
Betsy Has a Birthday—Fisher	81.3
Bill—Gale	80.0
Cinderella—Grimm	81.5
Constant Tin Soldier—Andersen	83.5
Dust—Lambert	80.0
Fiddle for Gladsome Tunes—Hall	92.2
Friends—Kelly	83.8
Gift of the Magi—Henry	82.5
Golden Touch—Hawthorne	81.2
Good Wits Jump—Kaye-Smith	92.0
Here Comes the King—Fuller	82.1
Intervention of Peter—Dunbar	80.8
Koyo the Singer—Gilbert	85.4
Love Letters of Smith—Bunner	92.1
Man in the House—Singmaster	83.7
Marjorie Daw—Aldrich	81.3
Mending the Clock—Barrie	81.2
Minuet—Dodge	85.4
Necklace—Maupassant	84.1
Other Wise Man—Van Dyke	77.2
Patchwork Quilt—Field	85.5
Perseus—Sabin	83.7
Piece of Red Calico—Stockton	86.8
Pygmalion—Baker	80.4
Race for the Silver Skates—Dodge	81.1
Return to Constancy—Chase	86.9
Revolt of Mother—Freeman	89.6
Robina's Doll—Andrews	83.6
Sheener—Williams	84.3
Steamer Child—Singmaster	83.5
Third Ingredient—Henry	89.0
Wee Willie Winkie—Kipling	81.9
Wild Horse—Balch	81.4

CHAPTER XV

Nonfiction (General) and Essays (Literary)

A COMPARISON OF THE TITLES INCLUDED ON THE RESTRICTED LISTS used in English classes in which teachers or curriculum makers have decided what shall be read with the titles students approve when free to choose their reading shows the superiority of young people's choices from the standpoint of interest. If these student-chosen selections are found to equal or surpass in quality the school-imposed titles, a drastic revision of the reading program would be in order if we believe that interest is an indispensable factor in effective learning. The current chapter will note the evidence for general nonfiction and literary essays.

NONFICTION (GENERAL). The average score given by students for the nonfiction (general) list chosen by teachers for class instruction is 62.4, placing this nonfiction average below the averages for seven of eight important literary types when only school-imposed selections were used. However, when the average score (91.7) of the ten most popular nonfiction titles found on the *final* list which includes pupil-chosen selections (free reading) is compared with the ten best-liked on the restricted list (79.1), we find the student-approved titles ranking 12.6 points higher. Obviously, the schools which imposed their reading lists failed to be guided by student interests.

If it is found that from the standpoint of quality, the titles chosen by students rank as high as the selections imposed by the schools, we may conclude that the schools erred with their imposed lists. High-ranking in interest on the school-required list are *North to the Orient* (Anne Lindbergh); "Shipwrecked in Southern Seas" (Lowell Thomas); *The Whitehouse Gang* (Earl Looker); and "Thomas A. Edison's First Workshop" (F. A. Jones). On the well-liked list added by students are: *Berlin Diary* (Shirer); *Rise and Fall of the Third Reich* (Shirer); and *Hiroshima* (Hersey). Comparisons for novels and short stories also provide very high quality on the student-approved lists.

ESSAYS (LITERARY). Upon first inspection, one might judge that the literary essay would be a favorable form for emphasis in the English class. The ten best-liked essays average 81.6 points in interest. However, an examination of the data provides important sidelights. Eight of the ten best-liked are humorous essays. *Only six* of the very large number tested rank in interest above 80.0. The essay which ranks twentieth on the extensive list rates below the 50 percentile among the titles of all types commonly read in English classes, indicating that young people turn from this highly sophisticated literary form. Only the rare high school student is interested. Even the majority of college graduates with their greater average intelligence and added years of training in English reject it.

An examination of the extended list of tested essays with their very low interest scores makes it evident that the literary essay should not receive major emphasis in the English program as it has in the past. The extremely limited list that has reached the minimum interest standard is a warning.

Our lists of approved nonfiction include 41 for use in mixed classes in grades 10 to 12; an additional 27 for boys only (total, 68); and 5 more for girls only (total, 46). In grades 7 to 9, there are 65 nonfiction titles for use with classes of boys and girls; 52 more for boys only (total, 117); 2 more for girls only (total, 67).

There are 37 literary essays on the list for mixed classes in grades 10 to 12, and 6 more approved by boys only (total, 43); 15 more approved by girls only (total, 52). In grades 7 to 9, there are 20 essays meeting the minimum standards for mixed classes with 6 more approved by boys (total, 26); girls approve 4 more (total, 24).

TABLE 15-1

Nonfiction (General) for Reading in Mixed Classes of Boys and Girls,
Grades 10 to 12

(This list approved for grades 10 to 12 should be checked with the list for grades 7 to 9 since some of these selections are better liked in junior high school.)

TITLE AND AUTHOR	Scores	
	Boys	Girls
Across—Earhart	82.3	73.5
Adrift on an Ice Pan—Grenfell	79.5	75.3
Aku-Aku—Heyerdahl	82.0	76.9
Berlin Diary—Shirer	85.5	85.0
Bring 'Em Back Alive—Buck	83.1	78.7
Circus Episode—White	80.0	80.8
Count Luckner the Sea Devil—Thomas	96.1	89.7
Danger Is My Business—Craig	82.2	78.7
Day Christ Died—Bishop	87.7	92.1
Day Lincoln Was Shot—Bishop	77.1	77.2
F.B.I.—Reynolds	76.3	74.4
F.B.I., the "G" Men's Weapons and Tactics—Colby	81.5	77.1
Great Blizzard—Garland	76.6	77.8
Guadalcanal Diary—Tregaskis	93.4	92.6
Hiroshima—Hersey	85.5	83.3
Inside Africa—Gunther	77.3	74.3
Inside Russia Today—Gunther	79.9	77.0
Kon-Tiki—Heyerdahl	83.9	76.9
Leopard on the Loose—Buck	93.2	91.0
Lindbergh Tells of It—Lindbergh	79.3	72.7
Man's Highest Trip—Taylor	93.4	81.3
Mystery of Paul Redfern—Taylor	95.1	93.5
Night to Remember—Lord	84.4	90.2
North to the Orient—Lindbergh	83.1	89.8
Our European Guides—Twain	84.9	84.5
Pledge of Allegiance	80.9	85.7
Preamble to the Constitution	77.0	77.5
Prodigal Son—The Bible	77.4	81.5
Raft—Trumbull	87.2	86.5
Rise and Fall of the Third Reich—Shirer	88.4	77.2
R.M.S. Titanic—Baldwin	93.4	88.5
Safari: a Saga of the African Blue—Johnson	86.6	78.3
Shepherd's Psalm—The Bible	74.5	82.4
Shipwrecked in Southern Seas—Thomas	91.0	81.8
Skyward—Byrd	79.3	73.4
Spirit of St. Louis—Lindbergh	77.2	73.3

TITLE AND AUTHOR	Scores	
	Boys	Girls
Test Pilot—Drake	93.4	78.5
They Were Expendable—White	94.5	90.2
Thirty Seconds Over Tokyo—Lawson	93.2	96.6
Thomas A. Edison's First Workshop—Jones	86.8	78.2
We—Lindbergh	78.5	74.7

TABLE 15–2

Nonfiction (General) Approved by Boys Only, Grades 10 to 12
(This list approved for grades 10 to 12 should be checked with the list for grades 7 to 9 since some of these selections are better liked in junior high school.)

TITLE AND AUTHOR	Scores
Abominable Snowman—Izzard	78.0
Aerobatics, Thirty Minutes—Lay	87.5
Boy Scout's Handbook	76.8
Brave Men—Pyle	79.9
Byrd Flies to the North Pole—Murphy	92.1
Cowboy—Hough	79.1
Crusade in Europe—Eisenhower	79.8
Day of Infamy—Lord	88.3
Elephant—Akeley	80.2
Flight to the South Pole—Byrd	86.1
Floods—Lindbergh	79.7
Flying over the North Pole—Byrd	83.7
Flying Saucers—Keyhoe	76.6
Humanity's First Wings—Charnley	88.6
Last March—Scott	80.2
Life's Picture History	85.3
Masters of Deceit—Hoover	85.6
Men on Bataan—Hersey	87.8
On the Bottom—Ellsburg	92.1
Pony Express—Chapman	76.8
PT 109: John F. Kennedy—Donovan	82.8
Second World War—Churchill	81.1
Silent World—Cousteau and Dumas	83.7
Snaring a Bushmaster—Beebe	79.0
Story of D-Day—Bliven	83.2
Up Front—Mauldin	83.0
Where Every Direction Is South—Peary	80.1

TABLE 15–3

Nonfiction (General) Approved by Girls Only, Grades 10 to 12
(This list approved for grades 10 to 12 should be checked with the list for grades 7 to 9 since some of these selections are better liked in junior high school.)

TITLE AND AUTHOR	Scores
Beatitudes—The Bible	78.6
Definition of a Gentleman—Newman	72.9
Greatest Story Ever Told—Oursler	89.4
Joseph the Dreamer—The Bible	81.2
Our Hearts Were Young and Gay—Skinner and Kimbrough	83.6

TABLE 16–1

Nonfiction (General) for Reading in Mixed Classes of Boys and Girls,
Grades 7 to 9
(This list approved for grades 7 to 9 should be checked with the list for grades 10 to 12 since some of the selections are better liked in the senior high school.)

TITLE AND AUTHOR	Scores	
	Boys	Girls
Adrift on an Ice Pan—Grenfell	81.5	79.0
Adventures of Buffalo Bill—Cody	86.8	75.8
Adventures of the Overland Road—Cody	90.8	78.7
Aku-Aku—Heyerdahl	82.9	80.5
Antelope Mother Faces Danger—Finley	89.3	83.7
Born Free—Adamson	80.7	90.5
Boy Scout with Byrd—Siple	82.6	81.7
Brin—Grenfell	82.4	83.1
Bring 'Em Back Alive—Buck	89.0	83.4
Bringing Back a Live Elephant—Buck	88.0	78.9
Brooklyn Dodgers—Graham	82.9	81.5
Caught in a Blizzard—Siple	94.1	89.3
Critical Moments with Wild Animals—Velvin	87.5	81.4
Cub Pilot—Twain	83.6	82.8
Daniel Boone Outwits the Indians—White	93.2	75.2
Day Christ Died—Bishop	88.0	92.3
Day Lincoln Was Shot—Bishop	81.7	81.6
Day's Pleasure—Garland	76.6	85.7
Dick, a Homing Pigeon—Gilbert	90.5	92.3
Facing Death Under the Sea—Adams	92.3	81.8
Father Sews On a Button—Day	91.3	92.5
F.B.I. Story—Whitehead	84.4	79.3

TITLE AND AUTHOR	Scores	
	Boys	Girls
Four-Footed Police of the Dog Patrol—Crump	92.0	81.0
God Is My Co-Pilot—Scott	93.9	92.0
Great Blizzard—Garland	76.5	75.8
Guadalcanal Diary—Tregaskis	98.0	89.9
Hero of the South Pole—Taylor	94.4	91.6
Indian Boy's Training—Eastman	78.3	74.7
Indian Captive—Lenski	76.8	81.6
Inside the U.S.A.—Gunther	73.8	73.7
Joseph and His Brethren—The Bible	78.0	86.6
Just Short of Eternity—Heiser	91.2	90.8
Kon-Tiki—Heyerdahl	87.3	75.3
Lincoln the Lawyer—Tarbell	82.0	82.3
Man's Highest Trip—Taylor	96.0	91.0
Mystery of Paul Redfern—Taylor	96.6	93.8
Nice Lion—Johnson	86.4	78.7
Night Ride in a Prairie Schooner—Garland	80.1	75.7
Night to Remember—Lord	90.2	87.5
Old Rattler and the King Snake—Jordan	90.7	72.8
Our Guides in Genoa—Twain	80.0	80.3
Pledge of Allegiance	81.1	81.8
Poor Richard's Epigrams—Franklin	83.5	85.2
Psalm 19—The Bible	74.5	85.1
Rabbit Roads—Sharp	86.0	73.8
Raft—Trumbull	87.1	80.3
Round Trip into the Ocean's Depths—Taylor	93.1	87.6
Shepherd's Psalm—The Bible	81.0	82.2
Spending a Day in an Igloo—Peary	89.6	93.6
Spirit of St. Louis—Lindbergh	80.9	75.2
Story of D-Day—Blivin	87.5	75.0
Tanganyika Lions—Johnson	90.4	76.5
They Bring Me Back Alive—Lay	96.0	85.9
They Were Expendable—White	92.6	82.6
Thirty Seconds Over Tokyo—Lawson	93.6	92.7
Thomas A. Edison's First Workshop—Jones	86.8	80.3
Through the Heart of Africa—Taylor	91.7	84.0
Turning the Grindstone—Franklin	80.3	83.2
Under the Sea—Craig	92.5	90.6
We—Lindbergh	79.3	74.3
We Capture Gorillas Alive—Johnson	89.9	78.3
Where Did You Go? Out—Smith	79.8	75.7
Whipped by Eagles—Sharp	83.0	77.0
Who Is My Neighbor—The Bible	82.9	86.1
Young Horseman—Steffens	82.4	89.6

TABLE 16–2

Nonfiction (General) Approved by Boys Only, Grades 7 to 9
(This list approved for grades 7 to 9 should be checked with the list for grades
10 to 12 since some of these selections are better liked in the senior high
school.)

TITLE AND AUTHOR	Scores
Abominable Snowman—Izzard	84.1
Adventure with a Lion—Livingston	78.0
Animal Sixth Sense—Hawkes	77.2
Army Ants in the Jungle—Beebe	72.7
Battle of the Ants—Thoreau	75.9
Battle of the Snakes—de Crèvecoeur	74.7
Boy Scout's Handbook	85.9
Brave Men—Pyle	79.0
Capturing the Wild Horse—Irving	78.6
Challenge of Fujiyama—Halliburton	81.0
Conquest of Space—Ley	82.3
Cowboys of the Skies—Poole	85.6
Coyote—Twain	74.8
Creature God Forgot—Johnson	76.6
Crusade in Europe—Eisenhower	82.0
Custer's Last Stand—Reynolds	82.6
Danger Is My Business—Craig	79.6
David and Goliath—The Bible	76.7
Day with an Eskimo Family—Stefansson	77.8
Diving for Gold—Ellsburg	85.2
Fighting Planes of the World—Law	79.3
Finding of Livingston—Stanley	74.6
Firearms—Colby	77.2
First Book of World War I—Snyder	81.6
First Book of World War II—Snyder	86.7
Flying Saucers—Keyhoe	78.8
Flying with a Test Pilot—Teale	83.0
Gold Seekers of '49—Sabin	77.0
How the Beavers Saved Their Homes—Mills	75.7
Jungle Camp—Buck	88.1
Last March—Scott	77.8
Life's Picture History	86.1
Log of a Cowboy—Adams	80.9
Men on Bataan—Hersey	89.1
New York to Paris—Lindbergh	88.4
Night with Ruff Grouse—Hawkes	77.9
Old Santa Fe Trail—Vestal	80.5
Our G Men—Crump	79.0

TITLE AND AUTHOR	Scores
Our Space Age Jets—Colby	76.6
Pony Express—Twain	79.0
Pony Express Rider—Walker	88.1
PT 109: John F. Kennedy—Donovan	84.3
Sheriff Roosevelt and the Thieves—Hagedorn	84.3
Silent World—Cousteau and Dumas	81.7
Story of Mankind—Van Loon	75.6
Story of the U.S. Marines—Hunt	79.3
Trail Signs and Indian Signals—Seton	75.2
Turkey Drive—Sharp	74.9
Twenty-five Years of Flight—Jacobs	83.8
Ways of Chipmunks—Harper	75.9
What Brings Them Home—Vance	78.9
Wrights Fly—Charnley	82.8

TABLE 16–3

Nonfiction (General) Approved by Girls Only, Grades 7 to 9
(This list approved for grades 7 to 9 should be checked with the list for grades 10 to 12 since some of these selections are better liked in the senior high school.)

TITLE AND AUTHOR	Scores
Beatitudes—The Bible	79.0
Charity—The Bible	73.9

TABLE 17–1

Literary Essays and Editorials, Letters, and Speeches for Reading in Mixed Classes of Boys and Girls, Grades 10 to 12
(This list approved for grades 10 to 12 should be checked with the list for grades 7 to 9 since some of the selections are better liked in the junior high school.)

TITLE AND AUTHOR	Scores	
	Boys	Girls
America on Wheels—Warfield	73.4	75.8
Argument with a Millionaire—Grayson	84.0	79.9
Asking for a Raise—Shumway	74.3	79.6
Babies—Twain	74.9	83.6
Bovine and Human Happiness—Phelps	73.8	81.5
Correct Behavior on a Picnic—Stewart	83.0	88.1
Dissertation on Roast Pig—Lamb	79.5	77.2
Dog in the House—Johnson	77.3	83.4

TITLE AND AUTHOR	Scores	
	Boys	Girls
Dying for Dear Old——Broun	82.8	73.4
Farewell to the Citizens of Springfield—Lincoln	72.9	75.0
Fifty-first Dragon—Broun	80.3	74.3
Frozen Words—Addison and Steele	79.1	79.6
Furnace and I—Bergengren	73.3	76.1
Gettysburg Address—Lincoln	88.9	90.0
Grand Vizier of the Furnace—Warner	72.8	80.3
Human Traits in the Farmyard—Derieux	89.2	89.0
I Entertain an Agent Unawares—Grayson	73.8	80.0
I'll Stay in Canada—Leacock	75.1	81.7
Imagine Yourself—Marquis	79.4	85.9
Joe Grimm—Broun	74.2	79.9
Letter to Mrs. Bixby—Lincoln	71.5	74.5
Letter to the President—Nye	80.2	75.2
Lure of the Labrador—Grenfell	76.8	75.2
Mary White—White	74.0	89.7
My Financial Career—Leacock	80.5	87.6
My Son Gets Spanked—Van de Water	73.2	76.3
New England Weather—Twain	76.3	78.8
Off for a Vacation—Jerome	83.0	86.4
Our European Guides—Twain	84.9	84.5
Saturday-Night Bath—Baker	81.4	85.6
Sleeping Outdoors—Allen	82.6	87.3
Southern Hospitality—Bangs	78.1	82.0
Spring Is Here—Rogers	87.3	87.9
Story of a Piebald Horse—Hudson	76.2	78.1
Symptoms—Jerome	76.9	85.7
Under the Barber's Knife—Leacock	80.3	75.6
What College Did to Me—Benchley	87.2	90.1

TABLE 17–2

Literary Essays and Editorials, Letters, and Speeches Approved by Boys Only, Grades 10 to 12
(This list approved by boys for grades 10 to 12 should be checked with the list for grades 7 to 9 since some of the selections are better liked in the junior high school.)

TITLE AND AUTHOR	Scores
Chirstmas Day at Sea—Conrad	74.3
Epic of the North—O'Brien	79.3
Great American Game—Phelps	77.2
Meaning of a Fragment—Merriam	74.5

TITLE AND AUTHOR	Scores
Message to Garcia—Hubbard	75.1
On Making Camp—White	74.8

TABLE 17–3

Literary Essays and Editorials, Letters, and Speeches Approved by Girls Only, Grades 10 to 12

(This list approved by girls for grades 10 to 12 should be checked with the list for grades 7 to 9 since some of the selections are better liked in the junior high school.)

TITLE AND AUTHOR	Scores
Christmas Shopping—Davenport	74.6
Claustrophobia—Goodloe	79.6
Dog—West	76.0
Dream Children—Lamb	74.8
Five Varieties—Lucas	81.0
Florist Shop—Hawkridge	79.9
Getting-Up-to-Date—Wayne	76.9
Holding a Baby—Broun	75.5
January Summer—Sharp	76.8
Julie—Morley	76.6
Not According to Hoyle—Benchley	77.2
Old Man Warner—Fisher	74.6
Old Romance—Twain	79.0
On Doors—Morley	75.9
Tooth, the Whole Tooth, and Nothing but the Tooth—Benchley	77.6

TABLE 18-1

Literary Essays and Editorials, Letters, and Speeches for Reading in Mixed Classes of Boys and Girls, Grades 7 to 9

(This list approved for grades 7 to 9 should be checked with the list for grades 10 to 12 since some of the selections are better liked in the senior high school.)

TITLE AND AUTHOR	Scores	
	Boys	Girls
A-Hunting of the Deer—Warner	79.8	73.7
Argument with a Millionaire—Grayson	75.6	79.8
Awful Fate of Melpomenous Jones—Leacock	79.7	84.7
Correct Behavior on a Picnic—Stewart	85.7	92.1

114   THE READING INTERESTS

TITLE AND AUTHOR	Scores	
	Boys	Girls
Correct Display of the Stars and Stripes—McCandless and Grosvenor	76.2	73.6
Dentist and the Gas—Leacock	88.3	90.1
Gettysburg Address—Lincoln	91.1	93.7
Hanging a Picture—Jerome	84.0	88.6
Horace Greeley's Ride—Ward	82.6	87.2
How I Killed a Bear—Warner	78.6	74.8
Letter to Mrs. Bixby—Lincoln	71.0	76.3
Liberty or Death—Henry	81.8	76.8
Mary White—White	74.9	89.2
My Financial Career—Leacock	79.7	89.5
On Cats and Dogs—Jerome	83.0	89.9
Return—Grayson	74.7	72.7
Skiing Party—Ford	75.0	75.7
Sleeping Outdoors—Allen	79.6	78.9
Stickeen—Muir	77.5	76.0
Symptoms—Jerome	79.3	86.7

TABLE 18-2

Literary Essays and Editorials, Letters, and Speeches Approved by Boys Only, Grades 7 to 9
(This list approved by boys for grades 7 to 9 should be checked with the list for grades 10 to 12 since some of the selections may be better liked in the senior high school.)

TITLE AND AUTHOR	Scores
Address to the Army—Albert	80.0
American Boy—Roosevelt	76.2
Cattle Drive—White	76.5
Don't Die on Third—Cameron	81.8
In the Wilderness—Warner	80.0
Meaning of a Fragment—Merriam	74.9

TABLE 18-3

Literary Essays and Editorials, Letters, and Speeches Approved by Girls Only, Grades 7 to 9
(This list approved by girls for grades 7 to 9 should be checked with the list for grades 10 to 12 since some of the selections may be better liked in the senior high school.)

TITLE AND AUTHOR	Scores
My Cats—Fabre	79.6
Pine Tree Shillings—Hawthorne	74.5
What America Means to Me—Thomas	77.8
With the Photographer—Leacock	85.9

CHAPTER XVI

Biography

BIOGRAPHY IS A SUPERIOR FORM OF NONFICTION FOR YOUNG PEO-
ple in the junior and senior high schools. The best-liked biographies
rank in interest with selections in any other reading field: novels,
short stories, and nonfiction adventure. Consequently, they are
highly useful in promoting reading, the most valuable of all the
outcomes of English classes. In stimulating and guiding the thinking
of adolescents the biography may well be the most useful of all
literary forms, and turning to it for recreation and inspiration may
well become a major lifelong habit.

Nevertheless, biography is a field that some authorities on high
school reading have declared to be unsatisfactory for high school
students. There seems little doubt that this conclusion has been
reached·because of biographies forced upon English classes in the
past. The great majority of adolescents lack the background to understand or to be interested in the details of history, political maneuver-
ing, scientific discovery, and the artistic and literary arguments
which fill so many pages of the classic lives of the great which English
teachers and curriculum makers demand. Actually, boys seldom
react favorably to a biography which is not also an adventure story.

For girls, romance as well as adventure adds to the possibility of a favorable verdict. An examination of the scores for the biographies most frequently used when the reading program was imposed shows how shockingly unsuited many of them are.

Not one of these books is liked. The average score (57.2) is scandalous. The average number of student reports (1102) is an indication of the frequency with which these books are required. The number of reports on some of the least enjoyed emphasizes the point: Franklin's *Autobiography*, 2280; Macaulay's *Johnson*, 1850. No wonder some authorities have doubted the importance of biography in the English class.

It should be noted that biography is fully as interesting to students in grades 7 to 9 as in grades 10 to 12.

Biography is a field which presents a special problem in English classes, arising form the rejection by boys of many excellent lives of women. Since girls give approval to many biographies of men, the teacher should have no difficulty in finding suitable biographies for reading in common in mixed classes. The problem arises from the probability that girls in mixed classes may miss such highly significant books as *The Diary of Anne Frank*, Helen Keller's *Story of My Life*, *The Helen Keller Story* by Peare, and *Flush* by Woolf.

A satisfactory solution might be to use part of the time to be devoted to the reading in this field to the group-reading by girls of outstanding women's biographies, while the boys read important books about men rejected by girls.

The approved lists of biographies for mixed classes include 21 for

TABLE 19

BIOGRAPHIES FREQUENTLY REQUIRED IN THE SENIOR HIGH SCHOOL

TITLE AND AUTHOR	SCORES BOYS AND GIRLS
Autobiography of Benjamin Franklin	51.3
Life of Johnson—Boswell	64.2
Essay on Johnson—Macaulay	61.9
Essay on Burns—Carlyle	53.0
Making of an American—Riis	65.9
Pepys's Diary	67.7
Son of the Middle Border—Garland	59.6
Emily Dickinson's School Days—Bianchi	46.8
Life and Letters of Walter H. Page—Hendrick	44.6
AVERAGE	57.2

grades 10 to 12 with boys approving 17 additional (total, 38), and girls approving 18 (total, 39). In grades 7 to 9, there are 49 listed for boys and girls; 22 more approved by boys (total, 71), and 18 by girls (total, 67).

TABLE 20–1

Biographies for Reading in Mixed Classes of Boys and Girls, Grades 10 to 12

(This list approved for grades 10 to 12 should be checked with the list for grades 7 to 9 since some of the biographies are better liked in the junior high school.)

TITLE AND AUTHOR	Scores	
	Boys	Girls
Abe Lincoln Grows Up—Sandburg	79.0	83.2
Boyhood on a Missouri Farm—Twain	78.3	82.2
Boy's Life of Edison—Meadowcroft	80.0	76.8
Buffalo Bill—Visscher	85.4	75.2
Cheaper by the Dozen—Gilbreth	75.1	81.4
Count Luckner, the Sea Devil—Thomas	96.1	89.7
Death Be Not Proud—Gunther	83.3	91.7
Diary of Anne Frank	77.4	90.4
Edith Cavell—Hagedorn	88.1	95.6
Helen Keller Story—Peare	75.3	87.9
I Married Adventure—Johnson	79.0	79.8
Knute Rockne, All American—Stuhldreher	92.0	82.8
Koch, the Death Fighter—De Kruif	77.9	75.3
Labrador Doctor—Grenfell	78.3	76.6
Life with Father—Day	79.3	78.6
Lone Cowboy—James	79.9	75.2
Lou Gehrig, a Quiet Hero—Graham	94.3	86.6
Man Called Peter—Marshall	80.2	88.8
Profiles in Courage—Kennedy	75.8	74.0
Story of Louis Pasteur—Gibney and Collins	90.5	91.5
Will Rogers—O'Brien	92.5	93.4

TABLE 20–2

Biographies Approved by Boys Only, Grades 10 to 12

(This list approved by boys for grades 10 to 12 should be checked with the list for grades 7 to 9 since some of these biographies are better liked in the junior high school.)

TITLE AND AUTHOR	Scores
Babe Ruth Story—Considine	77.6
Barnum—Werner	81.3
Benedict Arnold—Bradford	74.3
Boy's Life of Theodore Roosevelt—Hagedorn	80.3
Boys' Life of the Wright Brothers—Charnley	79.7
Daniel Boone, Wilderness Scout—White	79.1
Edison, Greatest American of the Century—Ludwig	76.8
Fulton's Folly—Sutcliffe	83.1
Kit Carson—Vestal	77.2
Knute Rockne—Van Riper	84.9
Life on the Mississippi—Twain	84.5
Lou Gehrig, Boy of the Sandlots—Van Riper	83.2
Microbe Hunters—De Kruif	78.1
Robert Fulton—Henry	74.1
Story of a Bad Boy—Aldrich	78.9
Swamp Fox of the Revolution—Brown	77.2
Wilbur and Orville Wright—Hagedorn	83.5

TABLE 20–3

Biographies Approved by Girls Only, Grades 10 to 12
(This list approved by girls for grades 10 to 12 should be checked with the
list for grades 7 to 9 since some of these biographies are better liked in the
junior high school.)

TITLE AND AUTHOR	Scores
Albert Schweitzer, Genius of the Jungle—Gollomb	74.4
Anna and the King of Siam—Landon	83.3
At School in the Promised Land—Antin	76.7
Autobiography of Lincoln Steffens	77.7
Belles on Their Toes—Gilbreth and Carey	80.7
Boys' Life of Mark Twain—Paine	74.9
First Woman Doctor—Baker	78.6
Florence Nightingale—Strachey	81.7
Flush, a Biography—Woolf	82.1
Girl in White Armor—Paine	78.9
How I Found America—Yezierska	81.1
I'll Cry Tomorrow—Roth	85.7
Lady with a Lamp—Strachey	80.2
Little Princesses—Crawford	74.0
Modeling My Life—Scudder	86.5
Story of Joan of Arc—Lang	82.5
Story of My Life—Keller	85.6
Too Much Too Soon—Barrymore and Frank	75.2

TABLE 21-1

Biographies for Reading in Mixed Classes of Boys and Girls, Grades 7 to 9

(This list approved for grades 7 to 9 should be checked with the list for grades 10 to 12 since some of the biographies are better liked in the senior high school.)

TITLE AND AUTHOR	Scores Boys	Girls
Abraham Lincoln—Hagedorn	90.7	91.2
Abe Lincoln Grows Up—Sandburg	82.1	82.3
Abraham Lincoln's Education—Tarbell	86.9	82.5
Andrew Jackson—Hagedorn	87.9	80.1
Babe Ruth—Meany	90.0	86.3
Blackbeard—Stockton	94.9	87.5
Book of Courage—Hagedorn	87.4	83.0
Boyhood on a Missouri Farm—Twain	75.8	75.1
Boy on Horseback—Steffens	93.7	95.0
Boy Scout's Life of Lincoln—Tarbell	75.5	73.1
Boys' Life of Abraham Lincoln—Nicolay	78.2	77.9
Boys' Life of Edison—Meadowcroft	86.1	81.6
Boys' Life of Mark Twain—Paine	89.7	84.4
Boy's Life of Theodore Roosevelt—Hagedorn	80.4	78.3
Clara Barton—Hagedorn	81.7	96.1
Daniel Boone—Daugherty	89.3	78.0
Daniel Boone—Hagedorn	91.7	83.5
David Livingston—Hagedorn	85.9	86.1
Davy Crockett—Rourke	83.4	75.3
Diary of Anne Frank	78.8	89.8
Edith Cavell—Hagedorn	74.6	88.9
George Washington—Hagedorn	89.2	85.5
Helen Keller Story—Peare	78.8	92.9
Hero of the South Pole—Taylor	94.4	91.6
I Married Adventure—Johnson	83.5	85.4
Joan of Arc—Hagedorn	77.1	82.7
King Albert of Belgium—Sanford and Owen	92.6	92.3
Kit Carson—Vestal	85.9	74.0
Labrador Doctor—Grenfell	81.3	78.7
Lincoln the Lawyer—Tarbell	82.0	82.3
Lindbergh—Hagedorn	92.4	90.1
Lone Cowboy—James	83.1	78.2
Lou Gehrig, a Quiet Hero—Graham	92.3	87.1
Lucky to Be a Yankee—DiMaggio	86.4	84.0
Mark Twain—Meigs	85.5	82.5
Mark Twain's Autobiography	75.0	75.4

TITLE AND AUTHOR	Scores	
	Boys	Girls
My Life Story—Joe Louis	86.6	80.8
Radisson—Laut	91.7	79.6
Raft—Trumbull	87.1	80.3
Robert E. Peary—Hagedorn	83.7	78.0
Robert Lee's Boyhood—Gilman	79.3	80.8
Spending a Day in an Igloo—Peary	89.6	93.6
Story of a Bad Boy—Aldrich	80.9	76.2
Story of Joan of Arc—Lang	76.8	85.2
Story of My Life—Keller	79.4	89.9
Tad Lincoln's Father—Bayne	82.7	91.0
Through the Heart of Africa—Taylor	91.7	84.0
Wilbur and Orville Wright—Hagedorn	87.6	79.1
Will Rogers—O'Brien	84.4	84.7

TABLE 21–2

Biographies Approved by Boys Only, Grades 7 to 9
(This list approved by boys in grades 7 to 9 should be checked with the list
for grades 10 to 12 since some of these biographies may be better liked in
the senior high school.)

TITLE AND AUTHOR	Scores
America's Paul Revere—Forbes	75.7
Babe Ruth Story—Considine	85.7
Boyhood in the Bush—LeBlanc	77.2
Boy Life on the Prairie—Garland	76.4
Boys' Life of the Wright Brothers—Charnley	76.5
Chinese Gordon—Hagedorn	79.5
Daniel Boone, Wilderness Scout—White	88.6
Davy Crockett—Rourke	83.4
Felix Von Luckner—Hagedorn	84.7
Francis Drake—Hagedorn	79.2
Hannibal—Hagedorn	77.2
Knute Rockne, All American—Stuhldreher	94.8
Lawrence of Arabia—Hagedorn	80.2
Paul Jones—Seawell	74.9
Robert E. Lee—Gilman	75.2
Robert E. Lee—Hagedorn	80.6
Robert Fulton—Sutcliffe	76.7
Story of Captain Kidd—Gilbert	87.7
Story of Thomas Alva Edison—Meadowcroft	77.1
Swamp Fox of the Revolution—Brown	80.9
Ted Williams Story—Schoor and Gilfond	75.1
Two Years Before the Mast—Dana	76.8

TABLE 21-3

Biographies Approved by Girls Only, Grades 7 to 9
(This list approved by girls in grades 7 to 9 should be checked with the list
for grades 10 to 12 since some of these biographies may be better liked in
the senior high school.)

TITLE AND AUTHOR	Scores
Albert Schweitzer, Genius of the Jungle—Gollomb	81.6
Amelia Earhart—Garst	76.0
Belles on Their Toes—Gilbreth and Carey	80.5
Clara Barton—Pace	77.5
Clara Barton and the Red Cross—Sweetser	77.1
Elizabeth of England—Hagedorn	78.1
First Woman Doctor—Baker	76.2
Florence Nightingale—Nolan	78.1
Franklin D. Roosevelt—Hatch	75.4
George Washington's Boyhood—Scudder	85.5
How I Found America—Yezierska	82.0
Invincible Louisa—Meigs	82.0
Life with Father—Day	86.4
Little Princesses—Crawford	75.7
Profiles in Courage—Kennedy	74.9
Real Story of Lucille Ball—Harris	77.4
'Twixt 12 and 20—Boone	80.4
Up from Slavery—Washington	77.9

CHAPTER XVII

Poetry and Plays

POETRY. THE HIGH IMPORTANCE WITH WHICH ENGLISH TEACHERS regard poetry is suggested by the number of poems for which we have test scores: 1183 in grades 10 to 12 and 944 in grades 7 to 9, a total of 2127. Unfortunately, only a few, comparatively, reach a satisfactory interest level. In the senior high school, only one in 16 ranks with the list recommended for use in mixed classes. Almost four of every five poems score below the midpoint for poems used in our public schools. In the junior high school, one poem in nine is listed for mixed classes. However, through careful choices, it is possible to provide an interesting experience in poetry in English classes. This success demands the most drastic revision of the current program.

The list approved by both boys and girls for grades 10 to 12 includes 85 poems; 29 additional poems approved by boys only (a total of 114). The total for girls is 185. In grades 7 to 9, the total listed for mixed classes is 103; for boys only, 19; the total for boys, 122. For girls, the total is 214.

It may be surprising to find that the proportion of approved poems is higher in the junior high school, particularly when it is recalled that on average students in grades 7 to 9 and in grades 10 to 12 enjoy poetry almost equally. The explanation may be that teachers of English in the higher grades are increasingly concerned with introducing young people to the artistic and sophisticated.

This massive rejection by students of the school's requirements in poetry makes it obvious that nothing short of a revolution can make this part of the program in literature even moderately acceptable if we rank enjoyment by students an essential factor of the outcome. Attention is called to the rejection by college graduates of poetry even as they rejected essays.

Though the relative number of disliked poems is very great, poetry has one advantage over the familiar essay: there are enough well-liked poems to provide satisfaction instead of boredom and disgust if teachers will make it a primary objective.

The addiction of English teachers to the fetish of high quality is so intense that students, particularly boys, become haters of poetry. A review of the chapter on literary quality (Chapter IX) provides overwhelming evidence. Teachers who wish to help their students enjoy poetry will find that choices for the most part will be restricted to poems of high quality rather than to masterpieces.

Of 750 lyrics, only one in seven scores in interest above the midpoint of the poetry scale, a low level. With boys *only*, approval of lyrics is very much rarer.

PLAYS. The play is another literary type which presents a special problem in the classroom. First, the play *on average* must be more interesting to the general public than the other literary types or it would not have survived the drastic testing every play must meet on the stage. As a result, most plays rate high in interest with young people when they become acquainted with them. On the other hand, the play, because of unusual difficulties in reading, is not often chosen by students in their free reading programs. The result of these factors has been that plays including those chosen by the schools when read and discussed under the teacher's direction have usually proved so interesting as to place the play second on the list of literary types in popularity in the senior high school. Several illustrations of the power of interest to offset difficulty are supplied by some of Shakespeare's plays.

The average score for the highest-ranking ten plays (omitting radio plays which would raise the score) is 88.7 points compared with 90.9 for novels, 93.5 for short stories, and 87.6 for biographies. The best-liked plays include two by O'Neill *(The Emperor Jones* and *In the Zone); The Boy Comes Home* (by Milne); and *Nathan Hale* (by Fitch).

The study of plays in the classroom should have special value in preparing young people not alone for the legitimate theater, but for motion pictures and television.

In grades 10 to 12, there are 42 plays recommended for use in mixed classes with 3 more approved by boys only, a total of 45 for boys. For girls, the total is 58. In grades 7 to 9, 11 plays meet the requirements for mixed classes; the total for boys, 12; and the total for girls, 21.

TABLE 22–1

Poems for Reading in Mixed Classes of Boys and Girls, Grades 10 to 12
(This list approved for grades 10 to 12 should be checked with the list for grades 7 to 9 since some of the poems are better liked in the junior high school.)

TITLE AND AUTHOR	Scores	
	Boys	Girls
Abou Ben Adhem—Hunt	75.6	77.4
America, the Beautiful—Bates	82.7	88.4
Ballad of Billy the Kid—Knibbs	92.7	89.1
Ballad of Hard Luck Henry—Service	75.7	83.3
Ballad of the Oysterman—Holmes	75.1	82.3
Barbara Frietchie—Whittier	84.9	86.9
Between Two Loves—Daly	76.8	89.7
Blindman—Allen	79.6	89.4
Blue and the Gray—Finch	76.4	80.0
Bombardment—Lowell	78.8	77.4
Boomer Johnson—Knibbs	84.2	85.8
Boys—Holmes	82.1	81.9
Casey at the Bat—Thayer	90.4	87.0
Cowboy's Dream—American Ballad	75.5	82.7
Cremation of Sam McGee—Service	90.3	83.3
Da Greata Stronga Man—Daly	88.3	85.1
Da Leetla Boy—Daly	81.4	89.4
Damming the Missouri—Guiterman	84.8	74.5
Da Younga 'Merican—Daly	83.8	90.0
Days of Forty-nine—American Ballad	84.7	78.4
Deacon's Masterpiece—Holmes	88.4	84.2
Dorlan's Home Walk—Guiterman	92.7	89.8
Dying Ranger—Cowboy Ballad	75.8	76.8
Elegy on the Death of a Mad Dog—Goldsmith	84.2	85.7
Farmer Remembers Lincoln—Bynner	80.5	79.0
First Snowfall—Lowell	78.3	83.2
Flag Goes By—Bennett	81.4	84.3
George Washington—Kirk	89.4	90.3

TITLE AND AUTHOR   Scores

	Boys	Girls
Gunga Din—Kipling	85.9	81.9
Height of the Ridiculous—Holmes	74.0	78.8
Highwayman—Noyes	83.1	88.8
Hindoo Legend—Birdseye	76.6	81.0
Home on the Range—Cowboy Ballad	86.4	75.7
Home Thoughts from Europe—Van Dyke	78.9	87.9
House with Nobody in It—Kilmer	81.0	93.8
How the Great Guest Came—Markham	76.0	90.4
If—Kipling	75.4	83.8
I Knew a Black Beetle—Morley	76.6	86.0
Incident of the French Camp—Browning	83.7	76.6
In Flanders Fields—McCrae	79.2	88.8
In Hardin County, 1809—Thompson	76.2	80.0
It's a Queer Time—Graves	86.0	79.8
Jesse James—Benét	88.2	81.2
Jest 'Fore Christmas—Field	79.3	87.7
Jim—Harte	78.3	81.4
King Robert of Sicily—Longfellow	77.8	78.9
Kit Carson's Ride—Miller	78.7	74.0
Larrie O'Dee—Fink	82.1	89.3
Leetla Giorgio Washeenton—Daly	81.6	88.7
Letter from Home—Irwin	78.7	87.4
Lincoln, the Man of the People—Markham	75.6	79.0
Little Lost Pup—Guiterman	78.1	88.4
Lone Dog—McLeod	79.4	77.8
Look What You Did, Christopher—Nash	85.2	85.5
Mandalay—Kipling	75.0	81.7
Men—Reid	80.9	83.6
Messages—Gibson	80.7	79.8
Mia Carlotta—Daly	76.9	80.0
O Captain! My Captain!—Whitman	82.8	89.9
Old Ironsides—Holmes	88.4	85.4
Old Man and Jim—Riley	79.8	79.2
Old Swimmin' Hole—Riley	79.9	84.1
Owl Critic—Field	81.6	82.2
Paul Revere's Ride—Longfellow	83.6	76.7
Pets—Weaver	75.9	80.9
Prayer of Cyrus Brown—Foss	81.5	89.2
Revenge of Hamish—Lanier	74.9	76.9
Reynard the Fox—Masefield	78.8	76.6
Sand Creek—Vestal	78.6	80.2
Science for the Young—Irwin	81.6	82.3
Shepherd's Psalm—The Bible	74.5	82.4
Simon Legree—Lindsay	83.6	79.7

TITLE AND AUTHOR	Scores	
	Boys	Girls
Smack in School—Palmer	75.7	89.5
So Glad for Spreeng—Daly	80.0	87.5
To an Athlete Dying Young—Housman	75.5	75.3
Tommy—Kipling	85.1	85.8
Trees—Kilmer	79.2	87.2
Twins—Leigh	85.4	92.3
Walking Man—Knibbs	85.2	79.4
When the Work's All Done This Fall—American Ballad	77.9	80.8
Wilbur Wright and Orville Wright—Benét	76.0	75.6
Wreck of the "Hesperus"—Longfellow	79.9	80.7
Yarn of the "Nancy Bell"—Gilbert	80.2	75.9
Young Fellow, My Lad—Service	82.8	89.5
Zebra Dun—Cowboy Ballad	83.0	81.9

TABLE 22-2

Poems Approved by Boys Only, Grades 10 to 12
(This list approved by boys for grades 10 to 12 should be checked with the list for grades 7 to 9 since some of the poems are better liked in the junior high school.)

TITLE AND AUTHOR	Scores
Ballad of East and West—Kipling	76.0
Ballad of John Silver—Masefield	78.9
Bill Peters—Cowboy Ballad	76.2
Billy the Kid—American Ballad	77.6
Bronco That Would Not Be Broken—Lindsay	75.4
Charge of the Light Brigade—Tennyson	80.2
Concord Hymn—Emerson	77.9
Congo—Lindsay	76.4
Darius Green and His Flying Machine—Trowbridge	76.4
Defense of the Alamo—Miller	75.3
Hervé Riel—Browning	77.6
Jim Bludso—Hay	82.0
Johnnie's First Moose—Drummond	77.0
Man from Snowy River—Paterson	78.2
Man He Killed—Hardy	79.7
Nautical Extravaganza—Irwin	78.0
On a Soldier Fallen in the Phillippines—Moody	78.7
Revenge—Tennyson	77.2
Robin Hood and Little John—British Ballad	78.8
Robin Hood Ballads—British Ballads	78.7

TITLE AND AUTHOR	Scores
Rounding the Horn—Masefield	75.6
Rudolph the Headsman—Holmes	76.7
Skeleton in Armor—Longfellow	77.0
Sohrab and Rustum—Arnold	75.5
Song of the Open Road—Whitman	75.2
Strawberry Roan—Cowboy Ballad	80.6
Valley That God Forgot—Knibbs	75.6
Water Hole—Barker	76.1
Working Party—Sassoon	78.5

TABLE 22–3

Poems Approved by Girls Only, Grades 10 to 12
(This list approved by girls for grades 10 to 12 should be checked with the list for grades 7 to 9 since some of these poems are better liked in the junior high school.)

TITLE AND AUTHOR	Scores
Abraham Lincoln—Malone	79.1
Annabel Lee—Poe	78.3
Ballad of Dennis McGinty—Burnet	83.1
Ballad of the Harp-Weaver—Millay	83.0
Barefoot Boy—Whittier	76.2
Boots—Kipling	75.5
Cerelle—Houston	85.2
Come Up from the Fields, Father—Whitman	80.2
Conquered Banner—Ryan	75.5
Courtin'—Lowell	80.6
Crossing the Bar—Tennyson	77.3
Cruel Brother—British Ballad	75.1
Day Is Done—Longfellow	79.6
Death at Evening—McGinley	75.8
Death of the Flowers—Bryant	79.9
Death of the Hired Man—Frost	78.6
Dorothy Q—Holmes	78.8
Een Napoli—Daly	77.0
Enchanted Shirt—Hay	81.6
Enoch Arden—Tennyson	85.2
Evangeline—Longfellow	75.0
Flathouse Roof—Crane	86.4
Fleurette—Service	88.3
Flower Factory—Evans	83.7
Fool's Prayer—Sill	75.4
For a New Year—Hinton	78.8

TITLE AND AUTHOR	Scores
Gareth and Lynette—Tennyson	79.2
Get Up and Bar the Door—British Ballad	80.3
Guinevere—Tennyson	75.1
Hannah Armstrong—Masters	75.7
Her Letter—Harte	85.0
House by the Side of the Road—Foss	79.6
In School Days—Whittier	87.5
In Service—Letts	77.8
Janitor's Boy—Crane	85.6
Jethro's Pet—Coffin	77.6
Kitty of Colraine—Shanley	75.7
Lady Clare—Tennyson	76.2
Lancelot and Elaine—Tennyson	86.6
Lasca—Desprez	76.1
Laugh and Be Merry—Masefield	77.7
Listeners—de la Mare	75.0
Little Boy Blue—Field	87.0
Little Boy in the Morning—Ledwidge	79.3
Little Orphant Annie—Riley	80.7
Lochinvar—Scott	80.2
Lord Chancellor's Song—Gilbert	80.7
Lost Chord—Proctor	85.0
Man with the Hoe—Markham	75.9
Matilda—Belloc	80.8
Maude Muller—Whittier	81.6
Moonlight—Weaver	77.9
Mother to Son—Hughes	75.3
Mrs. Judge Jenkins—Harte	76.0
My Aunt—Holmes	85.8
My Dog—Bangs	81.9
My Lost Youth—Longfellow	79.2
Nancy Hanks—Benét	77.5
Nightmare—Gilbert	80.4
Old Story—Robinson	77.0
On His Blindness—Milton	78.2
Only Seven—Leigh	80.5
Philosopher—Bangs	77.9
Pied Piper of Hamelin—Browning	80.9
Prayer—Untermeyer	77.3
Prayer for a Little Home—Bone	75.8
Psalm CXXI—The Bible	75.7
Pyramus and Thisbe—Saxe	75.5
Quest of the Ribband—Guiterman	84.1
Remarks from the Pup—Johnson	82.2
Renascence—Millay	75.4

TITLE AND AUTHOR	Scores
Road Not Taken—Frost	75.0
Roadways—Masefield	77.0
Robinson Crusoe's Story—Carryl	81.0
Roofs—Kilmer	76.1
Rouge Bouquet—Kilmer	75.1
Seaside Romance—Marquis	81.0
Seein' Things—Field	88.3
Short'nin' Bread—Negro Song	80.0
Silver—de la Mare	78.8
Smells (Junior)—Morley	75.8
Snow-Bound—Whittier	77.6
Song for a Little House—Morley	77.5
Song of the Old Mother—Yeats	79.4
Song of the Shirt—Hood	84.2
" 'Spacially Jim"—Morgan	83.2
Spires of Oxford—Letts	77.3
Stone—Gibson	80.0
Stopping by Woods—Frost	74.6
Suicide in the Trenches—Sassoon	82.3
Turning of the Babies in the Bed—Dunbar	83.6
Two Old Bachelors—Lear	82.6
Vive la France—Crawford	82.8
Wander thirst—Gould	78.5
We and They—Kipling	80.4
West Wind—Masefield	80.2
When I Was One and Twenty—Housman	75.9
When the Frost Is on the Punkin—Riley	79.2
Women—Aristophanes	81.5
Wynken, Blynken, and Nod—Field	75.6

TABLE 23-1

Poems for Reading in Mixed Classes of Boys and Girls, Grades 7 to 9
(This list approved for grades 7 to 9 should be checked with the list for grades 10 to 12 since some of the poems are better liked in the senior high school.)

TITLE AND AUTHOR	Scores	
	Boys	Girls
America—Smith	82.6	85.9
America for Me—Van Dyke	81.1	86.2
America the Beautiful—Bates	77.1	87.0
Ballad of Dennis McGinty—Burnet	77.3	85.0
Ballad of Ivan Petrovsky Skivar—American Ballad	86.3	84.1
Barbara Frietchie—Whittier	82.7	89.2

TITLE AND AUTHOR	Scores	
	Boys	Girls
Barefoot Boy—Whittier	78.7	87.5
Baseball in de Park—Guiterman	86.6	83.0
Between Two Loves—Daly	88.7	93.9
Bill Peters—American Ballad	86.3	81.2
Billy the Kid—American Ballad	85.9	79.6
Blind Men and the Elephant—Saxe	75.9	75.6
Boll Weevil Song—Negro Song	74.7	80.0
Boy and His Dog—Guest	79.0	83.8
Boy's Mother—Riley	83.5	93.6
Broken Sword—Markham	83.4	78.9
Bronc That Wouldn't Bust—Cowboy Ballad	88.7	86.8
Casey at the Bat—Thayer	91.5	90.4
Change About—Folk Rhyme	82.2	88.3
Clown's Baby—Vandergrift	75.3	85.3
Code of the Cow Country—Barker	83.4	78.7
Color-Bearer—Preston	78.3	79.3
Conductor Bradley—Whittier	80.5	78.8
Cowboy's Dream—Cowboy Ballad—Loman (Ed.)	75.9	80.2
Cremation of Sam McGee—Service	87.9	85.9
Da Greata Basaball—Daly	92.9	91.0
Da Greata Stronga Man—Daly	80.3	84.8
Da Horsa Race—Daly	87.1	91.0
Daniel Boone—Guiterman	78.3	75.5
Darius Green and His Flying Machine—Trowbridge	86.4	82.1
Deacon's Masterpiece—Holmes	79.7	81.1
Dying Ranger—Cowboy Ballad	76.1	87.7
Elegy on the Death of a Mad Dog—Goldsmith	81.9	86.7
Father William—Carroll	76.9	81.4
Flag Goes By—Bennett	81.0	78.9
For Want of a Nail—Mother Goose	84.7	85.8
George Washington—Kirk	89.8	91.8
Gol-Darned Wheel—Cowboy Ballad	87.8	86.2
Grandmother's Story of the Battle of Bunker Hill—Holmes	82.0	82.9
Gray Horse Troop—Chambers	82.1	81.6
Height of the Ridiculous—Holmes	79.9	84.6
Highwayman—Noyes	81.7	82.2
House with Nobody in It—Kilmer	74.2	90.2
How the Old Horse Won the Bet—Holmes	85.8	80.4
I Knew a Black Beetle—Morley	76.2	83.3
Inchcape Rock—Southey	77.3	75.1
In Flanders Fields—McCrae	79.3	82.8
In Hardin County, 1809—Thompson	76.6	83.9
Janitor's Boy—Crane	79.0	89.9

TITLE AND AUTHOR	Scores	
	Boys	Girls
Jean Desprez—Service	90.4	86.2
Jesse James—American Ballad	79.9	77.2
Jest 'Fore Christmas—Field	85.0	93.3
Jim Bludso—Hay	86.2	87.5
Jimsy—Burnet	77.3	91.4
Leak in the Dike—Cary	83.0	89.3
Leetla Giorgio Washeenton—Daly	86.8	94.9
Little Bateese—Drummond	75.5	84.0
Little Billee—Thackeray	77.3	79.0
Little Breeches—Hay	75.2	84.9
Little Lost Pup—Guiterman	75.3	82.0
Little Turtle—Lindsay	80.7	87.1
Low-Backed Car—Lover	78.6	86.3
Mia Carlotta—Daly	77.8	88.7
Mr. Hail Colomb—Daly	75.7	81.4
O Captain! My Captain!—Whitman	77.8	81.6
Old Chisholm Trail—Cowboy Ballad	78.3	78.9
Old Ironsides—Holmes	84.4	83.2
Old Swimmin' Hole—Riley	82.5	81.6
Oregon Trail—Guiterman	82.1	81.9
Owl Critic—Fields	77.4	79.9
Paul Revere's Ride—Longfellow	85.9	82.9
Pershing at the Front—Guiterman	91.1	89.6
Plantation Memories—Russell	76.6	83.5
Psalm Nineteen—The Bible	74.5	85.1
Raggedy Man—Riley	75.0	87.4
Rhyme of the Chivalrous Shark—Irwin	79.4	80.4
Robin Hood and Little John—British Ballad	79.8	75.0
Robin Hood and the Bishop—British Ballad	92.3	78.5
Robin Hood Ballads—British Ballads	90.7	79.3
Robin Hood Rescuing the Widow's Three Sons— British Ballad	78.3	76.8
Robin Hood's Birth—British Ballad	90.8	75.7
Robin Hood's Death and Burial—British Ballad	79.6	78.1
Robinson Crusoe's Story—Carryl	79.4	76.7
Rudolph the Headsman—Holmes	83.8	76.4
Sand Creek—Vestal	74.5	78.4
Science for the Young—Irwin	81.0	83.0
Shepherd's Psalm—The Bible	81.0	82.2
Somebody's Mother—Unknown	81.5	94.3
" 'Spacially Jim"—Morgan	85.4	92.9
Star-Spangled Banner—Key	78.6	85.8
Strictly Germ Proof—Guiterman	75.9	80.5
Suffering—Crane	80.1	84.3

TITLE AND AUTHOR	Scores	
	Boys	Girls
Texas Cowboy—Cowboy Ballad	77.2	78.3
Those Two Boys—Adams	85.4	89.1
To a Pack Horse—Carr	78.6	81.3
Tract for Autos—Guiterman	83.9	86.9
Twins—Leigh	87.8	94.8
When Malindy Sings—Dunbar	77.0	88.1
White-Footed Deer—Bryant	77.0	82.8
Wreck of the "Hesperus"—Longfellow	74.7	81.9
Yankee Doodle—Song	78.0	77.7
Young Fellow, My Lad—Service	89.1	93.2
Zebra Dun—Cowboy Ballad	92.2	85.5

TABLE 23-2

Poems Approved by Boys Only, Grades 7 to 9

(This list approved by boys for grades 7 to 9 should be checked with the list for grades 10 to 12 since some of these poems are better liked in the senior high school.)

TITLE AND AUTHOR	Scores
Ballad of East and West—Kipling	75.2
Charge of the Light Brigade—Tennyson	77.1
Charley Lee—Knibbs	76.0
Danny Deever—Kipling	78.1
Defense of the Alamo—Miller	76.3
Gunga Din—Kipling	78.0
Horatius at the Bridge—Macaulay	79.6
Incident of the French Camp—Browning	78.8
King John and the Abbot of Canterbury—British Ballad	75.6
Lincoln, the Man of the People—Markham	78.0
Railroad Corral—Cowboy Ballad	76.7
Revenge—Tennyson	76.8
Robin Hood and the Ranger—British Ballad	82.2
Sheridan's Ride—Read	79.0
Simon Legree—Lindsay	77.2
Some Call Him Brave—Barker	75.8
Spanish Waters—Masefield	76.0
Thinker—Braley	75.4
White Mustang—Barker	76.3

TABLE 23–3

Poems Approved by Girls Only, Grades 7 to 9
(This list approved by girls for grades 7 to 9 should be checked with the list for grades 10 to 12 since some of these poems are better liked in the senior high school.)

TITLE AND AUTHOR	Scores
Abou Ben Adhem—Hunt	80.6
Abraham Lincoln—Malone	77.2
Aladdin—Lowell	78.0
Ambitious Mouse—Farrar	78.4
Annabel Lee—Poe	84.6
Ballad of the Harp-Weaver—Millay	86.1
Book Houses—Johnston	84.4
Brook—Tennyson	75.6
Broomstick Train—Holmes	80.8
Calf Path—Foss	80.3
Cane-Bottomed Chair—Thackeray	78.9
Children's Hour—Longfellow	85.9
Coming of Spring—Perry	77.5
Congo—Lindsay	75.2
Courtin'—Lowell	77.8
Courtship of Miles Standish—Longfellow	82.8
Cruel Brother—British Ballad	80.1
Da Leetla Boy—Daly	83.9
Discovered—Dunbar	83.6
Dixie—Song	74.6
Does It Matter?—Sassoon	76.6
Duel—Field	75.5
Een Napoli—Daly	77.8
Enoch Arden—Tennyson	86.7
Etiquette—Guiterman	80.2
Evangeline—Longfellow	85.6
First Snowfall—Lowell	86.9
Flathouse Roof—Crane	88.5
Fleurette—Service	82.2
Flower of Liberty—Holmes	78.3
Four-Leaf Clovers—Higginson	80.1
Four Things—Van Dyke	81.3
Get Up and Bar the Door—British Ballad	81.1
Glove and the Lions—Hunt	75.7
Godfrey Gordon Gustavus Gore—Rands	78.4
Great Guest Comes—Markham	76.9
Hiawatha—Longfellow	78.1
Home, Sweet Home—Payne	75.0

TITLE AND AUTHOR	Scores
Home Thoughts from Europe—Van Dyke	79.5
House by the Side of the Road—Foss	80.5
How to Catch a Bird—Jacobs	79.8
If—Kipling	76.5
Incorrigible—Johnson	76.2
In Defense of Children—Guiterman	84.2
In Quebec—Kipling	82.0
In School Days—Whittier	84.6
It Couldn't Be Done—Guest	84.1
Jim—Belloc	80.5
Kentucky Babe—Buck	76.8
Lady Clara Vere de Vere—Tennyson	76.2
Lady Clare—Tennyson	79.3
Lady of Antigua—Monkhouse	86.2
Lady of Shalott—Tennyson	79.6
Landing of the Pilgrim Fathers—Hemans	77.9
Leetla Guiseppina—Daly	86.3
Letter from Home—Irwin	81.1
Little Brown Wren—Scollard	82.5
Little Giffin of Tennessee—Ticknor	77.0
Little Orphant Annie—Riley	88.6
Lochinvar—Scott	80.6
Long Time Ago—Prentiss	82.3
Lord Chancellor's Song—Gilbert	80.1
Lovers—Cary	75.9
Mandalay—Kipling	75.0
Matilda—Belloc	84.6
Maude Muller—Whittier	80.4
Meddlesome Mattie—Taylor	81.0
Miller of the Dee—Mackay	79.6
Modern Hiawatha—Strong	77.0
Moss, the Dentist—Wells	86.6
My Dog—Bangs	83.1
Nathan Hale—Finch	77.9
Old Susan—de la Mare	75.3
Opportunity—Braley	83.7
Opportunity—Markham	76.0
Out to Old Aunt Mary's—Riley	80.6
Owl and the Pussy Cat—Lear	87.3
Pied Piper of Hamelin—Browning	75.5
Plaint of the Camel—Carryl	78.1
Pobble Who Has No Toes—Lear	77.8
Poor Benighted Hindoo—Monkhouse	85.2
Prayer—Markham	75.9
Prayer of Cyrus Brown—Foss	86.9

TITLE AND AUTHOR	Scores
Psalm of Life—Longfellow	75.6
Pyramus and Thisbe—Saxe	86.4
Quest—Whittier	79.3
Rain Song—Loveman	79.7
Road to Vagabondia—Burnet	77.5
Robert of Lincoln—Bryant	81.1
Rose and the Gardener—Dobson	80.0
Runaway—Frost	92.7
Sally in Our Alley—Cary	86.5
Salute to the Trees—Van Dyke	80.6
Seein' Things—Field	82.0
September—Jackson	76.4
September Gale—Holmes	82.6
Singing Leaves—Lowell	78.2
Smack in School—Palmer	85.4
Song Against Children—Kilmer	81.0
Songs for my Mother—Branch	79.3
Spider and the Fly—Howitt	80.4
Spires of Oxford—Letts	78.8
Tales of a Wayside Inn—Longfellow	78.4
Thomson Green and Harriet Hale—Gilbert	81.6
To a Mountain Daisy—Burns	75.6
Trees—Kilmer	85.1
Tubby Hook—Guiterman	81.3
Village Blacksmith—Longfellow	78.0
What Is Good?—O'Reilly	75.8
Woman's Will—Unknown	81.0
Wreck of the "Julie Plante"—Drummond	80.1

TABLE 24-1

Plays for Reading in Mixed Classes of Boys and Girls, Grades 10 to 12
(This list approved for grades 10 to 12 should be checked with the list for grades 7 to 9 since some of these plays are better liked in the junior high school.)

TITLE AND AUTHOR	Scores	
	Boys	Girls
Abraham Lincoln—Drinkwater	76.3	74.7
Admirable Crichton—Barrie	80.7	84.3
Barretts of Wimpole Street—Besier	78.4	89.9
Beyond the Horizon—O'Neill	78.4	87.8
Boy Comes Home—Milne	87.5	90.6
Brink of Silence—Galbraith	84.0	85.8

TITLE AND AUTHOR	Scores	
	Boys	Girls
Cartwheel (Radio play)—Knight	80.8	86.6
Confessional—Wilde	75.1	80.3
Cyrano de Bergerac—Rostand	77.9	82.3
Eli Whitney, Man of Destiny (Radio play)	88.3	83.6
Emperor Jones—O'Neill	89.2	84.6
Finders—Keepers—Kelly	83.5	92.1
Finger of God—Wilde	81.7	90.6
Forgot in the Rains (Radio play)—Merrick	82.8	90.0
Grand Cham's Diamond—Monkhouse	75.2	80.3
Hamlet—Shakespeare	72.6	79.1
Hand of Siva—Goodman and Hecht	78.7	75.3
In the Zone—O'Neill	89.2	83.1
Journey's End—Sherriff	81.4	84.2
Kelly Kid—Norris and Totheroh	78.7	88.7
Macbeth—Shakespeare	74.4	78.1
Man with a Gun (Radio play)—Vanda and Johnson	88.8	86.8
Merton of the Movies—Kaufman and Connelly	83.4	88.1
Monsieur Beaucaire—Tarkington	79.5	77.8
Moonshine—Hopkins	85.4	79.4
My Fair Lady—Lerner	75.9	85.8
Nathan Hale—Fitch	85.6	88.5
One Special for Doc—Geiger	92.3	96.6
Passing of the Third Floor Back—Jerome	74.4	78.5
Pygmalion—Shaw	77.0	85.2
Seven Waves Away (Radio play)—Sale	91.9	90.5
She Stoops to Conquer—Goldsmith	74.2	84.4
Silver Box—Galsworthy	77.1	81.6
Sparkin'—Conkle	85.1	92.0
Taming of the Shrew (Radio play)—Barnoew	78.5	86.0
Trysting Place—Tarkington	77.2	80.4
Two Crooks and a Lady—Pillot	78.7	82.7
Two Slaps in the Face—Molnar	80.1	83.9
Unseen—Gerstenberg	74.6	81.8
Valiant—Hall and Middlemas	93.6	96.0
Yellow Jack—Howard and De Kruif	81.3	83.0
You Can't Take It with You—Hart and Kaufman	76.7	76.2

TABLE 24–2

Plays Approved by Boys Only, Grades 10 to 12

TITLE AND AUTHOR	Scores
Green Pastures—Connelly	75.0

TITLE AND AUTHOR	Scores
Night at an Inn—Dunsany	75.9
Robert E. Lee—Drinkwater	79.8

TABLE 24–3

Plays Approved by Girls Only, Grades 10 to 12
(This list approved by girls for grades 10 to 12 should be checked with the list for grades 7 to 9 since some of the plays are better liked in the junior high school.)

TITLE AND AUTHOR	Scores
Comedy of Errors—Shakespeare	79.1
Doll's House—Ibsen	75.9
Dulcy—Kaufman and Connelly	79.4
Elizabeth the Queen—Anderson	80.0
Helena's Husband—Moeller	81.5
Merchant of Venice—Shakespeare	72.8
Midsummer Night's Dream—Shakespeare	77.1
Old Lady Shows Her Medals—Barrie	81.8
Othello—Shakespeare	81.8
Quality Street—Barrie	86.7
Rivals—Sheridan	76.8
Romancers—Rostand	81.9
Romeo and Juliet—Shakespeare	85.1
Taming of the Shrew—Shakespeare	85.8
Trifles—Glaspell	78.7
Where But in America—Wolff	81.0

TABLE 25–1

Plays for Reading in Mixed Classes of Boys and Girls, Grades 7 to 9
(This list approved for grades 7 to 9 should be checked with the list for grades 10 to 12 since some of the plays are better liked in the senior high school.)

TITLE AND AUTHOR	Scores	
	Boys	Girls
Blue Bird—Maeterlinck	72.7	79.1
Brink of Silence—Galbraith	87.1	84.2
Grand Cham's Diamond—Monkhouse	83.6	87.8
Kelly Kid—Norris and Totheroh	89.0	96.5
Merchant of Venice—Shakespeare	73.7	78.6
Merry Adventures of Robin Hood (Radio play)— C.B. Co.	92.2	87.5

TITLE AND AUTHOR	Scores	
	Boys	Girls
Nathan Hale—Fitch	89.9	93.3
Not Quite Such a Goose—Gale	82.9	94.8
Seeing the Elephant—Totheroh	80.2	92.7
Travelling Man—Gregory	86.9	91.4
Two Crooks and a Lady—Pillot	85.9	84.7

TABLE 25-2

Play Approved by Boys Only, Grades 7 to 9

TITLE AND AUTHOR	Score
Night at an Inn—Dunsany	81.4

TABLE 25-3

Plays Approved by Girls Only, Grades 7 to 9
(This list approved by girls for grades 7 to 9 should be checked with the list for grades 10 to 12 since some of the plays may be better liked in the senior high school.)

TITLE AND AUTHOR	Scores
Knave of Hearts—Saunders	84.9
Maker of Dreams—Down	79.9
Midsummer Night's Dream—Shakespeare	76.8
My Fair Lady—Lerner	83.8
My Lady's Dress—Knoblock	84.8
Pyramus and Thisbe—Shakespeare	76.9
Romancers—Rostand	87.0
Trysting Place—Tarkington	90.3
Violin Maker of Cremona—Coppée	81.3
Where But in America—Wolff	77.4

CHAPTER XVIII

Periodicals in the Coming Curriculum

MAGAZINES AND NEWSPAPERS DOMINATE READING IN AMERICA. Are young people being prepared by our schools to meet this reality? Two investigations made a quarter of a century apart may suggest an answer.

This discussion will deal primarily with reports from junior and senior high schools; data for grades 3 to 6 obtained from similar investigations were published in 1966 in *Elementary English*. Four tables present the basic information. Table 26 reports the returns in 1936 from 3384 senior high school students in more than 30 high schools on 51 magazines. Table 27 records the 1936 reports from 2576 students in more than 30 junior high schools on 30 magazines. Table 28 presents 1962 data on 48 magazines from 3720 senior high school boys and girls in 148 classes. Table 29 gives the 1962 figures for 38 magazines from 3844 students in grades 7 to 9 in 150 classes. In each table, listing is in the order of popularity.

The same basic procedures were used in 1936 and 1962. Each student was given a list of magazines and asked to indicate his degree of interest in each one with which he was acquainted by checking in the appropriate column. The replies on a particular magazine were then expressed by formula as an interest score for boys, a score for girls, and a score for boys and girls.

Notable are the similarities and contrasts between the interests of boys and girls. Adult magazines edited for both men and women (*Reader's Digest, Atlantic Monthly*) range in interest, usually, from approximately equal approval by girls and boys to a difference of ten points. The average difference recorded for ten such magazines is 5.9 points in grades 7 to 9; and 5.2 points in grades 10 to 12. By contrast, nine magazines planned primarily for one sex (*McCall's, Popular Science*) differ in interest from 22 to 46 points in grades 10 to 12 with an average difference of 34.2 points. In grades 7 to 9 the corresponding average difference is 32.1 points.

Tables 26 to 29 offer insight into various bents and trends in young people's reading. (1) The contrasting attitudes of the girls of four groups toward four widely read women's magazines (*Better Homes and Gardens, Ladies' Home Journal, McCall's,* and *Vogue*) tested in 1936 and again in 1962 permits these tentative conclusions: senior high school girls are more interested in women's magazines than the younger girls, but girls of both ages today value women's magazines less highly than they did a quarter century ago. (2) Of the 14 magazines best liked by senior high school girls (1962), eight are published for women. (3) By contrast, boys show their aversion to women's magazines by placing them at the end in each of the four tables. This emphasis is especially noticeable in 1962 where the last nine of 48 on the senior list are women's or girls' magazines, and on the junior list where the last 8 are women's or girls' magazines. (4) Boys retain in senior high school intense interest in outdoor activities. (5) A comparison of the interests of boys and girls in five news magazines (1962) shows that in grades 7 to 9 boys rate such periodicals 5.9 points higher than do girls. In grades 10 to 12 boys' average interest is only 0.7 point higher than girls' interest in the same magazines. When girls' and boys' reports are combined, however, it is found that the interest of young people in news magazines has gained less than one point in the three years from grade 8 to grade 11. (6) In spite of the ambivalent attitudes of older adolescents toward the concerns of both childhood and age, they register in their choices a wavering advance toward maturity.

We expect to find the attitudes of children toward children's magazines differing from their attitudes toward adult magazines. However, some of the contrasts are surprising. In grades 4 to 6, boys place three adult magazines among the four best-liked, and seven adult magazines among the first 15. Girls in the same grades vote only one adult magazine (*National Georgraphic*) among the top four, but include six among the first 15. Even in grade 3, boys give the first three places to adult magazines: *Popular Science, National Geographic,* and *Popular Mechanics.*

Changes in age influence girls and boys more powerfully when choosing children's magazines than when choosing those edited for adults. Four magazines planned for children below junior high school *(Child Life, Children's Activities, Children's Digest,* and *My Weekly Reader)* lost an average of 16.0 points in interest from grade 3 to grade 5. By contrast, five adult magazines *(Life, Look, Popular Mechanics, Popular Science,* and *National Geographic)* during the same period changed in appeal by an average of only 2.9 points. Table 15 shows that for 13 adult magazines the average interest of boys and of girls remains almost unchanged from the elementary grades to junior high school, while from junior high school to senior high school there has been an average loss of interest of 2.5 points for the same magazines. That in the period of rapid maturation, from the elementary grades to senior high school, children have lost interest in representative adult magazines deserves thoughtful attention.

The fact that the *average* difference between the interests of girls and boys for the 13 magazines of Table 30 is only 2.0 points at its widest does not signify that there are not wide variations in interest in individual magazines. It simply records that among the 13 magazines those greatly preferred by girls are offset by others highly preferred by boys.

Table 31, which summarizes the data of four correlations at four age levels of the scores given by boys and girls in 1962, confirms that the opposition in reading interests of girls and boys in many magazines is marked from age 8, and therefore highly significant in determining choices for school libraries. The rank-difference method was used. Of the 48 magazines ranked in the senior high school list, 26 are edited for both men and women, or boys and girls; and 22, primarily for one sex. The coefficient of correlation was -0.246. In the junior high school, 21 magazines are designed for both sexes; 17 for one sex only. The extent of correlation was -0.404. Of the 31 magazines tested in the elementary grades, 20 make the broad appeal to both boys and girls; 11 aim primarily at one group. The coefficient of correlation was -0.091. The 12 magazines scored by children in grade 3 include a very large proportion (10) planned for both sexes. In spite of this, the coefficient of correlation was low, 0.241.

The contrast in magazine choices between girls and boys shown by these four correlations is marked. Three are negative. Even with the very young children in grade 3 where close correspondence might have been anticipated, basic cleavage is revealed. We must conclude that at every age level the register of periodicals should include those that have high appeal for both groups, those that enthrall girls only, and those that enthrall boys only.

Equal numbers of girls and boys in the study made possible an assessment of the comparative breadth of reading of magazines by the two groups at three age levels.[10] Only magazines of the 1962 study which were planned to appeal to both girls and boys or both women and men were used. Sixteen magazines tested in the elementary grades with total reports of 16,028 indicated that at ten years of age girls' reading was 95.8 percent of boys' reading. Reports (15,176) on 17 magazines in junior high school ranked girls' reading as 108.6 percent of boys' reading. In the senior high school with 22,852 reports on 19 magazines, the girls' position had advanced to 123.6 percent of the boys' reading.

The magazines used at the different grade levels were the same only in part. However, since four widely read adult magazines *(Life, Reader's Digest, Saturday Evening Post,* and *Time)* were rated at the three levels, additional computations were made for these four magazines only. For these, girls' percentages of boys' reading were: 94.5 in grades 4 to 6; 100.7 in grades 7 to 9; and 113.2 in grades 10 to 12.

The influence of intelligence on the choices of periodicals by superior, average, and slow students in grades 10 to 12 is reported in Table 32. It is evident from the data that there is no blanket rule as to differences in attitudes by the three groups of students toward the magazine field. In certain instances (e.g., *Reader's Digest, Saturday Evening Post),* variations are slight. In certain other cases, the differences are marked: nine light magazines as a group are much better liked by average students than by the superior (9.8 points), and are still better liked by the slow (15.4 points above the superior). Other examples: slow boys place *Boys' Life* 9.8 points higher than average boys, and 11.8 points higher than the superior; superior girls and boys, on the other hand, score five literary magazines more than six points higher than either the average or the slow pupils. High-grade newspapers are almost equally liked by the three groups, while tabloids find much less favor with the superior than with the average or slow.

The evidence suggests that the editors of general magazines of good quality have succeeded in preparing products which appeal almost equally to readers of high and low intellectual capacity; that

[10]Detailed data will be found in Table III of "The Challenge of Periodicals in Education," in *Elementary English,* April 1966.

trashy magazines and tabloids appeal strongly to weaker readers; and that magazines distinguished for literary quality or weighty content are most attractive to readers of superior ability.

The use of the same testing techniques with a number of the same magazines at an interval of 26 years has made possible the examination of a question which otherwise would have been very difficult or impossible to approach. The question: Has there been in a quarter of a century a significant change in young people's attitudes toward the reading of periodicals? Interest scores for 13 magazines tested in many junior high schools in 1936, and again in 1962, record an average loss of interest of 10.1 points. Only the *Saturday Evening Post* scored higher at the later date. In the senior high school, there were comparative scores for 21 widely tested magazines. The result, an average loss of reading interest of 12.5 points. Again, the *Saturday Evening Post* alone received a higher score in 1962.

The testimony of children in the elementary grades gathered in 1936 and 1962 by the methods used in the high schools showed an average loss for six magazines of 3.8 points. During the same interval, children of the same grades (1544 in 1936; 2666 in 1962) lowered their rating of *My Weekly Reader* from 85.0 to 67.0, a startling drop of 18 points.

Data are available also for changes in high school students' interests in two daily newspapers: the New York *Times* and the New York *Herald-Tribune* (Table 33). The votes for the two are combined. In 1936 junior high school boys and girls (1169) gave these papers a score of 81.3. In 1962 corresponding young people (1992) rated the same papers 68.0, a loss of 13.3 points. Senior high school students (1832) in 1936 scored them 82.8; in 1962 the score by 2797 young people of the same grades lowered the rating to 71.0, a loss of 11.8 points.

An unpublished study by the writer found that children's interest in books and other literary materials also have declined during the past quarter century, though the evidence did not indicate a decline in the *amount* of children's reading.

Is there a reasonable explanation for this apparent loss of interest in reading? No one doubts that scientific discoveries and instant, world-wide communication have increased sophistication at all ages. Among instrumentalities, the radio has been influential. Television has been more so. That children, particularly young children, are fascinated (or bewitched) by this transcendent gadget is not only obvious to parents; it is verified by the astonishing time youngsters devote to it, an average of three hours daily, and by the rating they give it. On reflection, does it not appear inevitable that news, formalized and relayed through inanimate print, should pale in children's eyes compared with the drama of life in action?

It is universally recognized that the newspaper is the favorite reading of adults. People who can read at all, almost invariably read newspapers, while seven in 20 fail to read any magazine. Eells reported in his 1936 study (No. 7) that secondary school students placed the daily newspaper higher than any magazines when asked to list the periodicals they "enjoyed and valued most." In 1936 the writer found not only that the newspaper was popular from the fourth to the twelfth grade, but that at 10 or 11 years, children are more interested in the daily paper than they ever will be again. In the elementary grades, 416 boys and girls rated eight large city newspapers 89.6; in the junior high school, 2475 young people rated 18 large city papers 81.4; and in the senior high school, 3430 students rated the same 18 city papers 81.2.

The interests of senior high school boys and girls in eight New York City papers (including two tabloids) are tabulated in Table 34, and comparable data for the same papers for young people in junior high school are given in Table 35. The schools reporting are principally in upstate New York. While the six regular newspapers do not vary greatly in their appeal, it is noteworthy that the New York *Times* ranks at the top (83.4) with both sexes in senior high school, and with boys (82.0) in junior high school. It is significant, too, that the tabloids rank lower than the others: the New York *Mirror* scoring 52.2 on 700 reports in grades 7 to 9, and 41.8 on 404 reports in grades 10 to 12. That the scores for tabloids in senior high school are markedly lower than the low ratings in junior high school is encouraging.

A wider view of newspaper reading is found in Table 36 which gives the reactions in grades 7 to 12 to various groups of newspapers. While students value small city dailies, large city dailies, and high-grade New York City papers almost equally, the 14 papers published in large cities of upstate New York achieve the highest endorsement (83.6). It may be that emphasis on local news in the communities represented more than offsets for area readers the greater coverage of national and world news offered by the metropolitan press. The average scores for the two tabloids (62.5 in junior high school; 54.0 in senior high school) demonstrates that this type occupies an inferior position in the view of adolescents.

The average score (81.8) by 2854 junior high school students, and the 79.8 rating by 3944 young people in senior high school given to 30 dailies representing a wide diversity of community and editorial policy, may be close to the true valuations which adolescents accord the newspaper. While these and other ratings indicate that students in grades 7 to 9 regard general newspaper reading slightly more favorably than older boys and girls, the ranking is reversed when the elite New York City papers are concerned.

If we recognize that a roster of erudite magazines which will lie untouched on the library shelves is little more than an unintentional sham, should we not ask, "How is the school to find the periodicals which will genuinely serve young people?" The Eells Scale demonstrates the outcome of relying on the consensus of 167 experts. Of 127 magazines on the official Scale, the highest third includes a surprising proportion which only the rare adolescent would choose to read. The lowest third includes many that not only rank high with young people, but are widely read and approved by the nation's college graduates.

Ironically, the country-wide study which produced the Eells Scale provided a second criterion that could have transformed and vitalized it. Coordinator Eells compiled a list of the magazines which 17,338 boys and girls placed highest when asked to name those both "enjoyed and valued." Had this list been used by the Committee for the Cooperative Study of Secondary School Standards to humanize the recommendations of their experts, a genuinely useful instrument would have been achieved.[11] Eells also compiled a second list of 108 periodicals which the same 17,338 students reported as "read fairly regularly," but omitting any with fewer than 30 reports. A comparison of this student list with the Eells Scale discloses that the educational specialists had placed on the *upper half* of their scale 22 magazines (not including library tools or teachers' journals) that *not one* student in 578 was making a practice of reading. One asks in wonder: With universal lip service to interest as basic in learning, why is the principle ignored in practice even when its use would appear unavoidable?

SUGGESTED PROCEDURE: To select periodicals for school use, go first directly to boys and girls to learn which ones they enjoy. Then ask educators and parents to delete those they are convinced would be harmful. When choosing the final list, include adequate representation from magazines edited for both sexes and popular with girls

[11]Two statistical sidelights on the conflict between the choices of experts and of young people: (1) A rank-difference correlation between the rankings of 34 magazines on the student-chosen list reported by Eells and the recommendations on the Eells Scale yields the low coefficient, 0.076. (2) Paul A. Witty and Anne Coomer reported the 15 magazines they found to be most frequently read by high school students (*Journal of Educational Psychology*, February, 1943). Thirteen appeared on the Eells Scale. A rank-difference correlation of the two rankings yields the emphatically negative coefficient, -0.445.

and boys; magazines highly approved by girls; and magazines highly approved by boys.

Students of periodical reading are widely agreed on the following:

1. Two of three adults read magazines, 95 percent read newspapers, and fewer than half read books.
2. Adult readers with an eighth grade education spend more than fourfold as much time on periodicals as on books.
3. Of the thousands of magazines published, young people and adults alike are largely uninformed as to which could serve them best.
4. Following school days, newspapers and magazines provide the most important means of lifetime education for Americans.
5. There are important values in periodicals of which the majority of readers are unaware.
6. Classroom instruction can improve taste, promote independent judgment in making choices, and develop efficient plans for reading periodicals.
7. Schools generally have made little effort to guide the reading of periodicals by girls and boys.

That most of this information has been available for many years, but has been largely ignored in planning school programs constitutes an indictment. Schools might well take these steps to answer the indictment:

(1) establish carefully planned, continuous (not haphazard) instruction in newspapers and magazines;
(2) aim specifically at the development of effective standards for choosing periodicals and efficient plans for reading them;
(3) provide a generous roster of adult and juvenile periodicals which *stimulate* and *delight* young people; and
(4) recognize that it is a primary function of public education to prepare young people for the useful intellectual activities that most will perform every day of their lives.

TABLE 26

INTERESTS OF BOYS AND OF GIRLS, GRADES 10 TO 12, IN 51 MAGAZINES, LISTED IN THE ORDER OF POPULARITY (1936)*

MAGAZINE	BOYS		MAGAZINE	GIRLS		MAGAZINE	BOYS AND GIRLS	
	NO.	SCORE		NO.	SCORE		NO.	SCORE
Sport Stories	286	93.6	Stage	180	93.9	Reader's Digest	3525	90.1
Popular Mechanics	1266	90.0	Reader's Digest	1827	91.0	National Geographic	1692	88.1
Popular Science	895	89.5	National Geographic	882	89.5	Fortune	501	87.6
Reader's Digest	1698	89.1	Fortune	258	88.0	Stage	288	86.1
Fortune	243	87.2	American Girl	326	86.2	American Magazine	2008	82.7
National Geographic	810	86.6	Vogue	407	86.2	Esquire	602	82.2
Esquire	366	86.5	Good Housekeeping	1543	85.8	Popular Science	1176	81.5
Open Road for Boys	216	84.0	Cosmopolitan	1009	84.7	Cosmopolitan	1318	78.0
American Boy	649	82.7	American Magazine	1154	84.4	Popular Mechanics	1646	77.9
Hunting and Fishing	209	82.5	McCall's	812	82.3	New Yorker	301	77.6
American Magazine	854	81.0	Woman's Home Companion	900	80.5	Time	1425	77.1
Newsweek	94	80.3	Harper's Bazaar	240	80.0	Radio Guide	264	76.4
Field and Stream	362	80.2	Red Book	319	80.0	Newsweek	198	76.0

*Since the number of reports by boys, or by girls, in particular instances were too few to yield reliable results, scores for them have been omitted. Consequently, there are 54 scores for boys, 53 for girls, and 51 for boys and girls.

TABLE 26 (continued)

MAGAZINE	BOYS NO.	SCORE	MAGAZINE	GIRLS NO.	SCORE	MAGAZINE	BOYS AND GIRLS NO.	SCORE
Boys' Life	700	79.9	Ladies' Home Journal	1176	79.7	Red Book	436	75.9
Stage	108	78.2	Photoplay	257	79.4	Scholastic	930	75.1
Time	665	77.8	Theatre Arts Monthly	149	78.9	Photoplay	392	73.6
New Yorker	148	77.4	Scholastic	494	78.8	Collier's	2160	73.0
Radio Guide	122	75.0	Movie Magazine	295	78.6	Harper's Bazaar	428	73.0
Collier's	987	74.8	Delineator	480	78.2	American Boy	836	72.8
Liberty	801	72.5	Esquire	236	77.8	Literary Digest	2206	72.2
Saturday Evening Post	1240	72.3	New Yorker	153	77.8	Current History	251	70.5
Red Book	117	71.8	Radio Guide	142	77.8	Harper's	489	70.5
Scholastic	436	71.4	Pictorial Review	479	77.5	Saturday Evening Post	2831	70.1
Cosmopolitan	309	71.2	Harper's	286	76.9	Liberty	1645	68.7
Literary Digest	853	70.2	Time	760	76.4	Movie Magazine	454	68.4
Current History	115	69.6	Golden Book	233	74.2	Boys' Life	814	68.0
Country Gentleman	143	69.2	Literary Digest	1353	74.1	Good Housekeeping	1908	67.9
Scientific American	163	68.4	Popular Science	281	73.5	Pictorial Review	568	67.1
Photoplay	135	67.8	Atlantic Monthly	340	72.6	Atlantic Monthly	628	66.6
Nature	135	67.4	Newsweek	104	71.6	Country Gentleman	282	65.7
Detective Stories	180	67.2	Better Homes and Gardens	355	71.4	Nature	237	65.6

TABLE 26 (continued)

MAGAZINE	BOYS NO.	SCORE	MAGAZINE	GIRLS NO.	SCORE	MAGAZINE	BOYS AND GIRLS NO.	SCORE
Scribner's	341	66.6	Scribner's	316	71.4	Scribner's	585	65.6
Current History	188	66.0	Current History	136	71.3	Golden Book	360	65.1
Collier's	203	64.0	Collier's	1173	71.1	Field and Stream	477	64.9
Saturday Evening Post	165	62.1	Saturday Evening Post	1591	67.8	Vogue	516	64.7
Travel	125	61.2	Travel	103	67.5	Better Homes and Gardens	504	63.2
Popular Mechanics	288	60.6	Popular Mechanics	380	65.7	McCall's	978	62.9
Liberty	269	59.7	Liberty	844	64.8	Forum	336	62.7
Nature	321	59.7	Nature	102	63.7	Detective Stories	252	62.4
Forum	159	58.2	Forum	171	63.2	Travel	206	62.4
American Boy	103	57.3	American Boy	187	62.8	Ladies' Home Journal	1466	62.1
Review of Reviews	89	56.7	Review of Reviews	162	62.7	Theatre Arts Monthly	242	62.1
Country Gentleman	127	55.9	Country Gentleman	139	62.2	Delineator	558	61.2
American Mercury	170	55.6	American Mercury	105	59.5	Woman's Home Companion	1171	61.0
True Story	149	55.0	True Story	618	59.5	American Mercury	230	60.4
True Romances	365	50.0	True Romances	144	58.0	True Story	939	59.6
Detective Stories	93	45.2	Detective Stories	72	57.6	Western Stories	521	59.4
Boys' Life	127	44.9	Boys' Life	114	56.1	Review of Reviews	332	59.2

MAGAZINE

Western Stories
Harper's Bazaar
Harper's
Forum

American Mercury

Atlantic Monthly
Scribner's
True Story
Movie Magazine
Travel

Pictorial Review

Golden Book
Review of Reviews

Better Homes and Gardens
Good Housekeeping
Theatre Arts Monthly
Asia

TABLE 26 (continued)

MAGAZINE	BOYS		MAGAZINE	GIRLS		MAGAZINE	BOYS AND GIRLS	
	NO.	SCORE		NO.	SCORE		NO.	SCORE
Ladies' Home Journal	290	44.5	Asia	145	52.4	Scientific American	251	57.5
Delineator	78	44.2	Western Stories	180	52.2	Asia	272	48.7
McCall's	166	43.4	True Confessions	256	51.8	True Confessions	389	43.2
Vogue	109	43.1	Field and Stream	115	49.6			
Woman's Home Companion	271	41.5	Scientific American	88	46.6			
True Confessions	133	34.6						

TABLE 27

INTERESTS OF BOYS AND OF GIRLS, GRADES 7 TO 9, IN 30 MAGAZINES LISTED IN THE ORDER OF POPULARITY (1936)*

MAGAZINE	BOYS NO.	SCORE	MAGAZINE	GIRLS NO.	SCORE	MAGAZINE	BOYS AND GIRLS NO.	SCORE
Popular Mechanics	1700	95.4	American Girl	1354	91.6	National Geographic	2319	87.3
Popular Science	931	93.6	Photoplay	149	90.9	Current Events	511	86.5
Sport Stories	135	92.6	Fortune	134	89.9	Fortune	271	86.0
Boys' Life	1755	91.4	Child Life	650	88.5	Popular Science	1275	85.3
Open Road for Boys	691	89.3	National Geographic	1142	87.4	Reader's Digest	1076	84.8
American Boy	978	88.9	Current Events	267	86.0	Detective Stories	230	83.0
Field and Stream	86	87.2	Good Housekeeping	1058	85.0	Popular Mechanics	2465	81.3
National Geographic	1177	87.1	Reader's Digest	542	85.0	American Boy	1237	79.2
Current Events	244	86.9	Cosmopolitan	392	83.3	Boys' Life	2118	78.4
Shadow	109	85.8	Vogue	105	82.9	New Yorker	289	76.4
Detective Stories	142	85.2	Red Book	120	82.5	American Magazine	1625	74.1
Reader's Digest	534	84.5	McCall's	498	81.2	Collier's	1221	73.9
Fortune	137	82.1	Detective Stories	88	80.7	Time	649	72.8
Western Stories	221	79.2	American Magazine	880	79.7	Cosmopolitan	492	71.2
New Yorker	174	78.4	Delineator	199	79.4	Western Stories	362	70.3
Hunting and						Saturday		

*Since the number of reports by boys, or by girls, in particular instances were too few to yield reliable results, scores for them have been omitted. As a result, there are 35 scores for boys, 37 for girls, and 30 scores for boys and girls.

TABLE 27 (continued)

MAGAZINE	BOYS NO.	SCORE	MAGAZINE	GIRLS NO.	SCORE	MAGAZINE	BOYS AND GIRLS NO.	SCORE
Fishing	142	74.6	Pictorial Review	224	78.8	Evening Post	2077	70.2
Time	330	73.5	St. Nicholas	358	78.8	Nature	447	69.9
Collier's	433	72.9	Ladies' Home Journal	613	77.6	Child Life	887	68.8
Pathfinder	152	71.7	Popular Science	344	77.0	Literary Digest	1286	68.4
Saturday Evening Post	915	69.0	Woman's Home Companion	406	76.7	Pathfinder	405	67.8
American Magazine	745	68.5	Nature	192	75.7	St. Nicholas	574	67.7
Literary Digest	617	67.0	Collier's	788	74.9	Liberty	1091	66.3
Liberty	515	66.4	New Yorker	115	74.3	True Story	652	65.8
Nature	255	64.1	Junior Red Cross Magazine	162	73.1	Junior Red Cross Magazine	315	65.2
True Story	203	59.1	True Story	449	72.4	Good Housekeeping	1294	63.0
Cosmopolitan	100	59.0	Time	319	72.1	Scholastic	567	62.3
Scholastic	271	57.9	Saturday Evening Post	1162	71.3	American Girl	1679	59.2
Junior Red Cross Magazine	153	57.2	Literary Digest	669	69.7	McCall's	619	57.8
St. Nicholas	216	56.5	American Boy	259	69.5	Ladies' Home Journal	792	57.5
Child Life	237	49.0	Better Homes and Gardens	104	68.3	Hygeia	202	49.6
Good Housekeeping	236	40.9	Popular Mechanics	765	67.1			
Hygeia	92	38.6	Scholastic	296	66.6			

TABLE 27 (continued)

MAGAZINE	BOYS NO.	SCORE	MAGAZINE	GIRLS NO.	SCORE	MAGAZINE	BOYS AND GIRLS NO.	SCORE
Ladies' Home Journal	179	37.4	Liberty	576	66.2			
McCall's	121	34.3	Boys' Life	363	65.4			
American Girl	325	26.8	Pathfinder	253	63.8			
			Western Stories	141	61.3			
			Hygeia	110	60.5			

TABLE 28

INTERESTS OF BOYS AND OF GIRLS, GRADES 10 TO 12, IN 48 MAGAZINES LISTED IN THE ORDER OF POPULARITY (1962)

MAGAZINE	BOYS		MAGAZINE	GIRLS		MAGAZINE	BOYS AND GIRLS	
	NO.	SCORE		NO.	SCORE		NO.	SCORE
Hot Rod	558	82.0	Seventeen	1559	88.2	Life	3080	81.6
Life	1448	79.4	Mademoiselle	436	83.8	Reader's Digest	2700	78.8
Popular Mechanics	1138	77.7	Life	1632	83.7	Look	2801	78.6
Popular Science	1005	77.4	Glamour	522	82.7	Saturday Evening Post	2445	76.3
Look	1260	76.7	Reader's Digest	1487	81.5	Time	1876	72.0
Reader's Digest	1213	76.1	Look	1541	80.5	Scientific American	448	69.8
Field and Stream	847	76.0	McCall's	1394	79.7	Newsweek	1749	67.7
Saturday Evening Post	1134	75.4	Saturday Evening Post	1311	77.2	Hot Rod	731	65.4
Time	942	72.8	Vogue	989	76.7	Current Events	1198	65.1
Scientific American	292	71.9	Ladies' Home Journal	1285	74.6	News Time	933	65.1
True	747	70.7	Time	934	71.1	Theatre Arts Monthly	317	64.8
Argosy	222	68.7	Harper's	582	70.3	Seventeen	1781	64.3
Newsweek	857	68.2	American Home	290	70.2	Current History	537	62.2
Flying	468	66.0	Good Housekeeping	1310	70.1	Popular Science	1307	61.8
News Time	484	65.8	Show	112	69.6	New Yorker	946	60.9
Aviation	388	65.5	Scientific			Mademoiselle	510	60.8

TABLE 28 (continued)

MAGAZINE	BOYS NO.	SCORE	MAGAZINE	GIRLS NO.	SCORE	MAGAZINE	BOYS AND GIRLS NO.	SCORE
Current History	294	63.8	American	156	67.6	McCall's	1859	60.6
Esquire	678	63.5	Newsweek	892	67.2	Saturday Review	192	60.5
Boys' Life	1161	63.4	Current Events	607	67.1	American Home	393	60.1
Current Events	591	63.1	Theatre Arts Monthly	193	67.1	Photoplay	1084	59.7
Theatre Arts Monthly	124	62.5	American Girl	1110	64.8	Scouting	199	59.7
Saturday Review	85	61.2	News Time	449	64.3	Scholastic	1023	59.2
Photoplay	441	60.0	Red Book	682	64.3	Show	179	58.7
New Yorker	453	57.9	New Yorker	493	63.8	Atlantic Monthly	349	58.3
Scouting	140	57.5	Better Homes and Gardens	1331	62.9	Vogue	1162	58.0
Scholastic	487	57.2	Scouting	59	61.9	True	956	57.6
Atlantic Monthly	182	56.6	Scholastic	536	61.1	Harper's	800	57.2
Model Airplane News	337	55.6	Woman's Home Companion	189	61.1	Argosy	287	57.1
True Story	321	50.5	Current History	243	60.5	Boys' Life	1520	56.0
Junior Red Cross Magazine	149	50.3	Atlantic Monthly	167	59.9	Esquire	1035	55.7
American Home	103	50.0	Junior Red Cross Magazine	214	59.8	Popular Mechanics	1413	55.6
Photoplay	280	48.8	Saturday Review	107	59.7	Glamour	591	55.5
Show	67	47.8	Photoplay	643	59.3	Field and Stream	1130	55.3
			Modern Screen	783	57.5			

TABLE 28 (continued)

MAGAZINE	BOYS NO.	BOYS SCORE	MAGAZINE	GIRLS NO.	GIRLS SCORE	MAGAZINE	BOYS AND GIRLS NO.	BOYS AND GIRLS SCORE
Fortune	300	46.3	Modern Screen	316	53.2	Junior Red Cross Magazine	363	55.1
True Story	218	44.0	Harper's	834	50.9	Ladies' Home Journal	1570	53.8
Hot Rod	339	42.0	True Confessions	173	48.8	Good Housekeeping	1739	53.4
Boys' Life	465	41.4	McCall's	359	48.5	Red Book	899	52.5
Esquire	552	41.2	Better Homes and Gardens	357	47.8	American Girl	1163	52.2
True Confessions	217	40.6	Red Book	917	46.8	Better Homes and Gardens	1883	52.1
Popular Science	222	40.3	Seventeen	302	46.2	Aviation	474	52.0
Argosy	53	39.6	American Girl	65	45.4	Modern Screen	1083	51.9
True	173	39.3	Vogue	209	44.5	Flying	537	51.1
Calling All Girls	74	37.8	Mademoiselle	421	42.0	Fortune	596	51.0
Model Airplane News	429	36.6	Good Housekeeping	75	40.7	True Story	1155	50.7
Aviation	285	33.0	Ladies' Home Journal	86	38.4	Model Airplane News	412	48.2
Flying	14	28.6	Calling All Girls	69	36.2	True Confessions	1256	44.4
Field and Stream	69	28.3	Glamour	283	34.6	Woman's Home Companion	237	40.0
Popular Mechanics	48	18.8	Woman's Home Companion	275	33.5	Calling All Girls	435	35.3

TABLE 29

INTERESTS OF BOYS AND OF GIRLS, GRADES 7 TO 9, IN 38 MAGAZINES LISTED IN THE ORDER OF POPULARITY (1962)*

MAGAZINE	BOYS		MAGAZINE	GIRLS		MAGAZINE	BOYS AND GIRLS	
	NO.	SCORE		NO.	SCORE		NO.	SCORE
Popular Science	852	83.3	Seventeen	979	90.4	Life	2406	81.4
Hot Rod	287	82.9	Life	1202	83.5	Saturday Evening Post	1747	79.4
Popular Mechanics	944	82.2	Reader's Digest	1068	81.3	Reader's Digest	2051	78.6
Field and Stream	697	81.7	Saturday Evening Post	881	81.2	Scientific American	359	75.4
Scientific American	229	79.9	Look	1017	77.6	Look	1966	74.9
Life	1204	79.3	American Girl	947	77.0	Popular Science	1071	71.1
Boys' Life	1125	78.0	McCall's	995	76.8	Photoplay	648	70.0
Saturday Evening Post	866	77.5	Mademoiselle	204	74.8	Time	1254	69.5
Flying	291	76.8	Modern Screen	435	72.3	Boys' Life	1367	68.6
Model Airplane News	308	76.5	Photoplay	418	72.1	Seventeen	1086	67.4
Reader's Digest	983	75.9	Vogue	624	71.8	News Time	590	65.9
Aviation	258	74.6	Ladies' Home Journal	715	71.2	Scouting	270	65.8
Time	662	73.0	Scientific American	130	70.8	Current History	189	65.3

*21 of the magazines are edited for both sexes; 17 for men or women.

TABLE 29 (continued)

MAGAZINE	BOYS NO.	SCORE	MAGAZINE	GIRLS NO.	SCORE	MAGAZINE	BOYS AND GIRLS NO.	SCORE
True	160	72.5	True Story	276	67.4	Hot Rod	314	64.6
Look	949	72.1	Time	592	66.0	Newsweek	1214	64.4
News Time	321	69.9	Calling All Girls	820	65.5	Field and Stream	844	63.5
Scouting	218	69.0	True Confessions	315	63.7	Current Events	726	63.2
Newsweek	663	67.8	Harper's	216	63.4	Modern Screen	587	62.8
Photoplay	230	67.8	T V Guide	353	63.3	Model Airplane News	349	62.7
Current History	99	67.7	Current History	90	62.8	True Story	413	62.4
Current Events	376	64.6	Scouting	52	62.5	Flying	309	62.0
Atlantic Monthly	129	62.8	Junior Scholastic	679	62.4	Aviation	317	61.5
New Yorker	362	62.7	News Time	269	61.9	New Yorker	709	61.0
T V Guide	296	57.9	Current Events	350	61.7	T V Guide	649	60.6
Junior Scholastic	595	57.8	Newsweek	551	61.0	Atlantic Monthly	218	60.4
True Story	137	57.3	New Yorker	347	59.2	Junior Scholastic	1274	60.1
Modern Screen	152	53.3	Boys' Life	242	59.1	True	206	59.6
Fortune	131	52.3	Popular Science	219	58.9	Popular Mechanics	1108	59.3
True Confessions	81	51.9	Atlantic Monthly	89	57.9	American Girl	986	59.0
Harper's	118	50.4	Better Homes and Gardens	739	55.6	True Confessions	396	57.8
Calling All Girls	57	45.6	Fortune	133	50.0	Harper's	334	56.9
Seventeen	107	44.4	Model Airplane News	41	48.8	Calling All Girls	877	55.6
Better Homes and Gardens	305	42.8	Aviation	59	48.3	McCall's	1331	55.5

TABLE 29 (continued)

MAGAZINE	BOYS		MAGAZINE	GIRLS		MAGAZINE	BOYS AND GIRLS	
	NO.	SCORE		NO.	SCORE		NO.	SCORE
American Girl	39	41.0	Flying	18	47.2	Vogue	719	53.0
McCall's	336	34.2	True	46	46.7	Ladies' Home Journal	895	52.3
Vogue	95	34.2	Hot Rod	27	46.3	Fortune	264	51.2
Ladies' Home Journal	180	33.3	Field and Stream	147	45.2	Better Homes and Gardens	1044	49.2
Mademoiselle	19	15.8	Popular Mechanics	164	36.3	Mademoiselle	223	45.3

TABLE 30

COMPARISONS OF THE INTERESTS OF BOYS AND GIRLS OF THREE GRADE LEVELS IN 13 ADULT MAGAZINES*

NO OF ADULT MAGAZINES	GRADES 4 TO 6 AVERAGE SCORES			GRADES 7 TO 9 AVERAGE SCORES			GRADES 10 TO 12 AVERAGE SCORES		
	BOYS	GIRLS	BOYS AND GIRLS	BOYS	GIRLS	BOYS AND GIRLS	BOYS	GIRLS	BOYS AND GIRLS
13	66.3	68.2	67.3	66.2	68.2	67.2	64.2	65.2	64.7

*The magazines: Better Homes and Gardens, Life, Look, McCall's, Modern Screen, Newsweek, Photoplay, Popular Mechanics, Popular Science, Reader's Digest, Saturday Evening Post, Time, True Confessions.

TABLE 31

CORRELATIONS OF THE RANKINGS OF MAGAZINES GIVEN BY BOYS AND GIRLS AT FOUR DIFFERENT GRADE LEVELS, USING THE RANK-DIFFERENCE METHOD

GRADE LEVEL	NO. OF MAGAZINES	COEFFICIENT OF CORRELATION
Grades 10 to 12	48	−0.246
Grades 7 to 9	38	−0.404
Grades 4 to 6	31	−0.091
Grade 3	12	+0.241

TABLE 32

INFLUENCE OF INTELLIGENCE ON THE CHOICES OF PERIODICALS BY SUPERIOR, AVERAGE, AND SLOW STUDENTS IN GRADES 10 TO 12 (1936)

PERIODICALS	NO. OF REPORTS	SCORE SUPERIOR STUDENTS	SCORE AVERAGE STUDENTS	SCORE SLOW STUDENTS	CHANGE SUPERIOR TO AVERAGE	CHANGE SUPERIOR TO WEAK
Reader's Digest	3525	91.1	89.5	89.2	−1.6	−1.9
Saturday Evening Post	2831	69.7	70.3	72.6	+0.6	+2.9
Good, Nonliterary Magazines (9)*	2194	66.6	62.3	61.4	−4.3	−5.2
Light Magazines (9)*	1967	57.0	66.8	72.4	+9.8	+15.4
Literary (5)*	2212	70.1	63.6	63.9	−6.5	−6.2
Boys' Life (boys only)**	700	73.7	75.7	85.5	+2.0	+11.8
Good Housekeeping (girls only)**	1543	83.7	87.2	84.7	+3.5	+1.0
Ladies' Home Journal (girls only)**	1176	80.8	78.0	81.4	−2.8	+0.6
Popular Mechanics (boys only)**	1266	85.9	92.2	93.3	+6.3	+7.4
Popular Science (boys only)**	895	84.6	91.5	96.6	+6.9	+12.0
High– Grade Newspapers (4)	2618	81.1	81.7	83.1	+0.6	+2.0
Tabloids (2)	1122	46.6	56.9	57.5	+10.3	+10.9

*When one periodical of a particular type lacked sufficient reports for dependable results, data for several periodicals were combined. The following groups were used: light magazines (nine of the following types—detective, motion picture, confession, and western story); good nonliterary magazines (nine of the following types—opinion and discussion, current history, travel, science, and theatre arts); literary (5); high-grade newspapers (4); tabloids (2).
**When the readership for a particular magazine was principally boys, or principally girls, the data used were restricted to one sex.

TABLE 33

COMPARISONS OF THE INTERESTS OF JUNIOR AND SENIOR HIGH SCHOOL BOYS AND GIRLS IN TWO NEWSPAPERS IN 1936 AND 1962*

| NEWSPAPERS | DATE | JUNIOR HIGH SCHOOL | | | | SENIOR HIGH SCHOOL | | | |
		TOTAL REPORTS	SCORES BOYS	SCORES GIRLS	AVG.	TOTAL REPORTS	SCORES BOYS	SCORES GIRLS	AVG.
N.Y. Herald-Tribune and N.Y. Times	1936	1169	81.2	81.4	81.3	1832	82.7	82.9	82.8
N.Y. Herald-Tribune and N.Y. Times	1962	1992	70.2	65.7	68.0	2797	71.3	70.6	71.0
Difference in Scores 1936 to 1962			11.0	15.7	13.4		11.4	12.3	11.9

*The two studies, using the same basic procedures, were carried out in more than 60 classes in representative high schools in 1936 and again in 1962.

TABLE 34

INTERESTS OF BOYS AND OF GIRLS, GRADES 10 TO 12, IN EIGHT NEWSPAPERS LISTED IN THE ORDER OF POPULARITY (1936)

NEWSPAPER	BOYS		NEWSPAPER	GIRLS		NEWSPAPER	BOYS AND GIRLS	
	NO.	SCORE		NO.	SCORE		NO.	SCORE
N.Y. Times	531	83.5	N.Y. Times	598	83.2	N.Y. Times	1129	83.4
N.Y. American	164	82.9	N.Y. Herald-Tribune	365	82.5	N.Y. Herald-Tribune	703	82.2
N.Y. Herald-Tribune	338	81.8	N.Y. American	227	80.4	N.Y. American	365	80.7
N.Y. Sun	190	78.9	N.Y. Sun	173	80.3	N.Y. Sun	363	79.6
N.Y. World-Telegram	196	77.8	N.Y. World-Telegram	201	78.4	N.Y. World-Telegram	423	79.1
N.Y. Journal	195	74.6	N.Y. Journal	217	77.6	N.Y. Journal	412	76.1
N.Y. News	373	62.9	N.Y. News	345	58.7	N.Y. News	718	60.8
N.Y. Mirror	228	46.9	N.Y. Mirror	176	36.6	N.Y. Mirror	404	41.8

TABLE 35

INTERESTS OF BOYS AND OF GIRLS, GRADES 7 TO 9, IN EIGHT NEWSPAPERS LISTED IN THE ORDER OF POPULARITY (1936)

NEWSPAPER	BOYS		NEWSPAPER	GIRLS		NEWSPAPER	BOYS AND GIRLS	
	NO.	SCORE		NO.	SCORE		NO.	SCORE
N.Y. Times	295	82.0	N.Y. American	129	89.1	N.Y. American	235	85.4
N.Y. American	106	81.6	N.Y. Times	340	85.3	N.Y. Times	635	83.7
N.Y. Journal	150	81.0	N.Y. Journal	193	80.3	N.Y. Journal	343	80.7
N.Y. Herald-Tribune	276	80.3	N.Y. Sun	168	80.1	N.Y. Sun	359	79.7
N.Y. Sun	191	79.3	N.Y. Herald-Tribune	258	77.5	N.Y. Herald-Tribune	534	78.9
N.Y. World-Telegram	158	79.1	N.Y. World-Telegram	143	76.9	N.Y. World-Telegram	301	78.0
N.Y. News	334	71.9	N.Y. News	323	74.1	N.Y. News	657	73.0
N.Y. Mirror	390	56.2	N.Y. Mirror	310	48.2	N.Y. Mirror	700	52.2

TABLE 36

INTERESTS OF BOYS AND GIRLS, GRADES 7 TO 12, IN GROUPS OF NEWSPAPERS (1936)

NEWSPAPERS	GRADES 10 TO 12		GRADES 7 TO 9	
	NO.	SCORE	NO.	SCORE
High Grade, New York City (4)	2618	81.9	1829	80.6
Newspapers (no tabloids) (30)	3944	79.8	2854	81.8
Large City (outside New York City) (14)	812	79.2	646	83.6
Small City Dailies (11)	370	75.5	379	81.2
Tabloids (2)	1122	54.0	1351	62.5

CHAPTER XIX

The Mass Media of Communication in the English Program

GREEK AND LATIN WERE CENTRAL IN EDUCATION THROUGHOUT the Western World for centuries after their primary justification had become invalid. Today our instructional system clings desperately to outgrown materials and methods. During a half century, changes in transportation, communication, and modes of living have transformed the civilized world—but not education. Changing a curriculum "is like moving a cemetery."

The Preface to *The Language Arts* (Volume I) calls for "reexamination of the program in English at all levels of instruction." Further, it points out: "The mass media of communication have become major sources of power, and consequently, ability to use radio, television, motion pictures, newspapers, and magazines wisely is a major goal of education." The reexamination reported here employs research in agreement with those who believe in evidence as guidance. While it is directed primarily to the field of English, the evidence has significance for the other school subjects.

How important in the lives of children and adults are the various means of communication? What, actually, is the school's program in this field? Is it succeeding? Should teachers of reading and literature aim primarily to develop critical readers of belles-lettres? Are young people entitled to training in helpful standards in the choice and use of the mass media of communication, as well as of books? Should the schools orient them to reality? Should the course in English prepare them to perform with success the useful activities in the field of communication in which they will engage throughout life?

The devotion of youth to the mass media of communication is a central feature of American life. What share of their time and energy do these media monopolize? To answer this question, the data of more than 30 investigations have been examined.

Many studies have concerned radio and television. Before television's advent, radio engaged approximately 2.5 hours of young people's time daily. Since television, there has been a marked reduction. The findings of the Northwestern University-Office of Education study,[12] in the light of other inquiries, appear conservative: 1.1 hours daily for radio and 3.0 hours for television.

How much time do children give daily to voluntary reading, and what part goes to the reading of books? The Northwestern University-Office of Education report, on page 67, makes a concise statement, based on carefully-gathered evidence. Children of the elementary and junior high school grades give to various forms of reading outside of school a total daily average of 1.1 hours. A number of studies provide evidence as to the time spent by children daily on *each* type of voluntary reading. From them we have the following conservative figures: newspapers (including comic strips) 20 to 25 minutes; youthful and adult magazines, 15 to 20 minutes; comic magazines, 20 to 25 minutes; and books, 20 to 22 minutes. Using the lower figure in each case, the total for newspapers, regular magazines, and comic magazines is 55 minutes. With a total of 66 minutes (1.1 hours) for all voluntary reading, less than 20 minutes would be left for books. However, in making comparison with the total time given to the mass media of communication, the larger figure for books (22 minutes daily) will be used.

As shown above, children give television three hours daily and radio, 1.1 hours. Added to the 55 minutes for regular periodicals and comic magazines (but disregarding the small daily average for motion pictures) we have more than five hours for the mass media of communication compared with 22 minutes for voluntary book reading, a ratio of 14 to 1. On a weekly basis, these forms of communica-

[12]Paul Witty. *A Study of the Interests Of Children and Youth.* Evanston: Northwestern University, 1961. (Henceforth referred to as No. 26.)

tion occupy more time than children spend in school.

The traditional approach to the program in reading and literature has been through literary materials approved by critics. Teaching procedures have emphasized the purpose of leading young people to the habit, in their voluntary reading, of choosing materials of high literary quality. Comparatively little attention has been given to their interest in these high grade materials. The careful testing of several thousands (more than 7,700) of the literary titles commonly used in grades 3 to 12 shows that a large proportion ranks low in popularity with young people.

This customary approach to literary study could be defended if it (1) caused young people to be discriminating in their reading, and (2) led to a love of belles-lettres. The present system has been firmly entrenched for many years. It is proper, therefore, to ask: How has it worked? What are the reading interests and habits of those who have had this special training for eight to sixteen years?

Table 37 made by the writer in 1962, is from a study of young people's interests in the four major school subjects. Pupils in grades 4 to 12 were asked to indicate how interested they were in classes in English, social studies, mathemtaics, and science. Although the data are from widely varying communities, the number of reports on each of the four subjects by pupils in grades 4 to 6 varied little; the same was true also in grades 7 to 9, and in grades 10 to 12. Therefore, as typical, the number of reports received for science at the three levels will be given: in the elementary grades, 3,223; in junior high school, 4,589; in senior high school, 4,635.

For the elementary grades, the total spread in interest in mathematics, science, and social studies is only 3.6 points with the average interest score for the three, 71.2 points. From the lowest of these three (social studies), there is a drop of 11.6 points to English. In grades 7 to 9, the drop from mathematics to English is 14.5 points. In the senior high school, English scores 8.8 points lower than social studies. A further occasion for thought is provided by these figures: English in the junior high school ranks 10.7 points lower in interest than it does in the elementary grades, and has a further three-point fall in the senior high school to an interest level of 44.0.

In *A Study of the Interests of Children and Youth,* cited earlier, 600 children in grades 7 and 8 were asked to name their best-liked school subject. The findings concur with the evidence reported in the current study: both boys and girls placed English lower than mathematics, science, and social studies.

In 1949 the writer questioned young people on their interests in a variety of activities. More than 1200 at *each* of three levels (grades

TABLE 37

PUPILS' INTERESTS IN CLASSES IN FOUR SUBJECTS AND IN GOING TO
SCHOOL, 1962

Grades 4–6		Grades 7–9		Grades 10–12	
Class	Score	Class	Score	Class	Score
Mathematics	72.9	Science	65.9	Science	57.2
Science	71.4	Social Studies	64.4	Mathematics	53.9
Social Studies	69.3	Mathematics	61.5	Social Studies	52.8
English	57.7	English	47.0	English	44.0
Going to School	65.7	Going to School	59.9	Going to School	61.2

4 to 6, grades 7 to 9, grades 10 to 12) replied, with a total of 3874. Table 38 presents a section of the results.

In grades 4 to 6, the radio, comic magazines, comic strips, and motion pictures score approximately 90.0 per cent in interest. The radio and motion pictures remain popular in junior and senior high school. Interest in comic strips wanes steadily to 70.0 per cent in the senior high school. The changes for comic magazines are spectacular: from 90.0 per cent in the elementary grades to 76.0 per cent in grades 7 to 9, and 46.0 per cent in grades 10 to 12. Short stories, too mature for the younger children, gain in interest with advancing age.

Of special significance are the data for magazine articles, and for the poems and essays taught in the schools. Magazine articles advance in interest from 65.0 per cent (grades 4 to 6) to 71.5 per cent in grades 10 to 12. School-chosen essays emphasizing literary quality receive the very low score of 51.0 in grades 10 to 12. Poetry, given the greatest stress in the school's program in literature, scores 56.5 in grades 4 to 6; falls to 45.0 in grades 7 to 9; and to 41.0 per cent in grades 10 to 12. Is it not shocking to find school-chosen poems under the continuous ministrations of devoted teachers descending year by year to a level which signifies disgust? How can we avoid the conclusion that these methods with literature help to explain (and produce) the plight of English revealed in Tables 37 and 38?

Do not misunderstand. An essential part of the reading program should be classic literature, but *only when it delights*. Fortunately there is an ample supply identified through careful testing. The school fails, and distaste and rejection follow, when the unsuitable is forced upon young people.[13]

Dr. Paul Witty (No. 25) reported in *Education* (October 1961) the

[13]See "Watchman, What of Literature in Our Schools?" by the writer in *The English Journal*, September 1963.

TABLE 38

Pupils' Interests in Various Activities in the Order of
Preference: Grades 4–6; Grades 7–9; and Grades 10–12 (1949)*

Grades 4–6 Activity	Percent	Grades 7–9 Activity	Percent	Grades 10–12 Activity	Percent
Radio**	93.0	Radio	93.0	Radio	91.0
Comic Magazines	90.0	Motion Pictures	88.0	Short Stories	86.0
Comic Strips	88.5	Comic Strips	83.0	Motion Pictures	83.5
Motion Pictures	88.5	Short Stories	76.5	Magazine Articles	71.5
Life Stories of		Comic Magazines	76.0	Comic Strips	70.0
Famous Men	75.0				
				Life Stories of	
Short Stories	68.5	Magazine Articles	70.5	Famous Men	63.5
Magazine Articles	65.0	Life Stories of		Essays	51.0
		Famous Men	64.0		
Poetry	56.5	Essays	45.0	Comic Magazines	46.0
Essays	47.5	Poetry	45.0	Poetry	41.0

*In this study, scores were rounded off to the nearest whole number. Boys' and girls'
scores were computed separately and averaged to give a combined score.
**In 1949 television was in its early development. With television's improvement,
radio lost interest markedly, particularly with the younger children.

preferred types of reading of young people in grades 9 to 12. Magazine and newspaper articles were placed first by 32.0 percent of the boys in grades 9 and 10. Following were fiction (31.3%), biography (22.4%), plays (5.7%), essays (5.4%), and poetry (3.2%). The older boys in grades 11 and 12 made only small changes from the reports given above. It is noticeable, however, that poetry, preferred by 3.2 percent of the younger boys, fell to 1.7 percent.

The girls placed fiction first with a vote of 30.4 per cent in grades 9 and 10, and 32.6 per cent in grades 11 and 12. Both groups of girls placed articles in magazines and newspapers second, followed by biographies, plays, poetry, and essays. Poetry declined in interest from 7.0 to 6.2 per cent with the older girls; essays declined from 5.4 to 4.6 per cent. These results, though obtained through an approach different from the one used by the writer, also show clearly the low estate of essays and poetry with high school students.

The evidence so far offered in this chapter has not dealt with pupils' responses to the individual selections studied in school. Attention is called to Table 7 in Chapter IX, which lists the scores for 24 titles which are disliked by young people (scores below 65.0), but are above average in quality, and therefore presumably of higher appeal to the superior. Not one of the 24 is rated "very interesting" by the superior; not one is satisfactory for class reading by the superior if enjoyment is a major aim.

In Table 6 of Chapter IX, the scores for 125 poems by 11 superior poets are given. The average score for the 125 is 54.3 with not one of the poems scoring "very interesting." The evidence appears irrefutable that a very large number of high school students are not ready to enjoy the literary refinements which appeal to critics and English teachers.

Most of the selections included in the two tables cited are widely used in English classes. A majority are classics. The scores provide contrasts of the interests of all senior high school students with the interests of the superior.

Perhaps the most striking data demonstrate the closeness of the scores by all and by the superior. The average for the 24 titles by I's (55.7) is only 0.3 point higher than the average by all students. Eleven of the 24, including Lamb's "Old China," *Julius Caesar, Lord Jim,* and *Walden* are better liked by all students.

It appeared useful to go further with the evidence. Keats and Shakespeare are awarded the highest poetic rank. Available were data on senior high school students' interests in a total of 11 poems by Keats (Chapter IX, Table 5) and 9 by Shakespeare (Table 4). Interest scores for the 20 were computed for I's and for all students. The average score given the 11 Keats poems by I's was 56.3; by all students, 54.5. Shakespeare's nine poems were rated 45.5 by I's and 48.2 by all.

Has there been a change in young people's attitudes toward the school's program in the past decade? The answer is *yes.* Table 39 is based upon a comparison of the writer's study cited above (see Table 37) of the principal school subjects, and an earlier study employing the same approach, made in 1951. From 1951 to 1962, young people in grades 7 to 9, and 10 to 12, lost interest in their school classes and in the total experience of going to school. It will be noted that in every instance the loss was substantial. Loss of interest in going to school at each level is not far from the average loss of interest in the four school subjects.

Attention is directed to the fact that in junior high school the loss of interest in English is more than twice as great as for any other subject. In the senior high school, the subject showing almost as great a loss as English is social studies, another *reading* subject. The combined results for the two levels reveal that mathematics, the subject requiring the least reading, and the subject least affected by radio and television, has maintained interest best. It is evident that not

TABLE 39

LOSSES IN INTEREST IN FOUR School SUBJECTS, AND IN GOING TO
SCHOOL, IN JUNIOR AND SENIOR HIGH SCHOOL, 1951 TO 1962*

SUBJECT	LOSS IN POINTS GRADES 7–9	LOSS IN POINTS GRADES 10–12
English	−22.5	−14.8
Mathematics	− 5.8	− 6.4
Science	− 5.6	− 11.1
Social Studies	− 8.9	− 14.6
Average, four subjects	−10.7	−11.7
Going to School	− 9.2	− 8.1

*The same approach was made in the two studies. The loss in each case is the difference between the score in 1951 and the score in 1962.

only is English the least liked school subject, it has deteriorated in interest most rapidly.

It might be thought that, even though young people fail to enjoy their study of literature in school, their early indoctrination would bear fruit in maturity. Let us look at the record.

The Language Arts (Volume I) makes the following comments: "Only a quarter of the adults in the United States were believed to read books at all—books for the most part of poor quality. Three-fourths were said to read magazines with the 'pulp' type leading in sales. Comic magazines sell hundreds of thousands of copies to one children's book" (pp. 391-392.) "Sixty million Americans (a majority of them adults) read comic magazines regularly" (p. 192.) "The people of the United States spend more money each year on Christmas cards than they do on books" (p. 49.)

Dean William S. Gray of the University of Chicago in his study of adult reading in Chicago found that of men and women with an eighth grade education, only one in seven would read more books even were they more easily available, and not one was interested in literary style.

Students of the reading habits of adult Americans have universally deplored what they found. The record is particularly black compared with that of other English-speaking countries. Dr. George H. Gallup has reported that in England three times as many people read books as in America; in Canada and Australia, almost twice as many.

Further evidence is provided by an unpublished study of adult reading by the writer, to which more than 3000 respondents from coast to coast contributed. The replies of mature men and women from all walks of life duplicate the unfavorable attitudes of children and young people. Actually, these adults score essays and poetry lower than do high school students.

Devotees to the fond theory that the way to make literature a delight and refreshment is to constrain children to center attention zealously on literature's aesthetic values maintain that "enough of this will surely succeed." Let us, then, consider the reactions of those who have had 16 years of such tutelage: the best educated group in America.

In his study cited above, Dean Gray reported as follows on the reading interests of college graduates living in two above average communities in Chicago: 50.5 per cent had *no* interest in poetry; 69 per cent had *no* interest in plays; 71 per cent had *no* interest in essays.

Table 40 presents the views of the 372 college graduates who participated in the writer's study of adult reading cited earlier. The combined interest scores of men and women (poetry, 50.2%; plays, 44.5%; essays, 37.8%) demonstrate that protracted indoctrination of superior young people fails to develop lovers of belles-lettres. It is equally clear that college graduates prefer to read periodicals (score, 76.8%) and light fiction (75.0%). Even among magazines, *Life* is given clear priority over *Harper's* Magazine. When teachers and other professional men and women *only* were questioned, they rated articles on literature 54.7 per cent in interest, and book reviews 50.0 per cent.

TABLE 40

INTERESTS OF COLLEGE GRADUATES, MEN AND WOMEN, IN VARIOUS
AREAS OF READING*

AREA OF READING	INTERESTS IN PERCENTS		
	COLLEGE GRADS. MEN	COLLEGE GRADS. WOMEN	COLLEGE GRADS. MEN AND WOMEN
Poetry	38.2	62.1	50.2
Essays	36.0	39.6	37.8
Plays	33.5	55.4	44.5
Comic Strips	54.2	42.2	48.2
Short Stories	68.4	81.6	75.0
Magazines	74.8	78.7	76.8
Harper's Magazine	60.4	67.3	63.9
Life	73.7	73.4	73.6

*The basic approach in this study was the same used by the writer in studying young people's reading interests in literary selections.

College students also rate essays and poetry very low. College men prefer *The Swiss Family Robinson,* a children's book, to Franklin's *Autobiography* or Shakespeare's *As You Like It;* and college girls prefer *Anne of Green Gables* to *The Idylls of the King* or *Alice in Wonderland.* Both groups agree with college graduates in placing *Life* higher than *Harper's* and the *Atlantic Monthly.*

George H. Gallup in a wide poll taken in 1953 found that 26 per cent of college graduates had not read a single book (the Bible not included) during the previous year. In a recent survey, he found that 77 per cent of adults in general had not read a book within the past year.

On the basis of many investigations by reputable students of the field, there is strong evidence to support the following:

Our schools' training in book reading during many decades has not led to wide reading of books by Americans, and not even to the choice of high quality books by our best educated groups—college students and college graduates.

The attention in English classes to book reading with emphasis on belles-lettres and literary criticism is vastly out of proportion to the voluntary intellectual activities of children and adults. The time young people devote to the mass media of communication each week is at least equal to the hours spent in school.

Classes in English in junior and senior high school rank in interest not only markedly below the other major subjects but, during the period 1951 to 1962, declined in interest much more rapidly than classes in mathematics or science, fields demanding hard digging and without claim to fostering delight.

Children's and adults' interests in essays and poetry are so low as to shock anyone who believes the present program is leading to a love of the schools' customary offerings in literature.

The great majority of people of all ages are deeply ignorant as to how to use newpapers, magazines, motion pictures, radio, and television to the best advantage. Yet these media receive from the schools a miniscule fraction of the time and attention to which they are entitled as "major sources of power" in American life.

Following school days, newspapers, magazines, the radio, and television rather than books are the principal educators of Americans.

The schools are under obligation to prepare young people to deal successfully with the intellectual activities in which they will engage every day of their lives.

What excuse do we have in the field of English for refusing to give the universal media of communication major treatment in guidebooks for teachers and in courses of study? It is too late to claim that radio, television, motion pictures, and periodicals are devoid of intellectual and artistic merit. These communicants range, as do books, from the trashy to the superb. They are the affable companions Americans demand for their entertainment, their information, and their inspiration. It is conservative to say that in the field of communication the school spends nine-tenths of its time on activities that occupy less than one-tenth of the public's interest and attention. *The Language Arts* (Volume I, p. 192) reminds that "the sole justification for the inclusion of any activity in the school program and the relative emphasis placed upon it are to be derived from the legitimate demands of everyday living."

Is it not time:

to recognize the school's failure to prepare young people adequately for life now and in the future;

to use only the classics which young people have endorsed;

to give a central place (instead of haphazard treatment as "adjuncts" of English) to the universal media of communication;

to teach reading primarily for use and for satisfaction rather than to make literary critics?

Is it not time to revolutionize the teaching of English?

INVESTIGATIONS REFERRED TO IN THE CURRENT STUDY

1. Abbott, Allan. "The Reading of High School Pupils." *School Review*, X (1902), pp. 585-600
2. Anderson, Roxanna E. "A Preliminary Study of the Reading Tastes of High School Pupils." *Pedagogical Seminary*, XIX (1912), pp. 438-460.
3. Atkinson, Dora. "An Investigation of the Reading Habits, Tastes and Attitudes of Junior High School Students as Revealed by Their Voluntary Reading." Master's thesis (unpublished), University of Southern California, 1932.
4. Coy, G. L. *The Interests, Abilities and Achievements of a Special Class of Gifted Children.* Contributions to Education, No. 131. New York: Bureau of Publications, Teachers College, Columbia University, 1923.
5. Crow, C. S. *Evaluation of English Literature in the High School.* Contributions to Education, No. 141. New York: Bureau of Publications, Teachers College, Columbia University, 1924.

6. Dunn, Fannie W. *Interest Factors in Primary Reading Material.* Contributions to Education, No. 113. New York: Bureau of Publications, Teachers College, Columbia University, 1921.
7. Eells, Walter C. "What Periodicals Do School Pupils Prefer?" *Wilson Bulletin,* 12 (December 1937), pp. 248-252.
8. Gray, William S. and Monroe, Ruth. *The Reading Interests and Habits of Adults.* New York: Macmillan Company, 1929.
9. Huber, M. B. *Influence of Intelligence upon Children's Reading Interests.* Contributions to Education, No. 312. New York: Bureau of Publications, Teachers College, Columbia University, 1928.
10. Huber, M. B., Bruner, H. B., and Curry, M. C. *Children's Interests in Poetry.* Chicago: Rand McNally and Company, 1927.
11. Jordan, A. M. *Children's Interests in Reading.* Contributions to Education, No. 107. New York: Bureau of Publications, Teachers College, Columbia University, 1921.
12. Mackintosh, Helen K. *A Critical Study of Children's Choices in Poetry.* Iowa City: University of Iowa, 1932.
13. McConn, C. M. "High School Students' Ratings of English Classics." Bulletin of the Illinois Association of Teachers of English (February 1912).
14. Norvell, G. W. "The Challenge of Periodicals in Education." *Elementary English* (April 1966), pp. 492-408.
15. ———, *What Boys and Girls Like to Read.* Morristown, et. al. Silver Burdett Company, 1958.
16. ———, "Wide Individual Reading Compared with the Traditional Plan of Studying Literature." *School Review,* XLIV (1941), pp. 603-613.
17. Richards, I. A. *Practical Criticism, a Study of Literary Judgment.* London: K. Paul, 1929.
18. Russell, J. E., and Bullock, R. W. "Some Observations of Children's Reading." N. E. A. Proceedings (1897), pp. 1015-1021.
19. Squire, James R. "The Response of Adolescents to Literature, Involving Selected Experiences in Personal Development." Doctoral dissertation (unpublished), University of California, Berkeley, 1956.
20. Terman, L. M., and Lima, M. *Children's Reading.* New York: D. Appleton and Company, 1925.
21. Thorndike, R. L. *Children's Reading Interests.* New York: Bureau of Publications, Teachers College, Columbia University, 1941.

22. Waples, D., and Tyler, R. *What People Want To Read About.* Chicago: University of Chicago Press, 1931.
23. Washburne, C., and Vogel, M. *Winnetka Graded Book List.* Chicago: American Library Association, 1926.
24. Wissler, Clark. "The Interests of Children in the Reading Work of the Elementary Schools." *Pedagogical Seminary,* V. (1897), pp. 523-540.
25. Witty, Paul A. "A Study of Pupils' Interests, Grades 9, 10, 11, 12." *Education,* 82 (October 1961), pp. 100-110.
26. ———, *A Study of the Interests of Children and Youth.* Evanston: Northwestern University, 1961.
27. Witty, P., Coomer, A., and McBean, D. "Children's Choices of Favorite Books: A Study Conducted in Ten Elementary Schools." Journal of Educational Psychology, XXVII (1946), pp. 266-278.

TABLE 41

Literary Selections with Scores, Grades 10–12
Ts and Ss = Teachers and Schools   S = Studied in Class
IR = Independent Reading   R = Read in Class

SELECTION—AUTHOR	Boys		Girls		Total		Ts & Ss	
	No.	%	No.	%	No.	Av. %		
A, B, and C—Stephen Leacock	301	67.1	365	66.3	666	66.7	25	S
Abe Lincoln Grows Up— Carl Sandburg	290	79.0	342	83.2	632	81.1	15	S
Abe Lincoln in Illinois— Robert Sherwood	256	70.5	293	73.4	549	72.0	44	IR
Abominable Snowman, The—Ralph Izzard	288	78.0	192	69.3	480	73.7		
Abou Ben Adhem— Leigh Hunt	180	75.6	250	77.4	430	76.5	18	S
Abraham Lincoln—John Drinkwater	452	76.3	528	74.7	980	75.5	41	S
Abraham Lincoln— Walter Malone	556	70.4	733	79.1	1289	74.8	29	R
Abraham Lincoln—Carl Schurz	359	62.3	164	61.6	523	62.0	15	S
Abraham Lincoln— Richard H. Stoddard	291	51.0	252	47.0	543	49.0	15	R
Abraham Lincoln— Woodrow Wilson	178	63.5	177	60.5	355	62.0	24	S
Abraham Lincoln's Autobiography	1342	76.3	1367	74.0	2709	75.2	46	R
Abraham Lincoln: The Prairie Years— Carl Sandburg	298	67.6	304	69.2	602	68.4		
Abraham Lincoln: The War Years—Carl Sandburg	351	73.4	230	68.3	581	70.9		
Abraham Lincoln Walks at Midnight— Vachel Lindsay	957	66.1	937	69.3	1894	67.7	44	R
Absalom and Achitophel —John Dryden	242	41.5	306	40.4	548	41.0	28	S
Abyss, The—Pio Barojo	286	59.3	364	59.9	650	59.6	13	R
Acme—John Galsworthy	327	71.8	401	79.1	728	75.5	31	S

180   THE READING INTERESTS

PUPILS' READING INTERESTS: GRADES 10-12
Ts and Ss = Teachers and Schools   S = Studied in Class
IR = Independent Reading   R = Read in Class

SELECTION—AUTHOR	Boys No.	Boys %	Girls No.	Girls %	Total No.	Total Av. %	Ts & Ss	
Acres of Diamonds—Russell H. Conwell	266	82.5	279	81.5	545	82.0	16	R
Across—Amelia Earhart	320	82.3	361	73.5	681	77.9	12	R
Address to the Army—Albert, King of the Belgians	273	67.1	318	56.8	591	62.0	14	R
Adjustment—Christopher Morley	302	47.0	297	54.0	599	50.5	12	R
Admirable Crichton, The—James M. Barrie	771	80.7	780	84.3	1551	82.5	59	R
Admiral's Ghost, The—Alfred Noyes	472	71.1	475	63.6	947	67.4	38	S
Adrift on an Ice Pan—Wilfred T. Grenfell	246	79.5	253	75.3	499	77.4	57	IR
Advancement—Unknown	273	48.4	309	57.9	582	53.2	13	R
Adventure of the Black Fisherman, The—Washington Irving	174	79.3	182	65.4	356	72.4	21	S
Adventure of the Mason, The—Washington Irving	201	80.3	253	78.3	454	79.3	14	R
Adventures of Odysseus (Retold)	148	65.2	208	62.5	356	63.9	56	IR
Adventures of Sherlock Holmes, The— A. Conan Doyle	462	96.2	265	93.0	727	94.6	33	IR
Advice to Small Children—Edward Anthony	188	49.7	244	60.5	432	55.1	15	S
Advise and Consent—Allen Drury	135	69.3	193	71.5	328	70.4		
A. E. F.—Carl Sandburg	339	38.4	387	33.0	726	35.7	14	R
Aesop's Fables	387	64.1	503	66.5	890	65.3		
Aes Triplex—Robert L. Stevenson	335	42.4	350	42.0	685	42.2	23	S
Aerobatics, Thirty Minutes—Beirne Lay	303	87.5	304	72.0	607	79.8	11	R
Affairs of the Morgans—Evelyn G. Klahr	302	59.6	193	73.8	495	66.7	14	S
African Queen, The—C. S. Forester	491	84.1	358	78.9	849	81.5		

PUPILS' READING INTERESTS: GRADES 10-12

Ts and Ss = Teachers and Schools S = Studied in Class

IR = Independent Reading R = Read in Class

SELECTION—AUTHOR	Boys		Girls		Total		Ts & Ss	
	No.	%	No.	%	No.	Av. %		
Aftermath—Siegfried Sassoon	203	73.4	223	70.6	426	72.0	16	S
Afternoon on a Hill— Edna St. V. Millay	251	41.4	489	67.9	740	54.7	31	S
After Twenty Years—O. Henry	277	96.8	366	96.0	643	96.4	15	R
Against Idleness—Michel Montaigne	201	40.0	312	32.5	513	36.3	13	R
Agincourt—Michael Drayton	197	36.8	211	39.1	408	38.0	21	S
Akond of Swat, The— Edward Lear	291	55.0	272	62.1	563	58.6	12	R
Aku-Aku—Thor Heyerdahl	348	82.0	212	76.9	560	79.5		
Alarmed Skipper, The— James T. Fields	309	62.3	367	59.5	676	60.9	12	R
Albert Schweitzer, Genius in the Jungle— Joseph Gollomb	540	73.1	485	74.4	1025	73.8		
Album Verses—Oliver W. Holmes	196	46.4	232	51.5	428	49.0	26	S
Alexander's Feast—John Dryden	263	63.3	186	54.0	449	58.7	21	S
Alfred (Comic Strip)	236	66.7	246	58.9	482	62.8	46	IR
Alice Adams—Booth Tarkington	60		407	63.5			125	IR
Alice's Adventures in Wonderland—Lewis Carroll	472	51.1	1145	62.4	1617	56.8	55	IR
All American—John R. Tunis	490	79.8	71				95	IR
All But Blind—Walter de la Mare	273	50.2	370	53.8	643	52.0	15	R
Alley Oop (Comic Strip)	928	55.2	1194	33.6	2122	44.4	55	IR
All God's Chillun Got Wings (Negro Song)	355	55.8	373	71.3	728	63.6	11	R
All Gold Canyon—Jack London	368	83.2	367	73.1	735	78.2	12	S
All Men Are Pioneers— Lionel Wiggam	403	40.2	423	35.7	826	38.0	13	R

PUPILS' READING INTERESTS: GRADES 10-12
Ts and Ss = Teachers and Schools   S = Studied in Class
IR = Independent Reading   R = Read in Class

SELECTION—AUTHOR	Boys		Girls		Total		Ts & Ss	
	No.	%	No.	%	No.	Av. %		
All Quiet on the Western Front—E. M. Remarque	541	82.7	219	69.4	760	76.1		
All's Well That Ends Well—William Shakespeare	92	65.2	248	71.4	340	68.3	120	IR
All This and Heaven Too —Rachel Field	15		204	80.9				
Alone—Richard E. Byrd	152	74.0	98					
Alysoun—Unknown	175	24.0	195	33.8	370	28.9	16	S
Ambitious Guest, The— Nathaniel Hawthorne	823	59.1	816	67.5	1639	63.3	54	S
Ambitious Haddock, The —Laura E. Richards	279	51.8	344	50.4	623	51.1	14	R
Amenities of Street-Car Travel—Unknown	336	38.4	337	57.7	673	48.1	14	R
America—Sidney Lanier	346	46.5	384	58.6	730	52.6	14	R
American and Briton— John Galsworthy	311	53.9	329	59.0	640	56.5	27	S
American Boy, The— Theodore Roosevelt	534	68.0	616	62.2	1150	65.1	41	S
American Dream, The— J. T. Adams	233	55.6	287	49.7	520	52.7	20	S
American Flag, The— Joseph R. Drake	324	63.9	410	66.3	734	65.1	14	R
Americanism—Theodore Roosevelt	497	61.7	619	67.4	1116	64.6	17	R
Americanization of Edward Bok, The— Edward Bok	172	66.6	167	68.9	339	67.8	23	S
American Mystic, An— Christopher Morley	303	43.9	298	49.7	601	46.8	12	R
American Quarter, An: Greenwich Village— Konrad Bercovici	193	61.9	219	68.9	412	65.4	14	S
American's Creed, The— William T. Page	337	83.5	373	78.4	710	81.0	14	R
American Slang—Henry L. Mencken	208	56.7	341	54.0	549	55.4	17	S
American Tragedy, An— Theodore Dreiser	108	66.7	210	76.7	318	71.7		

PUPILS' READING INTERESTS: GRADES 10-12

Ts and Ss = Teachers and Schools   S = Studied in Class

IR = Independent Reading   R = Read in Class

SELECTION—AUTHOR	Boys		Girls		Total		Ts & Ss	
	No.	%	No.	%	No.	Av. %		
America on Wheels—Frances Warfield	297	73.4	231	75.8	528	74.6	21	R
America's Paul Revere—Esther Forbes	279	66.3	176	62.2	455	64.3		
America's Robert E. Lee—Henry S. Commager	342	69.6	198	62.1	540	65.9		
America the Beautiful—Katherine L. Bates	301	82.7	480	88.4	781	85.6	29	S
Among the Corn Rows—Hamlin Garland	419	56.8	198	72.2	617	64.5	16	S
Anatomy of a Murder, The—Robert Traver	608	80.3	727	78.1	1335	79.2		IR
Ancient Mariner, The—Samuel T. Coleridge	602	60.7	655	61.1	1257	60.9	44	S
Andersonville—MacKinlay Kantor	167	84.7	146	78.1	313	81.4		IR
And Then There Were None—Agatha Christie	272	81.1	465	76.1	737	78.6		IR
And to Think That I Saw It on Mulberry Street—Dr. Seuss	140	64.3	241	69.5	381	66.9		IR
Angel on Skis—Betty Cavanna	29		309	64.6				IR
Angel Unawares—Dale E. Rogers	38		324	90.9				IR
Anglo-Saxon Chronicle, The	248	44.8	305	38.0	553	41.4	23	S
Anglo-Saxon Riddles	292	43.5	344	44.2	636	43.9	25	S
Angry Planet, The—John K. Cross	336	69.8	124	66.1	460	68.0		
Animal Farm—George Orwell	162	85.2	167	78.7	329	82.0		
Animals as Family Retainers—Mary E. Chase	235	58.7	221	57.9	456	58.3	20	R
Anna and the King of Siam—Margaret Landon	230	67.8	818	83.3	1048	75.6		
Annabel Lee—Edgar A. Poe	446	60.8	519	78.3	965	69.6	51	S

PUPILS' READING INTERESTS: GRADES 10-12

Ts and Ss = Teachers and Schools   S = Studied in Class
IR = Independent Reading   R = Read in Class

SELECTION—AUTHOR	Boys		Girls		Total		Ts & Ss	
	No.	%	No.	%	No.	Av. %		
Anna Karenina—Leo Tolstoy	56		150	82.0				
Anne of Green Gables— L. M. Montgomery	10		224	71.7				
Anne Rutledge—Edgar L. Masters	457	59.1	454	69.3	911	64.2	48	S
Annie Laurie—William Douglas	467	56.1	510	69.8	977	63.0	26	S
Annie Rooney (Comic Strip)	749	33.9	1356	50.6	2105	42.3	55	IR
Another Blue Day— Thomas Carlyle	281	46.8	295	51.7	576	49.3	12	R
Anthony Adverse— Hervey Allen	181	67.7	297	73.2	478	70.5	168	IR
Anything Can Happen— George and Helen Papashvily	117	63.2	321	72.7	438	68.0		
Apes and Ivory—Alfred Noyes	1191	38.7	1262	47.5	2453	43.1	32	R
Apology for Idlers, An— Robert L. Stevenson	325	58.9	221	53.2	546	56.1	28	S
Appetite—Hugh McNair Kahler	193	73.3	194	71.9	387	72.6	17	S
Apple that No One Ate, The—Christopher Morley	302	59.1	380	67.2	682	63.2	18	R
April Morning, An—Bliss Carman	334	56.9	387	73.0	721	65.0	27	S
April, North Carolina— Harriet Monroe	435	32.2	505	44.3	940	38.3	18	R
Arabian Nights, The	520	80.7	693	78.3	1213	79.5	60	IR
Arachne—Rannie B. Baker	252	39.1	304	51.0	556	45.1	11	R
Are Cats People?— Oliver Hereford	547	52.8	580	59.9	1127	56.4	16	R
Argument with a Millionaire, An—David Grayson	213	84.0	506	79.9	719	82.0	16	S
Ariel's Song—William Shakespeare	3369	27.4	3552	31.1	6921	29.3	122	R

PUPILS' READING INTERESTS: GRADES 10-12

Ts and Ss = Teachers and Schools   S = Studied in Class

IR = Independent Reading   R = Read in Class

SELECTION—AUTHOR	Boys		Girls		Total		Ts & Ss	
	No.	%	No.	%	No.	Av. %		
Around the World in Eighty Days—Jules Verne	255	79.0	189	71.7	444	75.4	126	IR
Arrow and the Song, The—Henry W. Longfellow	331	54.5	344	69.2	675	61.9	13	R
Arrowsmith—Sinclair Lewis	325	84.3	330	86.5	655	85.4	31	S
Arsenal at Springfield, The—Henry W. Longfellow	221	72.1	261	64.4	482	68.3	15	S
Art of Dating, The— Evelyn M. Duvall	98	58.7	369	65.2	467	62.0		
As a Dog Should— Charles Alexander	221	80.1	358	75.1	579	77.6	17	S
Asking for a Raise— Harry I. Shumway	251	74.3	277	79.6	528	77.0	20	S
Aspects of the Pines— Paul H. Hayne	227	53.5	308	62.0	535	57.8	24	S
Assignment in Brittany— Helen McInnes	187	81.8	406	83.0	593	82.4	48	IR
As the Earth Turns— Gladys H. Carroll	184	70.9	225	77.8	409	74.4	27	S
As Toilsome I Wandered Virginia's Woods— Walt Whitman	333	64.9	453	62.9	786	63.9	13	R
As You Like It—William Shakespeare	636	50.3	788	68.0	1424	59.2	65	S
Atalanta—Rannie B. Baker	289	58.3	338	67.2	627	62.8	15	R
Atalanta's Race—William Morris	204	56.1	227	64.5	431	60.3	23	S
At a Toy Shop Window— Charles S. Brooks	326	48.2	247	52.6	573	50.4	17	S
Athenian Boy's Oath, The	601	54.3	698	47.9	1299	51.1	34	R
At Home—Anton Chekhov	352	46.9	162	61.7	514	54.3	14	S
At Magnolia Cemetery— Henry Timrod	196	55.6	230	58.0	426	56.8	21	S

PUPILS' READING INTERESTS: GRADES 10-12

Ts and Ss = Teachers and Schools   S = Studied in Class
IR = Independent Reading   R = Read in Class

SELECTION—AUTHOR	Boys		Girls		Total		Ts & Ss	
	No.	%	No.	%	No.	Av. %		
At School in the Promised Land—Mary Antin	155	62.3	163	76.7	318	69.5	16	S
Attack, The—Siegfried Sassoon	264	72.7	313	60.7	577	66.7	19	S
At the Aquarium—Max Eastman	559	56.9	634	59.4	1193	58.2	35	S
At the Cenotaph—Siegfried Sassoon	304	41.0	390	45.6	694	43.3	16	R
At the Crossroads—Richard Hovey	289	65.9	290	74.0	579	70.0	27	S
Auld Lang Syne—Robert Burns	367	69.8	342	70.3	709	70.1	27	S
Auld Robin Gray—Anne Lindsey	209	55.7	203	63.3	412	59.5	21	S
Auntie Mame—Patrick Dennis	334	81.4	998	87.2	1332	84.3		
Author's Account of Himself, The—Washington Irving	303	55.1	188	52.9	491	54.0	22	S
Autobiography of Andrew Carnegie, The	244	70.3	251	63.3	495	66.8	62	S
Autobiography of Benjamin Franklin, The	1158	58.1	1122	44.4	2280	51.3	115	S
Autobiography of Lincoln Steffens, The	391	73.7	300	77.7	691	75.7	30	S
Autocrat of the Breakfast Table, The— Oliver W. Holmes	327	45.6	438	48.7	765	47.2	25	S
Autumn—Emily Dickinson	1092	35.7	1256	57.6	2348	46.7	30	R
Awakening, The—Robert Browning	267	35.0	377	48.4	644	41.7	13	R
Awful English of England, The—H. W. Seaman	227	63.9	255	62.5	482	63.2	18	S
Babbitt—Sinclair Lewis	207	76.1	249	67.5	456	71.8	20	S
Babe Ruth Story, The— Bob Considine	303	77.6	49					

PUPILS' READING INTERESTS: GRADES 10-12

Ts and Ss = Teachers and Schools   S = Studied in Class

IR = Independent Reading   R = Read in Class

SELECTION—AUTHOR	Boys		Girls		Total		Ts & Ss	
	No.	%	No.	%	No.	Av. %		
Babies, The—Mark Twain	241	74.9	313	83.6	554	79.3	15	R
Bacon and Beans and Limousines—Will Rogers	316	62.3	346	63.2	662	62.8	16	R
Ballad—Charles Calverley	328	44.7	333	64.0	661	54.4	13	R
Ballade—Catalogue of Lovely Things, A— Richard Le Gallienne	278	45.5	353	55.7	631	50.6	27	S
Ballad of Billy the Kid, The—Henry H. Knibbs	423	92.7	498	89.1	921	90.9	16	R
Ballad of Dennis McGinty, The—Dana Burnet	299	72.9	304	83.1	603	78.0	10	R
Ballad of East and West, The—Rudyard Kipling	450	76.0	634	71.8	1084	73.9	47	S
Ballad of Hard Luck Henry, The—Robert W. Service	282	75.7	333	83.3	615	79.5	10	R
Ballad of Ivan Petrofsky Skevar, The (American Ballad)	449	80.5	434	75.5	883	78.0	24	R
Ballad of Jack and Jill, The—Anthony C. Deane	234	53.6	268	67.7	502	60.7	19	S
Ballad of John Silver, A— John Masefield	561	78.9	648	68.2	1209	73.6	20	S
Ballad of Old Doc Higgins, The—Leonara Speyer	211	60.9	260	61.7	471	61.3	14	R
Ballad of Semmerwater, The—William Watson	383	31.7	458	43.0	841	37.4	18	R
Ballad of the Harp-Weaver, The— Edna St. V. Millay	534	59.3	784	83.0	1318	71.2	53	S
Ballad of the Hundred and Fifteen Horses— Lucy S. Mitchell	280	50.7	326	45.4	606	48.1	16	R
Ballad of the Oysterman, The—Oliver W. Holmes	739	75.1	886	82.3	1625	78.7	46	R
Ballet Shoes—Noel Streatfeild	15		215	57.9				

PUPILS' READING INTERESTS: GRADES 10-12
Ts and Ss = Teachers and Schools   S = Studied in Class
IR = Independent Reading   R = Read in Class

SELECTION—AUTHOR	Boys		Girls		Total		Ts & Ss
	No.	%	No.	%	No.	Av. %	
Bambi—Felix Salten	171	52.6	298	63.8	469	58.2	
Banks o' Doon, The—Robert Burns	276	51.1	304	57.7	580	54.4	24 S
Barbara Frietchie—John G. Whittier	198	84.9	412	86.9	610	85.9	18 S
Baree, Son of Kazan—Oliver Curwood	216	85.6	107	79.0	323	82.3	168 IR
Barefoot Boy, The—John G. Whittier	222	73.4	277	76.2	499	74.8	18 R
Barney Google and Snuffy Smith (Comic Strip)	735	63.8	884	35.0	1619	49.4	52 IR
Barnum—M. R. Werner	499	81.3	356	69.7	855	75.5	31 S
Barrel-Organ, The—Alfred Noyes	569	60.1	546	71.8	1115	66.0	47 S
Barretts of Wimpole Street, The—Rudolf Besier	218	78.4	416	˙89.9	634	84.2	25 S
Barter—Sara Teasdale	653	39.6	693	65.9	1346	52.8	34 R
Basquerie—Eleanor M. Kelly	142	63.4	428	88.4	570	75.9	20 S
Battle: Hit—Wilfred W. Gibson	209	66.5	234	57.7	443	62.1	15 S
Battle of Bannockburn, The—Robert Burns	228	57.7	252	57.3	480	57.5	26 S
Battle of Blenheim, The—Robert Southey	851	71.8	864	70.3	1715	71.1	43 R
Battle of Brunanburh, The—Alfred Tennyson	243	53.1	245	41.8	488	47.5	22 S
Battle Stations—Margaret Scoggin	216	79.2	17				
Beany Malone—Lenora M. Weber	5		222	59.0			
Bear's Heart—Stanley Vestal	364	65.4	413	55.7	777	60.6	13 R
Beat! Beat! Drums!—Walt Whitman	173	66.2	225	66.7	398	66.5	18 S
Beatitudes, The—The Bible	350	71.6	392	78.6	742	75.1	15 R

PUPILS' READING INTERESTS: GRADES 10-12
Ts and Ss = Teachers and Schools   S = Studied in Class
IR = Independent Reading   R = Read in Class

SELECTION—AUTHOR	Boys		Girls		Total		Ts & Ss	
	No.	%	No.	%	No.	Av. %		
Beau Geste—Percival C. Wren	263	90.3	232	87.7	495	89.0	41	IR
Beau of Bath, The— Constance D'Arcy Mackay	207	46.9	197	60.9	404	53.9	21	S
Beau's Head, A—Joseph Addison	262	47.9	302	40.9	564	44.4	13	R
Because of the Dollars— Joseph Conrad	144	61.6	242	63.6	386	62.6	17	S
Bedquilt, The—Dorothy C. Fisher	241	62.0	241	80.9	482	71.5	15	S
Bees' Song, The—Walter de la Mare	619	39.3	712	51.6	1331	45.5	29	R
Bee That Wished a Sting, The—Aesop	318	61.2	407	64.4	725	62.8	14	R
Beggar and the King, The—Winthrop Parkhurst	176	60.8	173	55.8	349	58.3	56	S
Behind the Closed Eye— Francis Ledwidge	229	43.4	255	59.6	484	51.5	13	S
Believe It or Not— Robert L. Ripley	221	78.7	104	68.3	325	73.5		
Believe Me, If All Those Endearing Young Charms—Thomas Moore	228	47.8	311	69.5	539	58.7	19	S
Bell and the Cat, The— Aesop	1027	55.4	1069	55.1	2096	55.3	43	R
Belles on Their Toes— Gilbreth and Carey	51		402	80.7				
Bell for Adano, A—John Hersey	269	76.0	261	73.3	530	74.7		
Bell of Atri, The—Henry W. Longfellow	330	61.8	414	73.9	744	67.9	74	S
Bells, The—Edgar A. Poe	245	64.5	366	72.5	611	68.5	23	S
Beloved Vagabond, The —William J. Locke	242	76.7	237	88.0	479	82.4	16	S
Ben and Me—Robert Lawson	445	67.9	505	67.6	950	67.8		
Benedict Arnold— Gamaliel Bradford	276	74.3	281	69.6	557	72.0	71	S

PUPILS' READING INTERESTS: GRADES 10-12
Ts and Ss = Teachers and Schools   S = Studied in Class
IR = Independent Reading   R = Read in Class

SELECTION—AUTHOR	Boys		Girls		Total		Ts & Ss	
	No.	%	No.	%	No.	Av. %		
Ben Hur—Lew Wallace	365	68.8	369	68.3	734	68.6	85	IR
Benjamin Franklin—Carl VanDoren	395	65.4	305	61.8	700	63.6		
Benjamin Franklin to Mr. Strahan	349	56.4	388	49.7	737	53.1	14	R
Bent Twig, The— Dorothy C. Fisher	105	61.4	308	93.3	413	77.4	23	S
Beowulf	441	67.0	457	62.3	898	64.7	39	S
Berlin Diary—William L. Shirer	368	85.5	324	85.0	692	85.3	194	IR
Bet, The—Anton Chekhov	431	76.6	313	77.6	744	77.1	41	S
Be True—Horatio Bonar	354	64.8	393	73.0	747	68.9	15	R
Better Known as Johnny Appleseed—Mabel L. Hunt	275	65.1	350	65.9	625	65.5		
Between Two Loves— Thomas A. Daly	396	76.8	414	89.7	810	83.3	19	R
Bewick Finzer—Edwin A. Robinson	365	62.7	381	61.5	746	62.1	34	S
Beyond the Horizon— Eugene O'Neill	222	78.4	242	87.8	464	83.1	66	S
Big Doc's Girl—Mary Medearis	33		167	68.6				
Big Fisherman, The— Lloyd C. Douglas	338	83.6	453	86.9	791	85.3		
Big Red—Jim Kjelgaard	265	73.0	163	73.0	428	73.0		
Bill—Zona Gale	368	71.1	468	87.0	836	79.1	18	S
Bill Peters (Cowboy Ballad)—John A. Lomax (Ed.)	384	76.2	487	68.1	871	72.2	16	R
Billy the Kid (American Ballad)	701	77.6	705	68.3	1406	73.0	37	R
Birches—Robert Frost	1008	66.6	966	74.4	1974	70.5	85	S
Birds' Christmas Carol, The—Kate D. Wiggin	299	69.1	778	84.8	1077	77.0	75	IR
Birthday, A—Christina G. Rossetti	164	48.8	225	72.4	389	60.6	15	S
Birthday, The—Thyra S. Winslow	169	60.0	185	80.1	354	70.1	15	S

PUPILS' READING INTERESTS: GRADES 10-12
Ts and Ss = Teachers and Schools   S = Studied in Class
IR = Independent Reading   R = Read in Class

SELECTION—AUTHOR	Boys		Girls		Total		Ts & Ss	
	No.	%	No.	%	No.	Av. %		
Bishop Murder Case, The —S. S. Van Dine	231	84.0	232	67.7	463	75.9	24	S
Bitter-Sweet—Fannie Hurst	395	56.5	349	77.2	744	66.9	20	S
Black Arrow, The— Robert L. Stevenson	472	77.1	256	73.6	728	75.4	98	IR
Black Ball Line, The (Sea Chantey)	258	31.6	267	37.3	525	34.5	14	R
Black Cat, The—Edgar A. Poe	275	85.3	246	85.2	521	85.3	21	S
Blackjack Bargainer, A— O. Henry	278	71.4	289	59.2	567	65.3	11	S
Black Stallion, The— Walter Farley	593	71.9	827	74.7	1420	73.3		
Black Vulture, The— George Sterling	214	54.9	234	46.2	448	50.6	17	S
Blades of Grass, The— Stephen Crane	535	52.7	538	71.8	1073	62.3	26	S
Blessed Damozel, The— Dante G. Rossetti	245	56.9	393	74.6	638	65.8	28	S
Blessing the Dance— Irwin Russell	405	46.8	427	58.4	832	52.6	22	R
Blind Girl, The—Nathalia Crane	280	46.3	321	68.7	601	57.5	18	R
Blindman—Hervey Allen	162	79.6	184	89.4	346	84.5		
Blind Men and the Elephant, The—John G. Saxe	393	73.9	416	72.5	809	73.2	16	R
Blondie (Comic Strip)	1029	74.7	1384	77.9	2413	76.3	55	IR
Blow, Blow, Thou Winter Wind—William Shakespeare	267	46.3	329	48.9	596	47.6	14	R
Blow the Man Down (Sea Chantey)	440	45.0	521	42.3	961	43.7	25	R
Blue and the Gray, The —Francis M. Finch	286	76.4	328	80.0	614	78.2	20	S
Blueberries—Robert Frost	395	29.6	453	38.4	848	34.0	13	R
Blue Bird, The—Maurice Maeterlinck	134	72.4	395	70.4	529	71.4	80	IR

PUPILS' READING INTERESTS: GRADES 10-12

Ts and Ss = Teachers and Schools   S = Studied in Class
IR = Independent Reading   R = Read in Class

SELECTION—AUTHOR	Boys		Girls		Total		Ts & Ss	
	No.	%	No.	%	No.	Av. %		
Blue Cross, The—Gilbert K. Chesterton	258	84.7	262	85.1	520	84.9	22	S
Blue Murder—Wilbur D. Steele	342	82.6	440	77.8	782	80.2	16	S
Blue Squills—Sara Teasdale	314	48.9	368	68.1	682	58.5	31	S
Boating—Oliver W. Holmes	299	64.7	333	58.9	632	61.8	28	S
Body of the Crime, The —Wilbur D. Steele	198	62.6	211	61.1	409	61.9	19	S
Bombardment—Amy Lowell	156	78.8	248	77.4	404	78.1	17	S
Bonjour Tristesse— Françoise Sagan	129	60.1	432	61.9	561	61.0		
Bonnie George Campbell (British Ballad)	26o	53.3	303	60.4	563	56.9	23	S
Boob, The—Walter DeLeon	247	82.6	256	90.0	503	86.3	19	S
Book, A.—Emily Dickinson	561	46.5	695	62.5	1256	54.5	40	S
Boomerang—Marion H. McNeely	248	95.2	267	99.3	515	97.3	14	R
Boomer Johnson—Henry H. Knibbs	291	84.2	422	85.8	713	85.0	13	R
Boor, The—Anton Chekhov	173	50.9	618	63.9	791	57.4	21	S
Boots—Rudyard Kipling	334	71.7	386	75.5	720	73.6	28	S
Boots and Her Buddies (Comic Strip)	394	28.0	793	67.0	1187	47.5	45	IR
Bovine and Human Happiness—William L. Phelps	334	73.8	381	81.5	715	77.7	14	R
Boy Comes Home, The— A. A. Milne	307	87.5	302	90.6	609	89.1	15	R
Boyhood on a Missouri Farm—Mark Twain	948	78.3	933	82.2	1881	80.3	61	S
Boy Life on the Prairie— Hamlin Garland	208	71.6	118	66.5	326	69.1	91	IR
Boy Next Door, The— Betty Cavanna	44		206	74.8				

PUPILS' READING INTERESTS: GRADES 10-12
Ts and Ss = Teachers and Schools   S = Studied in Class
IR = Independent Reading   R = Read in Class

SELECTION—AUTHOR	Boys		Girls		Total		Ts & Ss	
	No.	%	No.	%	No.	Av. %		
Boy on Horseback—Lincoln Steffens	118	66.5	164	69.8	282	68.2		
Boys, The—Oliver W. Holmes	266	82.1	290	81.9	556	82.0	28	S
Boy Scout's Handbook, The	600	76.8	49				57	IR
Boy Scout with Byrd, A —Paul Siple	366	75.1	54				300	IR
Boys' Life of Abraham Lincoln, The—Helen Nicolay	203	72.2	199	71.6	402	71.9	72	IR
Boys' Life of Edison, The —William H. Meadowcroft	303	80.0	155	76.8	458	78.4	46	IR
Boys' Life of Mark Twain, The—Albert B. Paine	201	71.9	221	74.9	422	73.4	19	S
Boy's Life of Theodore Roosevelt, The—Hermann Hagedorn	547	80.3	481	64.5	1028	72.4	22	S
Boys' Life of the Wright Brothers, The— Mitchell W. Charnley	305	79.7	89				281	IR
Brass Spittoons—Langston Hughes	299	68.6	321	57.6	620	63.1	18	S
Brave Men—Ernie Pyle	199	79.9	41					
Break, Break, Break—Alfred Tennyson	512	60.5	626	65.2	1138	62.9	44	S
Breaking and Entering—Frances L. Warner	378	72.6	371	70.5	749	71.6	10	R
Bred in the Bone—Elsie Singmaster	252	53.2	320	80.0	572	66.6	31	S
Bridge, The—Henry W. Longfellow	257	63.0	310	75.0	567	69.0	27	S
Bridge of San Luis Rey, The—Thornton Wilder	259	73.6	488	77.7	747	75.7	85	IR
Bridge of Sighs, The—Thomas Hood	191	50.3	196	73.2	387	61.8	18	S

PUPILS' READING INTERESTS: GRADES 10-12
Ts and Ss = Teachers and Schools   S = Studied in Class
IR = Independent Reading   R = Read in Class

SELECTION—AUTHOR	Boys		Girls		Total		Ts & Ss	
	No.	%	No.	%	No.	Av. %		
Bridge Over the River Kwai, The—Pierre Boulle	279	91.2	263	84.2	542	87.7		
Bridges of Toko-Ri, The —James A. Michener	778	85.2	352	79.3	1130	82.3		
Bring 'Em Back Alive— Frank Buck	500	83.1	279	78.7	779	80.9	131	IR
Bringing Up Father (Comic Strip)	894	71.9	1223	67.0	2117	69.5	53	IR
Brink of Silence, The— Esther E. Galbraith	228	84.0	260	85.8	488	84.9	15	S
Broken Arrow, The— Elliott Arnold	317	78.5	235	76.4	552	77.5		
Broken Sword, The— Edwin Markham	1211	62.5	1299	58.9	2510	60.7	33	R
Bronco Busting—Will James	296	69.1	313	58.1	609	63.6	10	R
Bronco That Would Not Be Broken, The— Vachel Lindsay	399	75.4	419	69.0	818	72.2	34	S
Brook, The—Alfred Tennyson	258	58.9	302	72.0	560	65.5	11	S
Brooklyn Bridge at Dawn—Richard Le Gallienne	196	45.2	324	59.1	520	52.2	16	S
Broom (British Ballad)	252	43.5	261	52.3	513	47.9	12	R
Brotherhood—Edwin Markham	239	55.4	265	61.1	504	58.3	22	S
Brothers, The— Björnstjerne Björnson	275	82.9	357	85.7	632	84.3	17	R
Brothers, The—Elias Lieberman	287	31.0	376	44.5	663	37.8	13	R
Brothers Karamazov, The—Fyodor Dostoevsky	232	72.6	342	74.3	574	73.5		
Brown Wolf—Jack London	253	95.7	381	92.7	634	94.2	13	R
Brute Neighbors—Henry D. Thoreau	372	71.4	382	60.2	754	65.8	27	S
Bubble Reputation, The —Walter P. Eaton	223	60.1	270	65.0	493	62.5	20	S

PUPILS' READING INTERESTS: GRADES 10-12
Ts and Ss = Teachers and Schools   S = Studied in Class
IR = Independent Reading   R = Read in Class

SELECTION—AUTHOR	Boys		Girls		Total		Ts & Ss	
	No.	%	No.	%	No.	Av. %		
Buff, a Collie—Albert P. Terhune	195	88.2	182	88.0	377	88.1	65	IR
Buffalo Bill—Ingri and Edgar d'Aulaire	183	58.5	41					
Buffalo Bill—Carl Sandburg	197	50.3	208	39.4	405	44.9	17	S
Buffalo Bill—William L. Visscher	611	85.4	292	75.2	903	80.3	73	R
Buffalo Dusk—Carl Sandburg	306	31.7	316	23.8	622	27.8	11	R
Bugle Song, The—Alfred Tennyson	187	52.7	229	59.2	416	56.0	27	S
Bull, The—Ralph Hodgson	287	66.9	294	59.9	581	63.4	18	S
Bumboat Woman's Story, The—William S. Gilbert	248	80.2	327	83.9	575	82.1	15	R
Bundle of Sticks, The— Aesop	1099	75.2	1118	73.4	2217	74.3	43	R
Bunker Hill Address, The —Daniel Webster	541	54.2	553	55.0	1094	54.6	51	S
Bunker Mouse, The— Frederick S. Greene	234	87.4	164	79.9	398	83.7	19	S
Buns for Tea—Dorothy M. Richardson	274	42.2	284	45.3	558	43.8	19	S
Burial of Sir John Moore, The—Charles Wolfe	263	70.2	304	68.4	567	69.3	11	S
Burke's Speech on Conciliation	465	49.9	607	36.2	1072	43.1	60	S
Business is Business— Ring Lardner	332	78.6	323	83.0	655	80.8	9	R
But He Didn't— Unknown	291	68.1	336	72.3	627	70.2	11	R
Buttons—Carl Sandburg	434	55.4	506	59.0	940	57.2	21	R
By Courier—O. Henry	322	88.5	343	96.8	665	92.7	12	R
By Love Possessed— James G. Cozzens	148	58.8	563	73.4	711	66.1		
Byrd Flies to the North Pole—C. J. V. Murphy	260	92.1	293	66.0	553	79.1	12	R

PUPILS' READING INTERESTS: GRADES 10-12
Ts and Ss = Teachers and Schools   S = Studied in Class
IR = Independent Reading   R = Read in Class

SELECTION—AUTHOR	Boys		Girls		Total		Ts & Ss
	No.	%	No.	%	No.	Av. %	
By the Banks of the Sacramento (Chantey)— Frank Shay, Ed.	255	41.8	345	41.6	600	41.7	11 R
By the Turret Stair (British Ballad)	306	24.0	338	40.2	644	32.1	17 R
Caine Mutiny, The— Herman Wouk	776	87.3	510	79.4	1286	83.4	
Calf Path, The—Sam W. Foss	295	69.7	305	69.3	600	69.5	13 R
Caliban in the Coal Mines—Louis Untermeyer	845	66.2	935	71.4	1780	68.8	43 S
Call Me Lucky—Bing Crosby	153	69.0	282	70.6	435	69.8	
Call of the Spring, The— Alfred Noyes	447	56.0	532	68.3	979	62.2	22 R
Call of the Wild, The— Jack London	203	91.1	243	87.4	446	89.3	25 S
Calvin—Charles D. Warner	200	59.5	279	63.6	479	61.6	15 S
Cannibal Flea, The— Thomas Hood	706	63.2	709	63.3	1415	63.3	27 R
Canterbury Tales, The— Geoffrey Chaucer	178	61.2	235	65.7	413	63.5	
Canvasser's Tale, The— Mark Twain	152	54.6	150	50.0	302	52.3	20 S
Captain Blood—Rafael Sabatini	346	91.2	240	82.5	586	86.9	37 R
Captain Horatio Hornblower—C. S. Forester	164	80.2	58				130 IR
Captains Courageous— Rudyard Kipling	539	70.6	386	64.4	925	67.5	
Caravan—Charles Merz	355	62.0	333	53.2	688	57.6	12 R
Cargoes—John Masefield	658	59.7	1104	64.8	1762	62.3	68 S
Carry On!—Robert W. Service	401	71.9	436	77.5	837	74.7	28 S
Cartwheel—Vic Knight	278	80.8	317	86.6	595	83.7	11 R
Casey at the Bat—Ernest L. Thayer	423	90.4	403	87.0	826	88.7	9 R

PUPILS' READING INTERESTS: GRADES 10-12

Ts and Ss = Teachers and Schools   S = Studied in Class
IR = Independent Reading   R = Read in Class

SELECTION—AUTHOR	Boys		Girls		Total		Ts & Ss	
	No.	%	No.	%	No.	Av. %		
Cask of Amontillado, The —Edgar A. Poe	445	68.7	486	60.3	931	64.5	28	S
Castaway, The—William Cowper	310	48.4	496	47.5	806	48.0	20	R
Catcher in the Rye, The —J. D. Salinger	151	83.1	289	84.8	440	84.0		
Cat's Meat—Harold Monro	1181	27.4	1383	32.2	2564	29.8	38	R
Cattle Range at Night, A —E. A. Brininstool	274	50.4	283	58.1	557	54.3	13	R
Cavalier's Escape, The— Walter Thornbury	256	59.6	289	52.1	545	55.9	12	R
Cavalier Tunes—Robert Browning	308	54.4	344	57.3	652	55.9	36	S
Celebrated Jumping Frog, The—Mark Twain	522	73.2	370	58.9	892	66.1	28	S
Celebrity, The—David Grayson	216	68.5	269	68.8	485	68.7	17	S
Century, The— Christopher Morley	258	65.7	302	63.9	560	64.8	22	S
Cerelle—Margaret B. Houston	281	65.8	340	85.2	621	75.5	14	R
Chambered Nautilus, The—Oliver W. Holmes	320	54.5	344	55.4	664	55.0	31	S
Chant of Loyalty, The— Elias Lieberman	323	44.4	340	60.6	663	52.5	12	R
Chant Out of Doors, A— Marguerite Wilkinson	260	37.1	436	50.6	696	43.9	17	R
Character of a Happy Life, The—Henry Wotton	284	57.6	351	67.9	635	62.8	30	S
Charge of the Light Brigade, The—Alfred Tennyson	247	80.2	586	73.7	833	77.0	26	S
Charity—Robert Burns	203	25.4	269	32.3	472	28.9	13	R
Charity—Joaquin Miller	360	57.4	420	69.2	780	63.3	28	S
Charleston—Henry Timrod	380	60.0	474	53.5	854	56.8	33	S
Charlie Lee—Henry H. Knibbs	284	66.0	337	57.4	621	61.7	10	R

PUPILS' READING INTERESTS: GRADES 10-12
Ts and Ss = Teachers and Schools   S = Studied in Class
IR = Independent Reading   R = Read in Class

SELECTION—AUTHOR	Boys		Girls		Total		Ts & Ss
	No.	%	No.	%	No.	Av. %	
Charlotte's Web—E. B. White	127	55.1	527	70.5	654	62.8	
Chartless—Emily Dickinson	664	49.2	831	62.1	1495	55.7	46	S
Chatterbox, The—A. Karaliychev	209	55.0	346	51.7	555	53.4	13	R
Cheaper by the Dozen— Frank B. Gilbreth, Jr.	387	75.1	1028	81.4	1415	78.3	
Cheerful Cherub, The — Rebecca McCann	408	61.8	512	79.4	920	70.6	16	R
Cherry-Ripe—Thomas Campion	266	45.3	306	59.0	572	52.2	25	S
Chewing Gum—Charles D. Warner	330	57.7	324	55.9	654	56.8	15	S
Chicago—Carl Sandburg	522	72.6	644	70.6	1166	71.6	59	S
Chicago via Cincinnati— Janet Scudder	488	51.9	485	83.6	973	67.8	41	S
Childe Harold's Pilgrimage—George G. Byron	332	52.1	388	56.7	720	54.4	31	S
Child of the Romans— Carl Sandburg	326	58.6	336	65.3	662	62.0	26	S
Children's Hour, The— Henry W. Longfellow	183	53.8	345	73.8	528	63.8	14	R
Child's Garden of Verses, A—Robert L. Stevenson	32		146	73.3			
Chinaman's Head, The— William R. Benét	333	68.0	502	71.8	835	69.9	15	R
Chinese Nightingale, The —Vachel Lindsay	137	37.2	294	61.6	431	49.4	81	IR
Choosing a President— Edward S. Martin	235	56.8	280	54.3	515	55.6	14	S
Christabel—Samuel T. Coleridge	170	54.7	220	74.8	390	64.8	20	S
Christmas—Washington Irving	291	51.0	229	53.9	520	52.5	22	S
Christmas Carol, A— Charles Dickens	797	74.3	1144	85.5	1941	79.9	54	IR
Christmas Day— Washington Irving	408	52.3	190	50.0	598	51.2	17	S

PUPILS' READING INTERESTS: GRADES 10-12
Ts and Ss = Teachers and Schools   S = Studied in Class
IR = Independent Reading   R = Read in Class

SELECTION—AUTHOR	Boys		Girls		Total		Ts & Ss	
	No.	%	No.	%	No.	Av. %		
Christmas Day at Sea— Joseph Conrad	300	74.3	415	65.1	715	69.7	31	S
Christmas Essays (Combined)—Washington Irving	1069	52.8	733	56.9	1802	54.9	41	S
Christmas Eve— Washington Irving	258	51.4	167	56.6	425	54.0	19	S
Christmas Shopping— Helen Davenport	157	45.9	280	74.6	437	60.3	14	S
Christopher Columbus— Rosemary C. and Stephen V. Benét	292	52.6	348	56.8	640	54.7	13	R
Cimarron—Edna Ferber	142	83.1	208	85.1	350	84.1	17	S
Circular Staircase, The— Mary R. Rinehart	138	78.6	684	83.6	822	81.1	192	IR
Circus Episode, A— William A. White	223	80.0	263	80.8	486	80.4	16	R
Circus-postered Barn, The—Elizabeth J. Coatsworth	304	40.6	342	51.2	646	45.9	13	R
Citadel, The—A. J. Cronin	154	73.1	234	82.1	388	77.6		
Cities—Boyce House	268	34.7	309	48.4	577	41.6	11	R
Citizen, The—James F. Dwyer	208	72.1	257	74.5	465	73.3	14	S
Citizen from Emporia, The—Elizabeth S. Sergeant	212	51.4	326	47.5	538	49.5	16	R
City Roofs—Charles H. Towne	168	55.4	250	70.2	418	62.8	17	S
City Sparrow—Alfred Kreymborg	262	68.1	302	69.4	564	68.8	20	S
City That Conquered Night, The—Vincent B. Ibanez	248	48.4	261	41.0	509	44.7	14	R
Clara Barton—Mildred Pace	23		245	69.8				
Classical Myths That Live Today—Frances E. Sabin	114	58.7	211	65.2	325	62.0	117	IR

PUPILS' READING INTERESTS: GRADES 10-12

Ts and Ss = Teachers and Schools   S = Studied in Class

IR = Independent Reading   R = Read in Class

SELECTION—AUTHOR	Boys		Girls		Total		Ts & Ss	
	No.	%	No.	%	No.	Av. %		
Claustrophobia—Abbie C. Goodloe	357	57.4	181	79.6	538	68.5	13	S
Clean-Up's Job in the "Pit"—Charles R. Walker, Jr.	175	73.2	200	47.3	375	60.3	17	S
Cleon and I—Charles MacKay	304	40.2	398	51.6	702	45.9	15	R
Clinker, The—Unknown	390	51.5	443	53.0	833	52.3	14	R
Clipper Ships and Captains—Rosemary C. and Stephen V. Benét	223	64.3	327	62.5	550	63.4	14	R
Clothes Make the Man— Booth Tarkington	245	76.1	332	84.0	577	80.1	24	S
Cloud, The—Percy B. Shelley	801	54.8	862	68.6	1663	61.7	45	S
Coddling in Education— Henry S. Canby	255	44.9	278	47.1	533	46.0	14	R
Code, The—Robert Frost	267	68.4	321	57.3	588	62.9	14	R
Code of Morals, A— Rudyard Kipling	250	54.6	323	57.6	573	56.1	14	R
Coin, A—Carl Sandburg	178	57.6	205	59.5	383	58.6	16	S
Coin, The—Sara Teasdale	281	58.7	281	73.1	562	65.9	29	S
Coliseum, The—George G. Byron	224	50.1	243	52.3	467	51.2	15	S
Colonial Printer and American Patriot— Benjamin Franklin	358	59.8	384	54.2	742	57.0	34	R
Columbus—Joaquin Miller	186	71.2	375	72.1	561	71.7	23	S
Comedy of Errors, The— William Shakespeare	177	70.6	342	79.1	519	74.9	197	IR
Comet—Samuel A. Derieux	192	88.8	242	90.7	434	89.8	24	R
Come Up from the Fields, Father—Walt Whitman	214	65.2	253	80.2	467	72.7	23	S
Comforter, The— Elizabeth Jordan	453	82.6	523	95.9	976	89.3	16	S

PUPILS' READING INTERESTS: GRADES 10-12
Ts and Ss = Teachers and Schools   S = Studied in Class
IR = Independent Reading   R = Read in Class

SELECTION—AUTHOR	Boys		Girls		Total		Ts & Ss	
	No.	%	No.	%	No.	Av. %		
Coming of Arthur, The—Alfred Tennyson	1042	61.0	1250	62.0	2292	61.5	88	S
Companions—Charles Calverly	478	28.8	561	56.6	1039	42.7	17	R
Compensation—Ralph W. Emerson	365	56.2	390	56.5	755	56.4	34	S
Compleat Angler, The—Izaak Walton	185	66.8	131	58.0	316	62.4	18	S
Compton's Encyclopedia	420	65.4	786	65.1	1206	65.3	43	IR
Comrades—An Episode—Robert Nichols	168	69.0	160	62.2	328	65.6	16	S
Comus—John Milton	378	45.2	428	60.8	806	53.0	62	S
Concerning X—Arthur Guiterman	298	67.4	313	76.5	611	72.0	10	R
Conclusion, The—Walter Raleigh	220	63.9	289	65.7	509	64.8	23	S
Concord Hymn—Ralph W. Emerson	504	77.9	601	73.0	1105	75.5	30	S
Confessional—Percival Wilde	223	75.1	251	80.3	474	77.7	26	S
Confidential Charles—Edward Anthony	289	47.1	422	53.8	711	50.5	13	R
Congo, The—Vachel Lindsay	760	76.4	748	74.3	1508	75.4	51	S
Connecticut Yankee in King Arthur's Court, A—Mark Twain	179	77.1	183	67.2	362	72.2	23	S
Conquered Banner, The—Abram J. Ryan	307	71.8	367	75.5	674	73.7	34	S
Consecration, A—John Masefield	321	61.8	355	64.5	676	63.2	31	S
Constant Lover, The—John Suckling	213	46.0	258	55.0	471	50.5	18	S
Contentment—Oliver W. Holmes	229	56.6	265	70.0	494	63.3	17	S
Contest Rider, The—Elliott C. Lincoln	541	68.1	552	60.1	1093	64.1	16	R
Contradiction—Christopher Morley	302	34.4	299	45.5	601	40.0	12	R

PUPILS' READING INTERESTS: GRADES 10-12

Ts and Ss = Teachers and Schools   S = Studied in Class

IR = Independent Reading   R = Read in Class

SELECTION—AUTHOR	Boys		Girls		Total		Ts & Ss	
	No.	%	No.	%	No.	Av. %		
Conversational Neighbor, A—Richard Kirk	212	61.1	261	74.5	473	67.8	16	R
Cool Tombs—Carl Sandburg	203	55.7	261	57.4	464	56.6	20	R
Cooper Union Address, The—Abraham Lincoln	228	71.7	224	64.3	452	68.0	39	S
Cop and the Anthem, The—O. Henry	197	85.5	236	81.4	433	83.5	68	IR
Coquette, The—John G. Saxe	518	39.4	571	65.7	1089	52.6	20	R
Coquette Conquered, A —Paul L. Dunbar	257	56.0	280	67.8	537	61.9	16	S
Coquette's Heart, A— Joseph Addison	237	51.1	264	67.6	501	59.4	28	S
Corazon—George Pattullo	236	79.4	275	66.2	511	72.8	30	S
Corinna's Going A-Maying—Robert Herrick	206	38.8	211	54.3	417	46.6	21	S
Correct Behavior on a Picnic—Donald O. Stewart	495	83.0	496	88.1	991	85.6	21	S
Cotter's Saturday Night, The—Robert Burns	373	68.5	300	74.8	673	71.7	42	S
Count Luckner, the Sea Devil—Lowell Thomas	319	96.1	281	89.7	600	92.9	24	S
Count of Monte Cristo, The—Alexandre Dumas	358	88.3	390	85.1	748	86.7	43	IR
Country of the Blind, The—H. G. Wells	162	68.8	194	71.4	356	70.1	17	S
Courtin', The—James R. Lowell	484	72.4	551	80.6	1035	76.5	54	S
Courtship of Miles Standish, The—Henry W. Longfellow	1123	55.6	1182	69.5	2305	62.6	67	S
Cowardice of Youth, The —London Times	148	50.7	155	60.6	303	55.7	20	S
Cowboy, The—Emerson Hough	287	79.1	327	52.6	614	65.9	11	R

PUPILS' READING INTERESTS: GRADES 10-12

Ts and Ss = Teachers and Schools   S = Studied in Class

IR = Independent Reading   R = Read in Class

SELECTION—AUTHOR	Boys		Girls		Total		Ts & Ss	
	No.	%	No.	%	No.	Av. %		
Cowboy's Dream, The—John A. Lomax (Ed.)	374	75.5	415	82.7	789	79.1	31	S
Cowboy's Life, The (Cowboy Ballad)	520	62.8	593	68.1	1113	65.5	19	R
Cow in Apple Time, The—Robert Frost	434	47.6	501	46.9	935	47.3	32	S
Coyote, The—Badger Clark	188	54.0	205	48.3	393	51.2	17	S
Crab and Its Mother, The—William E. Leonard	183	53.8	210	66.9	393	60.4	17	S
Cree Queery and Mysy Drolly—James M. Barrie	172	48.3	157	60.5	329	54.4	21	S
Cremation of Sam McGee, The—Robert W. Service	453	90.3	443	83.3	896	86.8	35	S
Cress Delahanty—Jessamyn West	48		205	60.5				
Crime and Punishment—Fyodor Dostoevsky	178	74.2	184	72.3	362	73.3		
Crisis, The—Winston Churchill	307	71.8	307	82.4	614	77.1	41	S
Crossing the Bar—Alfred Tennyson	468	63.9	601	77.3	1069	70.6	57	S
Cruel Brother, The (British Ballad)	197	52.0	259	75.1	456	63.6	15	R
Cruel Sea, The—Nicholas Mansarrat	172	76.5	46					
Crusade in Europe—Dwight D. Eisenhower	262	79.8	80					
Cry, the Beloved Country—Alan Paton	162	70.4	265	79.8	427	75.1		
Cuckoo Song—Unknown	6847	20.8	7980	26.1	14827	23.5	270	R
Curiosities of American Speech, The—New York Sun	185	65.7	210	68.1	395	66.9	22	S
Cyrano de Bergerac—Edmond Rostand	435	77.9	415	82.3	850	80.1	43	S
Daddy Long Legs—Jean Webster	271	55.0	1155	71.1	1426	63.1	82	IR

PUPILS' READING INTERESTS: GRADES 10-12
Ts and Ss = Teachers and Schools   S = Studied in Class
IR = Independent Reading   R = Read in Class

SELECTION—AUTHOR	Boys		Girls		Total		Ts & Ss	
	No.	%	No.	%	No.	Av. %		
Daffodils, The—William Wordsworth	1044	50.6	1418	69.2	2462	59.9	82	S
Da Greata Stronga Man —Thomas A. Daly	315	88.3	291	85.1	606	86.7	21	S
Daily Miracle, The— Arnold Bennett	278	52.0	285	56.7	563	54.4	15	S
Da Leetla Boy—Thomas A. Daly	395	81.4	399	89.4	794	85.4	31	S
Damming the Missouri— Arthur Guiterman	227	84.8	243	74.5	470	79.7	16	S
Danger Is My Business— John Craig	339	82.2	364	78.7	703	80.5	130	IR
Daniel Boone—Arthur Guiterman	354	70.5	403	64.6	757	67.6	17	R
Daniel Boone, Wilderness Scout— Stewart E. White	450	79.1	173	60.4	623	69.8	71	IR
Daniel Webster's Horses —Elizabeth J. Coatsworth	304	54.3	349	64.3	653	59.3	13	R
Danny Deever—Rudyard Kipling	312	71.8	476	70.0	788	70.9	20	S
Darest Thou Now, O Soul—Walt Whitman	296	43.2	366	53.4	662	48.3	26	S
Darius Green and His Flying Machine— John T. Trowbridge	373	76.4	329	72.9	702	74.7	12	R
Dark Brown Dog, A— Stephen Crane	247	84.6	309	89.3	556	87.0	13	R
Dark Hills, The—E. A. Robinson	241	54.6	271	59.0	512	56.8	26	S
Dark of the Dawn, The —Beulah M. Dix	311	73.3	359	70.9	670	72.1	31	S
Daughters of the Late Colonel, The— Rudyard Kipling	203	36.0	401	46.4	604	41.2	13	R
David and Goliath (Retold)	174	80.2	396	75.5	570	77.9	12	R
David Copperfield— Charles Dickens	934	74.3	874	88.8	1808	81.6	89	S

PUPILS' READING INTERESTS: GRADES 10-12
Ts and Ss = Teachers and Schools   S = Studied in Class
IR = Independent Reading   R = Read in Class

SELECTION—AUTHOR	Boys No.	Boys %	Girls No.	Girls %	Total No.	Total Av. %	Ts & Ss	
David Harum—Edward N. Westcott	206	73.5	333	71.3	539	72.4	92	IR
David Swan—Nathaniel Hawthorne	268	65.7	282	72.7	550	69.2	28	S
Day, A—Emily Dickinson	540	35.8	525	63.5	1065	49.7	23	S
Day Christ Died, The—Jim Bishop	159	87.7	261	92.1	420	89.9		
Day Is Done, The—Henry W. Longfellow	273	57.1	351	79.6	624	68.4	26	S
Day Lincoln Was Shot, The—Jim Bishop	524	77.1	492	77.2	1016	77.2		
Day of Infamy—Walter Lord	262	88.3	66					
Da Younga 'Merican—Thomas A. Daly	278	83.8	275	90.0	553	86.9	20	S
Days—Karle W. Baker	618	36.8	712	58.0	1330	47.4	18	R
Days—Ralph W. Emerson	309	30.3	321	44.5	630	37.4	14	R
Days of Forty-Nine, The (American Ballad)	301	84.7	333	78.4	634	81.6	14	R
Day's Pleasure, A—Hamlin Garland	247	62.8	310	80.6	557	71.7	30	R
Deacon's Masterpiece, The—Oliver W. Holmes	194	88.4	168	84.2	362	86.3	17	S
Dead, The—Rupert Brooke	222	56.1	277	62.0	499	59.1	29	S
Deadwood—Stanley Vestal	365	69.9	413	54.1	778	62.0	13	R
Dear Abby—Abigail Van Buren	64		252	75.4				
Dear and Glorious Physician—Taylor Caldwell	41		150	84.3				
Dear Brutus—James M. Barrie	167	58.4	192	65.6	359	62.0	21	S
Dear March, Come In—Emily Dickinson	435	31.3	504	45.0	939	38.2	18	R
Dear Teen-Ager—Abigail Van Buren	31		245	68.6				

PUPILS' READING INTERESTS: GRADES 10-12
Ts and Ss = Teachers and Schools   S = Studied in Class
IR = Independent Reading   R = Read in Class

SELECTION—AUTHOR	Boys		Girls		Total		Ts & Ss	
	No.	%	No.	%	No.	Av. %		
Death at Evening— Phyllis McGinley	303	64.2	378	75.8	681	70.0	14	R
Death Be Not Proud— John Gunther	114	83.3	313	91.7	427	87.5		
Death Comes for the Archbishop—Willa Cather	109	68.8	227	68.9	336	68.9		
Death of Caesar, The— Plutarch	325	64.8	365	61.1	690	63.0	12	R
Death of the Flowers, The—William C. Bryant	222	39.0	359	79.9	581	59.5	13	R
Death of the Hired Man, The—Robert Frost	306	71.1	304	78.6	610	74.9	25	S
Declaration of Independence, The	438	60.2	460	53.0	898	56.6	19	R
Decline of the Drama, The—Stephen Leacock	446	61.1	476	68.0	922	64.6	44	S
Deep River (Negro Spiritual)	353	39.9	370	51.8	723	45.9	11	R
Deerslayer, The—James F. Cooper	679	77.9	292	70.4	971	74.2	130	IR
Defense of Detective Stories, A—G. K. Chesterton	334	41.9	364	33.4	698	37.7	12	R
Defense of Nonsense, A —G. K. Chesterton	179	50.3	365	49.5	544	49.9	23	S
Defense of the Alamo, The—Joaquin Miller	467	75.3	525	69.1	992	72.2	40	S
Definition of a Gentleman—John H. Newman	213	68.3	238	72.9	451	70.6	25	S
De Fust Banjo—Irwin Russell	646	62.8	703	64.2	1349	63.5	27	R
De Gustibus—Robert Browning	330	42.3	442	55.2	772	48.8	50	S
Demagogue, The— Richard W. Gilder	540	60.6	556	60.4	1096	60.5	15	R
De Nice Leetle Canadienne—William H. Drummond	491	61.5	609	71.1	1100	66.3	20	R

PUPILS' READING INTERESTS: GRADES 10-12

Ts and Ss = Teachers and Schools   S = Studied in Class

IR = Independent Reading   R = Read in Class

SELECTION—AUTHOR	Boys		Girls		Total		Ts & Ss	
	No.	%	No.	%	No.	Av. %		
Dennis the Menace—Hank Ketcham	389	71.5	341	66.1	730	68.8		
Derelict—Young E. Allison	215	74.7	242	59.1	457	66.9	13	S
Description of Little America—Russell Owen	475	69.4	582	57.3	1057	63.4	14	S
Deserted—Madison Cawein	272	55.7	340	66.8	612	61.3	31	S
Deserted Village, The—Oliver Goldsmith	1135	51.2	1141	57.8	2276	54.5	118	S
Deserter, The—Richard H. Davis	285	74.0	341	71.0	626	72.5	19	S
Désirée—Annemarie Selinko	27		160	80.3				
Destruction of Sennacherib, The—George G. Byron	425	60.0	537	54.5	962	57.3	41	S
Destry Rides Again—Max Brand	171	69.9	162	68.8	333	69.4		
Determined Suicide, The—Don Marquis	174	67.8	191	66.0	365	66.9	16	R
Devil and Daniel Webster, The—Stephen V. Benét	525	85.9	622	84.4	1147	85.2	25	R
Devil and Tom Walker, The—Washington Irving	156	64.1	151	64.6	307	64.4	16	S
Diabolical Circle, The—Beulah Bornstead	96	63.5	570	68.4	666	66.0	17	R
Diary of Anne Frank, The	418	77.4	1484	90.4	1902	82.9		
Dickens in Camp—Bret Harte	354	49.9	393	55.1	747	52.5	18	R
Dick Tracy (Comic Strip)	959	70.6	1205	61.8	2164	66.2	54	IR
Difficult People—Anton Chekhov	114		147	51.3			22	R
Diogenes—Max Eastman	399	38.2	413	50.8	812	44.5	15	R
Dirge, A—Percy B. Shelley	3441	43.7	3558	51.2	6999	47.5	136	R

PUPILS' READING INTERESTS: GRADES 10-12

Ts and Ss = Teachers and Schools   S = Studied in Class

IR = Independent Reading   R = Read in Class

SELECTION—AUTHOR	Boys		Girls		Total		Ts & Ss	
	No.	%	No.	%	No.	Av. %		
Dirge for a Righteous Kitten, A—Vachel Lindsay	263	41.8	372	46.0	635	43.9	14	R
Discourager of Hesitancy, The—Frank R. Stockton	247	82.0	341	87.1	588	84.6	13	R
Discovered—Paul L. Dunbar	345	57.0	378	74.7	723	65.9	13	R
Discoverer, The— Nathalia Crane	372	48.5	420	51.3	792	49.9	17	R
Discovery—Georges Duhamel	274	43.2	281	45.7	555	44.5	16	S
Discovery of Guiana, The —Walter Raleigh	214	51.2	251	43.4	465	47.3	17	S
Dishonest Miller, The (American Ballad)	303	55.9	361	62.3	664	59.1	11	R
Dishwashing—Rebecca McCann	257	57.0	369	71.4	626	64.2	12	R
Disraeli—Louis N. Parker	128	62.9	173	72.3	301	67.6	71	IR
Disraeli and Victorian England—André Maurois	372	50.4	301	54.0	673	52.2	18	S
Disraeli in London— André Maurois	201	54.7	202	65.3	403	60.0	39	S
Dissection of a Beau's Head—Joseph Addison	279	52.9	325	64.6	604	58.8	26	S
Dissertation upon Roast Pig, A—Charles Lamb	1148	79.5	1259	77.2	2407	78.4	109	S
Dixie (Song)	781	67.7	1139	69.1	1920	68.4	54	IR
Doctor of Afternoon Arm, The—Norman Duncan	175	81.4	151	78.5	326	80.0	25	S
Does It Matter?— Siegfried Sassoon	270	74.6	316	81.2	586	77.9	18	S
Dog, The—George G. Vest	241	70.5	319	76.0	560	73.3	15	R
Dog in the House, A— Burges Johnson	532	77.3	463	83.4	995	80.4	11	R
Dog of Flanders, A— Ouida	258	80.6	385	80.9	643	80.8	55	IR

PUPILS' READING INTERESTS: GRADES 10-12

Ts and Ss = Teachers and Schools   S = Studied in Class

IR = Independent Reading   R = Read in Class

SELECTION—AUTHOR	Boys		Girls		Total		Ts & Ss	
	No.	%	No.	%	No.	Av. %		
Dog's Epitaph, A— William Watson	352	41.2	451	43.3	803	42.3	15	R
Doll's House, The— Henrik Ibsen	181	55.8	253	75.9	434	65.9	27	S
Donkey, The—G. K. Chesterton	331	62.4	360	62.6	691	62.5	26	S
Don Quixote—Miguel de Cervantes	375	61.7	254	64.8	629	63.3	130	IR
Don't Die on Third— William J. Cameron	386	77.7	434	63.9	820	70.8	16	R
Don't Get Lost—Robert Benchley	384	62.5	363	65.3	747	63.9	10	R
Don: The Story of a Lion Dog—Zane Grey	223	92.8	197	79.9	420	86.4	20	S
Dorlan's Home Walk— Arthur Guiterman	395	92.7	451	89.8	846	91.3	19	R
Dorothy Q—Oliver W. Holmes	412	51.8	427	78.8	839	65.3	22	S
Double Date—Rosamond Du Jardin	8		569	66.5				
Double Feature— Rosemond Du Jardin	6		373	68.5				
Dover Beach—Matthew Arnold	403	54.3	379	65.3	782	59.8	34	S
Do You Fear the Force of the Wind?— Hamlin Garland	231	64.3	267	66.1	498	65.2	13	S
Dragon Seed—Pearl Buck	163	78.8	398	85.5	561	82.2	130	IR
Dragonwyck—Anya Seton	78		199	81.9				
Drake's Drum—Henry Newbolt	205	66.6	241	53.3	446	60.0	16	S
Drama in the Lecture Field—Anna H. Shaw	334	55.2	655	67.9	989	61.6	30	S
Dream Children— Charles Lamb	478	52.3	530	74.8	1008	63.6	52	S
Dreamers—Herbert Kaufman	591	50.5	688	57.7	1279	54.1	19	R

PUPILS' READING INTERESTS: GRADES 10-12
Ts and Ss = Teachers and Schools　　　S = Studied in Class
IR = Independent Reading　　　　　　　R = Read in Class

SELECTION—AUTHOR	Boys		Girls		Total		Ts & Ss	
	No.	%	No.	%	No.	Av. %		
Dreamers—Siegfried Sassoon	393	51.0	413	65.4	806	58.2	22	S
Dream Pedlary—Thomas L. Beddoes	204	29.7	287	51.2	491	40.5	13	R
Dreams—Thomas De Quincey	167	50.6	190	52.9	357	51.8	22	S
Dr. Fu Manchu—Sax Rohmer	150	71.7	68					
Dr. Heidegger's Experiment—Nathaniel Hawthorne	347	61.8	343	65.5	690	63.7	31	S
Dr. Jekyll and Mr. Hyde —Robert L. Stevenson	270	84.4	320	82.0	590	83.2	25	S
Drowne's Wooden Image —Nathaniel Hawthorne	262	53.3	251	57.4	513	55.4	24	S
Dr. Zhivago—Boris Pasternak	147	67.0	164	73.2	311	70.1		
Drudgery as a Fine Art —Winifred Kirkland	129	51.6	353	68.8	482	60.2	22	S
Drums—James Boyd	758	84.1	429	77.9	1187	81.0	214	IR
Drums Along the Mohawk—Walter Edmonds	779	86.5	611	83.1	1390	84.8	130	IR
Ducks—F. W. Harvey	155	56.5	181	59.1	336	57.8	17	S
Duel, The—Eugene Field	325	57.7	466	71.4	791	64.6	23	S
Duel in the Sun—Niven Busch	181	68.8	80					
Dug-Out, The—Siegfried Sassoon	303	62.2	305	70.1	608	66.2	13	S
Duke of Plaza Toro, The —William S. Gilbert	1144	61.9	1206	63.0	2350	62.5	30	R
Dulcy—George S. Kaufman and Marc Connelly	165	71.2	187	79.4	352	75.3	18	S
Duncan Gray—Robert Burns	279	40.1	344	44.9	623	42.5	19	S
Dust—AE (G. W. Russell)	343	27.6	476	36.2	819	31.9	15	R
Dust of the Road— Kenneth S. Goodman	76		477	73.1				

PUPILS' READING INTERESTS: GRADES 10-12
Ts and Ss = Teachers and Schools   S = Studied in Class
IR = Independent Reading   R = Read in Class

SELECTION—AUTHOR	Boys		Girls		Total		Ts & Ss	
	No.	%	No.	%	No.	Av. %		
Duty—Ralph W. Emerson	1281	56.8	1383	67.7	2664	62.3	63	R
Dying for Dear Old— Heywood Broun	450	82.8	337	73.4	787	78.1	14	R
Dying Ranger, The (Cowboy Ballad)	227	75.8	244	76.8	471	76.3	24	S
Each and All—Ralph W. Emerson	178	51.4	232	61.2	410	56.3	24	S
Eagle, The—Alfred Tennyson	661	41.8	750	42.5	1411	42.2	35	S
Eagle and the Mole, The —Elinor Wylie	331	53.8	362	45.0	693	49.4	29	S
Eagle That Is Forgotten, The—Vachel Lindsay	227	56.8	207	57.7	434	57.3	22	S
Earning a Reputation— Otis Skinner	521	53.0	560	41.5	1081	47.3	62	S
East in Gold, The— William H. Davies	427	35.5	507	43.3	934	39.4	18	R
East of Eden—John Steinbeck	177	74.6	330	79.1	507	76.9		
Ecclesiastes 12—The Bible	166	46.1	223	61.4	389	53.8	16	S
Echo and Narcissus— Rannie B. Baker	245	43.1	294	62.4	539	52.8	11	R
Edison, Greatest American of the Century — Emil Ludwig	313	76.8	336	63.8	649	70.3	13	R
Edison's Personality— Francis A. Jones	179	72.1	203	67.7	382	69.9	15	S
Edith Cavell—Hermann Hagedorn	181	88.1	236	95.6	417	91.9	15	R
Educated Man, The— John H. Newman	240	64.2	300	61.0	540	62.6	22	S
Education—Gertrude Stein	393	41.7	483	39.5	876	40.6	20	R
Education of an American Boy, The— Unknown	182	76.2	215	79.3	397	77.8	18	S
Edward (American Ballad)	502	43.1	508	52.1	1010	47.6	29	R

PUPILS' READING INTERESTS: GRADES 10-12
Ts and Ss = Teachers and Schools   S = Studied in Class
IR = Independent Reading   R = Read in Class

SELECTION—AUTHOR	Boys		Girls		Total		Ts & Ss	
	No.	%	No.	%	No.	Av. %		
Een Napoli—Thomas A. Daly	400	68.5	441	77.0	841	72.8	30	S
Efficiency—Frank Crane	266	34.2	329	44.8	595	39.5	11	R
Effie—Randall Brown	210	71.2	227	74.7	437	73.0	17	S
Egg and I, The—Betty MacDonald	127	68.1	353	73.6	480	70.9		
Egyptian, The—Mika Waltari	185	75.7	197	80.2	382	78.0		
Eighteenth Century Autocrat, An—James Boswell	146	43.8	178	46.1	324	45.0	31	S
Eldorado—Edgar A. Poe	686	66.4	847	64.5	1533	65.5	45	S
Election Day Is a Holiday—Ogden Nash	281	56.9	335	61.2	616	59.1	10	R
Elegy in a Country Churchyard—G. K. Chesterton	389	45.6	404	56.8	793	51.2	11	R
Elegy on That Glory of Her Sex, Mrs. Mary Blaize—Oliver Goldsmith	339	47.6	374	70.1	713	58.9	12	R
Elegy on the Death of a Mad Dog, An— Oliver Goldsmith	367	84.2	436	85.7	803	85.0	27	S
Elegy Written in a Country Churchyard— Thomas Gray	1653	48.3	1532	51.2	3185	49.8	130	S
Elephant—Carl Akeley	399	80.2	485	68.2	884	74.2	37	S
Elephant Remembers, The—Edison Marshall	445	81.0	327	68.3	772	74.7	33	S
Elephants Are Different to Different People— Carl Sandburg	362	50.3	401	55.7	763	53.0	15	R
Eli Whitney, Man of Destiny (Radio Play)	244	88.3	427	83.6	671	86.0	10	R
Elizabeth the Queen— Maxwell Anderson	274	58.9	617	80.0	891	69.5	29	S
Ellis Park—Helen Hoyt	292	57.0	403	72.0	695	64.5	26	S
Elmer Gantry—Sinclair Lewis	190	77.6	168	70.5	358	74.1		

PUPILS' READING INTERESTS: GRADES 10-12

Ts and Ss = Teachers and Schools   S = Studied in Class
IR = Independent Reading   R = Read in Class

SELECTION—AUTHOR	Boys		Girls		Total		Ts & Ss	
	No.	%	No.	%	No.	Av. %		
"Elsie" Books, The—Martha Finley	2		207	65.5			52	IR
Emerson's Essays	215	46.5	222	51.4	437	49.0	24	S
Emily Dickinson's School Days—Martha D. Bianchi	265	33.2	296	60.3	561	46.8	28	S
Emperor Jones, The—Eugene O'Neill	446	89.2	410	84.6	856	86.9	44	S
Emperor's New Clothes, The—Hans C. Andersen	245	52.0	557	60.5	802	56.3	130	IR
Enchanted Shirt, The—John Hay	244	74.4	334	81.6	578	78.0	17	R
Enchanters, The—Angelo Patri	229	50.7	399	58.4	628	54.6	14	S
Encyclopaedia Britannica, The	714	67.6	1193	67.3	1907	67.5	73	IR
Endymion—John Keats	65	40.8	311	63.0	376	51.9	16	S
Enemy Below, The—D. A. Rayner	605	84.0	118	71.6	723	77.8		
Enemy of the People, An—Henrik Ibsen	205	72.2	193	63.5	398	67.9	16	S
England Before the War—Burton Hendrick	204	39.2	151	50.0	355	44.6	24	S
England to America—Margaret P. Montague	679	66.9	582	78.4	1261	72.7	42	S
English Undefiled—Kate D. Wiggin	800	45.0	783	53.9	1583	49.5	19	R
Enoch Arden—Alfred Tennyson	876	67.2	863	85.2	1739	76.2	65	S
Enter the Hero—Theresa Helburn	238	65.3	262	77.1	500	71.2	22	S
Epic of the North, An—Frank M. O'Brien	295	79.3	331	72.4	626	75.9	13	R
Epilogue to Asolando—Robert Browning	402	21.3	472	25.1	874	23.2	19	R
Episode of Sparrows, An—Rumer Godden	20		169	77.5				
Epitaph—Walter de la Mare	276	54.2	297	64.5	573	59.4	21	S
Epitaph (A bird, a man—)—Unknown	477	69.2	635	73.8	1112	71.5	23	R

PUPILS' READING INTERESTS: GRADES 10-12
Ts and Ss = Teachers and Schools   S = Studied in Class
IR = Independent Reading   R = Read in Class

SELECTION—AUTHOR	Boys		Girls		Total		Ts & Ss	
	No.	%	No.	%	No.	Av. %		
Epitaph of a Poor Man— Unknown	273	52.6	312	59.8	585	56.2	13	R
Epitaph of John Dale— Unknown	272	34.2	312	38.5	584	36.4	13	R
Epitaph on Charles II—J. Wilmot	401	58.0	496	61.8	897	59.9	25	R
Epitaphs for the Speed Age—Leonard H. Robbins	187	77.0	244	76.0	431	76.5	15	S
Erie Canal, The (Folk Song)	306	64.4	343	68.4	649	66.4	14	R
Escape—Arthur C. Benson	349	46.4	304	59.0	653	52.7	11	R
Essay on Burns—Thomas Carlyle	450	50.7	432	55.3	882	53.0	72	S
Essay on Johnson— Thomas B. Macaulay	928	60.2	922	63.6	1850	61.9	70	S
Essays: Of Books; Of Reading; Of Nations— John Ruskin	315	47.6	430	53.0	745	50.3	21	S
Ethan Frome—Edith Wharton	216	75.9	247	83.4	463	79.7	22	S
Ethics for Real People—Franklin H. Giddings	230	42.8	248	55.9	478	49.4	25	S
Etiquette—Arthur Guiterman	293	56.0	292	66.1	585	61.1	15	S
Etiquette—Emily Post	58		247	66.6				
Evangeline—Henry W. Longfellow	593	53.0	903	75.0	1496	64.0	37	S
Evelyn Hope—Robert Browning	371	27.6	434	61.5	805	44.6	15	S
Evening at the Farm— John T. Trowbridge	506	44.7	608	52.8	1114	48.8	25	R
Evening Clothes—Zona Gale	189	69.0	217	85.3	406	77.2	16	S
Eve of St. Agnes, The— John Keats	555	55.3	440	69.4	995	62.4	52	S
Eve of Waterloo, The— George G. Byron	266	66.2	281	62.5	547	64.4	16	S

PUPILS' READING INTERESTS: GRADES 10-12
Ts and Ss = Teachers and Schools   S = Studied in Class
IR = Independent Reading   R = Read in Class

SELECTION—AUTHOR	Boys		Girls		Total		Ts & Ss
	No.	%	No.	%	No.	Av. %	
Everyday Adventures— Samuel Scoville, Jr.	198	72.2	300	67.3	498	69.8	17 S
Everyman (Early English Play)	293	46.9	318	54.9	611	50.9	29 S
Every Man's Natural Desire to Be Somebody Else— Samuel McC. Crothers	272	59.6	253	64.7	525	62.2	38 S
Evolution—John B. Tabb	238	52.5	308	67.5	546	60.0	26 S
Evolution of the Gentleman, The— Samuel McC. Crothers	343	42.7	365	31.5	708	37.1	16 R
Example, The—William H. Davies	262	36.8	294	42.9	556	39.9	13 R
Excelsior—Henry W. Longfellow	655	50.5	598	66.7	1253	58.6	19 R
Exodus—Leon M. Uris	351	83.6	599	90.2	950	86.9	
Explorer, The—Rudyard Kipling	176	71.3	174	64.4	350	67.9	18 S
Express, The—William E. Leonard	177	51.7	200	46.3	377	49.0	17 S
Exultation—Shaemas O'Sheel	534	50.8	551	60.8	1085	55.8	16 R
Fable, A—Ralph W. Emerson	719	45.2	800	48.6	1519	46.9	36 R
Face in the Window, The—William D. Pelley	216	84.3	165	88.8	381	86.6	15 S
Factories—Margaret Widdemer	317	60.9	394	72.1	711	66.5	30 S
Facts of Life and Love for Teen Agers— Evelyn M. Duvall	188	66.8	324	71.3	512	69.1	
Faerie Queene, The— Edmund Spenser	340	48.4	357	57.3	697	52.9	31 S
Fair Enough—Westbrook Pegler	341	77.1	337	65.1	678	71.1	11 R
Fairy Tales—Hans C. Andersen	329	55.5	962	70.9	1291	63.2	
Fairy Tales—Grimm Brothers	340	55.4	988	67.9	1328	61.7	

PUPILS' READING INTERESTS: GRADES 10-12
Ts and Ss = Teachers and Schools   S = Studied in Class
IR = Independent Reading   R = Read in Class

SELECTION—AUTHOR	Boys		Girls		Total		Ts & Ss	
	No.	%	No.	%	No.	Av. %		
Falconer of God, The— William R. Benét	258	54.1	311	55.9	569	55.0	26	S
Fall of Heroes, The— William Watson	211	29.1	259	35.9	470	32.5	16	R
Fall of the City, The—Archibald MacLeish	303	40.9	297	37.5	600	39.2	14	R
Fall of the House of Usher, The—Edgar A. Poe	733	56.4	645	55.0	1378	55.7	62	S
Fame—Richard W. Gilder	547	49.8	540	56.4	1087	53.1	15	R
Fame—John B. Tabb	256	50.2	294	59.9	550	55.1	25	S
Fame's Little Day— Sarah O. Jewett	233	54.7	238	71.0	471	62.9	21	S
Family Fool, The— William S. Gilbert	508	47.3	602	49.3	1110	48.3	15	R
Famous Epigrams— Alexander Pope	774	42.4	938	50.8	1712	46.6	37	R
Fan Drill, The—Joseph Addison	232	46.3	229	60.0	461	53.2	18	S
Farewell Address, The— George Washington	728	53.7	702	53.3	1430	53.5	57	S
Farewell to America—H. W. Nevison	276	58.7	279	71.0	555	64.9	29	S
Farewell to Arms, A— Ernest Hemingway	255	77.8	649	84.4	904	81.1		
Farewell to the Citizens of Springfield— Abraham Lincoln	1146	72.9	1247	75.0	2393	74.0	43	R
Farmer Remembers Lincoln, A—Witter Bynner	262	80.5	307	79.0	569	79.8	29	S
Far-Sighted Muse, The— Dorothy Parker	185	59.2	204	69.9	389	64.6	17	S
Fast-Running Sheepherder, The—M. C. Boatright	248	60.9	343	56.8	591	58.9	11	R
Father, The— Björnstjerne Björnson	647	53.6	402	62.1	1049	57.9	44	S

PUPILS' READING INTERESTS: GRADES 10-12
Ts and Ss = Teachers and Schools   S = Studied in Class
IR = Independent Reading   R = Read in Class

SELECTION—AUTHOR	Boys		Girls		Total		Ts & Ss	
	No.	%	No.	%	No.	Av. %		
Father Duffy—Alexander Woollcott	417	71.7	442	73.3	859	72.5	21	R
Father of the Bride, The —Edward Streeter	85	61.8	422	75.1	507	68.5		
Father Opens My Mail— Clarence Day	178	74.2	208	85.1	386	79.7	15	R
Father William—Lewis Carroll	472	66.7	590	71.3	1062	69.0	16	R
Fathoms Deep—Octavus R. Cohen	175	80.9	181	70.4	356	75.7	15	S
Fat of the Land, The— Anzia Yezierska	482	68.7	448	82.6	930	75.7	50	S
F.B.I., The—Quentin Reynolds	403	76.3	86	74.4	489	75.4		
F.B.I., the "G Men's" Weapons and Tactics— Carroll B. Colby	1017	81.5	441	77.1	1458	79.3		
Feast of Ortolans, The— Maxwell Anderson	143	56.6	199	54.3	342	55.5	22	S
Federalist, The— Alexander Hamilton	245	32.4	307	23.6	552	28.0	21	R
Feud, The—Derrick Lohman	223	33.6	244	48.8	467	41.2	16	R
Feud Blood—Chester T. Crowell	238	72.7	295	75.1	533	73.9	30	S
Fiddler Jones—Edgar L. Masters	333	45.6	300	54.0	633	49.8	17	R
Fiddler of Dooney, The —William B. Yeats	192	50.3	254	56.5	446	53.4	20	S
Fiddlers Errant—Robert H. Schauffler	183	68.9	194	70.6	377	69.8	22	S
Fifteen—Beverly Cleary	19		294	79.9				
Fifty-first Dragon, The— Heywood Broun	1049	80.3	1235	74.3	2284	77.3	87	S
54–40 or Fight!— Emerson Hough	243	65.2	97	57.7	340	61.5		
Figureheads—Louise Saunders	82	66.5	708	76.2	790	71.4		
Find a Way—John G. Saxe	422	45.0	416	51.3	838	48.2	19	R

PUPILS' READING INTERESTS: GRADES 10-12
Ts and Ss = Teachers and Schools　　　S = Studied in Class
IR = Independent Reading　　　　　　　R = Read in Class

SELECTION—AUTHOR	Boys		Girls		Total		Ts & Ss	
	No.	%	No.	%	No.	Av. %		
Finders-Keepers—George Kelly	194	83.5	215	92.1	409	87.8	18	S
Finger of God, The—Percival Wilde	257	81.7	259	90.6	516	86.2	15	R
Finnigan to Flannigan—Strickland Gillilan	376	68.5	373	63.8	749	66.2	10	R
Firearms—Carroll B. Colby	193	74.4	10					
First Inaugural Address—Abraham Lincoln	225	64.2	193	59.8	418	62.0	19	S
First Snowfall, The—James R. Lowell	223	78.3	229	83.2	452	80.8	18	S
First Woman Doctor, The—Rachel Baker	37		292	78.6				
Fish Crier—Carl Sandburg	493	38.0	589	49.7	1082	43.9	19	R
Fish Story, A—Don Marquis	275	75.8	349	73.2	624	74.5	15	R
Five Little Peppers—Margaret Sidney	41		228	70.4				
Five Loaves—I. Creanga	287	65.3	392	61.4	679	63.4	14	R
Five Varieties, The—Edward V. Lucas	246	71.7	253	81.0	499	76.4	25	S
Flag Goes By, The—Henry H. Bennett	357	81.4	394	84.3	751	82.9	16	R
Flame, The—Louise McNeill	230	43.3	310	34.2	540	38.8	12	R
Flammonde—Edwin A. Robinson	246	49.8	268	63.8	514	56.8	19	S
Flathouse Roof, The—Nathalia Crane	563	66.4	750	86.4	1313	76.4	34	R
Fleurette—Robert W. Service	342	72.4	360	88.3	702	80.4	16	R
Flight—John Erskine	365	52.9	395	41.3	760	47.1	16	R
Flight to the South Pole—Richard E. Byrd	499	86.1	451	61.5	950	73.8	38	R
Flint and Fire—Dorothy C. Fisher	214	45.6	294	60.0	508	52.8	13	R
Floods, The—Anne M. Lindbergh	222	79.7	273	75.5	495	77.6	18	R

PUPILS' READING INTERESTS: GRADES 10-12

Ts and Ss = Teachers and Schools   S = Studied in Class

IR = Independent Reading   R = Read in Class

SELECTION—AUTHOR	Boys		Girls		Total		Ts & Ss	
	No.	%	No.	%	No.	Av. %		
Florence Nightingale—Jeannette C. Nolan	20		182	67.6				
Florence Nightingale—Lytton Strachey	235	65.1	230	81.7	465	73.4	28	S
Florist Shop, The—Winifred Hawkridge	223	60.3	219	79.9	442	70.1	17	S
Flower Drum Song—C. Y. Lee	157	72.0	305	84.1	462	78.1		
Flower Factory, The—Florence W. Evans	230	55.7	404	83.7	634	69.7	25	S
Flower in the Crannied Wall—Alfred Tennsyson	512	42.9	642	56.8	1154	49.9	35	S
Flush—Virginia Woolf	247	66.2	226	82.1	473	74.2	60	S
Fly, The—Katherine Mansfield	239	63.8	138	53.6	377	58.7		
Fly and a Flea, A—Unknown	423	58.0	499	62.9	922	60.4	11	S
Flying—Don Brown	180	78.9	218	70.4	398	74.7	18	S
Flying Over the North Pole—Richard E. Byrd	353	83.7	254	68.1	607	75.9	71	IR
Flying Saucers—Donald E. Keyhoe	199	76.6	26					
Flynn of Virginia—Bret Harte	671	57.8	718	57.2	1389	57.5	34	R
Fog—Carl Sandburg	548	65.4	762	69.2	1310	67.3	54	S
Fooling the People—Abraham Lincoln	1115	82.9	1173	87.2	2288	85.1	43	R
Fool's Prayer, The—Edward R. Sill	476	68.1	467	75.4	943	71.8	31	S
Football, American Style—Ilya Ilf and Eugene Petrov	243	77.8	313	66.8	556	72.3	13	R
Footfalls—Wilbur D. Steele	303	77.6	412	77.9	715	77.8	27	S
For a Lady I Know—Countee Cullen	990	33.3	1096	44.1	2086	38.7	29	R
For a New Year—Leonard Hinton	212	58.5	262	78.8	474	68.7	16	R
Forbearance—Ralph W. Emerson	407	38.9	522	52.3	929	45.6	27	S

PUPILS' READING INTERESTS: GRADES 10-12
Ts and Ss = Teachers and Schools   S = Studied in Class
IR = Independent Reading   R = Read in Class

SELECTION—AUTHOR	Boys		Girls		Total		Ts & Ss	
	No.	%	No.	%	No.	Av. %		
Forever Amber— Kathleen Winsor	38		208	73.1				
Forever Free—Honoré W. Morrow	102	72.5	207	78.0	309	75.3	253	IR
Forgot in the Rains (Radio Play)—William Merrick	229	82.8	294	90.0	523	86.4	13	R
Forsaken Merman, The— Matthew Arnold	257	50.6	370	65.8	627	58.2	22	S
For Those Who Fail— Joaquin Miller	777	61.4	858	61.7	1635	61.6	25	R
Fortitude—Hugh Walpole	150	76.3	256	88.7	406	82.5	32	S
Forty Singing Seamen— Alfred Noyes	243	62.0	245	59.6	488	60.8	15	R
For Whom the Bell Tolls —Ernest Hemingway	336	78.2	643	84.3	979	81.3		
Four-Leaf Clovers—Ella Higginson	322	43.9	339	59.1	661	51.5	19	R
Four-Line Philosophy, A —Joseph Anthony	186	53.8	239	65.7	425	59.8	15	S
Four Little Foxes—Lew Sarett	402	55.3	476	65.7	878	60.5	28	S
Fox Race—Roy Hilton	186	46.8	334	51.5	520	49.2	12	R
Freckles—Gene S. Porter	362	64.1	615	74.1	977	69.1	70	IR
Freckles and His Friends (Comic Strip)	531	68.3	835	69.9	1366	69.1	43	IR
Freshman Fullback, The —Ralph D. Paine	397	89.3	382	86.1	779	87.7	23	S
Friend of Napoleon, A— Richard Connell	214	76.9	232	87.1	446	82.0	15	S
Friends and Books—John Ruskin	536	60.4	538	65.5	1074	63.0	15	R
Frill, The—Pearl Buck	164	65.6	198	82.8	362	74.2	19	S
From "Byron"—Joaquin Miller	388	51.6	376	60.5	764	56.1	19	S
Frome's Plea for Falder —John Galsworthy	234	57.7	298	55.9	532	56.8	12	R
From Here to Eternity— James Jones	421	84.4	579	85.5	1000	85.0		

PUPILS' READING INTERESTS: GRADES 10-12

Ts and Ss = Teachers and Schools   S = Studied in Class
IR = Independent Reading   R = Read in Class

SELECTION—AUTHOR	Boys		Girls		Total		Ts & Ss	
	No.	%	No.	%	No.	Av. %		
Frost Tonight—Edith M. Thomas	212	44.8	226	58.8	438	51.8	21	S
Frozen Words—Joseph Addison and Richard Steele	170	79.1	169	79.6	339	79.4	24	S
Fulfillment—Dorothy Parker	744	35.4	813	53.0	1557	44.2	28	R
Fulton's Folly—Alice C. Sutliffe	304	83.1	320	69.1	624	76.1	46	S
Funny Business (Comic Strip)	148	61.5	193	63.5	341	62.5	112	IR
Furnace and I—Ralph Bergengren	290	73.3	245	76.1	535	74.7	27	S
Furrows—G. K. Chesterton	238	43.3	345	45.9	583	44.6	16	R
Fuzzy-Wuzzy—Rudyard Kipling	550	74.1	657	67.4	1207	70.8	45	S
Gala Dress, The—Mary E. W. Freeman	326	38.7	342	76.8	668	57.8	13	S
Gallegher—Richard H. Davis	428	87.9	468	82.3	896	85.1	41	S
Game, The—Grantland Rice	294	47.8	350	48.3	644	48.1	11	R
Game, The—Simeon Strunsky	119	64.3	234	59.6	353	62.0	21	S
Game of Chess, The— Kenneth S. Goodman	465	69.5	490	67.6	955	68.6	36	R
Gamesters All—DuBose Heyward	186	66.1	335	59.1	521	62.6	12	R
Gandhi: Fighter Without a Sword—Jeanette Eaton	178	71.9	136	68.8	314	70.4		
Garden by Moonlight, The—Amy Lowell	471	42.4	562	66.3	1033	54.4	41	S
Garden Party, The— Katherine Mansfield	206	54.4	197	77.1	403	65.8	18	S
Gareth and Lynette— Alfred Tennyson	1054	73.1	1315	79.2	2369	76.2	91	S
Gasoline Alley (Comic Strip)	841	62.8	1213	64.7	2054	63.8	44	IR

PUPILS' READING INTERESTS: GRADES 10-12
Ts and Ss = Teachers and Schools   S = Studied in Class
IR = Independent Reading   R = Read in Class

SELECTION—AUTHOR	Boys		Girls		Total		Ts & Ss	
	No.	%	No.	%	No.	Av. %		
Gaunt Gray Wolf, The—Hamlin Garland	245	57.8	324	51.2	569	54.5	11	R
Geese—W. H. Hudson	193	53.6	213	50.7	406	52.2	14	S
General William Booth Enters into Heaven—Vachel Lindsay	203	57.3	219	56.6	422	57.0	14	S
Genius in Exile—Lloyd Osborne	174	63.8	181	70.4	355	67.1	24	S
Gentleman from Indiana, The—Booth Tarkington	135	76.6	179	70.9	314	73.8	130	IR
Gentleman's Agreement —Laura Z. Hobson	92	66.8	197	73.4	289	70.1		
Gentlemen Prefer Blondes—Anita Loos	197	71.1	309	67.8	506	69.5		
George—Hilaire Belloc	500	58.8	505	64.8	1005	61.8	24	R
George Washington—William F. Kirk	307	89.4	347	90.3	654	89.9	10	R
George Washington, Country Gentleman—Paul L. Haworth	196	67.1	166	65.7	362	66.4	28	S
Georgia Autumn—Minnie H. Moody	423	35.1	504	43.6	927	39.4	18	R
Gerry's Rocks (American Ballad)	922	69.8	942	72.6	1864	71.2	32	R
Getting Up-to-Date—Roberta Wayne	199	57.0	337	76.9	536	67.0	13	R
Gettysburg—Percy Mackaye	195	52.8	199	54.5	394	53.7	16	R
Gettysburg Address, The —Abraham Lincoln	566	88.9	827	90.0	1393	89.5	43	S
Get Up and Bar the Door (British Ballad)	379	73.2	400	80.3	779	76.8	27	S
Ghost Horse—Long Lance	368	68.2	367	62.5	735	65.4	13	S
Ghosts of Indians—Witter Bynner	367	40.6	385	47.0	752	43.8	18	R
Giant—Edna Ferber	325	79.2	672	85.2	997	82.2		
Giant, The—Charles Mackay	347	54.9	404	58.2	751	56.6	12	R

PUPILS' READING INTERESTS: GRADES 10-12

Ts and Ss = Teachers and Schools   S = Studied in Class
IR = Independent Reading   R = Read in Class

SELECTION—AUTHOR	Boys		Girls		Total		Ts & Ss	
	No.	%	No.	%	No.	Av. %		
Giant Animals of Today—Raymond L. Ditmars	275	60.4	212	57.3	487	58.9		
Giants in the Earth—O. E. Rölvaag	479	75.1	671	84.4	1150	79.8	40	S
Gift of the Magi, The— O. Henry	680	70.4	764	87.1	1444	78.8	53	S
Gift of Tritemius, The— John G. Whittier	466	53.3	608	66.4	1074	59.9	19	R
Gifts—Ralph W. Emerson	396	58.7	395	67.3	791	63.0	38	S
Gipsying—Witter Bynner	283	43.8	281	53.7	564	48.8	13	R
Girl, A—Babette Deutsch	211	27.7	261	40.6	472	34.2	16	R
Girl Can Dream, A— Betty Cavanna	3		381	65.0				
Girl in White Armor, The—Albert B. Paine	25		225	78.9			109	IR
Girl Trouble—James L. Summers	18		293	61.6				
Glad Young Chamois, The—Burges Johnson	1349	52.3	1435	58.9	2784	55.6	36	R
Glenlogie (British Ballad)	365	48.8	383	64.4	748	56.6	13	R
Glorious Adventure, The —Richard Halliburton	279	76.5	271	78.0	550	77.3	87	IR
Glory Trail, The—Badger Clark	354	63.6	341	57.8	695	60.7	24	S
Glove and the Lions, The—Leigh Hunt	484	64.0	501	66.8	985	65.4	24	R
God of Quiet, The—John Drinkwater	158	37.3	252	43.3	410	40.3	15	S
Go Down, Moses (Negro Spiritual)	388	39.9	405	48.9	793	44.4	13	R
God's Little Acre— Erskine Caldwell	226	69.5	260	65.4	486	67.5		
God's World—Edna St. V. Millay	599	55.0	851	74.3	1450	64.7	55	S
Going on Sixteen—Betty Cavanna	7		563	64.3				
Going Steady—Anne Emery	14		178	69.4				

PUPILS' READING INTERESTS: GRADES 10-12
Ts and Ss = Teachers and Schools   S = Studied in Class
IR = Independent Reading   R = Read in Class

SELECTION—AUTHOR	Boys		Girls		Total		Ts & Ss	
	No.	%	No.	%	No.	Av. %		
Going Up to London— Nancy B. Turner	377	39.5	515	51.2	892	45.4	23	R
Gold Brick, The—Brand Whitlock	430	67.8	408	67.0	838	67.4	18	S
Gold Bug, The—Edgar A. Poe	304	81.3	322	66.8	626	74.1	32	S
Golden City of St. Mary, The—John Masefield	377	52.9	413	62.8	790	57.9	20	R
Golden Youth of Greece, The (Alcibiades) E. F. Benson	234	51.5	196	50.8	430	51.2	16	S
Gold-Mounted Guns— Frederick R. Buckley	297	79.6	411	74.2	708	76.9	23	S
Goliath—Thomas B. Aldrich	285	91.1	391	95.4	676	93.3	13	R
Go, Lovely Rose!— Edmund Waller	189	41.8	240	48.5	429	45.2	17	S
Gone With the Wind— Margaret Mitchell	360	82.2	906	93.8	1266	88.0	57	IR
Goodbye, Mr. Chips— James Hilton	124	80.2	301	76.9	425	78.6	30	IR
Good Bye, My Lady— James Street	54		189	61.3				
Goodbye, Old Paint (Cowboy Ballad)	243	50.0	316	49.4	559	49.7	12	R
Good Earth, The—Pearl Buck	259	76.8	630	85.7	889	81.3	67	IR
Good Morning, Miss Dove—Frances G. Patton	32		173	74.9				
Good Wits Jump—Sheila Kaye-Smith	349	57.7	160	66.6	509	62.2	16	S
Gospel Train, The (Negro Spiritual)	668	40.9	675	48.1	1343	44.5	36	R
Grand Cham's Diamond, The—Allan N. Monkhouse	347	75.2	330	80.3	677	77.8	31	S
Grand Vizier of the Furnace—Frances L. Warner	268	72.8	337	80.3	605	76.6	18	S

PUPILS' READING INTERESTS: GRADES 10-12
Ts and Ss = Teachers and Schools   S = Studied in Class
IR = Independent Reading   R = Read in Class

SELECTION—AUTHOR	Boys		Girls		Total		Ts & Ss
	No.	%	No.	%	No.	Av. %	
Grapes of Wrath, The—John Steinbeck	144	78.1	219	80.1	363	79.1	
Grass—Carl Sandburg	849	62.4	941	65.0	1790	63.7	70 S
Grass, The—Emily Dickinson	222	50.9	377	65.1	599	58.0	19 S
Great American Game, The—William L. Phelps	784	77.2	751	56.8	1535	67.0	68 S
Great Blizzard, The—Hamlin Garland	184	76.6	200	77.8	384	77.2	45 IR
Greatest of These Is Charity, The—Agnes L. Repplier	211	51.2	218	68.3	429	59.8	18 S
Greatest Story Ever Told—Fulton Oursler	75		232	89.4			
Great Inventors—Frank P. Bachman	167	67.7	52				
Great Lover, The—Rupert Brooke	232	46.3	279	66.5	511	56.4	26 S
Great Possessions—David Grayson	135	63.3	175	73.7	310	68.5	106 R
Great Stone Face, The—Nathaniel Hawthorne	162	64.2	184	81.0	346	72.6	16 S
Green Donkey Driver, The—Robert L. Stevenson	210	66.9	263	64.4	473	65.7	17 S
Green Grass of Wyoming, The—Mary O'Hara	97	72.2	179	74.9	276	73.6	
Green Grow the Rushes—Robert Burns	251	38.8	322	42.1	573	40.5	18 R
Green Mansions—William H. Hudson	151	74.5	218	80.0	369	77.3	16 S
Green Mountain Boys, The—D. P. Thompson	393	70.4	171	55.8	564	63.1	
Green Pastures, The—Marc Connelly	140	75.0	193	71.8	333	73.4	22 R
Green River—William C. Bryant	215	52.8	262	63.0	477	57.9	16 R
Greeting, A—William H. Davies	246	50.6	320	66.9	566	58.8	22 S

PUPILS' READING INTERESTS: GRADES 10-12

Ts and Ss = Teachers and Schools   S = Studied in Class
IR = Independent Reading   R = Read in Class

SELECTION—AUTHOR	Boys		Girls		Total		Ts & Ss	
	No.	%	No.	%	No.	Av. %		
Growth of the Soil, The —Knut Hamsun	135	58.9	151	62.3	286	60.6	156	IR
Guadalcanal Diary— Richard Tregaskis	242	93.4	263	92.6	505	93.0	17	IR
Guest, The—Edward Dunsany	340	60.6	391	75.3	731	68.0	14	R
Guinevere—Alfred Tennyson	269	53.2	295	75.1	564	64.2	30	S
Gulf Winds—Lafcadio Hearn	242	61.4	228	62.5	470	62.0	23	S
Gulliver's Travels— Jonathan Swift	422	71.3	308	62.8	730	67.1	33	S
Gulliver the Great— Walter A. Dyer	279	88.2	337	90.9	616	89.6	31	R
Gunga Din—Rudyard Kipling	1005	85.9	1017	81.9	2022	83.9	70	S
Guns of Bull Run, The— Joseph Altsheler	241	76.6	52					
Guns of Navarone, The (Book)—Alistair MacLean	225	90.4	129	82.9	354	86.7		
Guy Mannering—Walter Scott	223	68.8	80				108	IR
Gypsy Girl, The—Ralph Hodgson	293	51.7	321	66.0	614	58.9	14	R
Gypsy Trail, The— Rudyard Kipling	266	44.7	334	47.9	600	46.3	18	R
Haircut—Ring Lardner	266	83.8	313	79.1	579	81.5	11	R
Halcyon Days—Edwin M. Robinson	167	67.4	189	67.5	356	67.5	18	S
Half-Pint Flask, The— DuBose Heyward	447	75.4	502	76.3	949	75.9	17	R
Hallmarks of American— H. L. Mencken	317	48.3	376	48.1	693	48.2	14	R
Hamlet—William Shakespeare	708	72.6	622	79.1	1330	75.9	73	S
Hammers, The—Ralph Hodgson	230	58.5	249	56.0	479	57.3	15	S
Hammock Nights— William Beebe	302	60.1	348	48.0	650	54.1	19	R

PUPILS' READING INTERESTS: GRADES 10-12

Ts and Ss = Teachers and Schools   S = Studied in Class
IR = Independent Reading   R = Read in Class

SELECTION—AUTHOR	Boys		Girls		Total		Ts & Ss	
	No.	%	No.	%	No.	Av. %		
Hand of Siva, The—K. S. Goodman and Ben Hecht	211	78.7	269	75.3	480	77.0	18	S
Hannah Armstrong—Edgar L. Masters	270	63.0	455	75.7	725	69.4	21	R
Hans Brinker—Mary M. Dodge	134	63.4	222	73.0	356	68.2		
Happiness—Robert Burns	287	31.4	304	45.4	591	38.4	11	R
Happiness—Guy de Maupassant	256	48.2	284	69.4	540	58.8	24	S
Harbor, The—Carl Sandburg	362	48.2	427	53.5	789	50.9	41	S
Hardscrabble Hellas—Lucien Price	192	70.6	238	72.1	430	71.4	17	S
Hare and the Hounds, The—Aesop	478	62.7	560	54.0	1038	58.4	26	R
Hark! Hark! The Lark—William Shakespeare	3417	36.6	3523	49.1	6940	42.9	122	R
Haunted and the Haunters, The—Edward Bulwer-Lytton	167	78.7	144	77.8	311	78.3	16	S
Haunted Bookshop, The—Christopher Morley	121	71.9	369	74.8	490	73.4	119	IR
Haunted Palace, The—Edgar A. Poe	242	52.1	290	52.6	532	52.4	12	S
Havelok, The Dane—George P. Krapp	313	71.2	439	72.2	752	71.7	12	R
Hawaii—James A. Michener	225	88.4	355	88.7	580	88.6		
Heart of Little Shikara, The—Edison Marshall	276	79.5	337	82.9	613	81.2	23	S
He Asked the Dean—Benfield Pressey	172	59.3	376	67.8	548	63.6	13	S
Height of the Ridiculous, The—Oliver W. Holmes	327	74.0	346	78.8	673	76.4	24	S
Helena's Husband—Philip Moeller	204	69.9	246	81.5	450	75.7	16	S
Helen Keller Story, The—Catherine O. Peare	81	75.3	445	87.9	526	81.6		

PUPILS' READING INTERESTS: GRADES 10-12
Ts and Ss = Teachers and Schools   S = Studied in Class
IR = Independent Reading   R = Read in Class

SELECTION—AUTHOR	Boys		Girls		Total		Ts & Ss	
	No.	%	No.	%	No.	Av. %		
Hell-Gate of Soissons, The—Herbert Kaufman	415	79.3	412	63.3	827	71.3	16	R
Hem and Haw—Bliss Carman	438	67.6	465	70.1	903	68.9	22	S
Henry (Comic Strip)	859	66.2	1084	63.4	1943	64.8	54	IR
Henry V—William Shakespeare	222	53.2	301	53.3	523	53.3	21	S
Henry Ford—Edwin C. Hill	392	74.9	447	67.4	839	71.2	14	R
Hercules—Frances E. Sabin	278	59.0	448	44.3	726	51.7	13	R
Here's a Health to King Charles—Walter Scott	3342	49.5	3432	52.0	6774	50.8	118	R
Her First Ball—Katherine Mansfield	284	57.0	346	87.0	630	72.0	12	R
Her Letter—Bret Harte	249	61.5	266	85.0	515	73.3	18	S
Hero—Albert P. Terhune	502	87.1	551	88.8	1053	88.0	82	IR
Hervé Riel—Robert Browning	299	77.6	339	68.4	638	73.0	39	S
He Who Married a Dumb Wife—François Rabelais	295	34.1	310	35.3	605	34.7	15	R
Heyday of the Blood, The—Dorothy C. Fisher	338	71.8	288	74.5	626	73.2	28	S
He Wishes for the Cloths of Heaven— William B. Yeats	300	26.2	411	40.3	711	33.3	12	R
Hiawatha—Henry W. Longfellow	227	67.8	333	67.4	560	67.6	13	S
High Heart, The—Aline Kilmer	408	45.1	503	61.1	911	53.1	14	R
Highland Mary—Robert Burns	248	54.0	291	71.7	539	62.9	21	S
Highpockets—John R. Tunis	158	76.6	66					
Highwayman, The— Alfred Noyes	1109	83.1	1882	88.8	2991	86.0	95	S
Hills—Arthur Guiterman	292	65.4	235	69.6	527	67.5	22	S
Hindoo Legend, A— George Birdseye	239	76.6	294	81.0	533	78.8	19	R

PUPILS' READING INTERESTS: GRADES 10-12
Ts and Ss = Teachers and Schools   S = Studied in Class
IR = Independent Reading   R = Read in Class

SELECTION—AUTHOR	Boys		Girls		Total		Ts & Ss
	No.	%	No.	%	No.	Av. %	
Hiroshima—John Hersey	249	85.5	105	83.3	354	84.4	
His Mother's Son—Edna Ferber	287	73.5	294	84.2	581	78.9	14 S
History of the English Speaking Peoples—Winston Churchill	161	67.1	113	59.7	274	63.4	
Hohenlinden—Thomas Campbell	215	62.6	267	50.9	482	56.8	16 S
Holding a Baby—Heywood Broun	362	64.1	373	75.5	735	69.8	29 S
Holy Grail, The—Alfred Tennyson	179	67.6	285	66.5	464	67.1	21 S
Holy Ireland—Joyce Kilmer	267	74.7	277	78.7	544	76.7	29 S
Home Is the Sailor—Bill Adams	261	82.4	372	77.8	633	80.1	16 R
Home Life in the White House—Corinne R. Robinson	300	68.7	373	73.3	673	71.0	24 S
Home on the Range, A (Cowboy Ballad)	302	75.7	317	86.4	619	81.1	13 R
Homer and Humbug—Stephen Leacock	309	58.4	341	60.1	650	59.3	25 S
Home Song, A—Henry Van Dyke	1139	56.2	1213	71.6	2352	63.9	30 R
Home, Sweet Home—John H. Payne	362	51.1	456	70.1	818	60.6	23 R
Home Thoughts from Abroad—Robert Browning	869	47.9	976	64.4	1845	56.2	84 S
Home Thoughts from Europe—Henry Van Dyke	875	78.9	878	87.9	1753	83.4	29 R
Home Thoughts from the Sea—Robert Browning	172	55.2	215	60.7	387	58.0	29 S
Home Truths from Abroad—Unknown	346	38.6	397	49.0	743	43.8	16 R
Hopalong Cassidy—Clarence E. Mulford	149	47.0	119	40.8	268	43.9	

PUPILS' READING INTERESTS: GRADES 10-12
Ts and Ss = Teachers and Schools　　　S = Studied in Class
IR = Independent Reading　　　　　　R = Read in Class

SELECTION—AUTHOR	Boys		Girls		Total		Ts & Ss	
	No.	%	No.	%	No.	Av. %		
Horatius at the Bridge—Thomas B. Macaulay	238	73.7	299	63.7	537	68.7	22	S
Horrible Cow—Edward Lear	462	33.2	516	40.1	978	36.7	21	R
Horse, The—Oliver Hereford	338	44.8	385	41.4	723	43.1	13	R
Horse, The—Edward V. Lucas	228	47.6	231	54.5	459	51.1	13	S
Horseman in the Sky, The—Ambrose Bierce	533	69.7	520	63.0	1053	66.4	24	S
Horse Thief, The—William R. Benét	199	71.6	293	65.2	492	68.4	20	S
Hospital Song—Phyllis McGinley	286	51.2	337	70.5	623	60.9	10	R
Hosts and Guests—Max Beerbohm	154	47.7	285	54.2	439	51.0	14	S
Hot Rod—Henry G. Felsen	197	81.7	59					
Hot Weather Song, A—Don Marquis	352	52.6	360	66.1	712	59.4	11	R
Hound of the Baskervilles, The—A. Conan Doyle	279	77.4	196	71.4	475	74.4		
House by the Side of the Road, The— Sam W. Foss	204	62.3	213	79.6	417	71.0	17	S
Household Gods—E. V. Lucas	145	55.9	189	62.4	334	59.2	19	S
House of the Seven Gables, The— Nathaniel Hawthorne	2035	65.4	2469	81.3	4504	73.4	175	S
House on the Hill, The—Edwin A. Robinson	177	52.0	327	66.1	504	59.1	20	S
House with Nobody in It, The—Joyce Kilmer	271	81.0	324	93.8	595	87.4	13	R
How a Fisherman Corked Up His Foe in a Jar— Guy W. Carryl	319	56.1	297	56.7	616	56.4	12	R
How Come Christmas—Roark Bradford	170	69.7	174	68.1	344	68.9	89	R

PUPILS' READING INTERESTS: GRADES 10-12

Ts and Ss = Teachers and Schools   S = Studied in Class
IR = Independent Reading   R = Read in Class

SELECTION—AUTHOR	Boys		Girls		Total		Ts & Ss	
	No.	%	No.	%	No.	Av. %		
How Do I Love Thee?—Elizabeth B. Browning	271	49.8	422	73.9	693	61.9	28	S
How Gavin Birse Put It to Meg Lownie— James M. Barrie	465	46.1	434	57.7	899	51.9	41	S
How Green Was My Valley—Richard Llewellyn	169	66.6	457	84.9	626	75.8	48	IR
How I Found America—Anzia Yezierska	474	63.5	593	81.1	1067	72.3	30	S
How Oswald Dined with God—Edwin Markham	274	38.5	332	46.5	606	42.5	16	R
How Santa Claus Came to Simpson's Bar— Bret Harte	398	71.7	195	67.4	593	69.6	18	S
How Sleep the Brave—William Collins	541	55.5	554	56.9	1095	56.2	15	R
How the Great Guest Came—Edwin Markham	150	76.0	301	90.4	451	83.2	19	S
How the Locks of the Panama Canal Are Operated—Scientific American	150	71.3	163	36.2	313	53.8	17	S
How the Waters Came Down at Ladore—Robert Southey	350	25.9	406	49.8	756	37.9	10	R
How They Brought the Good News from Ghent to Aix—Robert Browing	336	72.5	368	70.8	704	71.7	45	S
How to Catch a Bird—Leland B. Jacobs	294	52.4	326	53.2	620	52.8	11	R
How to Eat Watermelon —William A. White	291	59.1	272	63.8	563	61.5	15	R
How to Make History Dates Stick—Mark Twain	206	59.7	413	67.1	619	63.4	20	S
How to Tell a Story—Mark Twain	156	70.2	144	73.6	300	71.9	24	S
How to Tell the Wild Animals—Carolyn Wells	298	44.6	310	57.6	608	51.1	15	R

PUPILS' READING INTERESTS: GRADES 10-12
Ts and Ss = Teachers and Schools   S = Studied in Class
IR = Independent Reading   R = Read in Class

SELECTION—AUTHOR	Boys		Girls		Total		Ts & Ss
	No.	%	No.	%	No.	Av. %	
How to Win Friends and Influence People— Dale Carnegie	154	64.9	285	64.4	439	64.7	
How to Write Short Stories—Ring Lardner	197	67.8	241	62.4	438	65.1	15	S
Huckleberry Finn—Mark Twain	255	91.2	301	90.5	556	90.9	21	S
Hugh Wynne—S. Weir Mitchell	351	62.7	258	61.8	609	62.3	27	S
Human—Zona Gale	260	68.1	285	83.0	545	75.6	14	R
Human Comedy, The— William Saroyan	196	81.1	551	85.5	747	83.3	52	IR
Humanity's First Wings —Mitchell W. Charnley	369	88.6	368	67.1	737	77.9	19	S
Human Saturation Point, The—Elwood Hendrick	256	57.2	301	54.0	557	55.6	17	R
Human Traits in the Farmyard—Samuel A. Derieux	334	89.2	373	89.0	707	89.1	14	R
Humble-Bee, The— Ralph W. Emerson	393	51.7	485	57.6	878	54.7	31	S
Humor as I See It— Stephen Leacock	188	62.5	228	65.8	416	64.2	18	S
Hunchback of Notre Dame, The—Victor Hugo	309	77.2	243	78.2	552	77.7	
Hundred Collars, A— Robert Frost	242	70.7	325	66.3	567	68.5	16	R
Hunger—Anzia Yezierska	364	50.5	277	69.9	641	60.2	29	S
Hungry Heart, The— Edna St. V. Millay	338	20.3	374	28.1	712	24.2	15	R
Hymn—Paul L. Dunbar	703	44.2	710	50.4	1413	47.3	31	R
Hymn to the Night— Henry W. Longfellow	173	52.0	197	64.0	370	58.0	15	S
Ice Cart, The—Wilfred W. Gibson	298	38.9	284	47.9	582	43.4	12	R
"Ice Water, Pl----!"— Fannie Hurst	426	60.0	381	83.9	807	72.0	33	S

PUPILS' READING INTERESTS: GRADES 10-12
Ts and Ss = Teachers and Schools   S = Studied in Class
IR = Independent Reading   R = Read in Class

SELECTION—AUTHOR	Boys		Girls		Total		Ts & Ss
	No.	%	No.	%	No.	Av. %	
Ides of March, The— Thornton Wilder	169	51.5	168	57.4	337	54.5	
I Do Not Love Thee— Thomas Brown	189	32.8	242	38.2	431	35.5	15 R
Idylls of the King, The— Alfred Tennyson	2255	62.6	2843	69.9	5098	66.3	190 S
I Entertain an Agent Unawares—David Grayson	590	73.8	517	80.0	1107	76.9	61 S
If—Rudyard Kipling	209	75.4	247	83.8	456	79.6	25 S
I Get a Colt to Break In —Lincoln Steffens	341	81.7	362	84.0	703	82.9	13 R
I Have a Rendezvous with Death—Alan Seeger	1238	67.4	1350	73.9	2588	70.7	79 S
I Hear America Singing —Walt Whitman	724	49.3	750	63.3	1474	56.3	39 S
I Kid You Not—Jack Paar	219	73.5	279	63.6	498	68.6	
I Knew a Black Beetle— Christopher Morley	385	76.6	392	86.0	777	81.3	16 R
Ile—Eugene O'Neill	718	74.3	1204	72.6	1922	73.5	59 S
Iliad, The—Homer	603	54.0	554	46.3	1157	50.2	75 S
I'll Cry Tomorrow— Lillian Roth	194	65.5	780	85.7	974	75.6	
I'll Stay in Canada— Stephen Leacock	376	75.1	369	81.7	745	78.4	10 R
Il Penseroso—John Milton	1263	50.8	1157	67.9	2420	59.4	135 S
I'm a Fool—Sherwood Anderson	399	89.7	488	87.1	887	88.4	18 R
Images—Richard Aldington	187	53.5	390	69.0	577	61.3	18 S
Imaginary Portrait— Rebecca McCann	254	48.6	367	63.7	621	56.2	11 R
Imagine Yourself—Don Marquis	356	79.4	410	85.9	766	82.7	16 R
I Married Adventure— Osa Johnson	219	79.0	389	79.8	608	79.4	54 IR
I. M. Margaritae Sorori— William E. Henley	376	48.0	509	60.8	885	54.4	29 S

PUPILS' READING INTERESTS: GRADES 10-12

Ts and Ss = Teachers and Schools   S = Studied in Class

IR = Independent Reading   R = Read in Class

SELECTION—AUTHOR	Boys		Girls		Total		Ts & Ss	
	No.	%	No.	%	No.	Av. %		
I'm Nobody! Who Are You?—Emily Dickinson	237	56.5	259	69.5	496	63.0	20	S
Importance of Being Earnest, The— Oscar Wilde	160	64.1	265	64.2	425	64.2		
In After Days—Austin Dobson	448	56.7	473	66.4	921	61.6	34	S
In a Restaurant—Wilfrid W. Gibson	194	52.8	358	61.5	552	57.2	19	S
In a Station of the Metro —Ezra Pound	431	16.5	426	21.9	857	19.2	28	R
Inchcape Rock, The— Robert Southey	570	69.2	611	63.0	1181	66.1	24	S
Incident of the French Camp, An— Robert Browing	840	83.7	1077	76.6	1917	80.2	76	S
Incorrigible—Burges Johnson	321	58.1	383	69.3	704	63.7	16	R
In Defense of Anglers— Izaak Walton	148	68.6	153	48.7	301	58.7	18	S
In Defense of Children— Arthur Guiterman	332	56.0	420	63.3	752	59.7	18	R
In Defense of Ignorance —Alfred G. Gardiner	124	52.8	323	55.6	447	54.2	17	S
Indian Burying Ground, The—Philip Freneau	390	67.6	467	61.2	857	64.4	38	S
Indian Serenade, The — Percy B. Shelley	176	49.1	229	61.4	405	55.3	19	S
Indian Summer—Emily Dickinson	396	59.8	399	65.5	795	62.7	32	S
Indian Summer—Lew Sarett	432	52.4	502	62.5	934	58.0	18	R
Indian Summer Day on the Prairie, An— Vachel Lindsay	257	61.9	300	70.0	557	66.0	19	S
In Explanation—Walter Learned	295	69.7	308	68.8	603	69.3	11	R
In Flanders Fields—John McCrae	506	79.2	569	88.8	1075	84.0	51	S
Information Please	263	69.0	329	70.7	592	69.9		

PUPILS' READING INTERESTS: GRADES 10-12
Ts and Ss = Teachers and Schools   S = Studied in Class
IR = Independent Reading   R = Read in Class

SELECTION—AUTHOR	Boys		Girls		Total		Ts & Ss	
	No.	%	No.	%	No.	Av. %		
Ingenue of the Sierras, An—Bret Harte	155	57.4	168	68.3	323	62.9	17	S
Ingo—Christopher Morley	408	65.0	293	72.9	701	69.0	33	S
In Hardin County, 1809—Lulu E. Thompson	743	76.2	846	80.0	1589	78.1	26	R
Initiative—Elbert Hubbard	644	51.3	734	54.8	1378	53.1	19	R
Inland Voyage, An— Robert L. Stevenson	401	53.9	359	46.0	760	50.0	35	S
Innocence—Rose W. Lane	168	59.8	289	72.1	457	66.0	19	S
Inn of the Two Witches, The—Joseph Conrad	239	65.9	190	58.7	429	62.3	17	S
In Praise of Izaak Walton — Herbert Hoover	264	67.6	240	53.1	504	60.4	25	S
In Quebec—Rudyard Kipling	636	65.6	691	69.3	1327	67.5	28	R
In Romney Marsh—John Davidson	243	51.2	311	56.4	554	53.8	21	S
In School Days—John G. Whittier	690	66.7	769	87.5	1459	77.1	31	S
Inscribed on the Collar of a Dog— Alexander Pope	1130	47.7	1238	62.8	2368	55.3	32	R
Inscription on the Ceiling of a Bedroom— Dorothy Parker	289	45.3	397	62.5	686	53.9	17	R
Insects Are Winning, The—William A. Du Puy	387	46.8	441	45.7	828	46.3	33	S
In Service—Winifred Letts	187	58.0	308	77.8	495	67.9	19	S
Inside Africa—John Gunther	229	77.3	173	74.3	402	75.8		
Inside Russia Today— John Gunther	199	79.9	161	77.0	360	78.5		
Insight—Dorothy Aldis	300	40.5	421	55.7	721	48.1	11	R
Instans Tyrannus— Robert Browing	173	53.5	214	53.0	387	53.3	21	S

PUPILS' READING INTERESTS: GRADES 10-12
Ts and Ss = Teachers and Schools   S = Studied in Class
IR = Independent Reading   R = Read in Class

SELECTION—AUTHOR	Boys		Girls		Total		Ts & Ss	
	No.	%	No.	%	No.	Av. %		
Instrument of the Gods, An—Lincoln Colcord	175	81.1	347	60.1	522	70.6	15	S
Interview with President Lincoln, An— Artemus Ward	362	50.4	387	56.1	749	53.3	12	R
In the City—T. B. C. Wilson	243	27.0	328	39.8	571	33.4	13	R
In the Garden of Proserpine—Algernon C. Swinburne	196	49.0	219	61.2	415	55.1	15	S
In the Light of Myth— Rannie B. Baker	130	45.4	180	62.8	310	54.1	30	IR
In the Matter of a Private—Rudyard Kipling	181	66.9	166	46.4	347	56.7	16	S
In the Time of the Breaking of Nations— Thomas Hardy	268	54.5	284	55.3	552	54.9	17	S
In the Zone—Eugene O'Neill	309	89.2	343	83.1	652	86.2	12	S
Introduction of Two Persons, An—Edward Bok	145	69.7	368	70.0	513	69.9	17	S
Introspective Reflections —Ogden Nash	280	38.2	337	51.9	617	45.1	10	R
Invictus—William E. Henley	724	58.4	967	65.8	1691	62.1	86	S
I Remember, I Remember—Thomas Hood	410	56.3	387	73.8	797	65.1	14	R
Iron Duke, The—John R. Tunis	201	75.6	17					
Irreverent Brahmin, The —Arthur Guiterman	278	49.3	330	58.2	608	53.8	14	R
I Saw a Man—Stephen Crane	210	53.6	193	35.9	403	44.8	16	S
I Shall Not Care—Sara Teasdale	575	52.2	691	69.3	1266	60.8	43	S
Israel Drake—Katherine Mayo	390	85.1	358	69.1	748	77.1	18	S

PUPILS' READING INTERESTS: GRADES 10-12
Ts and Ss = Teachers and Schools   S = Studied in Class
IR = Independent Reading   R = Read in Class

SELECTION—AUTHOR	Boys		Girls		Total		Ts & Ss	
	No.	%	No.	%	No.	Av. %		
Israfel—Edgar A. Poe	245	43.3	314	49.0	559	46.2	23	S
Is There a Santa Claus?—Francis P. Church	236	55.3	289	68.7	525	62.0	18	S
I Swim the Hellespont—Richard Halliburton	335	73.1	366	72.8	701	73.0	25	S
Italian in England, The—Robert Browing	213	65.3	245	73.9	458	69.6	29	S
It Is a Beauteous Evening—William Wordsworth	499	52.6	683	71.3	1182	62.0	57	S
It's a Queer Time—Robert Graves	258	86.0	300	79.8	558	82.9	11	S
It's So Hard to Make Them Happy— Hugh McN. Kahler	344	47.7	176	63.1	520	55.4	13	S
Ivanhoe—Walter Scott	765	80.1	778	73.7	1543	76.9	54	S
I Wanted to Be an Actress—Katherine Cornell	12		169	75.1			130	IR
I Was a Teen-Age Dwarf—Max Shulman	150	69.3	305	72.1	455	70.7		
Jabberwocky—Lewis Carroll	391	35.9	509	39.5	900	37.7	17	R
Jaffar—Leigh Hunt	454	29.7	447	35.5	901	32.6	14	R
Jalna—Mazo de la Roche	26		214	79.4			159	IR
Jane Addams of Hull House—Winifred E. Wise	103	52.9	651	72.4	754	62.7		
Jane Eyre—Charlotte Brontë	124	66.5	967	90.6	1091	78.6	91	IR
Jane Jones—Ben King	534	60.3	528	66.9	1062	63.6	20	R
Janice Meredith—Paul L. Ford	4		368	77.6			161	IR
Janitor's Boy, The—Nathalia Crane	568	73.0	921	85.6	1489	79.3	45	S
January Summer, A—Dallas Lore Sharp	201	60.7	315	76.8	516	68.8	16	S
Jason and the Argonauts—Frances E. Sabin	248	38.1	304	52.3	552	45.2	12	R
Jazz Fantasia—Carl Sandburg	268	60.8	298	56.9	566	58.9	22	S

PUPILS' READING INTERESTS: GRADES 10-12
Ts and Ss = Teachers and Schools S = Studied in Class
IR = Independent Reading R = Read in Class

SELECTION—AUTHOR	Boys		Girls		Total		Ts & Ss	
	No.	%	No.	%	No.	Av. %		
Jean—Robert Burns	256	46.5	296	62.0	552	54.3	16	S
Jean-ah Poquelin— George W. Cable	372	75.7	383	80.3	755	78.0	37	S
Jesse James (American Ballad)	520	68.5	506	71.5	1026	70.0	21	R
Jesse James—William Rose Benét	238	88.2	242	81.2	480	84.7	25	S
Jest 'Fore Christmas— Eugene Field	350	79.3	470	87.7	820	83.5	20	S
Jethro's Pet—Robert P. T. Coffin	408	72.2	425	77.6	833	74.9	13	R
Jim—Bret Harte	445	78.3	437	81.4	882	79.9	26	S
Jim Bludso—John Hay	921	82.0	929	73.5	1850	77.8	67	S
Jim Davis—John Masefield	466	80.4	312	75.2	778	77.8	217	IR
Jim Jay—Walter de la Mare	284	38.4	333	45.1	617	41.8	10	R
Joan, the Warrior Maid— Albert B. Paine	326	63.3	344	73.7	670	68.5	16	R
Jock o' Hazeldean— Walter Scott	190	52.4	237	53.0	427	52.7	17	S
Joe Grimm—Heywood Broun	324	74.2	365	79.9	689	77.1	12	R
Joe Palooka (Comic Strip)	916	71.0	1104	52.3	2020	61.7	54	IR
John Anderson, My Jo— Robert Burns	770	52.7	857	63.1	1627	57.9	57	S
John Brown's Body— Stephen V. Benét	178	69.4	157	60.8	335	65.1	19	S
John G.—Katherine Mayo	275	75.1	349	65.3	624	70.2	21	S
John Gilpin's Ride— William Cowper	186	72.6	145	73.8	331	73.2	25	S
John Henry and His Hammer—Harold W. Felton	190	77.6	47					
John Horace Burleson— Edgar L. Masters	181	48.9	241	54.2	422	51.6	19	S
Johnnie Armstrong (British Ballad)	345	61.2	361	47.8	706	54.5	13	R

PUPILS' READING INTERESTS: GRADES 10-12

Ts and Ss = Teachers and Schools   S = Studied in Class

IR = Independent Reading   R = Read in Class

SELECTION—AUTHOR	Boys		Girls		Total		Ts & Ss	
	No.	%	No.	%	No.	Av. %		
Johnnie Cock (British Ballad)	218	50.7	264	42.4	482	46.6	13	R
Johnnie's First Moose— William H. Drummond	599	77.0	608	68.7	1207	72.9	31	R
Johnny Tremain—Esther Forbes	197	75.4	217	76.7	414	76.1	130	IR
Johnson as a Conversationalist— James Boswell	149	36.9	176	44.0	325	40.5	23	S
Jonah—Lydia Gibson	282	38.3	335	38.1	617	38.2	11	R
Joseph the Dreamer— The Bible	227	73.1	468	81.2	695	77.2	10	R
Journey's End—R. C. Sherriff	354	81.4	374	84.2	728	82.8	32	S
Joys of the Road, The— Bliss Carman	127	57.1	253	70.8	380	64.0	18	S
Judge Lynch—J. Edgar Jones	226	75.0	225	61.1	451	68.1	19	S
Julie—Christopher Morley	185	54.3	367	76.6	552	65.5	17	S
Julius Caesar—William Shakespeare	3020	65.3	3315	61.1	6335	63.2	210	S
Jungle, The—Upton Sinclair	297	70.5	203	69.5	500	70.0		
Jungle Beach, A— William Beebe	223	60.1	344	53.9	567	57.0	17	S
Jungle Books, The— Rudyard Kipling	306	66.7	228	62.5	534	64.6		
Jungle Night—William Beebe	517	72.6	511	67.0	1028	69.8	57	S
Jungle Peace—William Beebe	182	64.0	205	48.0	387	56.0	15	S
Junior Miss—Sally Benson	44		1164	72.7				
Jury of Her Peers, A— Susan Glaspell	139	65.5	319	82.1	458	73.8	14	R
Just a Piece of Lettuce and Some Lemon Juice, Thank You—Ogden Nash	298	50.8	372	64.5	670	57.7	14	R
Justice—John Galsworthy	231	69.9	291	74.1	522	72.0	27	S

PUPILS' READING INTERESTS: GRADES 10-12
Ts and Ss = Teachers and Schools   S = Studied in Class
IR = Independent Reading   R = Read in Class

SELECTION—AUTHOR	Boys		Girls		Total		Ts & Ss	
	No.	%	No.	%	No.	Av. %		
Just Patty—Jean Webster	2		419	70.0			133	IR
Karen—Marie Killilea	5		212	83.0				
Katherine Jaffray (British Ballad)	192	48.2	233	68.5	425	58.4	20	S
Kazan—Oliver Curwood	264	89.2	138	87.3	402	88.3	70	IR
Keep a-Pluggin' Away—Paul L. Dunbar	305	54.8	350	59.4	655	57.1	14	R
Kelly Kid, The—Kathleen Norris and Dan Totheroh	312	78.7	265	88.7	577	83.7	12	R
Kentucky Babe—Richard H. Buck	664	51.4	747	71.1	1411	61.3	29	R
Kerry Drake (Comic Strip)	180	69.4	202	71.3	382	70.4	37	IR
Keys of the Kingdom, The—A. J. Cronin	205	86.1	722	92.3	927	89.2	67	IR
Kid Comes Back, The—John R. Tunis	224	71.4	18					
Kid from Tompkinsville, The—John R. Tunis	242	75.8	32					
Kidnapped—Robert L. Stevenson	284	73.5	275	75.1	559	74.3	26	S
Kids Say the Darndest Things—Art Linkletter	736	83.2	1090	84.9	1826	84.1		
Killers, The—Ernest Hemingway	203	79.6	290	79.7	493	79.7	13	R
Killers—Carl Sandburg	344	57.9	394	58.5	738	58.2	15	R
Kim—Rudyard Kipling	164	78.0	222	75.4	386	76.7	39	IR
King, The—Rudyard Kipling	271	25.8	331	34.4	602	30.1	18	R
King Lear—William Shakespeare	167	61.7	227	67.4	394	64.6	26	S
King Midas (Greek Myth)	217	46.5	249	57.8	466	52.2		
King of Boyville, The—William A. White	330	87.7	372	94.8	702	91.3	12	R
King of the Golden River, The—John Ruskin	194	64.7	329	65.2	523	65.0	54	IR
King Robert of Sicily—Henry W. Longfellow	200	77.8	408	78.9	608	78.4	24	S

PUPILS' READING INTERESTS: GRADES 10-12
Ts and Ss = Teachers and Schools   S = Studied in Class
IR = Independent Reading   R = Read in Class

SELECTION—AUTHOR	Boys No.	%	Girls No.	%	Total No.	Av. %	Ts & Ss	
King Solomon's Mines—H. Rider Haggard	502	89.7	215	73.0	717	76.9		
Kit Carson—Stanley Vestal	439	77.2	128	63.3	567	70.3	130	IR
Kit Carson's Ride—Joaquin Miller	371	78.7	313	74.0	684	76.4	26	S
Kit Carson, Trail Blazer—Doris S. Garst	389	56.7	115	41.9	504	49.3		
Kitchen Gods—Gulielma F. Alsop	167	41.0	300	68.7	467	54.9	14	S
Kitten, A—Agnes L. Repplier	442	55.8	517	71.3	959	63.6	52	S
Kitty Foyle—Christopher Morley	27		156	63.1				
Kitty of Coleraine—Charles D. Shanley	264	65.2	317	75.7	581	70.5	18	S
Knickerbocker History of New York, A—Washington Irving	179	57.8	229	61.4	408	59.6	20	S
Knight, The—Geoffrey Chaucer	194	29.9	302	26.7	496	28.3	19	R
Knives from Syria—Lynn Riggs	399	55.0	337	82.5	736	68.8	16	R
Knute Rockne—Guernsey Van Riper	195	84.9	53					
Knute Rockne, All American—Harry A. Stuhldreher	427	92.0	160	82.8	587	87.4	85	IR
Koch—The Death Fighter—Paul De Kruif	165	77.9	190	75.3	355	76.6	21	S
Kon-Tiki—Thor Heyerdahl	940	83.9	670	76.9	1610	80.4		
Krambambuli—Marie Ebner-Eschenbach	250	89.0	310	89.2	560	89.1	12	R
Kubla Khan—Samuel T. Coleridge	581	58.7	547	51.2	1128	55.0	43	S
La Belle Dame Sans Merci—John Keats	484	48.8	539	62.9	1023	55.9	48	S
Labor—Carl Sandburg	403	66.0	500	62.2	903	64.1	14	R

PUPILS' READING INTERESTS: GRADES 10-12
Ts and Ss = Teachers and Schools   S = Studied in Class
IR = Independent Reading   R = Read in Class

SELECTION—AUTHOR	Boys		Girls		Total		Ts & Ss	
	No.	%	No.	%	No.	Av. %		
Laboratory, The—Robert Browning	203	55.9	234	53.0	437	54.5	15	S
Labrador Doctor, A— Wilfred T. Grenfell	418	78.3	306	76.6	724	77.5	24	S
Lad and Wolf—Albert P. Terhune	326	85.7	262	85.3	588	85.5	66	IR
Laddie—Gene S. Porter	89	62.9	273	71.6	362	67.3		
Lady, A—Amy Lowell	344	45.5	323	71.7	667	58.6	29	S
Lady Clara Vere de Vere —Alfred Tennyson	220	43.9	293	64.8	513	54.4	20	R
Lady Clare—Alfred Tennyson	440	44.4	581	76.2	1021	60.3	26	R
Lady New Luck— Clinton Dangerfield	126	78.2	191	80.1	317	79.2	122	IR
Lady of Shalott, The— Alfred Tennyson	286	58.7	278	74.6	564	66.7	30	S
Lady of the Lake, The— Walter Scott	367	48.5	412	63.1	779	55.8	23	S
Lady or the Tiger, The— Frank R. Stockton	458	80.0	533	86.1	991	83.1	29	S
Lady with a Lamp, The —Lytton Strachey	331	59.1	351	80.2	682	69.7	18	S
Laffing—Josh Billings	240	70.8	332	70.9	572	70.9	16	R
Lake Isle of Innisfree, The—William B. Yeats	211	60.9	267	64.8	478	62.9	22	S
L'Allegro—John Milton	1235	53.5	1087	71.4	2322	62.5	127	S
Lancelot and Elaine— Alfred Tennyson	1127	71.4	1363	86.6	2490	79.0	90	S
Land—Sinclair Lewis	168	67.0	224	72.8	392	69.9	34	IR
Land of Heart's Desire, The—Myra Kelly	224	52.5	228	64.9	452	58.7	13	S
Land o' the Leal, The— Carolina Nairne	265	29.6	277	41.5	542	35.6	14	S
Lantern in Her Hand, A —Bess S. Aldrich	14		216	79.6			135	IR
Larrie O'Dee—William W. Fink	301	82.1	312	89.3	613	85.7	11	R
Lasca—Frank Desprez	335	70.6	351	76.1	686	73.4	27	S

PUPILS' READING INTERESTS: GRADES 10-12

Ts and Ss = Teachers and Schools   S = Studied in Class
IR = Independent Reading   R = Read in Class

SELECTION—AUTHOR	Boys		Girls		Total		Ts & Ss	
	No.	%	No.	%	No.	Av. %		
Lassie Come Home— Eric Knight	126	82.1	315	87.5	441	84.8	16	IR
Last Angry Man, The— Gerald Green	412	78.0	572	76.5	984	77.3		
Last Buccaneer, The— Charles Kingsley	275	71.5	294	58.5	569	65.0	14	S
Last Days of Pompeii, The— Edward Bulwer-Lytton	226	70.1	320	74.2	546	72.2	111	IR
Last Hurrah, The— Edwin O'Connor	159	70.8	178	69.1	337	70.0		
Last Leaf, The—O. Henry	170	80.3	190	90.3	360	85.3	16	S
Last Leaf, The—Oliver W. Holmes	287	68.0	398	73.2	685	70.6	35	S
Last Lesson, The— Alphonse Daudet	338	70.4	365	77.3	703	73.9	16	S
Last March, The—Robert F. Scott	363	80.2	385	70.1	748	75.2	14	R
Last of the Mohicans, The—James F. Cooper	603	89.5	442	76.6	1045	83.1	40	S
Laugh and Be Merry— John Masefield	203	67.0	264	77.7	467	72.4	19	S
Lavender and Old Lace —Myrtle Reed	54		183	68.3				
Law of the Jungle, The— Rudyard Kipling	333	57.2	453	57.7	786	57.5	24	R
Lead, Kindly Light— John H. Newman	239	55.6	321	69.5	560	62.6	21	S
Leaden-Eyed, The— Vachel Lindsay	265	27.7	385	30.8	650	29.3	21	R
Leaves Out of My Thrill Book—Irvin S. Cobb	152	61.5	164	65.9	316	63.7	23	S
Lee—Stephen V. Benét	224	56.5	296	55.4	520	56.0	18	S
Lee in Defeat—Thomas N. Page	377	68.4	389	64.9	766	66.7	30	S
Leetla Giorgio Washeenton—Thomas A. Daly	236	81.6	337	88.7	573	85.2	15	R

PUPILS' READING INTERESTS: GRADES 10-12
Ts and Ss = Teachers and Schools   S = Studied in Class
IR = Independent Reading   R = Read in Class

SELECTION—AUTHOR	Boys		Girls		Total		Ts & Ss	
	No.	%	No.	%	No.	Av. %		
Leetla Guiseppina—Thomas A. Daly	988	60.4	1103	74.2	2091	67.3	28	R
Lee Triumphant—Thomas N. Page	199	64.3	223	57.8	422	61.1	28	S
Legend Beautiful, The—Henry W. Longfellow	253	56.9	247	68.4	500	62.7	16	S
Legend of Sleepy Hollow, The—Washington Irving	476	79.1	179	67.6	655	73.4	24	S
Legend of the Moor's Legacy, The—Washington Irving	283	72.3	333	67.7	616	70.0	14	S
Leisure—William H. Davies	181	61.1	304	71.9	485	66.5	21	S
Le Morte D'Arthur—Thomas Malory	277	70.6	378	67.3	655	69.0	25	S
L'Envoi—Rudyard Kipling	426	65.0	513	77.0	939	71.0	33	S
Leopard on the Loose—Frank Buck	177	93.2	205	91.0	382	92.1		
Lepanto—G. K. Chesterton	219	55.9	200	55.3	419	55.6	23	S
Lesbia Railing—Caius V. Catullus	624	42.9	686	57.2	1310	50.1	21	R
Les Miserables—Victor Hugo	187	83.4	255	83.3	442	83.4	77	IR
Lesson in Fiction, A—Stephen Leacock	310	62.9	318	67.3	628	65.1	9	R
Let's Read Biography—Fred Eastman	517	56.1	522	62.7	1039	59.4	20	R
Letter from a Self-made Merchant to His Son, A—George H. Lorimer	246	71.0	232	73.5	478	72.3	22	S
Letter from Home, A—Wallace Irwin	310	78.7	325	87.4	635	83.1	12	R
Letter Home, A—Arnold Bennett	190	56.6	214	66.6	404	61.6	20	S
Letters to His Son—The Earl of Chesterfield	239	61.5	307	70.8	546	66.2	26	S

PUPILS' READING INTERESTS: GRADES 10-12
Ts and Ss = Teachers and Schools   S = Studied in Class
IR = Independent Reading   R = Read in Class

SELECTION—AUTHOR	Boys		Girls		Total		Ts & Ss	
	No.	%	No.	%	No.	Av. %		
Letter to Dr. Cochran—George Washington	232	52.4	287	62.2	519	57.3	21	S
Letter to Joseph Twitchell—Mark Twain	237	61.0	224	67.2	461	64.1	19	S
Letter to Lord Chesterfield—Samuel Johnson	315	52.4	298	46.3	613	49.4	24	S
Letter to Mrs. Bixby—Abraham Lincoln	246	71.5	282	74.5	528	73.0	16	S
Letter to Mrs. Clemm—Edgar A. Poe	233	60.7	242	71.5	475	66.1	18	S
Letter to Mrs. Felton—Charles Dickens	179	48.9	240	52.1	419	50.5	14	S
Letter to Napoleon III—Elizabeth B. Browning	234	54.1	241	60.6	475	57.4	18	S
Letter to the President of the United States—Bill Nye	237	80.2	250	75.2	487	77.7	19	S
Let the Hurricane Roar—Rose W. Lane	233	83.0	348	92.5	581	87.8	67	IR
Let Us Have Faith—Abraham Lincoln	565	57.5	661	62.3	1226	59.9	28	R
Leviathan—Joseph Husband	322	54.5	376	44.7	698	49.6	19	S
Liberal Education, A—Thomas H. Huxley	218	59.9	249	60.4	467	60.2	30	S
Liberty or Death—Patrick Henry	300	67.8	390	61.3	690	64.6	34	S
Life and Letters of Walter H. Page, The—Burton Hendrick	204	39.2	1515	50.0	355	44.6	24	S
Life in Inverted Commas—Eva Le Gallienne	68		343	58.5			15	S
Life in the South Seas—Charles Nordhoff and James Hall	346	82.4	308	75.3	654	78.9	62	IR
Life of Johnson, The—James Boswell	290	63.1	214	65.2	504	64.2	26	S
Life of Ma Parker—Katherine Mansfield	287	42.5	294	66.5	581	54.5	12	R

PUPILS' READING INTERESTS: GRADES 10-12
Ts and Ss = Teachers and Schools   S = Studied in Class
IR = Independent Reading   R = Read in Class

SELECTION—AUTHOR	Boys		Girls		Total		Ts & Ss	
	No.	%	No.	%	No.	Av. %		
Life of Robert E. Lee, The—Joseph and Mary Hamilton	283	70.0	155	67.1	438	68.6		
Life on the Mississippi—Mark Twain	216	84.5	269	70.1	485	77.3	18	S
Life's Picture History	160	85.3	53					
Life with Father—Clarence Day	208	79.3	553	78.6	761	79.0	73	IR
Light in the Forest, The—Conrad Richter	220	74.3	368	74.3	588	74.3		
Light of Other Days, The—Thomas Moore	182	54.3	184	69.6	366	62.0	18	S
Light That Failed, The—Rudyard Kipling	126	71.8	286	73.1	412	72.5	97	IR
'Lijah—Edgar V. Smith	309	74.3	351	84.8	660	79.6	24	S
Li'l Abner (Comic Strip)	902	76.8	1219	65.3	2121	71.1	26	IR
Lilacs—Amy Lowell	234	46.6	256	61.1	490	53.9	20	S
Lincoln—Vachel Lindsay	383	40.7	468	51.2	851	46.0	19	R
Lincoln—James R. Lowell	207	53.4	311	56.3	518	54.9	13	R
Lincoln's Addresses	308	57.8	320	56.7	628	57.3	28	S
Lincoln, the Man of the People—Edwin Markham	461	75.6	557	79.0	1018	77.3	44	S
Lindberg Flies Alone—H. M. Anderson	233	44.6	316	48.2	549	46.4	14	R
Lindbergh Tells of It—Charles A. Lindbergh	414	79.3	481	72.7	895	76.0	11	S
Lines Composed a Few Miles above Tintern Abbey—William Wordsworth	225	53.3	255	55.9	480	54.6	31	S
Lines Written in Early Spring—William Wordsworth	510	49.6	577	58.5	1087	54.1	45	S
Lion, The—Vachel Lindsay	261	60.3	371	56.9	632	58.6	14	R
Lion and the Mouse, The—Joseph B. Ames	163	81.6	274	78.3	437	80.0	14	S

PUPILS' READING INTERESTS: GRADES 10-12

Ts and Ss = Teachers and Schools   S = Studied in Class

IR = Independent Reading   R = Read in Class

SELECTION—AUTHOR	Boys		Girls		Total		Ts & Ss	
	No.	%	No.	%	No.	Av. %		
Listeners, The—Walter de la Mare	423	61.3	478	75.0	901	68.2	37	S
Little Boy Blue—Eugene Field	535	64.0	562	87.0	1097	75.5	41	S
Little Boy in the Morning, A— Francis Ledwidge	215	63.5	242	79.3	457	71.4	14	S
Little Breeches—John Hay	301	64.6	378	70.1	679	67.4	13	R
Little Britches—Ralph Moody	226	59.7	358	67.5	584	63.6		
Little Giffen of Tennessee— Francis O. Ticknor	340	54.7	416	60.6	756	57.7	13	R
Little Home in the Mountains, The— Arthur Guiterman	617	41.0	633	50.3	1250	45.7	23	R
Little Lord Fauntleroy— Frances H. Burnett	76		177	64.4				
Little Lost Pup, The— Arthur Guiterman	1237	78.1	1348	88.4	2585	83.3	35	R
Little Lulu (Comic Strip)	630	67.6	1085	74.7	1715	71.2	26	IR
Little Men—Louisa M. Alcott	258	62.0	737	78.4	995	70.2	138	IR
Little Minister, The— James M. Barrie	106	55.7	459	75.6	565	65.7	67	IR
Little Orphan Annie (Comic Strip)	814	28.2	1149	29.9	1963	29.1	51	IR
Little Orphan Annie— James W. Riley	472	58.4	647	80.7	1119	69.6	17	R
Little Peach, The— Eugene Field	222	59.2	355	65.5	577	62.4	15	R
Little Princesses, The— Marion Crawford	17		227	74.0				
Little Regiment, The— Stephen Crane	251	81.7	254	71.9	505	76.8	17	S
Little Roach, The— Christopher Morley	322	62.4	372	75.3	694	68.9	13	R
Little Scouts, The (Comic Strip)	316	76.3	348	74.9	664	75.6	43	IR

PUPILS' READING INTERESTS: GRADES 10-12
Ts and Ss = Teachers and Schools   S = Studied in Class
IR = Independent Reading   R = Read in Class

SELECTION—AUTHOR	Boys No.	Boys %	Girls No.	Girls %	Total No.	Total Av. %	Ts & Ss	
Little Song of Life, A—Lizette W. Reese	747	47.8	838	68.5	1585	58.2	44	S
Little While I Fain Would Linger Yet, A—Paul H. Hayne	201	52.7	258	66.7	459	59.7	23	S
Little Women—Louisa M. Alcott	63		538	90.4			27	IR
Lives of a Bengal Lancer (Book)— Francis Yates-Brown	286	70.8	90	54.4	376	62.6		
Lives of a Bengal Lancer (Motion Picture)	237	76.6	110	65.9	347	71.3		
Loan, The—Unknown	350	58.1	451	62.9	801	60.5	19	R
Lochinvar—Walter Scott	355	66.9	543	80.2	898	73.6	28	S
London, 1802—William Wordsworth	303	50.8	483	56.8	786	53.8	33	S
Lone Cowboy—Will James	328	79.9	151	75.2	479	77.6	124	IR
Lone Dog—Irene R. McLeod	257	79.4	288	77.8	545	78.6	17	S
Lone Ranger (Comic Strip)	683	58.6	868	47.5	1551	53.1	44	IR
Lonesome Road, The (Negro Song)	236	32.6	297	55.7	533	44.2	14	R
Long Pants—Irvin S. Cobb	305	85.1	344	84.3	649	84.7	23	S
Look, The—Sara Teasdale	367	53.5	397	74.7	764	64.1	12	R
Look Homeward, Angel —Thomas Wolfe	146	76.7	663	78.9	809	77.8		
Look What You Did, Christopher!—Ogden Nash	322	85.2	341	85.5	663	85.4	24	S
Lord Beichan and Susie Pye (British Ballad)	387	53.4	381	68.0	768	60.7	18	R
Lord Chancellor's Song, The—William H. Gilbert	1159	74.7	1182	80.7	2341	77.7	40	R
Lord Jim—Joseph Conrad	244	65.0	191	61.5	435	63.3		

PUPILS' READING INTERESTS: GRADES 10-12
Ts and Ss = Teachers and Schools   S = Studied in Class
IR = Independent Reading   R = Read in Class

SELECTION—AUTHOR	Boys		Girls		Total		Ts & Ss	
	No.	%	No.	%	No.	Av. %		
Lord Randal (British Ballad)	256	50.4	289	61.8	545	56.1	24	S
Lord Thomas and Fair Annette (British Ballad)	230	57.2	245	70.0	475	63.6	14	S
Lord Ullin's Daughter—Thomas Campbell	377	56.1	417	71.2	794	63.7	19	R
Lorna Doone—Richard Blackmore	260	78.0	522	77.6	782	77.8	72	IR
Lost—Carl Sandburg	236	60.6	293	66.7	529	63.7	16	S
Lost Chord, A—Adelaide A. Proctor	636	65.1	706	85.0	1342	75.1	22	R
Lost Horizon—James Hilton	360	72.2	646	79.0	1006	75.6		
Lost Leader, The—Robert Browning	246	62.2	327	62.1	573	62.2	31	S
Lost Phoebe, The—Theodore Dreiser	399	58.0	227	73.8	626	65.9	14	S
Lost Silk Hat, The—Edward Dunsany	345	56.5	905	50.0	1250	53.3	47	S
Lost Worlds—Anne T. White	161	74.8	67					
Lotus Eaters, The—Alfred Tennyson	334	35.3	332	35.8	666	35.6	20	S
Lou Gehrig, a Quiet Hero—Frank Graham	403	94.3	160	86.6	563	90.5	81	IR
Lou Gehrig, Boy of the Sand Lots— Guernsey Van Riper	158	83.2	26					
Louis Pasteur's Experiments—Samuel J. Holmes	480	67.3	437	60.1	917	63.7	26	S
Love Among the Ruins—Robert Browning	212	44.3	238	51.3	450	47.8	14	S
Love is Eternal—Irving Stone	32		449	78.8				
Love Letters of Smith, The—Henry C. Bunner	229	65.9	300	77.2	529	71.6	39	S
Loveliest of Trees—Alfred E. Housman	195	57.7	364	74.3	559	66.0	23	S

PUPILS' READING INTERESTS: GRADES 10-12

Ts and Ss = Teachers and Schools   S = Studied in Class
IR = Independent Reading   R = Read in Class

SELECTION—AUTHOR	Boys		Girls		Total		Ts & Ss	
	No.	%	No.	%	No.	Av. %		
Love of Home—Daniel Webster	326	51.4	362	58.6	688	55.0	14	R
Lovers, The—Phoebe Cary	299	60.2	320	60.9	619	60.6	17	R
Lover Tells of the Rose in His Heart, The— William B. Yeats	304	17.4	411	28.1	715	22.8	12	R
Love's Labor's Lost— William Shakespeare	58		158	69.3			210	IR
Love's Lasso—S. Omar Barker	321	52.5	396	62.0	717	57.3	25	S
Low-Backed Car, The— Samuel Lover	997	58.4	969	69.0	1966	63.7	29	R
Loyalties—John Galsworthy	164	74.1	218	66.7	382	70.4	21	S
Lucinda Matlock—Edgar L. Masters	385	52.7	420	70.0	805	61.4	37	S
Luck of Roaring Camp, The—Bret Harte	207	71.7	304	70.4	511	71.1	18	S
Lucy Gray—William Wordsworth	196	54.1	225	71.3	421	62.7	32	S
Lure of the Great North Woods, The— Kenneth Roberts	310	75.6	286	71.2	596	73.4	13	R
Lure of the Labrador, The— Wilfred T. Grenfell	758	76.8	639	75.2	1397	76.0	38	S
Lycidas—John Milton	358	46.8	317	55.5	675	51.2	51	S
Lyrical Epigram, A— Edith Wharton	212	33.7	253	49.0	465	41.4	16	R
Macbeth—William Shakespeare	2323	74.4	2556	78.1	4879	76.3	222	S
Madame Curie—Eve Curie	133	60.9	396	64.8	529	62.9		
Madman's Song—Elinor Wylie	223	43.3	284	43.8	507	43.6	16	S
Magic Ring, The— Kenneth Grahame	340	64.0	338	72.5	678	68.3	40	S
Magnificent Obsession— Lloyd C. Douglas	119	75.6	427	89.2	546	82.4		

PUPILS' READING INTERESTS: GRADES 10-12

Ts and Ss = Teachers and Schools   S = Studied in Class

IR = Independent Reading   R = Read in Class

SELECTION—AUTHOR	Boys No.	Boys %	Girls No.	Girls %	Total No.	Total Av. %	Ts & Ss	
Maid of Athens—George G. Byron	260	46.7	302	56.8	562	51.8	19	S
Main Street—Sinclair Lewis	148	66.9	256	67.8	404	67.4		
Maker of Dreams, The— Oliphant Down	249	56.6	273	68.8	522	62.7	23	S
Making of an American, The—Jacob Riis	520	68.8	538	62.9	1058	65.9	43	S
Maladie du Siecle— Christopher Morley	303	21.5	297	29.8	600	25.7	12	R
Mama's Bank Account— Kathryn Forbes	246	68.1	809	85.1	1055	76.6	130	IR
Mammon and the Archer —O. Henry	423	82.3	424	86.8	847	84.6	19	S
Man and His Dog, A— Thomas Mann	203	61.1	259	44.2	462	52.7	15	S
Man and the Lion, The— Aesop	275	63.5	307	64.5	582	64.0	16	R
Man Called Peter, A— Catherine Marshall	167	80.2	538	88.8	705	84.5		
Mandalay—Rudyard Kipling	594	75.0	737	81.7	1331	78.4	35	S
Mandrake the Magician (Comic Strip)	729	59.3	774	53.7	1503	56.5	54	IR
Man from Snowy River, The—Andrew B. Paterson	339	78.2	371	68.1	710	73.2	10	R
Man He Killed, The— Thomas Hardy	214	79.7	212	69.6	426	74.7	22	S
Man in Black, The— Oliver Goldsmith	201	62.4	270	68.0	471	65.2	16	S
Man in the Gray Flannel Suit, The— Sloan Wilson	369	65.7	653	69.7	1022	67.7		
Man in the House, A— Elsie Singmaster	234	60.0	259	77.4	493	68.7	16	R
Man's a Man for A' That, A—Robert Burns	532	58.3	542	56.9	1074	57.6	46	S
Man's Highest Trip into the Air—Irma Taylor	302	93.4	392	81.3	694	87.4	12	R

PUPILS' READING INTERESTS: GRADES 10-12

Ts and Ss = Teachers and Schools   S = Studied in Class
IR = Independent Reading   R = Read in Class

SELECTION—AUTHOR	Boys		Girls		Total		Ts & Ss	
	No.	%	No.	%	No.	Av. %		
Man Under the Yoke, The—Vachel Lindsay	361	61.4	429	71.6	790	66.5	32	S
Man Who Cursed the Lilies, The— Charles T. Jackson	219	74.7	145	62.1	364	68.4	17	S
Man Who Kept His Form, The—John Galsworthy	223	68.8	234	69.7	457	69.3	24	S
Man Who Married a Dumb Wife, The— Anatole France	154	51.9	191	45.6	345	48.8	23	S
Man Who Was, The— Rudyard Kipling	541	53.0	514	42.1	1055	47.6	45	S
Man With a Gun, The— Charles Vanda and Russ Johnson	282	88.8	315	86.8	597	87.8	11	R
Man Without a Country, The—Edward E. Hale	732	81.5	968	82.3	1700	81.9	37	S
Man with the Hoe, The —Edwin Markham	916	71.7	869	75.9	1785	73.8	78	S
Many Loves of Dobie Gillis, The— Max Shulman	165	78.8	179	72.6	344	75.7		
Marble Top—E. B. White	615	47.5	627	52.4	1242	50.0	23	R
Marching Along—Robert Browning	264	51.1	349	54.4	613	52.8	25	S
Maria Chapdelaine— Louis Hémon	57		299	73.9			42	IR
Marie Antoinette in the Temple— Hilaire Belloc	340	45.7	354	54.1	694	49.9	30	S
Marjorie Daw—Thomas B. Aldrich	368	47.6	425	68.0	793	57.8	31	S
Marjorie Morningstar— Herman Wouk	169	62.7	1043	82.7	1212	72.7		
Market, The—William McFee	160	41.6	313	49.2	473	45.4	26	S
Markheim—Robert L. Stevenson	283	61.0	233	63.1	516	62.1	33	S

PUPILS' READING INTERESTS: GRADES 10-12

Ts and Ss = Teachers and Schools   S = Studied in Class
IR = Independent Reading   R = Read in Class

SELECTION—AUTHOR	Boys		Girls		Total		Ts & Ss	
	No.	%	No.	%	No.	Av. %		
Marriage of Queen Victoria—Lytton Strachey	233	41.4	215	67.0	448	54.2	25	S
Marshes of Glynn, The— Sidney Lanier	241	52.3	274	54.9	515	53.6	20	S
Martin—Joyce Kilmer	457	62.5	544	72.4	1001	67.5	32	S
Mary—Katherine Mansfield	244	62.9	302	87.7	546	75.3	27	S
Mary Morrison—Robert Burns	351	41.6	401	51.6	752	46.6	14	S
Mary Smith—Booth Tarkington	229	68.1	249	75.3	478	71.7	23	S
Mary White—William A. White	1542	74.0	1698	89.7	3240	81.9	128	S
Masque of the Red Death, The—Edgar A. Poe	707	60.5	555	51.7	1262	56.1	49	S
Master, The—Edwin A. Robinson	285	64.2	269	69.3	554	66.8	26	S
Master, The—H. H. Tomlinson	207	73.4	282	70.4	489	71.9	16	R
Masters of Deceit—J. Edgar Hoover	170	85.6	64					
Masters of Science and Invention— Floyd L. Darrow	380	70.3	3				32	IR
Matilda—Hilaire Belloc	363	71.5	278	80.8	741	76.2	21	R
Maud Muller—John G. Whittier	521	62.4	517	81.6	1038	72.0	32	S
May I Drive You Home, Mrs. Murgatroyd— Ogden Nash	298	63.9	370	62.0	668	63.0	14	R
May Is Building Her House—Richard Le Gallienne	209	44.0	289	63.0	498	53.5	19	S
May Night—Sara Teasdale	401	52.9	501	70.7	902	61.8	14	R
Meadow Lark, The— Edna Ferber	183	65.3	334	69.8	517	67.6	95	IR

PUPILS' READING INTERESTS: GRADES 10-12

Ts and Ss = Teachers and Schools   S = Studied in Class
IR = Independent Reading   R = Read in Class

SELECTION—AUTHOR	Boys		Girls		Total		Ts & Ss	
	No.	%	No.	%	No.	Av. %		
Meaning of a Fragment, The—John C. Merriam	364	74.5	410	69.0	774	71.8	14	R
Meeting at Night— Robert Browning	219	50.9	244	66.2	463	58.6	15	S
Meeting-House Hill— Amy Lowell	191	48.2	196	52.0	387	50.1	21	S
Meet Me in St. Louis— Sally Benson	177	65.5	439	77.7	616	71.6		
Melting Pot, The—Israel Zangwill	166	67.5	194	77.8	360	72.7	26	S
Memory—Thomas B. Aldrich	208	61.1	289	71.8	497	66.5	20	S
Memory of Earth—AE (G. W. Russell)	161	49.1	188	55.1	349	52.1	19	S
Men—Dorothy E. Reid	337	80.9	382	83.6	719	82.3	22	S
Men Against the Sea— Nordhoff and Hall	294	84.0	44				82	IR
Mending Wall—Robert Frost	722	65.4	806	68.5	1528	67.0	64	S
Men on Bataan—John Hersey	197	87.8	41					
Merchant of Venice, The —William Shakespeare	3400	64.9	3309	72.8	6709	68.9	226	S
Merchants from Cathay —William R. Benét	190	55.0	202	51.0	392	53.0	20	S
Mermaid Tavern, The— John Keats	204	56.1	282	58.7	486	57.4	23	S
Merry Wives of Windsor, The— William Shakespeare	71		173	72.5			205	IR
Merton of the Movies— George S. Kaufman and Marc Connelly	337	83.4	412	88.1	749	85.8	24	S
Messages, The—Wilfrid W. Gibson	210	80.7	242	79.8	452	80.3	15	S
Message to Garcia, A— Elbert Hubbard	510	75.1	536	71.8	1046	73.5	47	S
Mia Carlotta—Thomas A. Daly	812	76.9	750	80.0	1562	78.5	61	S
Mice, The—Richard Kirk	211	51.9	260	66.3	471	59.1	16	R

PUPILS' READING INTERESTS: GRADES 10-12

Ts and Ss = Teachers and Schools   S = Studied in Class
IR = Independent Reading   R = Read in Class

SELECTION—AUTHOR	Boys		Girls		Total		Ts & Ss	
	No.	%	No.	%	No.	Av. %		
Michael—William Wordsworth	267	45.1	358	54.5	625	49.8	14	R
Mickey Mouse (Comic Strip)	841	64.5	1095	54.8	1936	59.7	54	IR
Microbe Hunters—Paul De Kruif	674	78.1	717	71.0	1391	74.6	72	S
Microbes Are a Menace (Pasteur)— Paul De Kruif	222	84.5	164	72.9	386	78.7	50	S
Midsummer Night's Dream, A—William Shakespeare	284	52.1	284	77.1	568	64.6	35	S
Milestones—Arnold Bennett and Edward Knoblock	306	60.5	334	72.2	640	66.4	15	R
Mile with Me, A—Henry Van Dyke	197	48.2	312	65.5	509	56.9	20	S
Milk for the Cat—Harold Monro	253	62.6	266	74.3	519	68.5	20	S
Miller, His Son and the Donkey, The—Aesop	1024	75.3	1120	77.0	2144	76.2	27	R
Miller of the Dee, The—Charles Mackay	333	71.8	367	71.5	700	71.7	16	R
Millionaire, The—Leopold Weiss	279	64.9	386	73.1	665	69.0	15	R
Mill on the Floss, The—George Eliot	209	53.1	381	74.0	590	63.6	82	IR
Milton's Minor Poems—John Milton	249	39.2	199	52.8	448	46.0	25	S
Minister's Black Veil, The— Nathaniel Hawthorne	176	56.5	182	66.5	358	61.5	21	S
Miniver Cheevy—Edwin A. Robinson	1228	59.8	1235	64.8	2463	62.3	83	S
Miracle of the Bells, The —Russell Janney	185	78.9	550	89.1	735	84.0		
Miracles—Walt Whitman	167	61.4	205	74.1	372	67.8	17	S
Miss Halloway's Goat—Luigi Pirandello	191	45.0	234	52.6	425	48.8	14	S
Miss Hinch—Henry S. Harrison	195	79.7	314	90.3	509	85.0	18	S

PUPILS' READING INTERESTS: GRADES 10-12
Ts and Ss = Teachers and Schools   S = Studied in Class
IR = Independent Reading   R = Read in Class

SELECTION—AUTHOR	Boys		Girls		Total		Ts & Ss	
	No.	%	No.	%	No.	Av. %		
Mission of Jane, The— Edith Wharton	136	50.0	165	73.3	301	61.7	21	S
Mississippi, The— Lafcadio Hearn	217	53.7	212	60.4	429	57.1	31	S
Miss Letitia's Profession —Lupton A. Wilkinson	546	64.9	573	79.0	1119	72.0	19	R
Miss Lulu Bett—Zona Gale	63		390	67.7			80	IR
Miss T—Walter de la Mare	382	21.6	485	33.9	867	27.8	16	R
Mister Hop-Toad—James W. Riley	205	65.1	189	75.9	394	70.5	17	S
Mob, The—John Galsworthy	168	65.8	176	63.4	344	64.6	53	IR
Moby Dick—Herman Melville	313	75.9	271	68.5	584	72.2	37	S
Modeling My Life—Janet Scudder	356	51.5	299	86.5	655	69.0	24	S
Modern Hiawatha— George A. Strong	481	55.2	578	59.9	1059	57.6	20	R
Modest Wit, A—Selleck Osborn	346	70.5	397	73.6	743	72.1	16	R
Molly McGuire, Fourteen —Frederick S. Greene	558	67.7	669	61.7	1227	64.7	45	S
Monkey, The—Nancy Campbell	266	40.0	299	62.9	565	51.5	12	R
Monkey's Paw, The— William W. Jacobs	1104	82.9	911	82.0	2015	82.5	66	S
Monsieur Beaucaire— Booth Tarkington	349	79.5	384	77.8	733	78.7	33	S
Moon, The—W. H. Davies	524	51.8	530	64.1	1054	58.0	36	S
Moon Is Up, The—Alfred Noyes	280	48.8	318	59.0	598	53.9	14	R
Moonlight—Bertha H. Nance	229	52.0	242	56.0	471	54.0	14	R
Moonlight—John V. A. Weaver	298	66.4	423	77.9	721	72.2	11	R
Moonshine—Arthur Hopkins	632	85.4	645	79.4	1277	82.4	49	S

PUPILS' READING INTERESTS: GRADES 10-12

Ts and Ss = Teachers and Schools   S = Studied in Class

IR = Independent Reading   R = Read in Class

SELECTION—AUTHOR	Boys		Girls		Total		Ts & Ss	
	No.	%	No.	%	No.	Av. %		
Morning—Emily Dickinson	297	49.8	421	65.9	718	57.9	11	R
Mother Goose	276	45.7	587	56.2	863	51.0		
Mother to Son— Langston Hughes	251	44.8	328	75.3	579	60.1	14	R
Moti Guj—Mutineer— Rudyard Kipling	311	81.8	287	82.4	598	82.1	18	S
Mountain Observatory, A —Alfred Noyes	173	65.0	257	62.5	430	63.8	18	S
Mountains Are a Lonely Folk, The— Hamlin Garland	311	30.1	325	44.9	636	37.5	15	R
Mountain Woman, The— DuBose Hayward	183	66.3	237	70.9	420	68.6	15	S
M'Pherson's Farewell— Robert Burns	187	55.3	205	57.3	392	56.3	18	S
Mr. Brisher's Treasure— H. G. Wells	173	75.7	178	71.9	351	73.8	20	S
Mr. Conley—Charles E. Van Loan	200	86.3	263	81.2	463	83.8	16	S
Mr. Dooley on Political Parades— Finley P. Dunne	434	41.9	461	46.9	895	44.4	12	R
Mr. Hail Colomb— Thomas A. Daly	394	74.4	388	77.1	782	75.8	13	R
Mr. Higginbotham's Catastrophe— Nathaniel Hawthorne	234	55.1	246	57.9	480	56.5	21	S
Mr. Rabbit Nibbles Up the Butter— Joel C. Harris	185	39.7	251	37.8	436	38.8	25	S
Mr. Roberts—Thomas Heggen	227	87.0	190	85.8	417	86.4		
Mrs. 'Arris Goes to New York—Paul Gallico	44		183	75.2				
Mrs. 'Arris Goes to Paris —Paul Gallico	51		291	75.3				
Mrs. Farnham's Secret—Dorothy C. Fisher	272	50.7	270	71.9	542	61.3	25	S

PUPILS' READING INTERESTS: GRADES 10-12
Ts and Ss = Teachers and Schools   S = Studied in Class
IR = Independent Reading   R = Read in Class

SELECTION—AUTHOR	Boys No.	Boys %	Girls No.	Girls %	Total No.	Total Av. %	Ts & Ss	
Mrs. Judge Jenkins—Bret Harte	267	66.3	321	76.0	588	71.2	15	R
Mrs. Mike—Benedict and Nancy Freedman	15		239	81.8				
Mrs. Miniver—Jan Struther	69		253	75.3				
Mrs. Wiggs of the Cabbage Patch— Alice H. Rice	311	57.2	920	74.0	1231	65.6	60	IR
Mr. Travers's First Hunt —Richard H. Davis	395	75.1	171	66.4	566	70.8	14	S
Much Ado About Nothing—William Shakespeare	147	62.9	437	72.8	584	67.9	328	IR
Mucker Pose, The— James T. Adams	235	53.6	140	47.1	375	50.4	15	R
Municipal Report, A—O. Henry	179	65.4	189	65.1	368	65.3	17	S
Mushy Seventies, The— George Ade	260	46.9	298	66.6	558	56.8	12	R
Music—Walter de la Mare	279	34.8	377	50.5	656	42.7	17	R
Music Man—Meredith Willson	119	77.7	238	80.0	357	78.9		
Music, When Soft Voices Die— Percy B. Shelley	519	50.5	630	72.6	1149	61.6	45	S
Mutiny on the Bounty— Nordhoff and Hall	609	86.6	355	78.5	964	82.6	139	S
My Antonia—Willa Cather	79		284	72.2			140	IR
My Aunt—Oliver W. Holmes	290	69.3	419	85.8	709	77.6	30	S
My Brother Henry— James M. Barrie	208	61.8	224	73.0	432	67.4	25	S
My Brother, Theodore Roosevelt— Corinne R. Robinson	300	68.7	373	73.3	673	71.0	24	S
My Dog—John K. Bangs	163	70.3	174	81.9	337	76.1	16	S

PUPILS' READING INTERESTS: GRADES 10-12

Ts and Ss = Teachers and Schools   S = Studied in Class
IR = Independent Reading   R = Read in Class

SELECTION—AUTHOR	Boys		Girls		Total		Ts & Ss	
	No.	%	No.	%	No.	Av. %		
My Double and How He Undid Me— Edward E. Hale	223	60.5	205	73.7	428	67.1	15	S
My Fair Lady—Alan J. Lerner	174	75.9	458	85.8	632	80.9		
My Favorite Flower— Christopher Morley	303	43.9	297	52.7	600	48.3	12	R
My Financial Career— Stephen Leacock	454	80.5	564	87.6	1018	84.1	32	S
My Friend Flicka—Mary O'Hara	543	93.4	1057	95.1	1600	94.3	50	IR
My Heart Leaps Up (Rainbow)— William Wordsworth	682	45.4	731	58.3	1413	51.9	67	S
My Heart's in the Highlands—Robert Burns	197	66.5	208	66.1	405	66.3	16	S
My Last Duchess— Robert Browning	835	57.2	966	70.1	1801	63.7	105	S
My Last Walk with the Schoolmistress— Oliver W. Holmes	240	51.9	263	63.9	503	57.9	19	S
My Lost Youth—Henry W. Longfellow	329	72.2	413	79.2	742	75.7	34	S
My Luve is Lika a Red, Red Rose— Robert Burns	511	42.9	585	58.9	1096	50.9	34	S
My Own True Ghost Story—Rudyard Kipling	223	61.0	241	60.0	464	60.5	31	S
Myrtle at 6 A.M.—Arnold Bennett	162	50.9	224	75.2	386	63.1	15	S
My Sculptor—Edward V. Lucas	381	40.3	406	51.6	787	46.0	11	R
My Senior Year at Knox College—S. S. McClure	295	56.9	268	61.0	563	59.0	24	S
My Silent Servants—John K. Bangs	278	51.8	256	66.4	534	59.1	27	S
My Sister Eileen—Ruth McKenney	42		308	80.0			130	IR
My Son Gets Spanked— Frederick F. Van de Water	192	73.2	217	76.3	409	74.8	16	S

PUPILS' READING INTERESTS: GRADES 10-12
Ts and Ss = Teachers and Schools   S = Studied in Class
IR = Independent Reading   R = Read in Class

SELECTION—AUTHOR	Boys		Girls		Total		Ts & Ss	
	No.	%	No.	%	No.	Av. %		
My Star—Robert Browning	374	17.4	431	38.9	805	28.2	13	R
Mysterious Card, The— Cleveland Moffett	277	90.6	335	89.9	612	90.3	10	R
Mysterious Island—Jules Verne	370	80.8	243	70.4	613	75.6		
Mysterious Mirage, The (Hungarian Folk Tale)	247	76.1	324	69.4	571	72.8	13	R
Mystery of Ah Sing, The —R. L. Duffus	269	45.0	310	63.7	579	54.4	14	S
Mystery of Paul Redfern, The—Irma Taylor	325	95.1	399	93.5	724	94.3	12	R
Mystery of Room 513, The—Corinne H. Markey	289	85.6	359	96.2	648	90.9	15	R
Mystified Quaker in New York, The—Unknown	221	71.7	221	73.1	442	72.4	14	R
Myths and Their Meanings—Max J. Herzberg	141	47.9	213	58.7	354	53.3	56	IR
My Uncle—Alvin S. Johnson	181	63.3	426	67.1	607	65.2	14	S
Naaman the Leper—The Bible	237	60.3	345	66.7	582	63.5	24	S
Naked and the Dead, The—Norman Mailer	275	77.1	173	67.3	448	72.2		
Name of Old Glory, The —James W. Riley	301	57.8	315	57.6	616	57.7	11	R
Namgay Doola—Rudyard Kipling	215	61.4	271	54.1	486	57.8	25	S
Nancy Hanks—Stephen and Rosemary Benét	228	63.2	256	77.5	484	70.4	17	S
Napoleon—Emil Ludwig	186	67.5	97	57.2	283	62.4		
Napoleon and Uncle Elby (Comic Strip)	278	50.9	287	38.9	565	44.9	44	IR
Nathan Hale—Clyde Fitch	413	85.6	377	88.5	790	87.1	38	S
National Velvet (Book)— Enid Bagnold	206	77.2	470	87.7	676	82.5	130	IR
National Velvet (Movie)	794	80.7	1072	92.7	1866	86.7	130	

PUPILS' READING INTERESTS: GRADES 10-12
Ts and Ss = Teachers and Schools   S = Studied in Class
IR = Independent Reading   R = Read in Class

SELECTION—AUTHOR	Boys		Girls		Total		Ts & Ss	
	No.	%	No.	%	No.	Av. %		
Nation's Prayer, The—Josiah G. Holland	496	44.5	585	53.1	1081	48.8	19	R
Nature—Henry W. Longfellow	164	54.3	253	69.2	417	61.8	14	S
Nature's Wisdom—Ellis P. Butler	575	45.7	646	55.3	1221	50.5	22	R
Nautical Extravaganza, A—Wallace Irwin	286	78.0	329	74.5	615	76.3	16	R
Nebuchadnezzar—Irwin Russell	606	62.2	640	61.6	1246	61.9	22	R
Necklace, The—Guy de Maupassant	848	66.5	780	86.6	1628	76.6	61	S
Negro Spirituals—Rosemary C. and Stephen V. Benét	386	35.2	414	50.2	800	42.7	16	R
Neighbors, The (Comic Strip)	330	65.9	527	69.1	857	67.5	41	IR
Never in This World—Stephen M. Avery	251	60.6	236	64.4	487	62.5	14	S
New Cat, The—Robert Lynd	191	64.7	587	76.0	778	70.4	16	S
New England Weather—Mark Twain	360	76.3	437	78.8	797	77.6	12	R
New Freedom, The—Woodrow Wilson	204	55.1	184	50.5	388	52.8	21	S
New International Encyclopedia, The	157	65.6	277	67.5	434	66.6	24	IR
New Master of Mount Vernon, The—Shelby Little	180	63.3	134	70.1	314	66.7	22	IR
New Mexican Bo-Peep, A—Arthur Guiterman	366	59.7	413	65.1	779	62.4	13	R
New Orleans—Lafcadio Hearn	246	50.8	243	56.8	489	53.8	29	S
New South, The—Henry W. Grady	285	63.5	342	59.9	627	61.7	33	S
New York Bootblack—Elias Lieberman	237	44.5	232	47.0	469	45.8	12	R
Niagara Falls—Rupert Brooke	199	66.6	207	63.8	406	65.2	19	S

PUPILS' READING INTERESTS: GRADES 10-12

Ts and Ss = Teachers and Schools   S = Studied in Class
IR = Independent Reading   R = Read in Class

SELECTION—AUTHOR	Boys		Girls		Total		Ts & Ss	
	No.	%	No.	%	No.	Av. %		
Nicholas Nye—Walter de la Mare	153	60.1	170	63.2	323	61.7	17	S
Night at an Inn, A— Edward Dunsany	696	75.9	764	71.6	1460	73.8	41	S
Night Flight—Antoine de Saint Exupéry	153	75.8	102	69.6	255	72.7		
Nightmare, A—William S. Gilbert	259	67.4	207	80.4	466	73.9	19	S
Night of the Storm, The —Zona Gale	293	86.0	393	96.4	686	91.2	14	R
Night Song at Amalfi— Sara Teasdale	226	46.5	205	62.9	431	54.7	17	S
Night Stuff—Carl Sandburg	333	27.2	336	43.5	669	35.4	13	R
Night To Remember, A —Walter Lord	195	84.4	158	90.2	353	87.3		
1984—George Orwell	266	82.0	157	80.9	423	81.5		
Noah an' Jonah an' Cap'n John Smith— Don Marquis	155	74.8	203	64.5	358	69.7	18	S
Nobody's Girl—Hector Malot	13		331	81.6			87	IR
Nocturne in a Deserted Brickyard— Carl Sandburg	311	33.6	373	44.0	684	38.8	9	R
Noiseless Patient Spider, A—Walt Whitman	377	41.6	455	44.8	832	43.2	40	S
Nonsense—Thomas Moore	477	29.8	555	41.7	1032	35.8	17	R
No. 1075 Packs Chocolates—Cornelia S. Parker	206	56.6	239	69.7	445	63.2	18	S
North to the Orient— Anne Lindbergh	186	83.1	210	89.8	396	86.5	20	S
Northwest Passage— Kenneth Roberts	722	89.1	545	81.2	1267	85.2	186	IR
Northwest Passage (Movie)	499	88.1	325	81.5	824	84.8	130	
Not According to Hoyle —Robert Benchley	159	69.8	311	77.2	470	73.5	15	S

PUPILS' READING INTERESTS: GRADES 10-12
Ts and Ss = Teachers and Schools   S = Studied in Class
IR = Independent Reading   R = Read in Class

SELECTION—AUTHOR	Boys		Girls		Total		Ts & Ss	
	No.	%	No.	%	No.	Av. %		
Not As a Stranger—Morton Thompson	59		255	83.9				
Notation on Immortality—Nancy B. Turner	174	46.0	183	51.4	357	48.7		
Note on the Essay, A—Carl Van Doren	276	38.8	366	44.0	642	41.4	24	S
Nothing Gold Can Stay—Robert Frost	247	23.5	240	34.2	487	28.9	13	R
No Time for Sergeants—Mac Hyman	967	88.6	914	81.1	1881	84.9		
Nun's Story, The—Kathryn Hulme	301	77.9	1299	90.9	1600	84.4		
Nurmi Breaks a Record—Robert Littell	237	73.2	270	61.1	507	67.2	15	R
Nutbrowne Mayde (British Ballad)	235	38.5	295	55.9	530	47.2	17	S
O Bury Me Not on the Lone Prairie (Cowboy Ballad)	269	49.1	353	63.9	622	56.5	16	R
O Captain! My Captain!—Walt Whitman	384	82.8	521	89.9	905	86.4	36	S
Ocean, The—George G. Byron	559	40.3	526	44.8	1085	42.6	23	R
Ocean, The—Moschus	270	43.9	318	54.9	588	49.4	20	S
Odd Ones, The—Ruth Suckow	268	31.2	258	50.6	526	40.9	12	R
Ode on a Grecian Urn—John Keats	861	48.7	1006	66.1	1867	57.4	73	S
Ode on Intimations of Immortality— William Wordsworth	148	52.4	166	62.7	314	57.6	28	S
Ode (The Poets)—Arthur O'Shaughnessy	230	53.0	381	65.0	611	59.0	21	S
Ode to a Nightingale—John Keats	477	57.3	504	71.9	981	64.6	43	S
Ode to Autumn—John Keats	258	43.8	318	58.0	576	50.9	27	S
Ode to the West Wind—Percy B. Shelley	793	51.3	858	57.6	1651	54.5	69	S

PUPILS' READING INTERESTS: GRADES 10-12
Ts and Ss = Teachers and Schools   S = Studied in Class
IR = Independent Reading   R = Read in Class

SELECTION—AUTHOR	Boys		Girls		Total		Ts & Ss	
	No.	%	No.	%	No.	Av. %		
Odyssey, The—Robert Fitzgerald	165	73.0	159	62.6	324	67.8		
Odyssey, The—Homer	346	61.3	490	57.0	836	59.2	47	S
Odyssey of K's, An— Wilbur D. Nesbit	387	51.8	393	60.4	780	56.1	22	R
Off for a Vacation— Jerome K. Jerome	423	83.0	477	86.4	900	84.7	14	R
Of Human Bondage—W. Somerset Maugham	97	68.5	324	82.1	421	75.2		
Of Riches—Francis Bacon	6897	25.2	7927	30.5	14824	27.9	270	R
Of Studies—Francis Bacon	6795	43.6	7867	50.5	14662	47.1	270	R
Oft in the Stilly Night— Thomas Moore	245	57.8	304	64.5	549	61.2	17	S
Of Truth—Francis Bacon	205	51.5	157	52.2	362	51.9	27	S
Old China—Charles Lamb	218	46.1	197	58.6	415	52.4	22	S
Old Chisholm Trail, The (Cowboy Ballad)	453	73.0	418	71.7	871	72.4	20	R
Old Christmas Morning —Roy Helton	281	61.0	333	65.5	614	63.3	14	R
Old Clothes Sensations— Unknown	304	36.2	283	42.9	587	39.6	19	R
Old Doc—Opie Read	239	77.2	258	69.8	497	73.5	16	S
Old Elizabeth—Hugh Walpole	208	70.0	208	85.1	416	77.6	15	R
Oldest Dog Story in Literature, The— Robert C. Holliday	184	63.9	211	69.9	395	66.9	15	R
Old Familiar Faces, The —Charles Lamb	320	65.2	356	73.6	676	69.4	23	S
Old-Fashioned Girl, An— Louisa M. Alcott	10		465	79.4			58	IR
Old Folks, The— Alphonse Daudet	372	46.4	184	63.9	556	55.2	15	S
Old Ironsides—Oliver W. Holmes	423	88.4	500	85.4	923	86.9	32	R

PUPILS' READING INTERESTS: GRADES 10-12
Ts and Ss = Teachers and Schools   S = Studied in Class
IR = Independent Reading   R = Read in Class

SELECTION—AUTHOR	Boys		Girls		Total		Ts & Ss	
	No.	%	No.	%	No.	Av. %		
Old Lady Shows Her Medals, The— James M. Barrie	341	67.2	337	81.8	678	74.5	25	S
Old Man and Jim, The— James W. Riley	543	79.8	563	79.2	1106	79.5	32	R
Old Man and the Sea, The—Ernest Hemingway	807	81.5	754	74.1	1561	77.8		
Old Man Warner— Dorothy C. Fisher	187	72.2	207	74.6	394	73.4	20	S
Old Navy, The— Frederick Marryat	521	64.7	541	55.5	1062	60.1	17	R
Old Oaken Bucket, The —Samuel Woodworth	342	49.1	301	56.8	643	53.0	12	R
Old Romance, An—Mark Twain	317	68.8	328	79.0	645	73.9	14	R
Old Saul—Lizette W. Reese	273	59.0	291	70.4	564	64.7	24	S
Old Story, An—Edwin A. Robinson	264	59.7	217	77.0	481	68.4	26	S
Old Susan—Walter de la Mare	277	51.3	328	70.7	605	61.0	22	S
Old Swimmin' Hole, The —James W. Riley	271	79.9	280	84.1	551	82.0	15	R
Old Time Sea Fight, An —Walt Whitman	271	64.0	368	37.4	639	50.7	14	R
Old Woman, The— Joseph Campbell	409	50.9	492	73.2	901	62.1	29	S
Old Woman of the Roads, An—Padraic Colum	364	58.4	347	66.3	711	62.4	23	S
Old Yeller—Fred Gipson	554	75.5	674	72.8	1228	74.2		
Oliver Goldsmith— William M. Thackeray	192	51.6	227	55.9	419	53.8	32	S
Oliver Twist—Charles Dickens	209	72.2	194	82.0	403	77.1	19	S
On a Certain Condescension in Foreigners— James R. Lowell	294	48.8	334	44.6	628	46.7	19	S

PUPILS' READING INTERESTS: GRADES 10-12
Ts and Ss = Teachers and Schools   S = Studied in Class
IR = Independent Reading   R = Read in Class

SELECTION—AUTHOR	Boys		Girls		Total		Ts & Ss	
	No.	%	No.	%	No.	Av. %		
On a Favorite Cat— Thomas Gray	185	62.2	228	68.2	413	65.2	17	S
On a Piece of Chalk— Thomas Huxley	189	67.5	242	52.5	431	60.0	29	S
On a Soldier Fallen in the Philippines— William V. Moody	216	78.7	245	70.4	461	74.6	17	S
On Carrying a Cane— Robert C. Holliday	341	51.9	355	54.6	696	53.3	29	S
On Destroying Books— J. C. Squire	178	71.9	159	73.3	337	72.6	16	S
On Doors—Christopher Morley	481	61.4	450	75.9	931	68.7	52	S
On Drawing—A. P. Herbert	242	61.4	257	66.5	499	64.0	23	S
One Hundred in the Dark—Owen Johnson	202	64.9	209	71.8	411	68.4	14	S
One Hundred Years of Pasteur—Edwin E. Slosson	382	71.3	354	64.8	736	68.1	12	R
One Million Pound Note, The—Mark Twain	200	85.0	198	78.0	398	81.5	74	IR
One Special for Doc— Milton Geiger	336	92.3	401	96.6	737	94.5	11	R
One Week—Carolyn Wells	280	63.8	435	72.1	715	68.0	17	R
One Word Is Too Often Profaned— Percy B. Shelley	175	56.9	247	65.2	422	61.1	22	S
One Word More—Robert Browning	128	48.8	231	66.5	359	57.7	27	S
On Finding Things— Edward V. Lucas	378	53.3	396	59.0	774	56.2	13	R
On First Looking into Chapman's Homer— John Keats	658	45.7	898	52.8	1556	49.3	63	S
On Flies—Stewart E. White	138	51.4	226	50.7	364	51.1	23	S
On Friendship—Francis Bacon	153	35.6	202	40.6	355	38.1	23	S

PUPILS' READING INTERESTS: GRADES 10-12

| Ts and Ss = Teachers and Schools | S = Studied in Class |
| IR = Independent Reading | R = Read in Class |

SELECTION—AUTHOR	Boys		Girls		Total		Ts & Ss	
	No.	%	No.	%	No.	Av. %		
On Getting Up on Cold Mornings—Leigh Hunt	379	65.2	316	69.6	695	67.4	36	S
On Going a Journey—William Hazlitt	673	52.0	737	52.4	1410	52.2	65	S
On Going a Journey—Robert C. Holliday	251	57.2	350	59.9	601	58.6	29	S
On His Blindness—John Milton	457	69.2	670	78.2	1127	73.7	61	S
On His Having Arrived at the Age of Twenty-three—John Milton	206	58.7	136	62.1	342	60.4	17	S
On His Seventy-fifth Birthday—Walter S. Landor	277	56.5	331	62.8	608	59.7	20	S
Only a Subaltern—Rudyard Kipling	353	71.7	385	67.9	738	69.8	27	S
On Lying Awake at Night—Stewart E. White	123	41.5	284	60.6	407	51.1	28	S
On Lying in Bed—G. K. Chesterton	450	54.6	480	67.0	930	60.8	49	S
Only Seven—Henry S. Leigh	290	60.5	354	80.5	644	70.5	16	R
On Making Camp—Stewart E. White	323	74.8	276	63.4	599	69.1	30	S
On Manners—Ralph W. Emerson	290	42.2	235	42.3	525	42.3	32	S
On Noses—Lucy E. Keeler	184	57.6	281	69.2	465	63.4	21	R
On Running After One's Hat—G. K. Chesterton	450	63.6	420	70.7	870	67.2	39	S
On Seeing a Wounded Hare—Robert Burns	221	44.1	336	42.1	557	43.1	13	R
On Self-Reliance—Ralph W. Emerson	380	57.5	370	62.0	750	59.8	48	S
Onset, The—Robert Frost	226	52.9	206	50.5	432	51.7	24	S
On Shakespeare—John Milton	145	58.3	188	68.6	333	63.5	17	S

PUPILS' READING INTERESTS: GRADES 10-12
Ts and Ss = Teachers and Schools   S = Studied in Class
IR = Independent Reading   R = Read in Class

SELECTION—AUTHOR	Boys		Girls		Total		Ts & Ss	
	No.	%	No.	%	No.	Av. %		
On the Beach—Nevil Shute	259	81.3	233	80.9	492	81.1		
On the Birth of His Son —Su Tung-p'o	167	53.6	197	58.6	364	56.1	19	S
On the Bottom—Edward Ellsburg	386	92.1	54				130	IR
On the Dodge—Will James	279	91.9	351	81.5	630	86.7	10	R
On the Grasshopper and the Cricket— John Keats	276	35.9	398	29.1	674	32.5	13	R
On the Knocking at the Gate in Macbeth— Thomas De Quincey	185	49.7	130	53.8	315	51.8	18	S
On the Receipt of My Mother's Picture— William Cowper	162	68.5	169	73.7	331	71.1	17	S
On the Stairs—Arthur Morrison	205	39.0	233	51.3	438	45.2	14	S
On the Vanity of Earthly Greatness— Arthur Guiterman	750	58.2	829	57.4	1579	57.8	28	R
On the Weather— Jerome K. Jerome	318	52.0	371	54.3	689	53.2	26	S
On Thumbing—Edward E. Whiting	164	67.4	199	62.6	363	65.0	16	S
On to Carson City— Mark Twain	208	75.7	259	64.7	467	70.2	17	S
On Unanswering Letters —Christopher Morley	1159	62.0	1211	71.9	2370	67.0	119	S
Opportunity—Edward R. Sill	471	62.8	566	67.9	1037	65.4	39	S
Ordeal at Mt. Hope— Paul L. Dunbar	332	69.4	285	71.6	617	70.5	13	R
Oregon Trail, The— Arthur Guiterman	309	70.2	352	63.1	661	66.7	17	R
Oregon Trail, The— Francis Parkman	282	60.5	159	60.7	441	60.6		
Oro Stage, The—Henry H. Knibbs	361	72.6	424	54.1	785	63.4	14	R

PUPILS' READING INTERESTS: GRADES 10-12

Ts and Ss = Teachers and Schools S = Studied in Class
IR = Independent Reading R = Read in Class

SELECTION—AUTHOR	Boys		Girls		Total		Ts & Ss	
	No.	%	No.	%	No.	Av. %		
Orphans, The—Wilfred W. Gibson	199	55.0	210	63.1	409	59.1	14	R
Orpheus—Rannie B. Baker	251	45.8	307	57.7	558	51.8	11	R
Orpheus with His Lute— William Shakespeare	277	20.2	350	28.4	627	24.3	14	R
Othello—William Shakespeare	167	72.2	278	81.8	445	77.0	103	IR
Other Men's Clover— Douglas Malloch	247	48.6	328	64.6	575	56.6	15	R
Other Wise Man, The— Henry Van Dyke	468	76.4	596	80.9	1064	78.7		
Our European Guides— Mark Twain	435	84.9	384	84.5	819	84.7	11	R
Our Hearts Were Young and Gay— Cornelia O. Skinner and Emily Kimbrough	144	68.4	880	83.6	1024	76.0	79	IR
Our Town—Thornton Wilder	748	64.0	1156	74.2	1904	69.1		
Outcasts of Poker Flat, The—Bret Harte	212	69.1	242	60.7	454	64.9	25	S
Outline of History— H. G. Wells	181	68.8	132	65.9	313	67.4		
Out Our Way (Comic Strip)	366	74.9	614	58.2	980	66.6	44	IR
Outstation, The—W. Somerset Maugham	159	74.8	195	60.5	354	67.7	15	S
Out to Old Aunt Mary's —James W. Riley	223	46.0	247	65.4	470	55.7	15	R
Out Where the West Begins—Arthur Chapman	909	63.9	971	68.5	1880	66.2	31	R
Overland Mail, The— Rudyard Kipling	431	57.0	427	56.6	858	56.8	13	R
Owl Critic, The—James T. Fields	421	81.6	479	82.2	900	81.9	15	R
Ox-Bow Incident, The—Walter Van T. Clark	622	73.6	240	65.2	862	69.4		

PUPILS' READING INTERESTS: GRADES 10-12
Ts and Ss = Teachers and Schools   S = Studied in Class
IR = Independent Reading   R = Read in Class

SELECTION—AUTHOR	Boys		Girls		Total		Ts & Ss	
	No.	%	No.	%	No.	Av. %		
Oxford as I See It—Stephen Leacock	324	55.4	281	66.2	605	60.8	34	S
Ozymandias—Percy B. Shelley	473	51.8	786	59.2	1259	55.5	53	S
Pack, The—John Galsworthy	370	63.8	435	56.0	805	59.9	18	S
Pair of Sexes, A—Franklin P. Adams	220	68.9	215	74.4	435	71.7	18	S
Paisley Shawl, The—Wilfrid W. Gibson	195	49.0	254	67.9	449	58.5	15	S
Palatine—Willa Cather	298	44.3	294	48.0	592	46.2	11	R
Pandora—Rannie B. Baker	256	48.6	309	64.9	565	56.8	11	R
Papa Was Foxy—George Milburn	308	75.5	400	81.4	708	78.5	12	R
Paradise Lost—John Milton	272	58.6	145	60.0	417	59.3	35	IR
Parody on "The Psalm of Life"—Phoebe Cary	248	48.4	350	58.1	598	53.3	11	R
Parody on Wordsworth—Hartley Coleridge	306	21.9	485	29.3	791	25.6	12	R
Parrot, The—Alfred Noyes	296	45.6	326	46.9	622	46.3	12	R
Parting at Morning—Robert Browning	315	39.8	440	48.1	755	44.0	21	R
Parting Guest, A—James W. Riley	267	50.9	291	67.0	558	59.0	22	S
Parting of Marmion and Douglas, The— Walter Scott	322	51.2	387	46.1	709	48.7	24	S
Passing of Arthur, The—Alfred Tennyson	969	71.1	1286	67.2	2255	69.2	90	S
Passing of Priscilla Winthrop, The— William A. White	286	35.8	313	45.4	599	40.6	18	R
Passing of the Third Floor Back, The—Jerome K. Jerome	205	74.4	186	78.5	391	76.5		

PUPILS' READING INTERESTS: GRADES 10-12

Ts and Ss = Teachers and Schools   S = Studied in Class
IR = Independent Reading   R = Read in Class

SELECTION—AUTHOR	Boys		Girls		Total		Ts & Ss	
	No.	%	No.	%	No.	Av. %		
Passionate Shepherd to His Love, The— Christopher Marlowe	430	47.2	546	61.6	976	54.4	39	S
Passion in the Desert, A —Honoré de Balzac	292	87.7	361	82.1	653	84.9	13	R
Pasteur and the Mad Dog—Paul De Kruif	353	87.0	256	82.2	609	84.6	80	S
Pasture, The—Robert Frost	271	64.9	427	70.0	698	67.5	30	S
Patchwork Quilt, The— Rachel Field	577	58.0	754	75.4	1331	66.7	70	S
Pathway to Truth, The— Stephen Crane	300	51.7	324	61.9	624	56.8	15	S
Patio, The—Carl Carmer	304	26.8	362	44.5	666	35.7	13	R
Patriot, The—Robert Browning	188	66.0	236	65.7	424	65.9	27	S
Patron of Art, A— Richard H. Davies	258	72.5	282	77.3	540	74.9	14	R
Patterns—Amy Lowell	181	57.2	331	84.3	512	70.8	25	S
Paul Jesperson's Masquerade—Hjalmar H. Boyesen	286	89.0	337	93.3	623	91.2	12	R
Paul Jones—Molly E. Seawell	290	67.1	86				191	IR
Paul Revere's Ride— Henry W. Longfellow	204	83.6	215	76.7	419	80.2	18	S
Paul's Case—Willa Cather	263	73.0	348	84.2	611	78.6	16	R
Peak in Darien, A— Richard Halliburton	371	76.8	342	75.9	713	76.4	25	R
Pearl, The—John Steinbeck	134	66.8	209	73.2	343	70.0		
Pearl, The—Unknown	267	30.2	268	45.7	535	38.0	18	R
Pear Tree, The—Edna St. V. Millay	397	57.3	405	72.8	802	65.1	29	S
Pecos Bill, Texas Cowpuncher—Harold W. Felton	283	58.5	149	47.7	432	53.1		
Pedigree—Emily Dickinson	250	58.2	279	65.6	529	61.9	20	S

PUPILS' READING INTERESTS: GRADES 10-12
Ts and Ss = Teachers and Schools   S = Studied in Class
IR = Independent Reading   R = Read in Class

SELECTION—AUTHOR	Boys		Girls		Total		Ts & Ss
	No.	%	No.	%	No.	Av. %	
Pegasus, The Winged Horse—Nathaniel Hawthorne	129	62.4	181	66.0	310	64.2	120 IR
Peggy Covers the News —Emma Bugbee	9		172	54.7			
Penalties of Artemis, The —Katherine F. Gerould	159	60.1	262	68.3	421	64.2	15 S
Penny Marsh, Public Health Nurse— Dorothy Deming	2		292	70.2			
Penrod—Booth Tarkington	363	84.6	408	83.3	771	84.0	38 IR
Penrod and Sam—Booth Tarkington	1351	85.2	1312	85.1	2663	85.2	88 S
Penrod's Busy Day— Booth Tarkington	483	82.3	376	91.2	859	86.8	36 S
People Next Door, The— Frank M. Colby	478	60.3	745	75.4	1223	67.9	36 S
People of Moronia, The —Eleanor R. Wimbridge	299	63.0	346	81.8	645	72.4	14 R
People, Yes, The—Carl Sandburg	135	66.7	190	67.6	325	67.2	
Pepys's Diary—Samuel Pepys	368	68.5	323	66.9	691	67.7	43 S
Perennial Bachelor, The —Anne Parrish	195	50.0	209	70.6	404	60.3	19 S
Perils of Thinking, The— Unknown	188	57.2	244	65.6	432	61.4	15 S
Pershing at the Front— Arthur Guiterman	253	87.3	387	92.4	640	89.9	16 R
Personal Recollections of Joan of Arc— Mark Twain	111	67.6	192	70.6	303	69.1	
Peter Projects—Marie L. Brady	232	85.6	319	90.6	551	88.1	14 S
Petit the Poet—Edgar L. Masters	238	36.8	262	45.4	500	41.1	20 S
Pets—John V. A. Weaver	299	75.9	424	80.9	723	78.4	11 R
Peyton Place—Grace Metalious	1029	67.3	1207	60.4	2236	63.9	

PUPILS' READING INTERESTS: GRADES 10-12
Ts and Ss = Teachers and Schools   S = Studied in Class
IR = Independent Reading   R = Read in Class

SELECTION—AUTHOR	Boys		Girls		Total		Ts & Ss	
	No.	%	No.	%	No.	Av. %		
Pheidippides—Robert Browning	157	54.5	197	54.8	354	54.7	26	S
Philosopher, A—John K. Bangs	445	62.6	454	77.9	899	70.3	15	R
Piece of String, The—Guy de Maupassant	213	68.1	341	75.1	554	71.6	28	S
Pied Piper of Hamelin, The—Robert Browning	268	72.2	290	80.9	558	76.6	48	S
Pig, The—Edward V. Lucas	375	58.1	429	59.9	804	59.0	25	S
Pigs Is Pigs—Ellis P. Butler	435	95.4	489	94.0	924	94.7	16	R
Pilgrim's Progress, The—John Bunyan	263	52.7	270	55.0	533	53.9	23	S
Pine at Timberline, The—Harriet Monroe	326	34.1	366	40.7	692	37.4	14	R
Pioneer: The Vignette of an Oil Well— Lexie D. Robertson	371	61.9	377	55.7	748	58.8	21	S
Piper, The—William Blake	143	46.2	188	46.8	331	46.5	16	S
Piper, The—Josephine P. Peabody	138	54.0	214	66.4	352	60.2	82	IR
Pipes at Lucknow, The—John G. Whittier	427	51.1	449	58.2	876	54.7	13	R
Pippa's Song—Robert Browning	2983	35.5	3427	51.2	6410	43.4	125	R
Pippi Longstocking—Astrid Lindgren	8		215	72.3				
Pirate Don Durk of Dowdee—Mildred P. Merryman	1140	58.4	1192	63.1	2332	60.8	27	R
Pit and the Pendulum, The—Edgar A. Poe	525	77.9	550	72.0	1075	75.0	53	S
Plain Language from Truthful James—Bret Harte	866	71.7	859	73.1	1725	72.4	48	S
Plaint of the Camel, The—Guy W. Carryl	737	66.9	944	67.7	1681	67.3	29	R

274   THE READING INTERESTS

PUPILS' READING INTERESTS: GRADES 10-12

Ts and Ss = Teachers and Schools   S = Studied in Class
IR = Independent Reading   R = Read in Class

SELECTION—AUTHOR	Boys		Girls		Total		Ts & Ss	
	No.	%	No.	%	No.	Av. %		
Plantation Play-Song— Joel C. Harris	239	60.3	273	71.6	512	66.0	12	S
Plantonio (Cowboy Ballad)	221	73.8	238	66.2	459	70.0	16	R
Plea for Gas Lamps, A— Robert L. Stevenson	209	61.7	232	58.4	441	60.1	17	S
Please Don't Eat the Daisies—Jean Kerr	351	71.9	878	74.7	1229	73.3		
Pledge of Allegiance, The—William T. Page	277	80.9	329	85.7	606	83.3	15	R
Plowman, The—Lizette W. Reese	401	49.5	503	47.2	904	48.4	14	R
Poem in Praise of Practically Nothing, A— Samuel Hoffenstein	362	63.4	423	72.8	785	68.1	14	R
Poetic People—Max Eastman	223	43.9	218	50.5	441	47.2	23	S
Point Bonita—Witter Bynner	277	71.5	285	57.4	562	64.5	13	R
Point of No Return— John P. Marquand	234	76.5	250	68.8	484	72.7		
Pollyanna—Eleanor H. Porter	107	59.3	383	71.1	490	65.2		
Polonius' Advice— William Shakespeare	339	43.4	345	54.8	684	49.1	12	R
Pony Express, The— Arthur Chapman	226	76.8	99	59.6	325	68.2	130	IR
Pony Express, The— Mark Twain	354	72.0	394	64.3	748	68.2	11	R
Poor Richard's Almanac —Benjamin Franklin	274	56.6	224	63.8	498	60.2	24	S
Poor Voter on Election Day, The—John G. Whittier	292	41.8	468	48.0	760	44.9	12	R
Popeye (Comic Strip)	889	59.2	1070	44.7	1959	52.0	54	IR
Porch Railery—Dorothy Scarborough	154	49.0	211	59.2	365	54.1	23	S
Porcupine, The—Oliver Hereford	336	49.3	381	57.2	717	52.3	13	R
Porgy—DuBose Heyward	118	69.5	257	77.4	375	73.5		

PUPILS' READING INTERESTS: GRADES 10-12
Ts and Ss = Teachers and Schools   S = Studied in Class
IR = Independent Reading   R = Read in Class

SELECTION—AUTHOR	Boys		Girls		Total		Ts & Ss	
	No.	%	No.	%	No.	Av. %		
Portrait of a Boy— Stephen V. Benét	321	72.0	348	73.7	669	72.9	30	S
Portrait of a Lady— Henry James	69		284	71.8				
Portrait of Jenny— Robert Nathan	60		430	77.2				
Possessions—Edward V. Lucas	239	53.6	243	68.7	482	61.2	29	S
Poster Girl, The— Carolyn Wells	437	34.0	513	43.8	950	38.9	16	R
Postman Always Rings Twice, The— James M. Cain	88		169	84.0				
Postmistress of Laurel Run, The—Bret Harte	423	67.0	326	76.5	749	71.8	23	S
Post Mortems—Devine	155	66.4	150	59.3	305	62.9	31	S
Powerful Eyes of Jeremy Tait, The— Wallace Irwin	346	74.7	366	69.4	712	72.1	13	R
Practically 17— Rosamond Du Jardin	3		366	69.8				
Prairie Battle—Stanley Vestal	365	59.0	413	36.6	778	47.8	13	R
Prayer—Louis Untermeyer	269	64.3	361	77.3	630	70.8	18	S
Prayer for a Little Home, A—Florence Bone	556	51.9	597	75.8	1153	63.9	20	R
Prayer of Cyrus Brown, The—Sam W. Foss	429	81.5	430	89.2	859	85.4	13	R
Prayers of Steel—Carl Sandburg	321	65.9	359	66.6	680	66.3	29	S
Preamble to the Constitution, The	276	77.0	331	77.5	607	77.3	15	R
Precious Words—Emily Dickinson	234	53.9	327	64.8	561	59.4	18	S
Preparedness—Edwin Markham	395	70.3	423	72.5	818	71.4	26	S
President's Lady, The— Irving Stone	13		172	78.5				

PUPILS' READING INTERESTS: GRADES 10-12
Ts and Ss = Teachers and Schools　　　S = Studied in Class
IR = Independent Reading　　　　　　　R = Read in Class

SELECTION—AUTHOR	Boys		Girls		Total		Ts & Ss	
	No.	%	No.	%	No.	Av. %		
Pretty Polly—E. M. Root	352	32.8	380	37.9	732	35.4	15	R
Pretty Words—Elinor Wiley	374	46.3	428	64.8	802	55.6	25	S
Pride and Prejudice— Jane Austen	213	58.9	793	70.9	1006	64.9		
Priest's Tale, The— Demetrios Bikelos	249	88.4	312	87.7	561	88.1	11	R
Prince and the Pauper, The—Mark Twain	366	75.8	715	81.3	1081	78.6	52	IR
Princess and the Puma, The—O. Henry	254	75.4	339	71.9	593	73.7	14	R
Printing Press, The— Robert H. Davis	545	70.5	550	72.5	1095	71.5	16	R
Prisoner of Chillon, The —George G. Byron	2069	66.4	1767	72.6	3836	69.5	142	S
Prisoner of Zenda, The— Anthony Hope	160	66.6	102	68.1	262	67.4		
Private Life of Helen of Troy, The— John Erskine	418	73.6	432	74.2	850	73.9		
Prodigal Son, The—The Bible	578	77.4	696	81.5	1274	79.5	23	S
Proem—Madison Cawein	200	42.2	262	50.0	462	46.1	18	S
Profiles in Courage— John F. Kennedy	298	75.8	277	74.0	575	74.9		
Program Notes— Stoddard King	398	61.9	448	77.0	846	69.5	13	R
Prologue to the Canterbury Tales, The— Geoffrey Chaucer	561	52.8	536	59.9	1097	56.4	62	S
Prom Trouble—James L. Summers	16		162	73.8				
Prophecy, A—Alfred Tennyson	529	45.1	545	52.8	1074	49.0	16	R
Prospice—Robert Browning	298	47.5	376	64.8	674	56.2	38	S
Protest of a Young Intellectual, The— Don Marquis	418	32.3	516	45.7	934	39.0	24	R

PUPILS' READING INTERESTS: GRADES 10-12

Ts and Ss = Teachers and Schools   S = Studied in Class
IR = Independent Reading   R = Read in Class

SELECTION—AUTHOR	Boys		Girls		Total		Ts & Ss	
	No.	%	No.	%	No.	Av. %		
Proud Maisie—Walter Scott	236	39.4	319	56.7	555	48.1	22	S
Prunier Tells a Story—T. Morris Longstreth	302	81.3	407	83.8	709	82.6	14	S
Psalm XIX—The Bible	565	53.6	642	67.4	1207	60.5	24	S
Psalm of David, A—The Bible	247	56.9	357	66.9	604	61.9	13	R
Psalm of Life, A—Henry W. Longfellow	461	46.7	482	65.7	943	56.2	17	R
Psalm I—The Bible	182	56.0	212	71.7	394	63.9	21	S
Psalm CXXI—The Bible	184	59.5	212	75.7	396	67.6	21	S
P. T. Barnum—R. F. Dibble	174	73.0	194	61.9	368	67.5	16	S
PT 109: John F. Kennedy—Robert J. Donovan	177	82.8	47					
Pudd'n Head Wilson— Mark Twain	303	82.5	312	78.7	615	80.6	82	IR
Pup-Dog, The—Robert P. Utter	460	71.4	579	69.7	1039	70.6	41	S
Pure Mathematician, A— Arthur Guiterman	251	40.8	325	41.1	576	41.0	14	R
Puritan's Ballad, The— Elinor Wylie	673	48.9	840	65.4	1513	57.2	27	R
Purloined Letter, The— Edgar A. Poe	314	68.8	297	64.7	611	66.8	40	S
Pursuit of Fire, The— Charles S. Brooks	201	55.5	478	68.3	679	61.9	20	S
Pusher in the Face, The —F. Scott Fitzgerald	188	91.5	322	86.2	510	88.9	14	R
Pygmalion—Rannie B. Baker	247	46.5	307	69.2	554	57.9	11	R
Pygmalion—George B. Shaw	141	77.0	325	85.2	466	81.1		
Pyramus and Thisbe— John G. Saxe	439	64.1	476	75.5	915	69.8	33	S
Pyramus and Thisbe— William Shakespeare	251	48.6	284	56.1	535	52.4	21	S
Quality—John Galsworthy	1281	74.4	1250	81.6	2531	78.0	98	S

PUPILS' READING INTERESTS: GRADES 10-12
Ts and Ss = Teachers and Schools   S = Studied in Class
IR = Independent Reading   R = Read in Class

SELECTION—AUTHOR	Boys No.	Boys %	Girls No.	Girls %	Total No.	Total Av. %	Ts & Ss	
Quality Street—James M. Barrie	284	63.2	364	86.7	648	75.0	46	S
Queed—Henry S. Harrison	327	70.2	464	74.9	791	72.6	28	S
Queen of the Mayhem, The—Margaret Fishback	294	41.7	345	58.7	639	50.2	17	R
Quentin Durward— Walter Scott	191	68.3	183	55.7	374	62.0	72	S
Quest of the Ribband, The—Arthur Guiterman	363	69.3	412	84.1	775	76.7	13	R
Quo Vadis—Henryk Sienkiewicz	167	81.1	169	82.5	336	81.8		
Rabbi Ben Ezra—Robert Browning	153	47.7	199	60.8	352	54.3	21	S
Rachel—Walter de la Mare	268	29.3	373	58.7	641	44.0	15	R
Radio—Harriet Monroe	296	67.1	315	66.4	611	66.8	14	R
Raft, The—Robert Trumbull	269	87.2	171	86.5	440	86.9	145	IR
Raggedy Man, The— James W. Riley	402	58.0	461	70.4	863	64.2	22	R
Railway Accident, A— Thomas Mann	183	67.8	225	68.7	408	68.3	17	R
Railway Train, The— Emily Dickinson	364	64.0	399	66.0	763	65.0	23	S
Rain (Essay)—Unknown	328	30.8	332	43.4	660	37.1	15	R
Rain Song, The—Robert Loveman	235	36.6	309	61.5	544	49.1	15	R
Raintree Country—Ross Lockridge, Jr.	309	70.6	670	76.4	979	73.5		
Rainy Day, The—Henry W. Longfellow	882	46.4	955	60.9	1837	53.7	32	R
Rally Round the Flag, Boys—Max Shulman	493	78.5	675	75.9	1168	77.2		
Ramona—Helen H. Jackson	103	72.8	732	81.4	835	77.1	201	IR
Ranchman's Ride, The— Larry Chittenden	387	66.4	455	61.2	842	63.8	30	S
Ransom of Red Chief, The—O. Henry	618	88.1	436	83.0	1054	85.6	33	S

PUPILS' READING INTERESTS: GRADES 10-12
Ts and Ss = Teachers and Schools   S = Studied in Class
IR = Independent Reading   R = Read in Class

SELECTION—AUTHOR	Boys		Girls		Total		Ts & Ss	
	No.	%	No.	%	No.	Av. %		
Rape of the Lock, The— Alexander Pope	259	45.2	128	53.5	387	49.4	19	S
Raven, The—Marquis James	189	57.1	241	62.2	430	59.7		
Raven, The—Edgar A. Poe	475	58.7	531	60.9	1006	59.8	42	S
Reading Boy, The— Nathalia Crane	346	53.8	394	69.9	740	61.9	15	R
Real Baseball, The— Arthur Guiterman	1036	74.5	1149	72.0	2185	73.3	36	R
Real Book of Submarines, The—Epstein and Williams	237	59.7	12					
Rear Guard, The— Siegfried Sassoon	491	71.0	537	72.2	1028	71.6	19	R
Reasonable Affliction, A —Matthew Prior	332	50.0	388	59.0	720	54.5	16	R
Rebecca—Daphne du Maurier	46		544	85.9				
Rebecca Nixon and Martha Waugh— Wilfred W. Gibson	298	48.5	368	63.3	666	55.9	14	R
Rebecca of Sunnybrook Farm—Kate D. Wiggin	40		203	68.5				
Recessional—Rudyard Kipling	747	65.1	794	73.1	1541	69.1	60	S
Red Badge of Courage, The—Stephen Crane	515	74.3	313	73.2	828	73.8	200	IR
Red-Headed League, The—A. Conan Doyle	375	79.7	338	72.5	713	76.1	40	S
Red Mark, The—Israel Zangwill	394	47.7	399	66.3	793	57.0	12	R
Red Ryder (Comic Strip)	678	62.2	784	47.6	1462	54.9	47	IR
Red Slippers—Amy Lowell	307	25.4	378	42.3	685	33.9	12	R
Reds of the Midi, The— Felix Gras	171	75.7	161	76.1	332	75.9	69	IR
Remarkable Wreck of the Thomas Hyke, The— Frank R. Stockton	202	81.4	131	61.8	333	71.6	16	S

PUPILS' READING INTERESTS: GRADES 10-12

Ts and Ss = Teachers and Schools   S = Studied in Class

IR = Independent Reading   R = Read in Class

SELECTION—AUTHOR	Boys		Girls		Total		Ts & Ss	
	No.	%	No.	%	No.	Av. %		
Remarks from the Pup—Burges Johnson	389	68.1	404	82.2	793	75.2	14	R
Remember Me to God—Myron S. Kaufman	41		139	82.3				
Renascence—Edna St. V. Millay	332	53.0	284	75.4	616	64.2	27	S
Requiem—Robert L. Stevenson	389	63.2	471	71.0	860	67.1	35	S
Requiem for a Nun, A—William Faulkner	57		164	82.3				
Requiescat—Oscar Wilde	513	54.7	541	69.2	1054	62.0	41	S
Reserved Coffin, The—Luigi Pirandello	171	57.9	189	51.3	360	54.6	70	IR
Retrieved Reformation, A—O. Henry	183	93.4	327	92.7	510	93.1	20	S
Return of a Private, The—Hamlin Garland	274	67.2	269	78.4	543	72.8	26	S
Return of the Native, The—Thomas Hardy	438	69.2	236	82.6	674	75.9	29	S
Reveille—Alfred E. Housman	530	60.7	590	57.1	1120	58.9	42	S
Revenge, The—Alfred Tennyson	279	77.2	202	63.6	481	70.4	30	S
Revenge of Hamish, The—Sidney Lanier	309	74.9	303	76.9	612	75.9	13	R
Revival Hymn—Joel C. Harris	244	52.5	277	65.9	521	59.2	13	S
Revolt of Mother, The—Mary E. W. Freeman	543	73.5	462	85.9	1005	79.7	36	S
Reynard the Fox—John Masefield	368	78.8	399	76.6	767	77.7	15	R
Rhinoceros, The—Ogden Nash	274	32.8	354	42.9	628	37.9	13	R
Rhodora, The—Ralph W. Emerson	318	52.4	433	62.0	751	57.2	25	S
Richard Cory—Edwin A. Robinson	701	64.2	833	69.2	1534	66.7	60	S
Rich Man, The—Franklin P. Adams	465	57.0	456	62.1	921	59.6	17	R

PUPILS' READING INTERESTS: GRADES 10-12

Ts and Ss = Teachers and Schools S = Studied in Class
IR = Independent Reading   R = Read in Class

SELECTION—AUTHOR	Boys		Girls		Total		Ts & Ss	
	No.	%	No.	%	No.	Av. %		
Riders of the Purple Sage—Zane Grey	255	85.1	241	78.6	496	81.9	58	IR
Riders to the Sea—J. M. Synge	352	52.4	279	55.3	631	53.9	36	S
Riding Song, A— Unknown	770	37.6	825	48.1	1595	42.9	27	R
Right Promethean Fire, The—George M. Martin	294	50.7	288	76.0	582	63.4	14	S
Ring Out, Wild Bells— Alfred Tennyson	249	50.0	278	66.0	527	58.0	16	S
Rip Van Winkle— Washington Irving	547	80.8	232	75.9	779	78.4	29	S
Rise and Fall of the Third Reich, The— William L. Shirer	176	88.4	114	77.2	290	82.8		
Rise of Silas Lapham, The—William D. Howells	162	69.1	594	67.9	756	68.5	35	S
Rising of the Moon, The —Augusta Gregory	499	67.0	473	67.2	972	67.1	31	S
Rivals, The—Richard B. Sheridan	342	68.9	366	76.8	708	72.9	31	S
Riverman, The—Stewart E. White	315	88.6	273	59.2	588	73.9	17	S
R. M. S. Titanic—Hanson W. Baldwin	311	93.4	365	88.5	676	91.0	15	R
Road, The—Siegfried Sassoon	168	43.2	215	46.5	383	44.9	15	R
Road Not Taken, The— Robert Frost	223	62.1	306	75.0	529	68.6	21	S
Road Race—Philip Harkins	214	77.6	22					
Roadways—John Masefield	230	72.6	224	77.0	454	74.8	15	S
Robe, The—Lloyd C. Douglas	192	88.3	596	90.4	788	89.4	71	IR
Robert E. Lee—John Drinkwater	181	79.8	129	68.2	310	74.0	29	S
Robert Fulton— Marguerite Henry	164	74.1	142	66.2	306	70.2	76	IR

282 THE READING INTERESTS

PUPILS' READING INTERESTS: GRADES 10-12
Ts and Ss = Teachers and Schools   S = Studied in Class
IR = Independent Reading   R = Read in Class

SELECTION—AUTHOR	Boys No.	%	Girls No.	%	Total No.	Av. %	Ts & Ss	
Robin Hood and Allan-a-Dale (British Ballad)	240	74.6	262	74.2	502	74.4	15	R
Robin Hood and Little John (British Ballad)	817	78.8	797	69.5	1614	74.2	49	S
Robin Hood Ballads, The (British Ballads)	635	78.7	516	74.4	1151	76.6	79	S
Robin Hood Rescuing the Widow's Three Sons (British Ballad)	224	70.1	252	68.7	476	69.4	17	S
Robin Hood's Death and Burial (British Ballad)	211	72.0	187	65.8	398	68.9	16	S
Robinson Crusoe—Daniel Defoe	799	84.9	716	78.7	1515	81.8	34	IR
Robinson Crusoe's Story —Charles E. Carryl	287	72.1	282	81.0	569	76.6	19	S
Roll a Rock Down— Henry H. Knibbs	447	71.7	444	60.0	891	65.9	22	R
Romance—Robert L. Stevenson	225	48.0	265	62.8	490	55.4	25	S
Romance—Simeon Strunsky	168	61.0	483	74.2	651	67.6	21	S
Romance—W. J. Turner	321	48.9	374	58.8	695	53.9	26	S
Romance of a Busy Broker, The—O. Henry	313	89.3	371	92.9	684	91.1	14	R
Romancers, The— Edmond Rostand	349	67.8	1050	81.9	1399	74.9	35	S
Romantic in the Rain, The—G. K. Chesterton	239	47.3	184	70.7	423	59.0	24	S
Romany of the Snows, A —Gilbert Parker	128	62.5	177	74.3	305	68.4	24	IR
Romeo and Juliet— William Shakespeare	822	70.5	872	85.1	1694	77.8	71	S
Rondeau (Jenny Kissed Me)—Leigh Hunt	548	34.2	616	43.4	1164	38.8	31	R
Roofs—Joyce Kilmer	302	62.6	324	76.1	626	69.4	28	S
Rose Aylmer—Walter S. Landor	211	42.7	265	54.0	476	48.4	17	S
Rouge Bouquet—Joyce Kilmer	232	73.9	295	75.1	527	74.5	26	S

PUPILS' READING INTERESTS: GRADES 10-12

Ts and Ss = Teachers and Schools   S = Studied in Class
IR = Independent Reading   R = Read in Class

SELECTION—AUTHOR	Boys		Girls		Total		Ts & Ss	
	No.	%	No.	%	No.	Av. %		
Round Columbus Circle—Christophei Morley	257	66.7	276	66.1	533	66.4	31	S
Rounding the Horn (From *Dauber*) John Masefield	289	75.6	288	69.6	577	72.6	34	S
Rudolph the Headsman —Oliver W. Holmes	266	76.7	376	66.2	642	71.5	13	R
Rule, Britannia—James Thomson	197	56.9	181	54.4	378	55.7	19	S
Rules for the Road— Edwin Markham	420	40.7	517	46.9	937	43.8	11	S
Runaway, The—Robert Frost	240	65.6	317	74.6	557	70.1	30	S
Running Wolf—Algernon Blackwood	216	79.4	376	78.3	592	78.9	15	S
Run Silent, Run Deep— Edward L. Beach	225	85.8	62					
Ruth—Thomas Hood	123	48.4	334	70.0	457	59.2	15	S
Sacrifice—Ralph W. Emerson	1124	45.5	1181	52.1	2305	48.8	43	R
Sad Tale of Mr. Mears, The—Unknown	335	56.6	402	65.2	737	60.9	13	R
Safari: A Saga of the African Blue—Martin Johnson	216	86.6	187	78.3	403	82.5	84	IR
Sage Counsel—Arthur T. Quiller-Couch	397	50.6	454	53.0	851	51.8	13	R
Saint Joan of Arc—Mark Twain	297	69.4	281	78.1	578	73.8	30	S
Sally in Our Alley— Henry Carey	222	68.7	246	71.3	468	70.0	19	S
Sam Houston—Rosemary C. and Stephen V. Benét	226	52.0	375	60.3	601	56.2	12	R
Samuel Brown—Phoebe Cary	411	33.1	461	47.6	872	40.4	15	R
Sand Creek—Stanley Vestal	365	78.6	414	80.2	779	79.4	13	R
Sandpiper, The—Celia Thaxter	368	38.7	397	52.2	765	45.5	22	R

PUPILS' READING INTERESTS: GRADES 10-12
Ts and Ss = Teachers and Schools　　　S = Studied in Class
IR = Independent Reading　　　　　　R = Read in Class

SELECTION—AUTHOR	Boys		Girls		Total		Ts & Ss	
	No.	%	No.	%	No.	Av. %		
Sands of Dee, The— Charles Kingsley	305	56.2	358	66.3	663	61.3	15	R
Santa Fé Trail, The— Samuel Adams	306	64.1	134	54.5	440	59.3		
Santa Fé Trail, The— Vachel Lindsay	298	72.5	328	71.2	626	71.9	28	S
Saturday-Night Bath, The —Helen C. Baker	223	81.4	222	85.6	445	83.5	27	S
Savage, A—John B. O'Reilly	440	68.7	429	62.9	869	65.8	15	R
Sayonara—James A. Michener	103	75.2	367	88.6	470	81.9		
Scaramouche—Rafael Sabatini	202	80.0	440	83.8	642	81.9	34	S
Scarecrow, The—Walter de la Mare	155	59.4	172	67.2	327	63.3	17	S
Scarlet Letter, The— Nathaniel Hawthorne	136	67.3	429	76.0	565	71.7	66	IR
Scarlet Pimpernel, The— Baroness Orczy	162	79.6	372	83.3	534	81.5	129	IR
Schoolboy Reads His Iliad, The—David Morton	219	53.9	249	59.2	468	56.6	13	S
Schoolmaster, The— Oliver Goldsmith	389	49.7	435	62.1	824	55.9	15	R
Science for the Young— Wallace Irwin	277	81.6	308	82.3	585	82.0	12	R
Scots Wha Hae Wi' Wallace Bled—Robert Burns	309	58.7	212	53.5	521	56.1	18	S
Scotty Bill—William H. Davies	460	45.9	513	46.5	973	46.2	21	R
Scum of the Earth— Robert H. Schauffler	310	62.7	387	65.2	697	64.0	33	S
Scythe Song—Andrew Lang	423	49.8	452	60.2	875	55.0	26	S
Sea, The—Eva L. Ogden	605	53.3	618	64.3	1223	58.8	21	R
Sea Around Us, The— Rachel Carson	202	72.0	142	63.7	344	67.9		

PUPILS' READING INTERESTS: GRADES 10-12

Ts and Ss = Teachers and Schools   S = Studied in Class

IR = Independent Reading   R = Read in Class

SELECTION—AUTHOR	Boys		Girls		Total		Ts & Ss	
	No.	%	No.	%	No.	Av. %		
Sea Dirge, A —William Shakespeare	188	61.7	248	58.3	436	60.0	23	S
Seafarer, The (Old English Poem)	225	58.2	296	60.0	521	59.1	23	S
Sea-Fever—John Masefield	1309	67.4	1603	72.0	2912	69.7	92	S
Sea Gypsy, The—Richard Hovey	382	51.8	495	56.4	877	54.1	31	S
Sea Lullaby—Elinor Wylie	294	60.2	337	72.7	631	66.5	27	S
Searchings of Jonathan, The—Elizabeth Woodbridge	243	52.7	311	62.1	554	57.4	16	R
Sea Serpent Chantey, The—Vachel Lindsay	461	53.4	460	49.1	921	51.3	20	R
Seaside Romance, A—Don Marquis	220	69.5	305	81.0	525	75.3	14	R
Sea Wolf, The—Jack London	605	80.3	130	62.7	735	71.5		
Second Inaugural Address—Abraham Lincoln	193	64.8	166	63.9	359	64.4	17	S
Second World War, The—Winston Churchill	206	81.1	43					
Securing Happiness—Benjamin Franklin	536	61.8	542	66.3	1078	64.1	15	R
See Here, Private Hargrove—Marion Hargrove	464	92.7	713	92.1	1177	92.4	62	IR
Seeing People Off—Max Beerbohm	179	59.5	220	66.4	399	63.0	26	S
Seein' Things—Eugene Field	448	74.2	429	88.3	877	81.3	31	S
Senator Rests, The—M. C. Blackman	250	60.8	239	64.9	489	62.9	25	S
Senior Prom—Rosamond Du Jardin	6		198	75.5				
Senior Year—Anne Emery	3		473	70.7				

PUPILS' READING INTERESTS: GRADES 10-12
Ts and Ss = Teachers and Schools   S = Studied in Class
IR = Independent Reading   R = Read in Class

SELECTION—AUTHOR	Boys		Girls		Total		Ts & Ss	
	No.	%	No.	%	No.	Av. %		
Sermon on the Mount, The—The Bible	626	56.9	740	67.4	1366	62.2	23	R
Servant Girl and Grocer's Boy—Joyce Kilmer	354	52.7	405	71.7	759	62.2	16	R
Sesame and Lilies—John Ruskin	179	41.1	224	44.4	403	42.8	21	R
Seventeen—Booth Tarkington	265	80.2	571	85.7	836	83.0	42	S
Seventeenth Summer— Maureen Daly	22		746	90.8			65	IR
Seven Waves Away (Radio Play)—Richard Sale	397	91.9	497	90.5	894	91.2	14	R
Shakespeare's Plays	163	59.2	231	65.2	394	62.2		
Sham—F. G. Tompkins	608	77.1	1246	78.1	1854	77.6	48	S
Shane—Jack Shaefer	495	79.6	312	75.3	807	77.5		
She Came and Went— James R. Lowell	201	56.7	186	65.6	387	61.2	16	S
She Dwelt Among the Untrodden Ways— William Wordsworth	333	42.6	452	55.2	785	48.9	30	S
Sheener—Ben A. Williams	360	73.6	311	82.2	671	77.9	24	S
Sheep—William H. Davies	439	56.5	512	58.7	951	57.6	26	S
Shell, The—James Stephens	232	52.6	263	67.1	495	59.9	22	S
Shepherd's Psalm, The— The Bible	304	74.5	415	82.4	719	78.5	16	R
Sheridan's Ride—Thomas B. Read	1100	74.6	1112	62.1	2212	68.4	30	R
She Stoops to Conquer— Oliver Goldsmith	1343	74.2	1438	84.4	2781	79.3	117	S
She Walks in Beauty— George G. Byron	429	47.4	525	65.9	954	56.7	37	S
She Was a Phantom of Delight— William Wordsworth	290	55.3	361	70.8	651	63.1	37	S

PUPILS' READING INTERESTS: GRADES 10-12

Ts and Ss = Teachers and Schools   S = Studied in Class

IR = Independent Reading   R = Read in Class

SELECTION—AUTHOR	Boys		Girls		Total		Ts & Ss	
	No.	%	No.	%	No.	Av. %		
Shield, The—Charlotte P. Stetson	278	44.4	292	51.5	570	48.0	16	R
Shipwrecked in Southern Seas—Lowell Thomas	189	91.0	184	81.8	373	86.4	20	S
Shoes—O. Henry	285	83.5	353	86.8	638	85.2	19	S
Short-Grass Country, The —E. A. Brininstool	281	51.6	285	53.2	566	52.4	13	R
Short'nin' Bread—Negro Song	237	73.0	302	80.0	539	76.5	14	R
Show Boat (Book)—Edna Ferber	138	69.2	282	84.8	420	77.0	130	IR
Show Boat (Movie)	423	70.2	498	86.2	921	78.2	130	
Side Glances (Comic Strip)	172	64.5	337	70.6	509	67.6	37	
Siege of Berlin, The— Alphonse Daudet	194	78.4	210	82.9	404	80.7	15	R
Silas Marner—George Eliot	5259	75.0	5065	90.1	10324	82.6	306	S
Silence—Edgar Lee Masters	243	68.5	272	70.5	515	69.5	28	S
Silent Brothers, The— Arnold Bennett	222	75.0	225	82.7	447	78.9	26	S
Silent World, The— Cousteau and Dumas	150	83.7	28					
Silver—Walter de la Mare	465	66.1	562	78.8	1027	72.5	42	S
Silver Box, The—John Galsworthy	170	77.1	239	81.6	409	79.4	19	S
Silver Chalice, The— Thomas B. Costain	351	80.2	674	86.6	1025	83.4		
Silver Lining, The— Constance D'Arcy Mackay	214	55.8	249	65.9	463	60.9	14	S
Simon Legree, a Negro Sermon—Vachel Lindsay	646	83.6	747	79.7	1393	81.7	21	R
Singing Leaves, The— James R. Lowell	151	54.3	324	71.1	475	62.7	72	S
Singing Lesson, The— Katherine Mansfield	415	37.3	248	66.1	663	51.7	17	S

PUPILS' READING INTERESTS: GRADES 10-12
Ts and Ss = Teachers and Schools   S = Studied in Class
IR = Independent Reading   R = Read in Class

SELECTION—AUTHOR	Boys		Girls		Total		Ts & Ss
	No.	%	No.	%	No.	Av. %	
Sioux Chief's Daughter, The—Joaquin Miller	254	64.4	313	68.1	567	66.3	17	S
Sire de Malétroit's Door, The—Robert L. Stevenson	931	72.2	716	77.2	1647	74.7	55	S
Sir Gawain and the Green Knight (Old English Tale)	318	71.7	327	72.9	645	72.3	17	S
Sir Patrick Spens (British Ballad)	605	58.8	557	56.6	1162	57.7	49	S
Sir Roger at Church— Joseph Addison	253	69.4	245	71.2	498	70.3	22	S
Sir Roger at the Theatre —Joseph Addison	237	59.9	125	65.2	362	62.6	18	S
Sir Roger de Coverley Papers, The— Addison and Steele	301	48.3	334	56.0	635	52.2	34	S
Sisterly Scheme, A—H. C. Bunner	516	66.8	360	87.2	876	77.0	27	S
Skeleton in Armor, The —Henry W. Longfellow	389	77.0	460	74.8	849	75.9	38	S
Sketch Book, The— Washington Irving	483	64.8	365	65.3	848	65.1	34	S
Skin of Our Teeth, The— Thornton Wilder	77		158	68.4			108	IR
Skipper Ireson's Ride— John G. Whittier	216	71.8	387	66.9	603	69.4	30	S
Skippy (Comic Strip)	605	45.7	877	41.7	1482	43.7	42	
Skunk Cabbage—Henry S. Canby	176	54.3	210	58.3	386	56.3	20	S
Skyscraper—Carl Sandburg	351	68.5	322	67.1	673	67.8	23	S
Skyward—Richard E. Byrd	358	79.3	177	73.4	535	76.4	145	IR
Slave, The—James Oppenheim	173	65.6	175	68.0	348	66.8	18	S
Sleeper, The—Walter de la Mare	270	33.0	374	43.4	644	38.2	15	R
Sleeping Outdoors— Frederick L. Allen	382	82.6	351	87.3	733	85.0	18	R

PUPILS' READING INTERESTS: GRADES 10-12

Ts and Ss = Teachers and Schools   S = Studied in Class

IR = Independent Reading   R = Read in Class

SELECTION—AUTHOR	Boys		Girls		Total		Ts & Ss	
	No.	%	No.	%	No.	Av. %		
Smack in School, The— William P. Palmer	348	75.7	421	89.5	769	82.6	14	R
Small Vocabulary May Have a Big Kick, A— Ring Lardner	412	70.6	448	75.1	860	72.9	16	R
Smells (Junior)— Christopher Morley	209	64.6	228	75.8	437	70.2	24	S
Smilin' Jack (Comic Strip)	996	73.6	1273	74.2	2269	73.9	54	IR
Smoke and Steel—Carl Sandburg	337	64.4	320	63.8	657	64.1	24	S
Smoky—Will James	314	86.1	194	79.1	508	82.6	32	S
Snake, The—Stephen Crane	400	77.4	537	68.6	937	73.0	21	R
Snake, The—Emily Dickinson	376	64.1	392	63.3	768	63.7	26	S
Snake Pit, The—Mary J. Ward	107	64.0	185	84.9	292	74.5		
Snakes—W. H. Hudson	280	62.0	338	63.8	618	62.9	17	S
Snare, The—James Stephens	467	50.6	431	56.0	898	53.3	18	R
Snaring a Bushmaster— William Beebe	188	79.0	196	65.3	384	72.2	21	S
Snow-Bound—John G. Whittier	224	68.8	268	77.6	492	73.2	29	S
Snow Dog—Jim Kjelgaard	150	76.3	141	70.9	291	73.6		
Snows of Kilamanjaro, The—Ernest Hemingway	317	81.4	248	76.2	565	78.8		
Snow Storm, The—Ralph W. Emerson	437	49.8	475	53.3	912	51.6	25	R
Snow-White and the Seven Dwarfs—Grimm Brothers	1078	46.4	1905	63.3	2983	54.9		
So Big—Edna Ferber	481	70.8	546	88.5	1027	79.7	47	S
Society upon the Stanislaus, The—Bret Harte	432	71.9	528	70.5	960	71.2	28	S
So Glad for Spreeng— Thomas A. Daly	302	80.0	307	87.5	609	83.8	11	R

PUPILS' READING INTERESTS: GRADES 10-12
Ts and Ss = Teachers and Schools   S = Studied in Class
IR = Independent Reading   R = Read in Class

SELECTION—AUTHOR	Boys		Girls		Total		Ts & Ss	
	No.	%	No.	%	No.	Av. %		
Sohrab and Rustem (Prose)—Firdausi	271	88.4	322	90.5	593	89.5	13	R
Sohrab and Rustum— Matthew Arnold	2531	75.5	2282	70.4	4813	73.0	145	S
Soldier, The—Rupert Brooke	801	69.6	907	71.2	1708	70.4	73	S
Soldier, Rest—Walter Scott	580	58.4	570	58.7	1150	58.6	22	R
Soldier's Dream, The— Thomas Campbell	288	67.0	325	69.1	613	68.1	15	S
Solitaire—Amy Lowell	211	49.3	219	56.6	430	53.0	22	S
Solitary Reaper, The— William Wordsworth	244	58.8	365	67.0	609	62.9	32	S
Solo—Rebecca McCann	246	41.7	281	70.7	527	56.2	12	R
Some Came Running— James Jones	252	73.0	466	78.6	718	75.8		
Some Nonsense about a Dog—Harry E. Dounce	428	60.6	505	69.9	933	65.3	40	S
Song—Rupert Brooke	272	38.2	366	54.4	638	46.3	11	R
Song—John Suckling	536	44.8	540	51.4	1076	48.1	15	R
Song—William Watson	158	49.4	244	60.2	402	54.8	14	S
Song Against Children— Aline Kilmer	246	41.1	370	62.7	616	51.9	20	R
Song for a Little House— Christopher Morley	201	52.0	402	77.5	603	64.8	11	R
Song in France, A— Walter Henry	464	89.2	532	89.8	996	89.5	32	R
Song My Paddle Sings, The—Josephine Johnson	282	43.6	278	53.2	560	48.4	13	R
Song of Bernadette, The —Franz Werfel	200	81.8	801	91.5	1001	86.7	67	IR
Song of Myself—Walt Whitman	332	33.4	365	44.1	697	38.8	24	S
Song of Sherwood, A— Alfred Noyes	268	60.6	251	62.2	519	61.4	16	S
Song of the Chattahoochee—Sidney Lanier	333	58.3	349	65.3	682	61.8	27	S
Song of the Old Mother, The—William B. Yeats	229	63.8	267	79.4	496	71.6	23	S

PUPILS' READING INTERESTS: GRADES 10-12
Ts and Ss = Teachers and Schools   S = Studied in Class
IR = Independent Reading   R = Read in Class

SELECTION—AUTHOR	Boys		Girls		Total		Ts & Ss	
	No.	%	No.	%	No.	Av. %		
Song of the Open Road —Walt Whitman	248	75.2	286	72.2	534	73.7	21	S
Song of the Shirt, The— Thomas Hood	188	65.7	219	84.2	407	75.0	18	S
Song of Wandering Angus, The—William B. Yeats	257	49.6	295	56.8	552	53.2	12	R
Song in a Showerbath— Christopher Morley	296	42.2	297	47.0	593	44.6	12	R
Sonnet—Rupert Brooke	349	45.1	349	52.4	698	48.8	20	S
Sonnet from an Oil Field —Dorothy McFarlane	304	53.8	361	77.6	665	65.7	13	R
Sonnets—William Shakespeare	151	46.4	213	63.4	364	54.9	17	S
Sonnets—William Wordsworth	143	54.5	254	66.7	397	60.6	16	S
Sonnets from the Portuguese—Elizabeth B. Browning	184	45.1	362	74.2	546	59.7	21	S
Sonnets in a Lodging House—Christopher Morley	316	54.9	352	66.8	668	60.9	14	R
Sonny's Christenin'— Ruth McE. Stuart	349	53.2	184	58.4	533	55.8	13	S
Son of the Middle Border, A—Hamlin Garland	894	65.2	846	54.0	1740	59.6	58	S
Son of the Wolf, The— Jack London	239	78.7	245	66.3	484	72.5	16	S
So Now You've Graduated—Elsie Robinson	220	66.4	225	68.9	445	67.7	18	S
Sorority Girl—Anne Emery	2		433	68.9				
So Runs the World Away —Thomas L. Mason	230	53.3	247	54.5	477	53.9	16	S
Soul of Jeanne D'Arc, The—Theodosia Garrison	305	37.7	357	51.4	662	44.6	12	R
Soul of the Great Bell, The—Lafcadio Hearn	384	63.3	372	82.1	756	72.7	15	S

PUPILS' READING INTERESTS: GRADES 10-12
Ts and Ss = Teachers and Schools   S = Studied in Class
IR = Independent Reading   R = Read in Class

SELECTION—AUTHOR	Boys		Girls		Total		Ts & Ss	
	No.	%	No.	%	No.	Av. %		
Sounds—Henry D. Thoreau	242	61.2	275	66.0	517	63.6	36	S
Source of Irritation, A— Stacy Aumonier	206	71.1	262	75.0	468	73.1	19	S
Southern Hospitality— John K. Bangs	167	78.1	206	82.0	373	80.1	16	S
" 'Spacially Jim"—Bessie Morgan	1067	70.6	1198	83.2	2265	76.9	30	R
Spanish Johnny—Willa Cather	649	53.5	629	54.9	1278	54.2	27	R
Spanish Waters—John Masefield	445	65.3	504	62.0	949	63.7	21	S
Sparkin'—Ellsworth P. Conkle	312	85.1	333	92.0	645	88.6	18	S
Spark Neglected, A—Leo Tolstoy	553	70.3	624	71.5	1177	70.9	17	R
Spartacus to the Gladiators—Elijah Kellogg	349	66.3	416	58.3	765	62.3	19	R
Specimen Jones—Owen Wister	246	87.6	266	74.3	512	81.0	12	S
Speckled Band, The—A. Conan Doyle	1129	89.2	788	87.8	1917	88.5	68	S
Specter Bridegroom, The —Washington Irving	462	60.7	431	64.2	893	62.5	41	S
Speech of Logan, the Mingo Chief, The	353	58.2	385	48.4	738	53.3	17	R
Speed of Light, The— Richard T. Cox	213	51.4	305	27.0	518	39.2	13	R
Spires of Oxford, The— Winifred Letts	247	70.6	346	77.3	593	74.0	18	S
Spirit of St. Louis, The— Charles A. Lindbergh	588	77.2	279	73.3	867	75.3		
Spirit of the Herd, The— Dallas L. Sharp	389	67.6	173	48.0	562	57.8	15	S
Spreading the News— Augusta Gregory	325	69.5	347	71.5	672	70.5	42	S
Spring—Richard Hovey	192	45.6	231	53.9	423	49.8	19	S
Spring—Louis Untermeyer	387	32.4	477	46.3	864	39.4	16	R

PUPILS' READING INTERESTS: GRADES 10-12

Ts and Ss = Teachers and Schools   S = Studied in Class
IR = Independent Reading   R = Read in Class

SELECTION—AUTHOR	Boys		Girls		Total		Ts & Ss	
	No.	%	No.	%	No.	Av. %		
Spring Comes to Thumping Dick— Walter P. Eaton	163	59.8	258	59.9	421	59.9	14	S
Spring Is Here—Will Rogers	393	87.3	526	87.9	919	87.6	43	S
Spy, The—James F. Cooper	593	77.3	306	72.4	899	74.9	83	S
Stage Coach, The— Washington Irving	481	60.3	262	59.5	743	59.9	19	S
Stage-Coach Journey, The—Richard Steele	276	60.0	247	57.1	523	58.6	24	S
Stage Driver's Story, The —Bret Harte	223	74.4	265	74.3	488	74.4	13	R
Stars—Sara Teasdale	543	49.6	663	65.4	1206	57.5	44	S
Stein Song—Richard Hovey	259	65.1	271	62.2	530	63.7	21	S
Stone, The—Wilfrid W. Gibson	268	67.4	240	80.0	508	73.7	26	S
Stopping by Woods on a Snowy Evening— Robert Frost	551	51.1	703	74.6	1254	62.9	32	S
Story of a Bad Boy, The —Thomas B. Aldrich	168	78.9	245	71.8	413	75.4	43	IR
Story of Abe, The— Alice Brown	265	73.2	310	70.0	575	71.6	13	R
Story of a Piebald Horse, The— W. H. Hudson	206	76.2	256	78.1	462	77.2	25	S
Story of a Thousand-Year Pine, The — Enos A. Mills	265	73.4	350	61.9	615	67.7	14	R
Story of Clara Barton, The — Jeannette C. Nolan	32		402	67.4				
Story of D-Day, The — Bruce Blivin	274	83.2	55					
Story of Eleanor Roosevelt, The — Jeanette Eaton	61		171	71.3				
Story of Joan of Arc, The — Andrew Lang	166	71.1	489	82.5	655	76.8	46	IR

PUPILS' READING INTERESTS: GRADES 10-12
Ts and Ss = Teachers and Schools   S = Studied in Class
IR = Independent Reading   R = Read in Class

SELECTION—AUTHOR	Boys		Girls		Total		Ts & Ss	
	No.	%	No.	%	No.	Av. %		
Story of Louis Pasteur, The — Sheridan Gibney and Pierre Collings	199	90.5	240	91.5	439	91.0	14	R
Story of My Life, The — Helen Keller	361	58.0	499	85.6	860	71.8	33	S
Story of the Salmon, The — Rex Beach	294	72.6	358	51.0	652	61.8	10	R
Story of Thomas Alva Edison, The— Enid Meadowcroft	222	73.2	134	70.9	356	72.1		
Stove, The — Marjorie Pickthall	486	66.2	509	83.9	995	75.1	48	S
Stover at Yale — Owen Johnson	168	72.3	54				77	IR
Strange Wild Song, A — Lewis Carroll	399	42.7	427	47.3	826	45.0	9	R
Stratford-on-Avon — Washington Irving	282	59.8	135	57.0	417	58.4	17	S
Strawberry Roan (Cowboy Ballad)	304	80.6	367	70.7	671	75.7	11	R
Street Rod — Henry G. Felsen	291	76.1	76					
Strenuous Life, The — Theodore Roosevelt	321	65.7	265	60.4	586	63.1	29	S
Strictly Germ-Proof — Arthur Guiterman	615	70.0	766	74.2	1381	72.1	23	R
Strife — John Galsworthy	327	60.1	240	53.8	567	57.0	27	S
Struggle for Life, A — Thomas B. Aldrich	164	70.4	219	75.3	383	72.9	17	S
Struggles and Triumph of Isidro de los Maestros, The — James M. Hopper	325	67.7	335	63.4	660	65.6	14	S
Stub-Book, The — Pedro A. de Alarcón	295	53.7	385	56.8	680	55.3	13	R
Student of Languages, A — Elsie Singmaster	190	45.3	329	64.3	519	54.8	22	S
Stung —Heywood Broun	258	62.2	272	66.7	530	64.5	13	R
Stupidity Street — Ralph Hodgson	537	59.4	553	63.7	1090	61.6	24	R

PUPILS' READING INTERESTS: GRADES 10-12
Ts and Ss = Teachers and Schools   S = Studied in Class
IR = Independent Reading   R = Read in Class

SELECTION—AUTHOR	Boys		Girls		Total		Ts & Ss	
	No.	%	No.	%	No.	Av. %		
Substitute, The — François Coppée	263	71.3	254	68.7	517	70.0	38	S
Successful Failure, A — Glenn Frank	263	45.4	387	42.0	650	43.7	17	R
Sue Barton (Books) — Helen D. Boylston	37		925	85.4			47	IR
Suffering — Nathalia Crane	749	51.5	822	71.8	1571	61.7	24	R
Suicide in the Trenches — Siegfried Sassoon	250	71.6	316	·823	566	77.0	14	R
Sun, The — Emily Dickinson	299	52.2	410	64.4	709	58.3	11	R
Sun Also Rises, The— Ernest Hemingway	169	75.1	369	71.4	538	73.3		
Sunday—E. B. White	430	41.6	504	62.8	934	52.2	18	R
Sunday in London— Washington Irving	228	45.2	265	57.9	493	51.6	29	S
Sunrise—Katherine Kosmak	343	38.0	401	54.6	744	46.3	12	R
Sunrise in Louisiana— Lafcadio Hearn	380	58.7	358	71.0	738	64.9	44	S
Superannuated Man, The —Charles Lamb	314	52.5	377	53.8	691	53.2	32	S
Superman (Comic Strip)	247	61.9	266	62.2	513	62.1	17	IR
Surrender Books— Thomas L. Mason	136	42.6	346	56.8	482	49.7	14	R
Swamp Fox of the Revolution, The— Marion M. Brown	327	77.2	98	62.7	425	70.0		
Sweet Afton—Robert Burns	187	70.6	192	72.9	379	71.8	17	S
Sweet Peas—John Keats	277	47.1	311	58.2	588	52.7	16	R
Swing Low Sweet Chariot (Negro Spiritual)	1004	49.9	1064	61.4	2068	55.7	39	R
Swiss Family Robinson— Johann D. Wyss	466	85.5	636	80.9	1102	83.2	45	IR
Sycophantic Fox and the Gullible Raven, The— Guy W. Carryl	221	73.3	227	74.2	448	73.8	17	S

PUPILS' READING INTERESTS: GRADES 10-12
Ts and Ss = Teachers and Schools   S = Studied in Class
IR = Independent Reading   R = Read in Class

SELECTION—AUTHOR	Boys		Girls		Total		Ts & Ss
	No.	%	No.	%	No.	Av. %	
Symptoms—Jerome K. Jerome	639	76.9	667	85.7	1306	81.3	35 R
Syntax for Cynics— Christopher Morley	235	52.6	282	61.2	517	56.9	14 R
Tactfulness—Arthur C. Benson	176	51.7	238	60.9	414	56.3	16 S
Take the Witness— Robert Benchley	382	66.2	370	73.0	752	69.6	10 R
Tale of Two Cities, A— Charles Dickens	2635	77.0	3062	83.2	5697	80.1	134 S
Tales—Edgar A. Poe	323	88.9	409	85.5	732	87.2	
Tales from Shakespeare —Charles and Mary Lamb	174	63.8	469	75.3	643	69.6	151 IR
Tales of a Wayside Inn— Henry W. Longfellow	250	69.4	401	74.1	651	71.8	122 IR
Tales of the South Pacific —James A. Michener	206	78.2	219	84.7	425	81.5	
Talisman, The—Walter Scott	148	67.9	107				
Taming of the Shrew, The—William Shakespeare	156	68.9	219	85.8	375	77.4	21 S
Taming of the Shrew, The (Radio Play)— Eric Barnoew	275	78.5	304	86.0	579	82.3	14 R
Tam o' Shanter—Robert Burns	313	57.7	235	56.2	548	57.0	31 S
Tanglewood Tales— Nathaniel Hawthorne	181	66.0	418	67.2	599	66.6	149 IR
Tarentella—Hilaire Belloc	359	47.8	329	58.7	688	53.3	11 R
Tarry Buccaneer, The— John Masefield	274	71.9	308	66.2	582	69.1	17 S
Tartary—Walter de la Mare	329	60.2	416	65.5	745	62.9	22 S
Tarzan (Book)—Edgar R. Burroughs	1067	74.6	578	65.3	1645	70.0	192 IR
Tarzan (Comic Strip)	1579	58.0	1477	42.3	3056	50.2	184 IR
Tarzan (Movie)	1240	66.1	1271	60.3	2511	63.2	130

PUPILS' READING INTERESTS: GRADES 10-12

Ts and Ss = Teachers and Schools   S = Studied in Class
IR = Independent Reading   R = Read in Class

SELECTION—AUTHOR	Boys		Girls		Total		Ts & Ss	
	No.	%	No.	%	No.	Av. %		
Teaching in the University of California— Cornelia S. Parker	240	54.8	257	64.4	497	59.6	17	S
Teahouse of the August Moon—John Patrick	200	68.3	411	80.9	611	74.6		
Tears—Lizette W. Reese	378	51.7	613	71.7	991	61.7	38	S
Tears, Idle Tears—Alfred Tennyson	258	42.8	276	57.6	534	50.2	17	S
Tea Trader, The—Daniel Henderson	460	55.8	511	68.0	971	61.9	20	R
Telephonics—Edward V. Lucas	335	57.8	398	65.2	733	61.5	35	S
Telling the Bees—John G. Whittier	226	57.5	266	72.2	492	64.9	23	S
Tell-Tale Heart, The— Edgar A. Poe	187	82.9	224	84.8	411	83.9	20	S
Tempest, A—Emily Dickinson	198	34.9	245	55.9	443	45.4	14	R
Tempest, The—Charles Lamb	287	58.2	262	67.7	549	63.0	15	R
Tempest, The—William Shakespeare	149	64.4	354	69.8	503	67.1	114	IR
Tender Heart, The— Helen G. Cone	286	48.3	313	59.7	599	54.0	12	R
Tennessee's Partner— Bret Harte	555	69.9	495	60.6	1050	65.3	50	S
Tenor, The—Henry C. Bunner	314	45.1	314	64.5	628	54.8	15	S
Terrible Infant, A— Frederick Locker-Lamson	307	63.8	412	75.0	719	69.4	16	R
Terrible Night, A—Anton Chekhov	256	90.4	336	94.6	592	92.5	13	R
Terry and the Pirates (Comic Strip)	851	80.7	1060	84.7	1911	82.7	44	
Test, The—J. M. Witherow	211	80.6	318	82.9	528	81.8	14	S
Test Pilot—James Collins	255	72.7	53					
Test Pilot—Francis V. Drake	264	93.4	325	78.5	589	86.0	14	R

PUPILS' READING INTERESTS: GRADES 10-12
Ts and Ss = Teachers and Schools   S = Studied in Class
IR = Independent Reading   R = Read in Class

SELECTION—AUTHOR	Boys		Girls		Total		Ts & Ss	
	No.	%	No.	%	No.	Av. %		
Texas—Amy Lowell	395	33.5	454	36.0	849	34.8	13	R
Texas Cowboy, The (Cowboy Ballad)	591	68.9	611	63.8	1202	66.4	32	R
Thanatopsis—William C. Bryant	303	54.6	398	64.2	701	59.4	40	S
That Brute Simmons— Arthur Morrison	265	61.5	218	68.9	483	65.2	20	S
Theobald Smith—Paul De Kruif	190	73.4	222	70.7	412	72.1	19	R
Theology—Joyce Kilmer	1078	39.2	1225	51.9	2303	45.6	29	R
There Once Was a Packer of York— Unknown	197	58.4	308	62.5	505	60.5	13	R
There Was an Old Man of Calcutta—Unknown	351	54.7	387	61.1	738	57.9	15	R
There Was an Old Man of the Cape— Robert L. Stevenson	233	51.5	325	56.5	558	54.0	14	R
There Was an Old Man of Thermopylae— Edward Lear	436	46.6	516	42.7	952	44.7	11	R
There Was an Old Man Who Said How— Edward Lear	462	33.2	516	40.1	978	36.7	21	R
There Was an Old Man With a Beard— Edward Lear	625	59.2	684	64.3	1309	61.8	29	R
There Was a Young Lady Named Perkins— Unknown	201	68.4	311	75.7	512	72.1	13	R
Theseus—Frances E. Sabin	248	46.6	310	44.2	558	45.4	11	R
They Grind Exceeding Small—Ben A. Williams	470	73.6	631	80.1	1101	76.9	43	R
They Were Expendable —William L. White	573	94.5	505	90.2	1078	92.4	83	IR
Things—Aline Kilmer	303	56.9	359	71.7	662	64.3	28	S
Thinker, The—Berton Braley	776	67.9	778	67.7	1554	67.8	24	R

PUPILS' READING INTERESTS: GRADES 10-12
Ts and Ss = Teachers and Schools   S = Studied in Class
IR = Independent Reading   R = Read in Class

SELECTION—AUTHOR	Boys		Girls		Total		Ts & Ss	
	No.	%	No.	%	No.	Av. %		
Thin Man, The—Dashiell Hammett	252	70.4	265	73.6	517	72.0		
Third Ingredient, The— O. Henry	1170	72.0	1170	87.2	2340	79.6	100	S
Thirty Seconds Over Tokyo—Ted W. Lawson	205	93.2	311	96.6	516	94.9	17	IR
Thomas A. Edison's First Workshop— Francis A. Jones	714	86.8	662	78.2	1376	82.5	44	S
Those Two Boys— Franklin P. Adams	334	75.8	371	77.6	705	76.7	26	S
Thread That Runs So True, The—Jesse Stuart	420	60.4	547	69.3	967	64.9		
Three Arshins of Land— Leo Tolstoy	500	76.2	542	72.0	1042	74.1	17	R
Three Bells—John G. Whittier	389	43.3	435	48.5	824	45.9	14	R
Three Days to See— Helen Keller	187	71.9	276	82.1	463	77.0	16	R
Three Musketeers, The— Alexandre Dumas	174	82.8	188	82.7	362	82.8	23	S
Three Questions—Leo Tolstoy	467	80.4	559	80.3	1026	80.4	18	S
Three Ravens, The (British Ballad)	560	45.5	634	47.1	1194	46.3	22	R
Three Strangers, The— Thomas Hardy	1190	64.3	778	62.8	1968	63.6	81	S
Three to One—D. Maitland Busby	201	76.1	247	62.8	448	69.5	26	S
Thrice-Promised Bride, The—Cheng Chin Hsing	82	53.7	428	61.4	510	57.6		
Thunderhead—Mary O'Hara	117	87.2	240	83.1	357	85.2	17	IR
Thunder Road—William C. Gault	434	80.1	128	70.3	562	75.2		
Ticket Agent, The— Edmund Leamy	585	61.5	636	67.5	1221	64.5	33	S
Tiger, The—William Blake	328	53.4	294	55.4	622	54.4	35	S

PUPILS' READING INTERESTS: GRADES 10-12

Ts and Ss = Teachers and Schools   S = Studied in Class

IR = Independent Reading   R = Read in Class

SELECTION—AUTHOR	Boys		Girls		Total		Ts & Ss	
	No.	%	No.	%	No.	Av. %		
Tiger Lilies—Thomas B. Aldrich	424	31.0	419	55.3	843	43.2	15	R
Tillie the Toiler (Comic Strip)	531	42.8	1084	65.5	1615	54.2	44	IR
Time, You Old Gypsy Man—Ralph Hodgson	367	58.9	386	72.4	753	65.7	23	S
Timid Sex, The—Robert M. Gay	415	59.5	446	67.8	861	63.7	23	R
Tired Tim—Walter de la Mare	1125	48.2	1290	58.3	2415	53.3	32	R
To a Blockhead— Alexander Pope	1135	40.7	1228	51.7	2363	46.2	32	R
To a Louse—Robert Burns	403	71.0	460	72.7	863	71.9	42	S
To Althea from Prison— Richard Lovelace	166	64.2	216	70.6	382	67.4	22	S
To a Mountain Daisy— Robert Burns	329	45.6	226	60.6	555	53.1	21	S
To a Mouse—Robert Burns	861	60.4	798	68.2	1659	64.3	67	S
To an Athlete Dying Young—Alfred E. Housman	551	75.5	581	75.3	1132	75.4	35	S
To a Post-Office Inkwell —Christopher Morley	251	64.1	261	72.4	512	68.3	16	S
To a Skylark—Percy B. Shelley	630	56.7	798	73.4	1428	65.1	66	S
To a Snowflake—Francis Thompson	144	56.9	272	70.4	416	63.7	21	S
To a Waterfowl—William C. Bryant	455	53.3	604	60.9	1059	57.1	46	S
To Be Read Only by Serious Stupid Persons— Charles S. Brooks	166	48.2	181	58.0	347	53.1	20	S
To Build a Fire—Jack London	305	87.5	311	80.6	616	84.1	22	R
To Celia—Ben Johnson	561	53.0	621	70.0	1182	61.5	60	S
To Have and to Hold— Mary Johnston	152	83.9	190	87.1	342	85.5	29	S
To Helen—Edgar A. Poe	386	43.7	708	67.0	1094	55.4	34	S

PUPILS' READING INTERESTS: GRADES 10-12
Ts and Ss = Teachers and Schools   S = Studied in Class
IR = Independent Reading   R = Read in Class

SELECTION—AUTHOR	Boys		Girls		Total		Ts & Ss	
	No.	%	No.	%	No.	Av. %		
Token, The—Joseph Hergesheimer	500	56.5	431	77.0	931	66.8	27	S
Tol'able David—Joseph Hergesheimer	314	88.1	424	82.9	738	85.5	19	S
To Lucasta, On Going to the Wars— Richard Lovelace	312	55.9	338	59.3	650	57.6	34	S
To Make a Prairie— Emily Dickinson	249	42.4	318	54.9	567	48.7	26	S
To Mary in Heaven— Robert Burns	167	52.7	197	71.3	364	62.0	17	S
Tom Brown's School Days—Thomas Hughes	227	77.8	320	76.1	547	77.0	45	IR
Tom Cat, The—Don Marquis	308	59.4	404	62.0	712	60.7	20	R
Tommy—Rudyard Kipling	466	85.1	502	85.8	968	85.5	33	S
Tomorrow—John Masefield	222	41.0	315	52.7	537	46.9	15	R
Tom Sawyer—Mark Twain	1047	87.6	1280	87.0	2327	87.3	65	IR
Tom Sawyer Abroad— Mark Twain	345	80.0	249	79.7	594	79.9	81	IR
To Night—Percy B. Shelley	230	48.9	298	66.3	528	57.6	24	S
Tony Kytes—Thomas Hardy	206	78.9	216	85.9	422	82.4	23	S
Too Much Too Soon— Barrymore and Frank	80	58.8	254	75.2	334	67.0		
Tooth, the Whole Tooth, and Nothing but the Tooth, The—Robert Benchley	446	71.6	494	77.6	940	74.6	22	R
Topper—Thorne Smith	172	72.1	172	64.8	344	68.5		
To Sidney Lanier—John B. Tabb	209	45.2	262	50.6	471	47.9	23	S
To Springvale for Christmas—Zona Gale	414	60.7	224	74.8	638	67.8	13	S
To Tell Your Love— Mary S. Stolz	5		177	76.3				

PUPILS' READING INTERESTS: GRADES 10-12
Ts and Ss = Teachers and Schools   S = Studied in Class
IR = Independent Reading   R = Read in Class

SELECTION—AUTHOR	Boys		Girls		Total		Ts & Ss	
	No.	%	No.	%	No.	Av. %		
To the Dandelion—James R. Lowell	339	49.4	429	65.7	768	57.6	25	S
To the Fringed Gentian—William C. Bryant	137	47.8	372	69.2	509	58.5	16	S
To the Memory of My Beloved Master, William Shakespeare—Ben Jonson	221	56.6	274	63.7	495	60.2	24	S
To the Moon—Percy B. Shelley	219	47.5	218	58.0	437	52.8	18	S
To the Skylark—William Wordsworth	193	57.8	172	68.3	365	63.1	26	S
To the Terrestrial Globe—William S. Gilbert	271	44.8	316	47.8	587	46.3	17	S
To Virgins to Make Much of Time— Robert Herrick	389	47.2	542	60.2	931	53.7	36	S
Tract for Autos, A—Arthur Guiterman	374	61.5	412	63.3	786	62.4	13	R
Trades—Amy Lowell	278	22.3	352	22.7	630	22.5	13	R
Trades Winds—John Masefield	296	43.8	309	61.8	605	52.8	13	R
Tragic Story, A—William M. Thackeray	351	51.1	360	66.5	711	58.8	11	R
Trail Makers, The—Henry H. Knibbs	202	63.1	219	52.5	421	57.8	16	S
Traits of Indian Character—Washington Irving	259	65.5	302	62.6	561	64.1	24	S
Tramp Transfigured, The —Alfred Noyes	177	50.8	178	60.7	355	55.8	19	S
Translating Literature into Life— Arnold Bennett	398	38.2	356	48.0	754	43.1	28	S
Trap-Lines North—Stephen W. Meader	153	88.2	20				130	IR
Travel—Edna St. V. Millay	352	56.4	379	67.4	731	61.9	32	S
Traveling Afoot—John H. Finley	219	69.9	200	66.3	419	68.1	23	S

PUPILS' READING INTERESTS: GRADES 10-12
Ts and Ss = Teachers and Schools   S = Studied in Class
IR = Independent Reading   R = Read in Class

SELECTION—AUTHOR	Boys		Girls		Total		Ts & Ss	
	No.	%	No.	%	No.	Av. %		
Travels with a Donkey—Robert L. Stevenson	674	63.5	696	63.6	1370	63.6	55	S
Treasure Island—Robert L. Stevenson	252	91.1	155	78.7	407	84.9	22	S
Treasurer's Report, The—Robert Benchley	442	52.5	489	60.5	931	56.5	25	R
Tree Grows in Brooklyn, A—Betty Smith	113	64.6	434	78.6	547	71.6		
Trees—Bliss Carman	217	55.1	387	76.4	604	65.8	12	R
Trees—Joyce Kilmer	525	79.2	465	87.2	990	83.2	42	S
Trees and the Intruders, The— Joseph Auslander	217	39.6	386	59.2	603	49.4	12	R
Trees at Timberline—Enos A. Mills	171	66.4	221	57.9	392	62.2	16	S
Treme Market—Carl Carmer	307	34.2	364	45.6	671	39.9	13	R
"Tremolino," The—Joseph Conrad	213	64.6	224	60.3	437	62.5	27	S
Trial in Tom Belcher's Store, The— Samuel A. Derieux	186	89.8	342	87.1	528	88.5	12	S
Tribute to Lincoln—James R. Lowell	207	53.4	311	56.3	518	54.9	13	R
Trifles—Susan Glaspell	587	66.9	615	78.7	1202	72.8	63	S
Trysting Place, The—Booth Tarkington	372	77.2	383	80.4	755	78.8	21	S
Tsar Oleg—J. J. Kennealy	322	41.9	339	46.8	661	44.4	11	R
Tubby Hook—Arthur Guiterman	325	56.2	335	70.0	660	63.1	10	R
Tuft of Flowers, The—Robert Frost	180	58.9	265	69.1	445	64.0	23	S
Tulip Garden, A—Amy Lowell	514	44.0	569	61.5	1083	52.8	31	S
Turkey Red—Frances G. Wood	524	68.6	437	72.9	961	70.8	30	S
Turmoil, The—Booth Tarkington	714	80.4	1009	90.0	1723	85.2	57	S
Turning of the Babies in the Bed, The— Paul L. Dunbar	306	63.7	342	83.6	648	73.7	22	S

PUPILS' READING INTERESTS: GRADES 10-12
Ts and Ss = Teachers and Schools   S = Studied in Class
IR = Independent Reading   R = Read in Class

SELECTION—AUTHOR	Boys		Girls		Total		Ts & Ss	
	No.	%	No.	%	No.	Av. %		
Turning the Grindstone—Benjamin Franklin	479	74.6	556	78.1	1035	76.4	26	R
Turtle Eggs for Agassiz—Dallas L. Sharp	248	73.2	252	73.6	500	73.4	17	S
Twa Corbies, The (British Ballad)	338	45.9	354	52.0	692	49.0	18	S
Twa Sisters, The (British Ballad)	280	45.9	312	66.2	592	56.1	18	S
Twelfth Night—William Shakespeare	368	55.7	527	66.5	895	61.1	33	S
Twelve-Pound Look, The —James M. Barrie	274	55.8	254	66.3	528	61.1	21	R
Twenty Cigarettes—Philip Wylie	284	96.5	386	95.3	670	95.9	13	R
Twenty Thousand Leagues Under the Sea—Jules Verne	454	81.8	238	67.6	692	74.7		
Twenty Years at Hull House—Jane Addams	51		154	64.0				
Twice—Told Tales—Nathaniel Hawthorne	237	70.5	414	68.6	651	69.6	150	IR
Twins, The—Henry S. Leigh	6874	85.4	7972	92.3	14846	88.9	270	R
'Twixt 12 and 20—Pat Boone	71		200	65.0				
Two Automobilists, The —Carolyn Wells	308	57.3	297	54.5	605	55.9	16	R
Two Crooks and a Lady —Eugene Pillot	211	78.7	240	82.7	451	80.7	31	S
Two 'Mericana Men—Thomas A. Daly	308	77.6	349	80.2	657	78.9	30	S
Two of Them—James M. Barrie	310	48.2	356	67.7	666	58.0	24	S
Two Old Bachelors—Edward Lear	326	71.0	330	82.6	656	76.8	13	R
Two Red Roses—William Morris	173	50.9	241	63.3	414	57.1	21	S
Two Slaps in the Face—Ferenc Molnar	196	80.1	246	83.9	442	82.0	15	S

PUPILS' READING INTERESTS: GRADES 10-12

Ts and Ss = Teachers and Schools   S = Studied in Class

IR = Independent Reading   R = Read in Class

SELECTION—AUTHOR	Boys		Girls		Total		Ts & Ss	
	No.	%	No.	%	No.	Av. %		
Two Years Before the Mast—Richard H. Dana	427	82.4	224	69.4	651	75.9	122	IR
Typee—Herman Melville	216	73.6	282	60.8	498	67.2	22	S
Typhoon—Joseph Conrad	204	83.1	171	82.5	375	82.8	60	IR
Ugly American, The— Lederer and Burdick	306	83.3	403	81.5	709	82.4		
Ugly Wild Boy, The— Frank H. Cushing	205	67.6	223	68.2	428	67.9	16	S
Ultimate Atrocity, The— Siegfried Sassoon	302	40.6	391	43.5	693	42.1	16	R
Ulysses—Alfred Tennyson	413	54.7	505	54.5	918	54.6	47	S
Umbrella, The—Arnold Bennett	348	70.8	173	78.9	521	74.9	13	S
Uncle Remus—Joel C. Harris	647	68.5	973	62.8	1620	65.7	132	IR
Uncle Tom's Cabin— Harriet B. Stowe	351	72.4	745	80.3	1096	76.4	54	IR
Under a Telephone Pole —Carl Sandburg	548	69.0	552	69.8	1100	69.4	15	R
Under the Barber's Knife —Stephen Leacock	277	80.3	240	75.6	517	78.0	16	R
Under the Greenwood Tree—William Shakespeare	233	52.6	267	60.9	500	56.8	33	S
Under the Lion's Paw— Hamlin Garland	300	75.0	373	68.5	673	71.8	26	S
Underwater Adventure— Willard deM. Price	170	77.4	34					
Unknown Soldier, The— James T. Adams	374	52.4	351	57.3	725	54.9	11	R
Unrhymed Limerick, An —William S. Gilbert	328	49.8	371	50.3	699	50.1	16	R
Unseen, The—Alice Gerstenberg	118	74.6	667	81.8	785	78.2	22	S
Untouchables, The—Ness and Fraley	296	87.8	110	78.2	406	83.0		
Up at a Villa—Down in the City— Robert Browning	337	58.9	419	67.2	756	63.1	52	S

PUPILS' READING INTERESTS: GRADES 10-12
Ts and Ss = Teachers and Schools   S = Studied in Class
IR = Independent Reading   R = Read in Class

SELECTION—AUTHOR	Boys		Girls		Total		Ts & Ss	
	No.	%	No.	%	No.	Av. %		
Up from Slavery—Brooker T. Washington	408	71.1	362	72.8	770	72.0	31	S
Up Front—Bill Mauldin	188	83.0	49					
Uprooted—Ruth Suckow	349	44.8	188	60.1	537	52.5	13	S
Urban Chanticleer—Joyce Kilmer	160	59.7	299	65.9	459	62.8	17	S
U. S. Grant Meets Robert E. Lee— U. S. Grant	279	71.1	341	51.0	620	61.1	11	R
Vagabond, The—Robert L. Stevenson	196	59.7	242	66.9	438	63.3	21	S
Vagabond Song, A—Bliss Carman	317	58.8	415	72.9	732	65.9	29	S
Valentine's Day—Charles Lamb	196	48.2	219	59.8	415	54.0	14	S
Valiant, The—Holworthy Hall and Robert Middlemas	259	93.6	275	96.0	534	94.8	18	S
Valley of Humiliation, The—John Bunyan	279	43.9	259	37.6	538	40.8	15	R
Valley of the Shadow, The—John Galsworthy	729	47.5	644	57.8	1373	52.7	21	R
Valley That God Forgot, The—Henry H. Knibbs	248	75.6	285	70.5	533	73.1	18	S
Valuation—John G. Whittier	225	48.0	368	56.0	593	52.0	11	R
Vanity Fair—John Bunyan	198	59.6	254	59.6	452	59.6	16	R
Vanity Fair—William M. Thackeray	123	59.8	252	63.9	375	61.9	62	IR
Velvet Shoes—Elinor Wylie	205	45.1	264	62.9	469	54.0	14	S
Vermont—Dorothy C. Fisher	170	57.9	176	60.8	346	59.4	16	S
Vicar of Bray, The—Langford Reed	244	51.0	336	52.1	580	51.6	15	R
Vicar of Wakefield, The—Oliver Goldsmith	274	61.5	287	62.7	561	62.1	83	S
Victory Ball, The—Alfred Noyes	480	61.7	605	71.8	1085	66.8	22	R

PUPILS' READING INTERESTS: GRADES 10-12
Ts and Ss = Teachers and Schools   S = Studied in Class
IR = Independent Reading   R = Read in Class

SELECTION—AUTHOR	Boys No.	Boys %	Girls No.	Girls %	Total No.	Total Av. %	Ts & Ss	
Virginian, The—Owen Wister	1102	82.8	840	83.3	1942	83.1	69	S
Virtue—George Herbert	144	48.6	203	53.7	347	51.2	22	S
Vision of Mirza, The—Joseph Addison	226	61.7	271	65.1	497	63.4	29	S
Vision of Sir Launfal, The—James R. Lowell	925	59.8	966	64.4	1891	62.1	91	S
Vive La France!—Charlotte H. Crawford	260	67.1	357	82.8	617	75.0	11	R
Vocabulary and Success—Johnson O'Connor	329	60.3	338	48.8	667	54.6	19	R
Voyage, The—Washington Irving	332	60.8	118	61.0	450	60.9	14	S
Vulture, The—Hilaire Belloc	507	55.4	516	55.1	1023	55.3	18	R
Wagner Matinee, A—Willa Cather	508	41.3	322	65.5	830	53.4	21	S
Walden—Henry D. Thoreau	163	55.8	202	59.7	365	57.8		
Walking Man, The—Henry H. Knibbs	322	85.2	276	79.4	598	82.3	11	R
Walrus and the Carpenter, The—Lewis Carroll	270	62.4	422	71.0	692	66.7	21	S
Walter Reed—Paul De Kruif	216	80.8	208	76.9	424	78.9	19	S
Waltz, The—Dorothy Parker	198	79.0	217	88.7	415	83.9	18	R
Wanderer's Song, A—John Masefield	526	64.4	500	69.4	1026	66.9	31	S
Wander Thirst—Gerald Gould	199	69.8	265	78.5	464	74.2	14	S
Wanted: a Secretary of Athletics— Thomas L. Mason	180	60.0	191	45.5	371	52.8	19	S
War—Jack London	167	87.7	199	71.6	366	79.7	15	S
War—Jonathan Swift	260	45.0	292	36.6	552	40.8	16	R
War and Peace—Leo Tolstoy	389	74.5	494	76.9	883	75.7		

PUPILS' READING INTERESTS: GRADES 10-12

Ts and Ss = Teachers and Schools   S = Studied in Class
IR = Independent Reading   R = Read in Class

SELECTION—AUTHOR	Boys		Girls		Total		Ts & Ss	
	No.	%	No.	%	No.	Av. %		
War of the Worlds—H. G. Wells	637	81.6	112	73.7	749	77.7		
Washington—James R. Lowell	330	50.6	318	54.4	648	52.5	15	R
Washington—Nancy B. Turner	307	56.7	334	73.5	641	65.1	11	R
Washington on Horseback—Henry A. Ogden	150	66.7	160	60.6	310	63.7	45	S
Water—Hilda Conkling	320	50.0	306	61.4	626	55.7	18	S
Water Hole, The—S. Omar Barker	357	76.1	413	64.1	770	70.1	28	S
Wayfarer, The—Stephen Crane	338	62.0	400	68.9	738	65.5	27	S
We—Charles A. Lindbergh	267	78.5	176	74.7	443	76.6	146	IR
We and They—Rudyard Kipling	354	65.0	364	80.4	718	72.7	11	R
We Are Seven—William Wordsworth	114	68.9	289	79.9	403	74.4	27	S
Weathers, The—Thomas Hardy	241	51.7	312	60.9	553	56.3	21	S
Week-Ender, The— Edgar J. Goodspeed	154	61.7	263	66.2	417	64.0	16	S
Wee Willie Winkie— Rudyard Kipling	198	74.5	341	80.5	539	77.5	23	S
Well, The—W. W. Jacobs	241	66.4	272	76.6	513	71.5	13	S
Well of St. Keyne, The— Robert Southey	277	62.8	321	65.6	598	64.2	21	R
West for Me, The—E. A. Brininstool	278	49.8	285	54.7	563	52.3	13	R
Westminster Abbey— Washington Irving	216	66.7	150	61.3	366	64.0	18	S
West Point Plebe— Russell P. Reeder	208	73.3	114	75.0	322	74.2		
West Point Story— Russell P. Reeder	357	72.8	168	74.7	525	73.8		
Westward Ho!—Charles Kingsley	312	69.1	326	66.3	638	67.7		

PUPILS' READING INTERESTS: GRADES 10-12

Ts and Ss = Teachers and Schools   S = Studied in Class
IR = Independent Reading   R = Read in Class

SELECTION—AUTHOR	Boys No.	Boys %	Girls No.	Girls %	Total No.	Total Av. %	Ts & Ss	
Westward Ho!—Joaquin Miller	361	52.6	423	54.4	784	53.5	16	R
Westward to the Indies— Washington Irving	176	71.6	162	61.7	338	66.7	114	IR
West Wind, The—John Masefield	157	68.0	374	80.2	531	74.1	17	S
Wet Sheet and a Flowing Sea, A— Allan Cunningham	346	61.0	417	53.2	763	57.1	19	S
What a College Education Should Give— David S. Jordan	215	58.8	236	66.5	451	62.7	22	S
What Americans Believe In—Charles W. Eliot	322	53.7	356	54.8	678	54.3	13	R
What College Did to Me —Robert Benchley	294	87.2	434	90.1	728	88.7	13	R
What Constitutes a State —William Jones	217	33.2	304	36.7	521	35.0	15	R
What Every Woman Knows—James M. Barrie	227	57.3	256	70.3	483	63.8	29	S
What I Live For— George L. Banks	297	48.3	320	64.4	617	56.4	15	R
What Is Good?—John B. O'Reilly	6847	57.8	7949	74.7	14796	66.3	270	R
What Is Youth?— Clemence Dane	406	44.8	442	64.7	848	54.8	15	R
What Makes Sammy Run —Budd Shulberg	154	71.4	208	64.9	362	68.2		
What Men Live By— Christopher Morley	206	53.9	214	57.5	420	55.7	30	S
What Mr. Robinson Thinks—James R. Lowell	217	55.1	237	51.9	454	53.5	21	S
What Tomas an Buile Said in a Pub— James Stephens	298	68.1	277	69.5	575	68.8	16	S
What Was It?— Fitz-James O'Brien	284	69.2	338	69.5	622	69.4	24	S
When Gran'pa Logged for Paul—Homer A. Watt	155	84.5	209	64.1	364	74.3	19	R

PUPILS' READING INTERESTS: GRADES 10-12
Ts and Ss = Teachers and Schools   S = Studied in Class
IR = Independent Reading   R = Read in Class

SELECTION—AUTHOR	Boys		Girls		Total		Ts & Ss	
	No.	%	No.	%	No.	Av. %		
When Icicles Hang by the Wall— William Shakespeare	418	52.8	480	57.3	898	55.1	27	R
When I Have Fears— John Keats	196	59.7	223	68.2	419	64.0	22	S
When I Heard the Learn'ed Astronomer— Walt Whitman	243	50.6	308	58.3	551	54.5	24	S
When I Loved You— Thomas Moore	535	55.9	542	70.8	1077	63.4	15	R
When in Disgrace with Fortune and Men's Eyes —William Shakespeare	201	44.0	261	60.3	462	52.2	25	S
When I Saw You Last, Rose—Austin Dobson	347	35.3	462	55.3	809	45.3	14	R
When I Was in Love— Alfred E. Housman	661	48.0	772	61.2	1433	54.6	49	S
When I Was One-and-Twenty—Alfred E. Housman	477	71.2	543	75.9	1020	73.6	44	S
When Mickey Mouse Speaks—Andrew R. Boone	280	67.0	344	57.7	624	62.4	11	R
When One Loves Tensely—Don Marquis	524	66.2	512	73.0	1036	69.6	21	R
When Patty Went to College—Jean Webster	5		447	78.4			100	IR
When the Frost Is on the Punkin— James W. Riley	463	71.7	414	79.2	877	75.5	35	S
When the Green Gits Back in the Trees— James W. Riley	228	60.7	273	70.3	501	65.5	17	S
When the Work's All Done This Fall (American Ballad)	305	77.9	369	80.8	674	79.4	11	R
When We Were Very Young—A. A. Milne	30		162	72.5				
When You Are Old— William B. Yeats	304	31.4	420	53.0	724	42.2	14	R
Where But in America— Oscar M. Wolff	505	62.1	581	81.0	1086	71.6	33	S

PUPILS' READING INTERESTS: GRADES 10-12

Ts and Ss = Teachers and Schools   S = Studied in Class
IR = Independent Reading   R = Read in Class

SELECTION—AUTHOR	Boys		Girls		Total		Ts & Ss	
	No.	%	No.	%	No.	Av. %		
"Where Did You Go?" "Out." "What Did You Do?" "Nothing."—Robert P. Smith	214	73.6	293	71.3	507	72.5		
Where Every Direction Is South— Robert E. Peary	386	80.1	372	66.1	758	73.1	17	R
Where I Lived and What I Lived For— Henry D. Thoreau	229	47.2	199	52.0	428	49.6	18	S
Where Love Is, There God Is Also— Leo Tolstoy	433	83.0	439	91.8	872	87.4	13	R
Where the Cross Is Made—Eugene O'Neill	705	74.7	588	78.7	1293	76.7	36	S
Where the Sagebrush Billows Roll— E. A. Brininstool	275	48.7	282	53.7	557	51.2	13	R
Whirligig of Life, The— O. Henry	246	75.4	386	75.0	632	75.2	23	S
White Fang—Jack London	329	90.9	169	85.5	498	88.2	58	IR
White Hawk, The— Harry Kemp	126	53.9	310	64.2	436	59.1	15	S
White Horse Winter— Wilbur D. Steele	191	71.2	190	75.8	381	73.5	17	S
White House Gang, The —Earl Looker	260	84.4	316	85.1	576	84.8	75	S
White Silence, The—Jack London	214	82.0	200	74.8	414	78.4	20	S
Who Is My Neighbor?— The Bible	713	64.1	776	72.5	1489	68.3	24	R
Who Is Sylvia?—William Shakespeare	476	49.3	485	67.8	961	58.6	36	S
Whoopee Ti Yi Yo, Git Along Little Dogies (Cowboy Ballad)	401	59.0	337	61.3	738	60.2	13	R
Who Owns the Mountains?—Henry Van Dyke	874	55.0	1118	61.4	1992	58.2	68	S

PUPILS' READING INTERESTS: GRADES 10-12

Ts and Ss = Teachers and Schools   S = Studied in Class

IR = Independent Reading   R = Read in Class

SELECTION—AUTHOR	Boys		Girls		Total		Ts & Ss	
	No.	%	No.	%	No.	Av. %		
Why a Classic Is a Classic—Arnold Bennett	253	32.6	244	37.5	497	35.1	27	S
Why Are Women Like That?—Irvin S. Cobb	206	80.6	219	75.3	425	78.0	14	S
Why Old Songs Live— Richard Le Gallienne	217	39.4	255	56.9	472	48.2	14	S
Why So Pale and Wan?— John Suckling	401	41.9	472	54.9	873	48.4	33	S
Why Tigers Can't Climb —Arthur Guiterman	339	61.8	373	63.5	712	62.7	14	R
Widow Malone, The— Charles J. Lever	251	52.6	324	60.5	575	56.6	14	R
Widow's Cruise, The— Frank R. Stockton	157	61.1	162	63.9	319	62.5	17	S
Wife of Usher's Well, The (British Ballad)	206	36.2	235	54.9	441	45.6	14	S
Wiffenpoof Island—Ellis P. Butler	174	82.8	179	76.5	353	79.7	16	S
Wilbur and Orville Wright—Hermann Hagedorn	339	83.5	141	69.5	480	76.5	203	IR
Wilbur Wright and Orville Wright— Rosemary C. and Stephen V. Benét	217	76.0	375	75.6	592	75.8	12	R
Wild Animals I Have Met—Carolyn Wells	271	38.9	304	51.2	575	45.1	12	R
Wild Bill Hickok—Doris S. Garst	503	58.7	153	45.1	656	51.9		
Wild Honeysuckle, The— Philip Freneau	179	48.3	211	64.2	390	56.3	18	S
Wild Ride, The—Louise I. Guiney	159	45.o	190	47.9	349	46.5	20	S
Will o' the Mill—Robert L. Stevenson	258	45.7	251	49.6	509	47.7	20	S
Will Ray (American Ballad)	301	62.6	369	76.6	670	69.6	11	R
Will Rogers—Patrick J. O'Brien	479	92.5	384	93.4	863	93.0	80	IR

PUPILS' READING INTERESTS: GRADES 10-12
Ts and Ss = Teachers and Schools   S = Studied in Class
IR = Independent Reading   R = Read in Class

SELECTION—AUTHOR	Boys		Girls		Total		Ts & Ss	
	No.	%	No.	%	No.	Av. %		
Will Wimble—Joseph Addison	291	57.0	248	31.5	539	44.3	16	R
Wind in the Willows, The—Kenneth Grahame	125	69.2	256	75.6	381	72.4		
Wings of Lead—Nathalia Crane	326	62.3	368	59.9	694	61.1	22	S
Winnowers, The—Robert Bridges	244	48.6	309	57.9	553	53.3	21	S
Winter Moon—Langston Hughes	400	34.3	501	47.6	901	41.0	14	R
Winthrop Woman, The—Anya Seton	47		180	74.4				
Wise King, The—Kahlil Gibran	214	53.5	255	58.4	469	56.0	15	S
With Helmet and Hose—William Beebe	255	72.7	317	63.3	572	68.0	17	S
With the Photographer—Stephen Leacock	446	86.8	431	92.4	877	89.6	13	R
Wolf, the Storm Leader—Frank Caldwell	202	88.1	128	86.3	330	87.2	75	IR
Woman's Will—Unknown	6749	61.5	7915	75.9	14664	68.7	270	R
Women, The—Aristophanes	622	70.8	688	81.5	1310	76.2	20	R
Wonder Book, The—Nathaniel Hawthorne	84		187	66.3			200	IR
Woodman, Spare that Tree—George P. Morris	370	59.2	360	63.9	730	61.6	15	R
Wood-Pile, The—Robert Frost	177	61.0	201	59.0	378	60.0	16	S
Work—Henry Van Dyke	205	63.4	268	71.3	473	67.4	23	S
Workhouse Ward, The—Augusta Gregory	131	50.0	394	42.5	525	46.3	16	R
Working Party, A—Siegfried Sassoon	297	78.5	390	71.4	687	75.0	16	R
World Almanac, The	394	68.9	335	70.6	729	69.8		
World Book (Encyclopedia)	254	61.6	501	66.8	755	64.2	39	IR
World Is Too Much with Us, The— William Wordsworth	467	48.3	679	60.4	1146	54.4	66	S

314 THE READING INTERESTS

PUPILS' READING INTERESTS: GRADES 10-12
Ts and Ss = Teachers and Schools   S = Studied in Class
IR = Independent Reading   R = Read in Class

SELECTION—AUTHOR	Boys		Girls		Total		Ts & Ss	
	No.	%	No.	%	No.	Av. %		
Wouter Van Twiller— Washington Irving	299	65.6	340	59.1	639	62.4	31	S
Wreck of the "Hesperus," The— Henry W. Longfellow	182	79.9	205	80.7	387	80.3	19	S
Wreck of the Mary Deare—Ralph Hammond-Innes	237	74.5	184	70.4	421	72.5		
Written in March— William Wordsworth	4186	51.7	4156	60.2	8342	56.0	130	R
Wuthering Heights— Emily Brontë	169	62.7	678	85.7	847	74.2	130	IR
Wuthless Dog, The— Franklin Holt	245	81.8	209	90.7	454	86.3	13	R
Wynken, Blynken, and Nod—Eugene Field	323	60.7	437	75.6	760	68.2	20	R
Yankee Doodle (Song)	755	71.1	1092	71.8	1847	71.5	54	IR
Yarn of the "Nancy Bell," The— William S. Gilbert	164	80.2	441	75.9	605	78.1	20	S
Yearling, The—Marjorie K. Rawlings	230	70.0	467	76.3	697	73.2		
Yearnings—Rebecca McCann	244	35.2	282	61.3	526	48.3	12	R
Year the Yankees Lost the Pennant, The— Douglass Wallop	439	77.9	192	70.3	631	74.1		
Yellow Cat, The—Wibur D. Steele	356	87.4	373	75.6	729	81.5	14	R
Yellow Jack—Sidney Howard and Paul De Kruif	257	81.3	306	83.0	563	82.2	21	S
You Can't Take It with You—Hart and Kaufman	148	76.7	305	76.2	453	76.5		
Young Fellow, My Lad— Robert W. Service	343	82.8	449	89.5	792	86.2	20	R
Young Grimes—B. L. Taylor	351	49.1	360	64.2	711	56.7	11	R
Young Lady of Niger— Cosmo Monkhouse	6804	64.4	7960	69.5	14764	67.0	270	R

PUPILS' READING INTERESTS: GRADES 10-12
Ts and Ss = Teachers and Schools   S = Studied in Class
IR = Independent Reading   R = Read in Class

SELECTION—AUTHOR	Boys		Girls		Total		Ts & Ss	
	No.	%	No.	%	No.	Av. %		
Young Lions, The—Irwin Shaw	175	83.7	134	50.3	309	67.0		
Young Man Axelbrod— Sinclair Lewis	384	66.8	246	65.4	630	66.1	27	S
Yussouf—James R. Lowell	122	49.6	201	50.0	323	49.8	19	R
Zebra Dun, The (Cowboy Ballad)	440	83.0	464	81.9	904	82.5	15	R
Zenobia's Infidelity— Henry C. Bunner	587	77.9	505	77.4	1092	77.7	53	S
Zodomirsky's Duel— Alexandre Dumas	263	74.7	182	67.6	445	71.2	29	S

TABLE 42
LITERARY SELECTIONS WITH SCORES, GRADES 7–9

Ts and Ss = Teachers and Schools   S = Studied in Class
IR = Independent Reading   R = Read in Class

SELECTION—AUTHOR	Boys		Girls		Total		Ts & Ss	
	No.	%	No.	%	No.	Av. %		
Abe Lincoln Grows Up— Carl Sandburg	291	82.1	291	82.5	582	82.3	22	S
Abe Lincoln: Log Cabin to White House— Sterling North	375	69.2	283	71.9	658	70.6		
Ab Kills a Hyena— Stanley Waterloo	314	77.2	320	71.7	634	74.5	13	R
Abominable Snowman— Ralph Izzard	337	84.1	213	71.8	550	78.0		
Abou Ben Adhem— Leigh Hunt	262	72.0	266	80.6	528	76.3	21	S
Abraham Lincoln— Genevieve Foster	279	72.6	191	66.8	470	69.7		
Abraham Lincoln— Hermann Hagedorn	389	90.7	348	91.2	737	91.0		IR
Abraham Lincoln— Walter Malone	1123	67.5	1112	77.2	2235	72.4	51	R
Abraham Lincoln— Richard H. Stoddard	248	69.0	207	72.9	455	71.0	21	S
Abraham Lincoln— Woodrow Wilson	203	75.4	213	70.2	416	72.8	15	S
Abraham Lincoln's Education—Ida M. Tarbell	332	86.9	277	82.5	609	84.7	12	R
Abraham Lincoln to John D. Johnston	501	60.9	461	58.5	962	59.7	20	R
Abraham Lincoln Walks at Midnight— Vachel Lindsay	482	64.0	442	73.1	924	68.6	32	S
Acres of Diamonds— Russell Conwell	293	76.5	373	72.5	666	74.5		IR
Actor and the Pig, The— Phaedrus	298	77.3	316	80.5	614	78.9	13	R
Address to the Army— Albert, King of the Belgians	247	80.0	260	68.3	507	74.2	18	S

PUPILS' READING INTERESTS: GRADES 7-9

Ts and Ss = Teachers and Schools   S = Studied in Class
IR = Independent Reading   R = Read in Class

SELECTION—AUTHOR	Boys		Girls		Total		Ts & Ss	
	No.	%	No.	%	No.	Av. %		
Adrift on an Ice Pan— Wilfred T. Grenfell	390	81.5	250	79.0	640	80.3		IR
Adventure of the Mason —Washington Irving	394	85.2	371	85.9	765	85.6	19	R
Adventure of the Norwood Builder, The— A. Conan Doyle	673	83.4	609	81.8	1282	82.6	33	S
Adventure of the One Penny Black, The— Ellery Queen	203	89.8	193	92.2	396	91.0	20	R
Adventures of Buffalo Bill, The— William F. Cody	186	86.8	184	75.8	370	81.3	17	S
Adventures of Joe Dobson, The—Unknown	308	65.9	306	80.7	614	73.3	13	R
Adventures of Odysseus and the Tale of Troy, The—Padriac Colum	162	79.3	123	64.6	285	72.0		
Adventures of Sherlock Holmes, The— A. Conan Doyle	539	90.5	401	87.4	940	89.0	44	IR
Adventures of the Overland Road— William F. Cody	233	90.8	211	78.7	444	84.8	19	S
Adventures of Thor (Norse Mythology)	388	72.7	473	64.8	861	68.8	22	S
Adventure with a Lion, An—David Livingston	225	78.0	225	69.8	450	73.9	15	R
A. E. F.—Carl Sandburg	517	50.2	505	42.1	1022	46.2	23	R
Aesop's Fables	424	71.5	581	73.8	1005	72.7	86	IR
African Queen, The—C. S. Forester	248	83.5	154	77.3	402	80.4		
Afternoon—Fannie S. Davis	326	41.1	412	72.3	738	56.7	26	S
Afternoon on a Hill— Edna St. V. Millay	512	49.2	471	65.4	983	57.3	34	S
After Twenty Years—O. Henry	699	94.6	655	93.6	1354	94.1	29	R
A-Hunting of the Deer— Charles D. Warner	601	79.8	602	73.7	1203	76.8	64	S

PUPILS' READING INTERESTS: GRADES 7-9
Ts and Ss = Teachers and Schools   S = Studied in Class
IR = Independent Reading   R = Read in Class

SELECTION—AUTHOR	Boys		Girls		Total		Ts & Ss	
	No.	%	No.	%	No.	Av. %		
Aku-Aku—Thor Heyerdahl	245	82.9	192	80.5	437	81.7		
Aladdin—James R. Lowell	1620	65.0	1645	78.0	3265	71.5	142	S
Aladdin and the Wonderful Lamp— Arabian Nights	438	86.2	445	93.6	883	89.9	18	R
Albert Schweitzer, Genius of the Jungle— Joseph Gollomb	197	72.8	177	81.6	374	77.2		
Alfred (Comic Strip)	273	67.4	309	66.0	582	66.7	70	IR
Ali Baba and the Forty Thieves— Arabian Nights	350	87.3	400	84.4	750	85.9	29	S
Alice's Adventures in Wonderland— Lewis Carroll	842	57.2	1501	70.9	2343	64.1	83	IR
All American—John R. Tunis	514	82.8	127	79.9	641	81.4	128	IR
Allan-a-Dale—Walter Scott	366	40.8	425	47.8	791	44.3	14	R
All Animals Are Brothers —H. L. Durov	285	51.0	273	50.7	558	50.9	16	R
Alley Cat—Esther V. Georges	335	44.2	330	50.2	665	47.2	13	R
Alley Oop (Comic Strip)	435	61.3	480	41.9	915	51.6	25	IR
All Quiet on the Western Front—E. M. Remarque	437	84.4	140	67.5	577	76.0		
All This My Pencil Sees —Elinor Coleman	307	34.4	346	47.4	653	40.9	17	R
Alone in a Roomful of Rats—Dan Beard	223	75.6	241	70.3	464	73.0	21	R
Amahl and the Night Visitors— Gian-Carlo Menotti	285	58.8	347	70.9	632	64.9		
Ambitious Guest, The— Nathaniel Hawthorne	396	56.6	390	61.4	786	59.0	31	S
Ambitious Haddock, The —Laura E. Richards	384	49.4	359	57.4	743	53.4	12	R
Ambitious Mouse, The— John Farrar	294	66.8	356	78.4	650	72.6	12	R

PUPILS' READING INTERESTS: GRADES 7-9
Ts and Ss = Teachers and Schools   S = Studied in Class
IR = Independent Reading   R = Read in Class

SELECTION—AUTHOR	Boys		Girls		Total		Ts & Ss	
	No.	%	No.	%	No.	Av. %		
Amelia Earhart—Doris S. Garst	47		171	76.0				
America—Franklin K. Lane	299	72.2	267	66.1	566	69.2	15	R
America—Samuel F. Smith	339	82.6	319	85.9	658	84.3	25	S
America—Edward Steiner	195	75.6	212	80.0	407	77.8	17	S
America for Me—Henry Van Dyke	438	81.1	452	86.2	890	83.7	34	S
American Boy, The—Theodore Roosevelt	283	76.2	281	64.8	564	70.5	18	S
American Flag, The—Joseph R. Drake	859	67.6	848	65.7	1707	66.7	39	R
American's Creed, The—William T. Page	1303	73.6	1338	72.3	2641	73.0	85	R
American, Sir!—Mary R. S. Andrews	372	80.6	412	79.2	784	79.9	16	S
America's Answer—R. W. Lilliard	554	73.8	555	76.1	1109	75.0	55	S
America's Paul Revere—Esther Forbes	767	75.7	486	68.8	1253	72.3		
America's Robert E. Lee—Henry S. Commager	332	73.9	138	61.2	470	67.6		
America the Beautiful—Katharine L. Bates	1053	77.1	1000	87.0	2053	82.1	96	S
Ancient Mariner, The—Samuel T. Coleridge	3596	64.9	3435	66.4	7031	65.7	200	S
Andrew Jackson—Hermann Hagedorn	219	87.9	123	80.1	342	84.0	69	IR
Androclus and the Lion—Michel de Montaigne	499	70.4	461	69.6	960	70.0	9	R
And To Think That I Saw It on Mulberry Street—Dr. Seuss	336	67.4	587	67.1	923	67.3		
And You Become King—Bruce Barton	339	38.9	352	42.8	691	40.9	16	R
Angel on Skis—Betty Cavanna	90	72.2	497	79.3	587	75.8		

PUPILS' READING INTERESTS: GRADES 7-9
Ts and Ss = Teachers and Schools   S = Studied in Class
IR = Independent Reading   R = Read in Class

SELECTION—AUTHOR	Boys		Girls		Total		Ts & Ss	
	No.	%	No.	%	No.	Av. %		
Angler's Wish, An— Henry Van Dyke	223	52.0	244	59.4	467	55.7	14	R
Angry Planet, The—John K. Cross	276	76.3	94	67.6	370	72.0		
Animal Sixth Sense, The—Clarence Hawkes	263	77.2	277	70.9	540	74.1	18	R
Annabel Lee—Edgar A. Poe	438	68.5	505	84.6	943	76.6	27	S
Anna Mareea—Esther Tiffany	365	45.5	324	72.5	689	59.0	11	R
Anne of Green Gables— L. M. Montgomery	133	82.3	297	97.8	430	90.1	51	S
Annie Laurie—William Douglas	304	40.8	325	65.4	629	53.1	18	R
Annie Rooney (Comic Strip)	336	47.8	520	65.8	856	56.8	25	IR
Another Blue Day— Thomas Carlyle	667	40.4	672	55.6	1339	48.0	24	R
Antelope Mother Faces Danger, An— William and Irene Finley	321	89.3	344	83.7	665	86.5	22	R
Apes and Ivory—Alfred Noyes	242	53.3	239	63.4	481	58.4	13	S
Apollo—Frances Sabin	249	63.5	281	74.7	530	69.1	24	S
Apple Orchard in the Spring, An— William W. Martin	356	33.6	360	51.7	716	42.7	18	R
April Weather—Lizette W. Reese	397	58.3	419	70.2	816	64.3	20	R
Arabian Nights, The	606	82.5	682	82.0	1288	82.3	105	IR
Arachne—Rannie B. Baker	381	36.7	336	49.7	717	43.2	17	R
Argument with a Millionaire, An— David Grayson	470	75.6	484	79.8	954	77.7	25	S
Ariel's Song—William Shakespeare	4083	30.8	4107	36.9	8190	33.9	173	R
Army Ants in the Jungle —William Beebe	311	72.7	276	55.4	587	64.1	19	S

PUPILS' READING INTERESTS: GRADES 7-9

Ts and Ss = Teachers and Schools   S = Studied in Class
IR = Independent Reading   R = Read in Class

SELECTION—AUTHOR	Boys		Girls		Total		Ts & Ss	
	No.	%	No.	%	No.	Av. %		
Arnold Von Winkelried—James Montgomery	339	65.2	323	58.0	662	61.6	13	R
Around the World in Eighty Days—Jules Verne	959	80.9	805	79.6	1764	80.3		
Arrow and the Song, The—Henry W. Longfellow	293	64.9	361	68.6	654	66.8	20	S
Arsenal at Springfield, The—Henry W. Longfellow	228	57.5	272	55.1	500	56.3	14	R
As a Beauty I'm Not a Great Star— Anthony Euwer	347	66.3	393	80.8	740	73.6	11	R
As You Like It—Charles Lamb	291	53.8	290	71.0	581	62.4	56	IR
As You Like It—William Shakespeare	1177	52.1	1168	72.6	2345	62.4	97	S
Atalanta—Rannie B. Baker	378	54.8	374	69.1	752	62.0	17	R
Atalanta's Race—William Morris	337	46.9	285	46.7	622	46.8	11	R
At a Toy Shop Window—Charles S. Brooks	330	58.0	339	72.0	669	65.0	21	S
Athenian Boy's Oath, The—Unknown	1283	55.2	1258	44.1	2541	49.7	51	R
At Night—Frances Cornford	397	41.7	418	49.3	815	45.5	22	R
At the Crossroads—Richard Hovey	353	53.7	336	67.1	689	60.4	21	S
At Twilight—Harriet Monroe	313	41.2	338	57.1	651	49.2	17	R
Auntie Mame—Patrick Dennis	288	83.3	768	86.5	1056	84.9		
Autobiography—Abraham Lincoln	314	62.3	380	55.9	694	59.1	12	R
Automobile, The—Percy MacKaye	319	26.8	343	24.1	662	25.5	15	R
Autumn—Emily Dickinson	360	45.6	404	67.3	764	56.5	20	R

PUPILS' READING INTERESTS: GRADES 7-9
Ts and Ss = Teachers and Schools   S = Studied in Class
IR = Independent Reading   R = Read in Class

SELECTION—AUTHOR	Boys		Girls		Total		Ts & Ss	
	No.	%	No.	%	No.	Av. %		
Autumn—Jean S. Untermeyer	277	60.0	278	72.7	555	66.4	16	R
Aviation Cadet—Henry Lent	159	69.5	10					
Awakening, The—Robert Browning	324	22.1	333	40.2	657	31.2	18	R
Away All Boats— Kenneth Dodson	237	77.8	26					
Away Goes Sally— Elizabeth J. Coatsworth	22		221	63.6				
Awful Fate of Melpomenous Jones, The — Stephen Leacock	408	79.7	397	84.7	805	82.2	24	R
Babe Ruth—Tom Meany	1077	90.0	466	86.3	1543	88.2	129	IR
Babe Ruth Story, The— Bob Considine	493	85.2	132	66.3	625	75.8		
Babies, The—Mark Twain	300	62.0	314	72.3	614	67.2	16	R
Baby Lon (British Ballad)	258	61.6	179	71.2	437	66.4	16	S
Baby Sylvester Leaves the Mining Camp— Bret Harte	363	80.3	360	82.5	723	81.4	13	R
Back to Treasure Island —Harold Calahan	605	75.5	386	64.8	991	70.2		
Baker, Manager—Robert L. Voorhees	268	84.1	307	77.2	575	80.7	23	S
Baldy of Nome—Esther B. Darling	283	87.1	244	84.6	527	85.9	55	R
Ballad of Dennis McGinty, The—Dana Burnet	198	77.3	203	85.0	401	81.2	14	S
Ballad of East and West, The—Rudyard Kipling	1459	75.2	1019	68.4	2478	71.8	109	S
Ballad of Father Gilligan, The— William B. Yeats	440	38.4	447	63.2	887	50.8	17	R
Ballad of Ivan Petrofsky Skevar (American Ballad)	393	86.3	414	84.1	807	85.2	15	R
Ballad of Jean La Fitte— Loia C. Cheaney	388	65.1	431	66.7	819	65.9	25	S

PUPILS' READING INTERESTS: GRADES 7-9

Ts and Ss = Teachers and Schools   S = Studied in Class

IR = Independent Reading   R = Read in Class

SELECTION—AUTHOR	Boys		Girls		Total		Ts & Ss	
	No.	%	No.	%	No.	Av. %		
Ballad of John Silver, A—John Masefield	230	66.7	277	62.6	507	64.7	20	S
Ballad of London, A—Richard Le Gallienne	248	44.6	329	58.7	577	51.7	16	S
Ballad of Sportsmanship, A—Thomas A. Daly	396	35.1	393	38.9	789	37.0	15	R
Ballad of the Boston Tea Party, The— Oliver W. Holmes	400	72.9	397	72.2	797	72.6	42	S
Ballad of the Circus, A—Charles H. Towne	461	53.9	470	70.9	931	62.4	15	R
Ballad of the Harp-Weaver, The—Edna St. V. Millay	391	70.6	396	86.1	787	78.4	24	S
Ballad of the Hundred and Fifteen Horses—Lucy S. Mitchell	227	65.9	220	66.1	447	66.0	15	S
Ballad of the Oysterman, The—Oliver W. Holmes	444	64.2	435	76.3	879	70.3	38	S
Ballet Shoes—Noel Streatfeild	17		296	64.4				
Bambi—Felix Salten	355	75.9	415	74.6	770	75.3	66	IR
Barbara Frietchie—John G. Whittier	1359	82.7	1449	89.2	2808	86.0	127	S
Barbed Wire—Lawrence Perry	350	84.3	399	80.7	749	82.5	22	S
Barclay of Ury—John G. Whittier	166	48.5	212	50.2	378	49.4	22	S
Barefoot Boy, The—John G. Whittier	485	78.7	502	87.5	987	83.1	45	S
Barker's Luck—Bret Harte	221	80.3	273	82.1	494	81.2	14	S
Barney Google and Snuffy Smith (Comic Strip)	359	65.7	413	48.3	772	57.0	23	IR
Barrel-Organ, The—Alfred Noyes	607	49.1	646	61.5	1253	55.3	29	S
Barter—Sara Teasdale	299	47.5	296	63.9	595	55.7	19	S
Baseball in de Park—Arthur Guiterman	318	86.6	342	83.0	660	84.8	26	S

PUPILS' READING INTERESTS: GRADES 7-9
Ts and Ss = Teachers and Schools   S = Studied in Class
IR = Independent Reading   R = Read in Class

SELECTION—AUTHOR	Boys		Girls		Total		Ts & Ss	
	No.	%	No.	%	No.	Av. %		
Battle of Bannockburn, The—Robert Burns	189	72.5	170	58.5	359	65.6	15	S
Battle of Blenheim, The —Robert Southey	249	60.4	256	60.0	505	60.2	26	S
Battle of Otterburn, The (British Ballad)	268	61.9	201	43.3	469	52.6	21	S
Battle of the Ants, The— Henry D. Thoreau	456	75.9	438	60.0	894	68.0	30	S
Battle of the Snakes, The — Hector St.J. de Crèvecoeur	458	74.7	438	57.0	896	65.9	19	S
Battle Stations—Margaret Scoggin	317	79.3	29					
Bayliffe's Daughter of Islington, The (British Ballad)	404	51.1	659	63.6	1063	57.4	22	S
Beany Malone—Lenora M. Weber	9		426	70.4				
Bear Hunt, A—Leo Tolstoy	331	93.4	388	87.8	719	90.6	13	R
Beatitudes, The—The Bible	745	70.3	727	79.0	1472	74.7	29	R
Beau Geste—Percival C. Wren	410	86.3	175	75.7	585	81.0	266	IR
Beautiful Joe—Marshall Saunders	126	82.1	278	87.9	404	85.0	88	IR
Bedquilt, The—Dorothy C. Fisher	357	54.9	323	78.2	680	66.6	19	S
Bee's Knees, The—Alida Hurtebise	254	63.4	322	68.6	576	66.0	12	R
Bees' Song, The—Walter de la Mare	538	45.6	564	49.5	1102	47.6	26	R
Bee That Wished a Sting, The—Aesop	826	75.2	841	77.6	1667	76.4	33	R
Behind the Closed Eye— Francis Ledwidge	229	58.1	231	660	460	62.1	14	S
Believe It or Not— Robert L. Ripley	389	81.4	281	73.5	670	77.5		
Bell and the Cat, The— Aesop	1536	66.2	1548	66.8	3084	66.5	62	R

PUPILS' READING INTERESTS: GRADES 7-9
Ts and Ss = Teachers and Schools   S = Studied in Class
IR = Independent Reading   R = Read in Class

SELECTION—AUTHOR	Boys		Girls		Total		Ts & Ss	
	No.	%	No.	%	No.	Av. %		
Bell Buoy, The—Rudyard Kipling	289	65.7	329	65.7	618	65.7	26	S
Belles on Their Toes— Gilbreth and Carey	31		218	80.5				
Bell of Atri, The—Henry W. Longfellow	568	64.1	624	72.4	1192	68.3	45	S
Bells, The—Edgar A. Poe	155	50.3	181	72.4	336	61.4	16	S
Ben and Me—Robert Lawson	628	74.3	765	69.9	1393	72.1		
Ben Hur—Lew Wallace	257	77.8	219	71.5	476	74.7	117	IR
Benjamin Franklin to Mr. Strahan	649	66.4	652	64.6	1301	65.5	22	R
Beowulf—Francis B. Gummere	149	82.2	337	65.0	486	73.6	13	S
Best and Worst Nail in the Ark, The— Arthur Guiterman	285	73.7	262	73.7	547	73.7	15	S
Best Bait for Mosquitoes, The—Henry S. Canby	330	69.5	211	65.2	541	67.4	13	S
Beth Gêlert—William R. Spencer	373	67.7	415	73.7	788	70.7	26	S
Be True—Horatio Bonar	1363	51.4	1332	63.1	2695	57.3	72	R
Betsy Has a Birthday— Dorothy C. Fisher			650	81.3			28	R
Betsy-Tacy—Maud Lovelace	13		270	63.1				
Better Known as Johnny Appleseed— Mabel L. Hunt	233	60.1	291	64.1	524	62.1		
Between Planets—Robert Heinlein	157	72.0	46					
Between Two Loves— Thomas A. Daly	300	88.7	336	93.9	636	91.3	15	R
Bewick and Grahame (British Ballad)	192	55.7	136	46.7	328	51.2	17	S
Big Baboon, The — Hilaire Belloc	389	55.5	358	65.4	747	60.5	15	R
Big Doc's Girl—Mary Medearis	17		153	73.9				

PUPILS' READING INTERESTS: GRADES 7-9
Ts and Ss = Teachers and Schools   S = Studied in Class
IR = Independent Reading   R = Read in Class

SELECTION—AUTHOR	Boys No.	Boys %	Girls No.	Girls %	Total No.	Total Av. %	Ts & Ss	
Big Fisherman, The— Lloyd C. Douglas	375	85.5	392	85.7	767	85.6		
Big Red—Jim Kjelgaard	296	80.2	256	72.5	552	76.4		
Bill—Zona Gale	289	62.5	288	80.0	577	71.3	15	S
Bill Brown's Test— Cleveland H. Moffett	274	79.7	271	76.0	545	77.9	12	R
Bill Peters (Cowboy Ballad)—John A. Lomax (Ed.)	267	86.3	314	81.2	581	83.8	19	S
Billy, the Dog That Made Good— Ernest T. Seton	467	89.9	427	86.3	894	88.1	16	R
Billy the Kid—American Ballad	428	85.9	479	79.6	907	82.8	18	R
Billy Topsail—Norman Duncan	212	85.4	251	78.7	463	82.1	17	R
Biography of a Grizzly, The—Ernest T. Seton	173	89.9	173	89.0	346	89.5	17	S
Biography of a Puppy, The—Albert P. Terhune	246	91.5	283	95.6	529	93.6	12	R
Birches—Robert Frost	381	55.9	383	63.7	764	59.8	29	S
Birds' Christmas Carol, The—Kate D. Wiggin	175	72.0	162	95.0	337	83.5	24	S
Birds of Killingworth, The—Henry W. Longfellow	625	57.4	734	58.7	1359	58.1	74	S
Bishop's Silver Candlesticks, The— Victor Hugo	258	78.3	275	85.3	533	81.8	27	S
Bison Track, The— Bayard Taylor	304	58.9	321	48.8	625	53.9	10	R
Black Arrow, The— Robert L. Stevenson	345	70.3	347	66.9	692	68.6	20	S
Blackbeard—Frank R. Stockton	305	94.9	324	87.5	629	91.2	16	R
Black Beauty—Anna Sewell	439	80.5	467	86.1	906	83.3	35	S
Black Beaver—Samuel Scoville, Jr.	336	87.6	313	83.9	649	85.8	11	R

PUPILS' READING INTERESTS: GRADES 7-9
Ts and Ss = Teachers and Schools   S = Studied in Class
IR = Independent Reading   R = Read in Class

SELECTION—AUTHOR	Boys		Girls		Total		Ts & Ss
	No.	%	No.	%	No.	Av. %	
Black Buccaneer, The—Stephen W. Meader	175	76.9	56				
Black Duck Dinner, The —James Stevens	394	74.1	242	58.1	636	66.1	21	S
Black Eagle—Sewell Ford	316	94.8	301	89.4	617	92.1	16	R
Black Gold—Marguerite Henry	109	67.9	207	77.1	316	72.5		
Black Hero of the Ranges, The—Enos A. Mills	398	96.0	417	84.5	815	90.3	19	R
Black Stallion, The— Walter Farley	852	75.1	972	78.7	1824	76.9		
Black Stallion's Sulky Colt, The— Walter Farley	150	68.0	337	74.9	487	71.5		
Blacktail Deer—Lew Sarett	241	63.1	287	60.8	528	62.0	14	S
Blazed Trail, The— Stewart E. White	270	72.4	128	65.2	398	68.8		
Blessing the Dance— Irwin Russell	397	58.1	418	59.3	815	58.7	20	R
Blind Colt, The—Glen Rounds	192	78.6	276	82.2	468	80.4		
Blind Girl, The—Nathalia Crane	300	40.8	339	59.0	639	49.9	16	R
Blind Men and the Elephant, The— John G. Saxe	230	75.9	199	75.6	429	75.8	15	S
Blind Setter, The— Samuel A. Derieux	197	94.9	164	92.1	361	93.5	18	S
Blondie (Comic Strip)	1225	83.2	1264	85.2	2489	84.2	78	IR
Blow, Blow, Thou Winter Wind— William Shakespeare	914	50.1	959	58.2	1873	54.2	51	S
Blow the Man Down (Sea Chantey)	583	47.7	571	50.8	1154	49.3	20	R
Blue and the Gray, The —Francis M. Finch	482	67.2	461	68.5	943	67.9	35	R

PUPILS' READING INTERESTS: GRADES 7-9
Ts and Ss = Teachers and Schools　　　S = Studied in Class
IR = Independent Reading　　　　　　R = Read in Class

SELECTION—AUTHOR	Boys		Girls		Total		Ts & Ss	
	No.	%	No.	%	No.	Av. %		
Blue Bird, The—Maurice Maeterlinck	229	72.7	576	79.1	805	75.9	96	IR
Blue Fairy Book, The— Andrew Lang	34		236	58.5				
Blue Squills—Sara Teasdale	394	32.2	386	51.3	780	41.8	18	R
Blue Willow—Doris Gates	32		377	70.8				
Boarded-up House, The —Augusta H. Seaman	109	77.5	415	88.0	524	82.8	122	IR
Bobbsey Twins, The (Stories)—Laura L. Hope	159	40.6	665	56.3	824	48.5		
Bob, Son of Battle— Alfred Ollivant	181	85.4	123	86.6	304	86.0	53	IR
Bob White—A Vanishing Game Bird— Dallas L. Sharp	173	67.3	180	60.3	353	63.8	15	S
Boggles—Unknown	319	50.0	341	67.0	660	58.5	10	R
Boggs on Dogs—Norman H. Crowell	379	76.7	384	69.9	763	73.3	29	S
Boll Weevil Song, The (Negro Folk Song)	314	74.7	325	80.0	639	77.4	20	S
Bonny Barbara Allen (British Ballad)	220	46.2	515	66.0	735	56.1	23	S
Book Houses—A. F. Johnston	341	63.1	358	84.4	699	73.8	19	S
Book of Courage, The— Hermann Hagedorn	199	87.4	169	83.1	368	85.3	82	IR
Book of Indians, The— Holling C. Holling	165	55.5	43					
Book of Knowledge, The	398	82.5	449	80.1	847	81.3	118	IR
Boomerang—Marion H. McNeely	365	83.0	355	96.3	720	89.7	12	R
Boots—Rudyard Kipling	297	51.7	329	67.5	626	59.6	10	R
Boots and Her Buddies (Comic Strip)	254	55.5	440	76.7	694	66.1	21	IR
Born Free—Joy Adamson	145	80.7	189	90.5	334	85.6		
Borrowers, The—Mary Norton	25		149	68.2				

PUPILS' READING INTERESTS: GRADES 7-9

Ts and Ss = Teachers and Schools   S = Studied in Class
IR = Independent Reading   R = Read in Class

SELECTION—AUTHOR	Boys		Girls		Total		Ts & Ss	
	No.	%	No.	%	No.	Av. %		
Boy and a Pup, A— Arthur Guiterman	404	52.4	415	59.5	819	56.0	26	S
Boy and His Dog, A— Edgar A. Guest	466	79.0	471	83.8	937	81.4	26	R
Boy at Gettysburg, A— Elsie Singmaster	209	71.5	103	65.5	312	68.5		
Boyhood in the Bush, A —Thomas LeBlanc	404	77.2	371	64.0	775	70.6	12	R
Boyhood of Lincoln, The — Godfrey R. B. Charnwood	549	73.9	534	73.5	1083	73.7	26	R
Boyhood on a Missouri Farm—Mark Twain	490	75.8	562	75.1	1052	75.5	76	S
Boy in the Model T, The—Stephen Longstreet	167	79.6	58					
Boy Life on the Prairie—Hamlin Garland	297	76.4	282	71.1	579	73.8	27	S
Boy Next Door, The— Betty Cavanna	39		576	79.9				
Boy on Horseback, A— Lincoln Steffens	358	93.7	378	95.0	736	94.4	14	R
Boys, The—Oliver W. Holmes	275	75.6	323	74.8	598	75.2	22	S
Boy Scout's Handbook, The	545	85.9	41				74	IR
Boy Scout's Life of Lincoln, The— Ida Tarbell	427	75.5	185	73.1	612	74.3	307	IR
Boy Scout with Byrd, A —Paul Siple	311	82.6	109	81.7	420	82.2	180	IR
Boys' Life of Abraham Lincoln, The— Helen Nicolay	569	78.2	479	77.9	1048	78.1	216	IR
Boys' Life of Edison, The — William H. Meadowcroft	339	86.1	187	81.6	526	83.9	112	IR
Boys' Life of Mark Twain, The— Albert B. Paine	271	89.7	212	84.4	483	87.1	48	IR

PUPILS' READING INTERESTS: GRADES 7-9
Ts and Ss = Teachers and Schools   S = Studied in Class
IR = Independent Reading   R = Read in Class

SELECTION—AUTHOR	Boys		Girls		Total		Ts & Ss	
	No.	%	No.	%	No.	Av. %		
Boy's Life of Theodore Roosevelt— Hermann Hagedorn	342	80.4	161	78.3	503	79.4	117	IR
Boys' Life of the Wright Brothers, The—Mitchell V. Charnley	323	76.5	106	72.6	429	74.6	244	IR
Boy's Mother, A—James W. Riley	384	83.5	381	93.6	765	88.6	13	R
Boy's Song, A—James Hogg	412	63.1	408	72.3	820	67.7	15	R
Boys Will Be Boys—Irvin S. Cobb	328	86.7	305	83.4	633	85.1	19	S
Boy Trouble—Rosamond Du Jardin	23		382	80.9				
Boy Wanted—Frank Crane	172	75.0	202	81.9	374	78.5	18	S
Boy Who Cried Wolf, The—Aesop	179	62.3	189	68.3	368	65.3	16	R
Brave Men—Ernie Pyle	157	79.0	32					
Break, Break, Break— Alfred Tennyson	450	37.4	480	48.1	930	42.8	14	R
Bridges at Toko-Ri, The —James A. Michener	462	86.9	115	80.9	577	83.9		
Brin—Wilfred T. Grenfell	333	82.4	350	83.1	683	82.8	10	R
Bring 'Em Back Alive— Frank Buck	693	89.0	347	83.4	1040	86.2	129	IR
Bringing Back a Live Elephant—Frank Buck	380	88.0	413	78.9	793	83.5	11	R
Bringing In a Gusher— Upton Sinclair	350	79.1	341	66.9	691	73.0	11	R
Bringing Up Father (Comic Strip)	389	73.0	521	76.1	910	74.6	24	IR
Brink of Silence, The— Esther E. Galbraith	400	87.1	404	84.2	804	85.7	19	S
Broken Sword, The— Edwin Markham	271	83.4	218	78.9	489	81.2	15	S
Bronco Busting—Will James	328	72.7	356	58.8	684	65.8	12	R

PUPILS' READING INTERESTS: GRADES 7-9

Ts and Ss = Teachers and Schools   S = Studied in Class
IR = Independent Reading   R = Read in Class

SELECTION—AUTHOR	Boys		Girls		Total		Ts & Ss	
	No.	%	No.	%	No.	Av. %		
Bronco That Would Not be Broken, The— Vachel Lindsay	316	61.6	302	63.1	618	62.4	20	S
Bronc That Wouldn't Bust, The (Cowboy Ballad)	451	88.7	501	86.8	952	87.8	19	R
Brook, The—Alfred Tennyson	280	60.9	367	75.6	647	68.3	27	S
Brooklyn Dodgers, The— Frank P. Graham	589	82.9	173	81.5	762	82.2	132	IR
Broom (British Ballad)	461	59.8	431	69.5	892	64.7	21	R
Broomstick Train, The— Oliver W. Holmes	811	70.7	850	80.8	1661	75.8	72	S
Buff, a Collie—Albert P. Terhune	239	90.8	275	90.9	514	90.9	19	R
Buffalo, The—Francis Parkman	251	71.7	286	59.6	537	65.7	25	S
Buffalo Bill—Ingri and Edgar d'Aulaire	850	73.9	372	56.7	1222	65.3		
Bugles of Dreamland, The—Fiona MacLeod	337	39.9	324	60.8	661	50.4	13	R
Bugle Song, The—Alfred Tennyson	223	62.1	234	64.7	457	63.4	23	S
Builders, The—Henry W. Longfellow	304	63.5	327	63.0	631	63.3	26	S
Building of the Ship, The —Henry W. Longfellow	285	70.4	288	69.3	573	69.9	27	S
Bundle of Sticks, The— Aesop	1353	78.4	1394	76.1	2747	77.3	56	R
Bunker Mouse, The— Frederick S. Greene	196	85.5	164	77.7	360	81.6	30	R
Burial of Moses, The— Cecil F. Alexander	264	46.8	246	51.6	510	49.2	14	R
Burial of Sir John Moore, The—Charles Wolfe	331	72.1	361	68.6	692	70.4	14	R
Burning Gold—Burr Leyson	342	96.1	310	80.2	652	88.2	11	R
Business in Mississippi— Irwin Russell	248	71.4	268	72.4	516	71.9	22	S
Busy—A. A. Milne	415	57.0	402	67.7	817	62.4	20	R

PUPILS' READING INTERESTS: GRADES 7-9
Ts and Ss = Teachers and Schools   S = Studied in Class
IR = Independent Reading   R = Read in Class

SELECTION—AUTHOR	Boys		Girls		Total		Ts & Ss	
	No.	%	No.	%	No.	Av. %		
Caddie Woodlawn—Carol R. Brink	59		471	91.9			92	IR
Caine Mutiny, The—Herman Wouk	259	84.2	177	76.3	436	80.3		
Calf Path, The—Sam W. Foss	230	72.6	208	80.3	438	76.5	16	S
Caliban in the Coal Mines—Louis Untermeyer	377	60.6	416	66.0	793	63.3	21	R
Calico Captive—Elizabeth G. Speare	13		189	81.0				
Call It Courage—Armstrong Sperry	191	73.8	152	70.1	343	72.0		
Call Me Lucky—Bing Crosby	133	66.9	198	73.2	331	70.1		
Call of Spring, The—Alfred Noyes	277	59.9	312	73.4	589	66.7	19	R
Call of the Wild, The—Jack London	160	90.9	274	89.1	434	90.0	36	S
Camping Trip, A—Hamlin Garland	462	74.8	518	66.9	980	70.9	29	S
Candy Kane—Janet Lambert	8		162	72.2				
Cane Bottom'd Chair, The—William H. Thackeray	340	71.3	405	78.9	745	75.1	24	S
Canner, Exceedingly Canny, A—Carolyn Wells	429	73.4	436	80.8	865	77.1	19	R
Cannibal Flea, The—Thomas Hood	317	63.3	360	65.3	677	64.3	10	R
Captain Blood—Rafael Sabatini	429	85.1	212	77.1	641	81.1	128	IR
Captain Horatio Hornblower—C. S. Forester	251	76.1	97	70.1	348	73.1		
Captain Lincoln—Helen Nicolay	320	68.0	319	60.8	639	64.4	11	R
Captains Courageous—Rudyard Kipling	271	83.9	194	73.7	465	78.8	69	IR

PUPILS' READING INTERESTS: GRADES 7-9
Ts and Ss = Teachers and Schools   S = Studied in Class
IR = Independent Reading   R = Read in Class

SELECTION—AUTHOR	Boys No.	%	Girls No.	%	Total No.	Av. %	Ts & Ss	
Capturing the Wild Horse—Washington Irving	325	78.6	329	60.5	654	69.6	15	R
Carry On!—Robert W. Service	200	72.5	179	72.1	379	72.3	15	S
Casabianca—Felicia D. Hemans	281	54.4	319	69.3	600	61.9	12	R
Casey at the Bat—Ernest L. Thayer	559	91.5	600	90.4	1159	91.0	33	S
Cat in the Hat, The—Dr. Seuss	192	45.8	328	52.1	520	49.0		
Cat's Meat—Harold Monro	399	62.7	398	71.5	797	67.1	25	S
Cattle Drive, The—Stewart E. White	360	76.5	371	56.9	731	66.7	28	S
Cat Who Walked by Himself, The—Rudyard Kipling	149	72.8	173	75.7	322	74.3	78	IR
Cat Who Went to Heaven, The—Elizabeth Coatsworth	149	66.8	363	69.1	512	68.0	132	IR
Caught in a Blizzard—Paul Siple	304	94.1	321	89.3	625	91.7	12	R
Cave Twins, The—Lucy F. Perkins	319	69.6	454	73.5	773	71.6	76	IR
Celebrated Jumping Frog, The—Mark Twain	1935	76.4	1906	66.7	3841	71.6	146	S
Centennial Hymn—John G. Whittier	319	44.4	347	50.0	666	47.2	23	R
Central—J. C. Underwood	272	41.7	304	49.5	576	45.6	15	R
Century, The—Christopher Morley	580	64.8	562	60.7	1142	62.8	31	S
Challenge of Fujiyama, The— Richard Halliburton	231	81.0	209	73.2	440	77.1	14	R
Chambered Nautilus, The—Oliver W. Holmes	775	50.1	775	57.5	1550	53.8	65	S
Champion of Honor—Mary R. Parkman	311	61.4	318	62.0	629	61.7	21	S

PUPILS' READING INTERESTS: GRADES 7-9
Ts and Ss = Teachers and Schools   S = Studied in Class
IR = Independent Reading   R = Read in Class

SELECTION—AUTHOR	Boys		Girls		Total		Ts & Ss	
	No.	%	No.	%	No.	Av. %		
Change About (Old Folk Rhyme)	384	82.2	379	88.3	763	85.3	13	R
Chant of Loyalty, A— Elias Lieberman	284	51.4	302	56.1	586	53.8	17	R
Chant of the Colorado, The—Gale Y. Rice	298	39.9	275	48.0	573	44.0	11	R
Chaparral Christmas Gift, A—O. Henry	331	78.9	275	77.8	606	78.4	35	S
Chaparral Prince—O. Henry	359	62.0	347	76.5	706	69.3	19	S
Charge of the Light Brigade, The— Alfred Tennyson	528	77.1	542	59.0	1070	68.1	33	S
Charity—The Bible	376	64.0	356	73.9	732	69.0	10	R
Charity—Robert Burns	370	27.8	388	36.3	758	32.1	18	R
Charlie Lee—Henry H. Knibbs	210	76.0	236	71.2	446	73.6	14	S
Charlotte's Web—E. B. White	142	71.5	551	76.5	693	74.0		
Charm, A—Christopher Morley	317	40.2	188	46.8	505	43.5	14	R
Chartless—Emily Dickinson	384	41.3	352	54.1	736	47.7	20	S
Cher Ami—Alice Gall and Fleming Crew	337	95.3	332	93.1	669	94.2	14	R
Chewing Gum—Charles D. Warner	314	56.5	318	54.7	632	55.6	18	R
Chewing Gum Tree, The —Alida Hurtebise	356	67.1	382	75.7	738	71.4	15	R
Child Is Introduced to the Cosmos at Birth, The (Indian Lyric)	280	28.2	282	36.3	562	32.3	17	S
Child Pioneer—Honoré W. Morrow	365	90.1	388	95.2	753	92.7	13	R
Children's Hour, The— Henry W. Longfellow	604	71.2	608	85.9	1212	78.6	38	S
Child's Dream of a Star, A—Charles Dickens	473	45.5	483	70.2	956	57.9	34	S
Child's Garden of Verses, A— Robert L. Stevenson	297	62.5	892	70.2	1189	66.4	81	IR

PUPILS' READING INTERESTS: GRADES 7-9
Ts and Ss = Teachers and Schools   S = Studied in Class
IR = Independent Reading   R = Read in Class

SELECTION—AUTHOR	Boys		Girls		Total		Ts & Ss	
	No.	%	No.	%	No.	Av. %		
Chimes—Alice Meynell	324	39.8	343	54.1	667	47.0	19	R
Chinese Gordon— Hermann Hagedorn	359	79.5	318	71.1	677	75.3	32	R
Chiquita—Bret Harte	301	57.0	286	57.7	587	57.4	16	R
Chivalry—Hendrick W. Van Loon	241	56.2	232	44.4	473	50.3	18	R
Chopin Prelude— Eleanor Norton	333	29.1	393	48.0	726	38.6	17	R
Christmas Carol, A— Charles Dickens	2567	74.9	2449	83.2	5016	79.1	217	S
Christmas Night with Satan—John Fox, Jr.	242	67.6	309	73.6	551	70.6	22	S
Christmas Present for a Lady, A— Myra Kelly	266	78.0	230	93.9	496	86.0	13	R
Chu Chu—Bret Harte	209	47.1	250	53.4	459	50.3	17	S
Chums—Arthur Guiterman	467	69.0	457	76.1	924	72.6	21	R
Cinderella—Grimm Brothers	1350	59.6	2031	81.5	3381	70.6	83	IR
Circular Staircase, The— Mary R. Rinehart	134	85.0	525	89.2	659	87.1	132	IR
Circus, The—Tom Prideaux	490	55.8	516	59.2	1006	57.5	16	R
Circus Day Parade, The —James W. Riley	622	48.2	636	60.7	1258	54.5	18	R
Citizen, The—James F. Dwyer	298	62.8	240	66.9	538	64.9	14	S
Citizenship: the Northfield Ideal— William Heyliger	211	82.9	204	90.0	415	86.5	16	S
City Afternoon, A—Edith Wyatt	348	33.5	391	37.9	739	35.7	15	R
Clara Barton—Hermann Hagedorn	342	81.7	332	91.1	674	86.4	31	R
Clara Barton—Mildred Pace	328	57.5	1585	77.5	1913	67.5		
Clara Barton and the Red Cross— Kate D. Sweetser	170	66.8	166	77.1	336	72.0	19	S

PUPILS' READING INTERESTS: GRADES 7-9
Ts and Ss = Teachers and Schools   S = Studied in Class
IR = Independent Reading   R = Read in Class

SELECTION—AUTHOR	Boys		Girls		Total		Ts & Ss	
	No.	%	No.	%	No.	Av. %		
Classical Myths That Live Today— Frances E. Sabin	170	63.8	236	75.4	406	69.6	81	IR
Class Ring—Rosamond Du Jardin	14		425	84.2				
Cleon and I—Charles Mackay	249	58.6	285	69.3	534	64.0	12	R
Climbing Mount Olympus—Richard Halliburton	281	64.8	299	60.7	580	62.8	12	R
Clothes Make the Man—Booth Tarkington	626	83.9	597	93.8	1223	88.9	19	R
Cloud, The—Percy B. Shelley	221	49.1	273	57.0	494	53.1	33	S
Clown's Baby, The— Margaret Vandergrift	295	75.3	276	85.3	571	80.3	13	R
C'n I Have a Dog?— Marion H. McNeely	274	90.3	277	93.5	551	91.9	11	R
Coaly Bay, the Outlaw Horse—Ernest T. Seton	1123	87.9	1097	81.5	2220	84.7	87	S
Code of the Cow Country, The—S. Omar Barker	340	83.4	350	78.7	690	81.1	23	S
Collie in the Desert, A— Enos A. Mills	495	88.5	461	84.9	956	86.7	12	R
Colonial Twins of Virginia, The— Lucy F. Perkins	214	61.9	660	75.5	874	68.7	175	IR
Color-Bearer, The— Margaret J. Preston	376	78.3	430	79.3	806	78.8	23	S
Colors of Animals, The— John Lubbock	460	63.0	421	46.4	881	54.7	17	R
Columbus—Joaquin Miller	471	73.0	638	71.8	1109	72.4	39	S
Columbus—Annette Wynne	259	49.4	246	60.4	505	54.9	16	S
Columbus Sails—C. Walter Hodges	223	59.0	110	65.0	333	62.0		

PUPILS' READING INTERESTS: GRADES 7-9

Ts and Ss = Teachers and Schools   S = Studied in Class
IR = Independent Reading   R = Read in Class

SELECTION—AUTHOR	Boys		Girls		Total		Ts & Ss	
	No.	%	No.	%	No.	Av. %		
Combat with the Octopus, The—Victor Hugo	463	93.3	392	78.7	855	86.0	28	S
Comet—Samuel A. Derieux	239	92.3	783	89.2	1022	90.8	24	S
Coming of Arthur, The—Thomas Malory	405	79.5	351	68.8	756	74.2	38	S
Coming of Spring, The—Hamlin Garland	670	58.7	685	55.2	1355	57.0	21	R
Coming of Spring, The—Nora Perry	853	58.9	883	77.5	1736	68.2	88	S
Coming of the Circus, The—Hamlin Garland	345	56.4	368	60.6	713	58.5	13	R
Compton's Encyclopedia	341	80.6	412	82.4	753	81.5	98	IR
Concord Hymn—Ralph W. Emerson	8896	60.4	8888	62.7	17784	61.6	339	R
Conductor Bradley—John G. Whittier	321	80.5	358	78.8	679	79.7	28	S
Congo, The—Vachel Lindsay	376	68.1	365	75.2	741	71.7	12	R
Connecticut Yankee in King Arthur's Court, A—Mark Twain	1143	83.3	1073	82.1	2216	82.7	278	IR
Conquest of Space, The—Willy Ley	141	82.3	23					
Consecration, A—John Masefield	425	53.1	252	48.4	677	50.8	13	R
Constant Tin Soldier, The—Hans C. Andersen	363	72.7	279	83.5	642	78.1	12	R
Contentment—Oliver W. Holmes	835	63.5	834	74.6	1669	69.1	80	S
Contrary Mary, or Words—Nancy B. Turner	393	50.0	346	74.0	739	62.0	25	R
Cop and the Anthem, The—O. Henry	329	76.3	337	76.0	666	76.2	14	R
Coquette, The—John G. Saxe	438	38.0	502	61.6	940	49.8	16	R
Coral Island—R. M. Ballantyne	183	79.2	130	68.8	313	74.0		

PUPILS' READING INTERESTS: GRADES 7-9
Ts and Ss = Teachers and Schools   S = Studied in Class
IR = Independent Reading   R = Read in Class

SELECTION—AUTHOR	Boys		Girls		Total		Ts & Ss	
	No.	%	No.	%	No.	Av. %		
Cornaylius Ha-Ha-Ha Hannigan—Thomas A. Daly	434	58.3	466	73.2	900	65.8	17	R
Corn Song, The—John G. Whittier	366	48.4	392	56.3	758	52.4	17	R
Correct Behavior on a Picnic— Donald O. Stewart	307	85.7	267	92.1	574	88.9	13	R
Correct Display of the Stars and Stripes, The— McCandless and Grosvenor	643	76.2	639	73.6	1282	74.9	17	R
Count of Monte Cristo, The—Alexandre Dumas	254	88.4	186	83.9	440	86.2	76	IR
Courage—John Galsworthy	457	34.1	477	35.5	934	34.8	16	R
Courtin', The—James R. Lowell	635	59.9	634	77.8	1269	68.9	48	S
Courtship of Miles Standish, The— Henry W. Longfellow	2493	72.0	2519	82.8	5012	77.4	209	S
Covered Wagon, The— Emerson Hough	572	86.2	156	79.5	728	82.9	33	S
Cowboy, The—John Antrobus	395	60.1	377	63.3	772	61.7	13	R
Cowboy's Christmas Ball, The— Larry Chittenden	288	52.4	300	53.8	588	53.1	13	R
Cowboy's Dream, The (Cowboy Ballad), John A. Lomax (Ed.)	276	75.9	330	80.2	606	78.1	27	S
Cowboy's Life, The (Cowboy Ballad)	386	71.2	363	64.3	749	67.8	22	R
Cowboys of the Skies— Ernest Poole	202	85.6	149	65.8	351	75.7	17	S
Coyote, The—Mark Twain	326	74.8	328	60.2	654	67.5	14	R
C. Q. D.—Henry W. Lanier	302	92.7	273	88.4	575	90.6	21	R
Crafty Farmer, The (British Ballad)	290	62.4	303	68.0	593	65.2	12	R

PUPILS' READING INTERESTS: GRADES 7-9

Ts and Ss = Teachers and Schools   S = Studied in Class
IR = Independent Reading   R = Read in Class

SELECTION—AUTHOR	Boys		Girls		Total		Ts & Ss	
	No.	%	No.	%	No.	Av. %		
Creature God Forgot, The—Martin Johnson	197	76.6	223	71.7	420	74.2	17	S
Cree Queery and Mysy Drolly—James M. Barrie	418	36.1	487	48.5	905	42.3	33	S
Cremation of Sam McGee, The—Robert W. Service	531	87.9	644	85.9	1175	86.9	47	S
Crimson Sweater, The—Ralph H. Barbour	225	81.1	217	76.5	442	78.8	92	IR
Critical Moments with Wild Animals— Ellen Velvin	279	87.5	274	81.4	553	84.5	13	R
Crossing the Bar—Alfred Tennyson	279	36.6	291	54.7	570	45.7	11	R
Crossing the Plains—Joaquin Miller	314	43.5	275	41.5	589	42.5	19	R
Cruel Brother, The (British Ballad)	187	62.0	382	80.1	569	71.1	17	S
Cruel Moon, The—Robert Graves	305	43.4	334	51.3	639	47.4	14	R
Cruel Sea, The—Nicholas Monsarrat	166	77.4	47					
Crusade in Europe—Dwight D. Eisenhower	194	82.0	50					
Cub Pilot, The—Mark Twain	542	83.6	516	82.8	1058	83.2	21	R
Cuckoo Song—Unknown	3095	45.5	3052	50.3	6147	47.9	41	R
Cucumber, The—Unknown	350	40.1	377	46.6	727	43.4	18	R
Cupid and Psyche—Rannie B. Baker	342	47.1	299	72.4	641	59.8	16	R
Custer's Last Stand—Quentin Reynolds	193	82.6	26					
Czar and the Angel, The (Cossack Folk Tale)	371	85.2	353	89.9	724	87.6	12	R
Daddy-Long-Legs—Jean Webster	146	54.1	477	75.2	623	64.7	63	IR
Daffodils, The—William Wordsworth	9331	43.4	9488	69.5	18819	56.5	374	R

PUPILS' READING INTERESTS: GRADES 7-9
Ts and Ss = Teachers and Schools   S = Studied in Class
IR = Independent Reading   R = Read in Class

SELECTION—AUTHOR	Boys		Girls		Total		Ts & Ss	
	No.	%	No.	%	No.	Av. %		
Da Greata Basaball— Thomas A. Daly	291	92.9	302	91.0	593	92.0	17	S
Da Greata Stronga Man —Thomas A. Daly	274	80.3	283	84.8	557	82.6	13	S
Da Horsa Race—Thomas A. Daly	321	87.1	316	91.0	637	89.1	23	S
Da Leetla Boy—Thomas A. Daly	290	73.3	254	83.9	544	78.6	20	S
Dance of the Snake—D. Maitland Bushby	169	53.3	199	41.7	368	47.5	18	S
Danger Is My Business— John Craig	301	79.6	190	69.5	491	74.6		
Daniel Boone—James Daugherty	993	89.3	755	78.0	1748	83.7	56	R
Daniel Boone—Arthur Guiterman	537	78.3	469	75.5	1006	76.9	16	R
Daniel Boone—Hermann Hagedorn	427	91.7	398	83.5	825	87.6	43	R
Daniel Boone—Theodore Roosevelt	437	70.8	163	59.5	600	65.2		
Daniel Boone Outwits the Indians— Stewart E. White	387	93.2	369	75.2	756	84.2	10	R
Daniel Boone, Wilderness Scout— Stewart E. White	338	88.6	293	66.7	631	77.7	35	S
Dan McGann Declares Himself—Edgar A. Guest	636	77.1	622	74.0	1258	75.6	25	R
Danny Deever—Rudyard Kipling	354	78.1	382	74.2	736	76.2	25	S
Danny Dunn and His Homework Machine— Williams and Abrashkin	331	73.9	378	71.7	709	72.8		
Darius Green and His Flying Machine— John T. Trowbridge	516	86.4	438	82.1	954	84.3	38	S
Dark Brown Dog, A— Stephen Crane	484	85.6	480	91.4	964	88.5	11	R
Dark Flight—John J. Floherty	351	79.1	332	66.6	683	72.9	13	R

PUPILS' READING INTERESTS: GRADES 7-9

Ts and Ss = Teachers and Schools   S = Studied in Class
IR = Independent Reading   R = Read in Class

SELECTION—AUTHOR	Boys		Girls		Total		Ts & Ss	
	No.	%	No.	%	No.	Av. %		
Dark Frigate, The—Charles B. Hawes	200	81.0	76				173	IR
Dark Mountains, The—Gunnar Gunnarsson	293	61.9	307	55.2	600	58.6	15	S
Dark of the Dawn, The—Beulah M. Dix	140	72.1	175	74.3	315	73.2	103	IR
David and Goliath—The Bible	688	76.7	806	68.5	1494	72.6	33	R
David Copperfield—Charles Dickens	488	75.4	663	86.6	1151	81.0	73	S
David Livingston—Hermann Hagedorn	177	85.9	198	86.1	375	86.0	27	R
Davy Crockett—Constance Rourke	875	83.4	388	75.3	1263	79.4	129	IR
Dawn Wind, The—Rudyard Kipling	331	44.4	183	47.3	514	45.9	12	R
Day, A—Emily Dickinson	410	49.3	382	59.9	792	54.6	25	S
Day and the Work, The—Edwin Markham	373	49.9	332	58.6	705	54.3	18	R
Day Christ Died, The—Jim Bishop	287	88.0	446	92.3	733	90.2		
Day Is Done, The—Henry W. Longfellow	243	58.8	276	73.7	519	66.3	12	R
Day Lincoln Was Shot, The—Jim Bishop	534	81.7	497	81.6	1031	81.7		
Day of the Circus Horse, The—T. A. Daly	187	73.8	176	71.9	363	72.9	18	S
Day's Pleasure, A—Hamlin Garland	310	76.6	291	85.7	601	81.2	13	S
Day with an Eskimo Family, A— Vilhjalmur Stefansson	385	77.8	363	74.9	748	76.4	30	S
Deacon's Masterpiece, The—Oliver W. Holmes	2424	79.7	2291	81.1	4715	80.4	208	S
Dear Abby—Abigail Van Buren	62		328	85.8				
Dear Land of All My Love—Sidney Lanier	325	56.2	297	64.1	622	60.2	15	R

PUPILS' READING INTERESTS: GRADES 7-9
Ts and Ss = Teachers and Schools   S = Studied in Class
IR = Independent Reading   R = Read in Class

SELECTION—AUTHOR	Boys		Girls		Total		Ts & Ss	
	No.	%	No.	%	No.	Av. %		
Dear Teen-Ager—Abigail Van Buren	65		362	83.7				
Death of a Prince, The—Felix Salten	204	66.9	211	69.4	415	68.2	19	S
Death of the Flowers, The—William C. Bryant	283	45.8	285	62.8	568	54.3	16	R
Declaration of Independence, The	680	64.1	675	53.0	1355	58.6	24	R
Deerslayer, The—James F. Cooper	1063	83.0	453	76.3	1516	79.7	248	IR
Defense of the Alamo, The—Joaquin Miller	276	76.3	291	55.3	567	65.8	22	S
Definition of a Gentleman—John H. Newman	380	52.4	362	52.5	742	52.5	23	S
De Fust Banjo—Irwin Russell	277	61.6	279	63.1	556	62.4	12	R
Delicatessen—Joyce Kilmer	354	40.3	356	49.9	710	45.1	15	R
Demon Ship, The—Thomas Hood	345	57.2	282	57.4	627	57.3	13	R
De Nice Leetle Canadienne— William H. Drummond	444	66.1	405	75.1	849	70.6	13	R
Dennis the Menace—Hank Ketcham	819	72.3	849	71.6	1668	72.0		
Dentist and the Gas, The —Stephen Leacock	350	88.3	313	90.1	663	89.2	26	S
Descent into the Maelstrom, A—Edgar A. Poe	324	73.9	319	55.6	643	64.8	27	S
Deserted—Madison Cawein	223	62.6	245	70.2	468	66.4	14	S
Deserted House, The—Mary E. Coleridge	286	51.6	287	52.8	573	52.2	13	R
Desert Gold—Zane Grey	228	85.5	165	79.4	393	82.5	124	IR
Destruction of Sennacherib, The—George G. Byron	1052	58.7	1097	54.0	2149	56.4	51	R

PUPILS' READING INTERESTS: GRADES 7-9
Ts and Ss = Teachers and Schools   S = Studied in Class
IR = Independent Reading   R = Read in Class

SELECTION—AUTHOR	Boys		Girls		Total		Ts & Ss	
	No.	%	No.	%	No.	Av. %		
Determined Suicide, The —Don Marquis	292	66.1	286	66.5	578	66.3	13	R
Diary of Anne Frank, The	278	78.8	1125	89.8	1403	84.3		
Dick, a Homing Pigeon —F. M. Gilbert	298	90.5	318	92.3	616	91.4	21	R
Dickens in Camp—Bret Harte	423	48.2	391	56.6	814	52.4	10	R
Dick Tracy (Comic Strip)	1096	80.4	1058	76.1	2154	78.3	77	IR
Dinosaurs—Herbert S. Zim	320	62.5	97	49.0	417	55.8		
Dirge, A—Percy B. Shelley	10749	26.0	10652	32.4	21401	29.2	422	R
Discourager of Hesitancy, The— Frank R. Stockton	413	82.4	417	91.0	830	86.7	17	R
Discovered—Paul L. Dunbar	523	69.6	548	83.6	1071	76.6	23	R
Discoverer, The— Nathalia Crane	238	36.1	248	52.0	486	44.1	15	R
Dissertation upon Roast Pig, A— Charles Lamb	190	67.6	219	73.7	409	70.7	24	S
Diving for Gold— Edward Ellsberg	418	85.2	377	65.9	795	75.6	100	IR
Dixie (Song)	915	70.8	1113	74.6	2028	72.7	77	IR
Dobry—Monica Shannon	122	74.6	200	72.3	322	73.5	99	IR
Does It Matter?— Siegfried Sassoon	207	61.1	263	76.6	470	68.9	15	S
Dog, The—George G. Vest	585	81.0	697	77.1	1282	79.1	34	R
Dog of Flanders, A— Ouida	592	81.2	687	83.9	1279	82.6	83	IR
Dog That Lied, The— George M. Mitchell	298	78.2	321	86.1	619	82.2	10	R
Dog That Saved the Bridge, The— Charles B. D. Robbins	382	93.3	352	87.9	734	90.6	13	R
Donkey, The—G. K. Chesterton	552	52.3	388	48.8	940	50.6	22	R

PUPILS' READING INTERESTS: GRADES 7-9
Ts and Ss = Teachers and Schools   S = Studied in Class
IR = Independent Reading   R = Read in Class

SELECTION—AUTHOR	Boys		Girls		Total		Ts & Ss	
	No.	%	No.	%	No.	Av. %		
Don Quixote—Miguel de Cervantes	323	58.9	191	57.3	514	58.1	117	IR
Don't Die on Third—William Cameron	630	81.8	547	67.6	1177	74.7	33	S
Don: the Story of a Lion Dog—Zane Grey	254	95.9	225	82.2	479	89.1	15	R
Double Date—Rosamond Du Jardin	20		391	83.8				
Double Feature—Rosamond Du Jardin	9		348	84.3				
Double Wedding—Rosamond Du Jardin	6		333	83.9				
Doubting Castle—John Bunyan	332	70.3	341	64.4	673	67.4	14	R
Douglas Tragedy, The (British Ballad)	199	55.5	510	71.4	709	63.5	22	S
Down Hill on a Bicycle—Louis Untermeyer	371	58.2	330	66.8	701	62.5	23	S
Do You Fear the Force of the Wind?— Hamlin Garland	400	51.1	419	54.1	819	52.6	26	S
Dragon Seed—Pearl Buck	210	79.8	364	87.7	574	83.8	60	IR
Dreamers, The—Theodosia Garrison	184	38.9	195	63.6	379	51.3	17	S
Dream Pedlary—Thomas L. Beddoes	506	25.8	550	38.0	1056	31.9	26	R
Dr. Fu-Manchu—Sax Rohmer	182	82.4	125	81.2	307	81.8	102	IR
Dr. Grenfell—Hermann Hagedorn	479	78.9	435	72.2	914	75.6	17	R
Dr. Jekyll and Mr. Hyde—Robert L. Stevenson	445	82.7	310	80.0	755	81.4		
Drums—James Boyd	158	75.6	71					
Drums Along the Mohawk—Walter D. Edmonds	766	82.6	350	68.3	1116	75.5		
Duel, The—Eugene Field	420	63.7	413	75.5	833	69.6	34	S

PUPILS' READING INTERESTS: GRADES 7-9
Ts and Ss = Teachers and Schools   S = Studied in Class
IR = Independent Reading   R = Read in Class

SELECTION—AUTHOR	Boys		Girls		Total		Ts & Ss	
	No.	%	No.	%	No.	Av. %		
Duna—Marjorie L. C. Pickthall	377	48.7	371	60.5	748	54.6	20	R
Dust—Clara Lambert	345	71.9	327	80.0	672	76.0	15	R
Dutch Picture, A—Henry W. Longfellow	200	50.5	232	54.1	432	52.3	15	S
Duty—Ralph W. Emerson	1268	51.9	1256	60.8	2524	56.4	52	R
Dying Ranger, The (Cowboy Ballad)	207	76.1	232	87.7	439	81.9	16	R
Each and All—Ralph W. Emerson	422	48.7	407	55.2	829	52.0	17	R
Eagle, The—Alfred Tennyson	956	37.2	968	37.4	1924	37.3	38	R
Earl o' Quarterdeck, The —George Macdonald	336	44.2	353	49.6	689	46.9	11	R
Echo and Narcissus— Rannie B. Baker	269	42.8	251	54.6	520	48.7	14	R
Echoes—Edwin J. Houston	292	56.7	291	50.7	583	53.7	17	S
Echo Mountain Grizzly, The—Enos A. Mills	240	79.2	238	74.6	478	76.9	17	S
Edith Cavell—Hermann Hagedorn	262	74.6	302	88.9	564	81.8	26	S
Education—Gertrude Stein	406	36.2	446	48.9	852	42.6	20	R
Edward (American Ballad)	489	51.8	452	61.0	941	56.4	17	R
Edward (British Ballad)	328	47.0	318	56.6	646	51.8	13	R
Edward Randolph's Portrait—Nathaniel Hawthorne	319	43.6	313	47.9	632	45.8	23	S
Een Napoli—Thomas A. Daly	288	67.4	270	77.8	558	72.6	24	S
Efficiency—Frank Crane	399	24.6	446	28.0	845	26.3	15	R
Egg and I, The—Betty MacDonald	120	70.4	262	75.2	382	72.8		
Eggstravagance, An— Oliver W. Holmes	500	64.0	545	69.6	1045	66.8	23	R
Eight Cousins—Louisa M. Alcott	59		992	81.4			137	IR

PUPILS' READING INTERESTS: GRADES 7-9
Ts and Ss = Teachers and Schools   S = Studied in Class
IR = Independent Reading   R = Read in Class

SELECTION—AUTHOR	Boys		Girls		Total		Ts & Ss	
	No.	%	No.	%	No.	Av. %		
Eldorado—Edgar A. Poe	779	64.2	868	65.5	1647	64.9	37	R
Elegy on the Death of a Mad Dog, An— Oliver Goldsmith	276	81.9	330	86.7	606	84.3	11	R
Elegy Written in a Country Churchyard— Thomas Gray	159	35.5	177	41.8	336	38.7	31	IR
Elephant Remembers, The—Edison Marshall	1301	81.2	1348	68.4	2649	74.8	89	S
Elephants That Struck, The—Samuel W. Baker	530	73.4	486	67.5	1016	70.5	30	S
Elizabeth of England— Hermann Hagedorn	194	66.5	226	78.1	420	72.3	83	IR
Ellen McJones Aberdeen —William S. Gilbert	737	59.1	761	64.8	1498	62.0	30	R
Ellis Park—Helen Hoyt	328	57.9	337	68.0	665	63.0	19	R
Eloise (Stories)—Kay Thompson	81	61.7	431	75.8	512	68.8		
Emperor's New Clothes, The—Hans C. Andersen	1002	65.8	1739	67.7	2741	66.8	146	IR
Enchanted Shirt, The— John Hay	438	66.1	401	73.8	839	70.0	23	R
Encyclopaedia Britannica, The	214	70.5	258	73.6	472	72.1	57	IR
Enemy Below, The—D. A. Rayner	319	88.6	60					
English Fairy Tales— Joseph Jacobs	46		202	62.9				
English Undefiled—Kate D. Wiggin	318	33.4	290	37.8	608	35.6	14	R
Enoch Arden—Alfred Tennyson	279	71.9	308	86.7	587	79.3	31	S
Enough Gold to Load a Packhorse— J. Frank Dobie	269	87.4	273	68.9	542	78.2	16	R
Epic of the North, An— Frank M. O'Brien	547	76.5	519	66.1	1066	71.3	19	R
Epitaph (A bird, a man . . .), An—Unknown	461	56.5	452	59.4	913	58.0	26	R

PUPILS' READING INTERESTS: GRADES 7-9

Ts and Ss = Teachers and Schools   S = Studied in Class

IR = Independent Reading   R = Read in Class

SELECTION—AUTHOR	Boys		Girls		Total		Ts & Ss	
	No.	%	No.	%	No.	Av. %		
Epitaph on a Politician, An—Hilaire Belloc	388	53.1	357	58.0	745	55.6	15	R
Erudite Ermine, The— Unknown	281	52.5	318	62.9	599	57.7	15	R
Escape at Bedtime— Robert L. Stevenson	422	42.5	438	52.6	860	47.6	24	R
Esther—The Bible	233	71.7	422	85.2	655	78.5	121	IR
Etiquette—Arthur Guiterman	478	69.1	430	80.2	908	74.7	27	S
Evangeline—Henry W. Longfellow	1788	68.2	1855	85.6	3643	76.9	173	S
Evening at the Farm— John T. Trowbridge	509	41.7	520	55.5	1029	48.6	18	R
Eve of Waterloo, The— George G. Byron	512	65.9	471	53.8	983	59.9	58	S
Example, The—William H. Davies	276	46.4	286	63.6	562	55.0	14	R
Excavation, The—Max Endicoff	230	32.2	273	30.4	503	31.3	12	R
Excelsior—Henry W. Longfellow	401	47.3	370	50.4	771	48.9	13	R
Exodus—Leon M. Uris	304	87.7	476	91.2	780	89.5		
Fable, A—Ralph W. Emerson	1074	56.9	1157	57.3	2231	57.1	43	R
Face in the Window, The—William D. Pelley	385	94.4	371	95.4	756	94.9	13	R
Facing Death Under the Sea—Gunner Adams	294	92.3	289	81.8	583	87.1	18	R
Factories—Margaret Widdemer	173	50.0	190	67.1	363	58.6	16	S
Facts of Life and Love for Teen Agers— Evelyn M. Duvall	140	78.6	195	78.2	335	78.4		
Fairies Have Never a Penny to Spend, The— Rose Fyleman	245	49.0	256	65.4	501	57.2	20	S
Fairy Tales—Hans C. Andersen	154	74.7	480	82.1	634	78.4	61	IR
Fairy Tales—Grimm Brothers	370	67.8	844	78.1	1214	73.0	74	IR

PUPILS' READING INTERESTS: GRADES 7-9
Ts and Ss = Teachers and Schools   S = Studied in Class
IR = Independent Reading   R = Read in Class

SELECTION—AUTHOR	Boys		Girls		Total		Ts & Ss
	No.	%	No.	%	No.	Av. %	
Falcons of France—Nordhoff and Hall	161	77.3	22				
Falling Asleep—Siegfried Sassoon	467	45.1	489	51.4	956	48.3	24 R
Fall of the House of Usher, The—Edgar A. Poe	236	50.6	242	53.9	478	52.3	16 S
Family Nobody Wanted, The—Helen Doss	34		156	83.0			
Farewell to the Citizens of Springfield— Abraham Lincoln	1163	72.3	1272	71.8	2435	72.1	51 R
Farmer Remembers Lincoln, A—Witter Bynner	268	69.8	277	72.6	545	71.2	22 S
Father Domino—J. Berg Esenwein	291	75.1	281	80.4	572	77.8	11 R
Father Duffy—Alexander Woollcott	401	71.4	404	67.0	805	69.2	19 R
Father Sews On a Button —Clarence Day	363	91.3	373	92.5	736	91.9	13 R
Father William—Lewis Carroll	481	76.9	529	81.4	1010	79.2	31 R
Fat Wife—Unknown	301	77.9	324	88.0	625	83.0	15 R
Fawn, The—Marjorie K. Rawlings	371	85.3	362	90.1	733	87.7	11 R
F.B.I. Story, The—Don Whitehead	1289	84.4	376	79.3	1665	81.9	
Feathertop—Nathaniel Hawthorne	282	63.7	301	71.6	583	67.7	19 S
Feigned Courage— Charles and Mary Lamb	593	48.3	665	53.8	1258	51.1	22 R
Felix Von Luckner— Hermann Hagedorn	176	84.7	88				128 IR
Ferdinand—Munro Leaf	143	60.5	196	68.1	339	64.3	
Few Proverbs of Solomon, A—The Bible	264	41.7	269	50.9	533	46.3	15 R
Fiddle for Gladsome Tunes, A—Esther G. Hall	323	76.3	327	92.2	650	84.3	11 R

PUPILS' READING INTERESTS: GRADES 7-9
Ts and Ss = Teachers and Schools   S = Studied in Class
IR = Independent Reading   R = Read in Class

SELECTION—AUTHOR	Boys		Girls		Total		Ts & Ss	
	No.	%	No.	%	No.	Av. %		
Fiddler Jones—Edgar L. Masters	364	42.2	390	44.7	754	43.5	15	R
Fifteen—Beverly Cleary	19		401	84.3				
Fighting Planes of the World—Bernard Law	227	79.3	2					
Fighting Soul, The— William Heyliger	251	87.5	308	81.8	559	84.7	15	R
Fighting Temeraire, The —Henry Newbolt	344	68.5	379	62.3	723	65.4	22	S
Fight with a Cannon, A —Victor Hugo	316	68.2	342	49.7	658	59.0	12	R
Fight with a Grizzly, A— Theodore Roosevelt	745	73.8	815	57.2	1560	65.5	43	S
Fight with a Hawk, The —Helen O. Watson	459	91.3	502	84.1	961	87.7	21	R
Fight with a Whale, A— Frank T. Bullen	439	79.8	412	62.4	851	71.1	18	R
Find a Way—John G. Saxe	423	63.9	480	59.2	903	61.6	25	R
Finding of Livingston, The—Henry M. Stanley	244	74.6	226	61.5	470	68.1	35	R
Finding of the Lyre, The —James R. Lowell	294	64.6	268	68.3	562	66.5	23	S
Firearms—Carroll B. Colby	237	77.2	4					
Fire Down Below (Sea Chantey)	304	62.3	312	59.3	616	60.8	19	S
Fireflies—Carolyn Hall	370	47.6	390	61.7	760	54.7	20	R
Firefly Song (Indian Lyric)	292	42.8	289	52.1	581	47.5	19	S
First Bluebird, The— James W. Riley	280	57.1	329	67.6	609	62.4	22	S
First Book of World War I—Louis Snyder	318	81.6	46					
First Book of World War II—Louis Snyder	162	86.7	24					
First Bow and Arrow, The—Stanley Waterloo	589	86.1	526	77.6	1115	81.9	29	S
First Christmas Tree, The—Henry Van Dyke	245	53.7	312	58.2	557	56.0	20	S

PUPILS' READING INTERESTS: GRADES 7-9
Ts and Ss = Teachers and Schools   S = Studied in Class
IR = Independent Reading   R = Read in Class

SELECTION—AUTHOR	Boys		Girls		Total		Ts & Ss	
	No.	%	No.	%	No.	Av. %		
First Potter, The—Hanford Montrose Burr	418	60.9	377	67.4	795	64.2	27	S
First Robin, The—Heywood Broun	276	49.8	315	57.3	591	53.6	12	R
First Snowfall, The—James R. Lowell	1750	60.6	1756	86.9	3506	73.8	148	S
First Woman Doctor, The—Rachel Baker	45		286	76.2				
Fir Tree, The—Hans C. Andersen	268	60.8	360	69.2	628	65.0	47	S
Fisherman and the Genie, The—Arabian Nights	194	77.8	204	79.4	398	78.6	18	S
Fish Story, A—Don Marquis	315	70.3	297	72.6	612	71.5	13	R
Five Boys in a Cave—Richard Church	145	74.5	109	61.9	254	68.2		
Five Little Peppers—Margaret Sidney	151	59.3	956	70.9	1107	65.1		
Five Thousand Dollars Reward—Melville D. Post	234	83.8	172	80.2	406	82.0	18	S
Five Weeks in a Balloon—Jules Verne	185	82.7	71					
Flag, The—Arthur Macy	511	68.4	466	70.3	977	69.4	19	R
Flag Goes By, The—Henry H. Bennett	927	81.0	717	78.9	1644	80.0	52	S
Flag o' My Land—Thomas A. Daly	351	57.7	318	69.7	669	63.7	15	R
Flags on Fifth Avenue, The—Christopher Morley	233	63.1	223	72.0	456	67.6	17	R
Flannan Isle—Wilfred W. Gibson	271	67.0	254	67.7	525	67.4	12	R
Flathouse Roof, The—Nathalia Crane	190	65.3	231	88.5	421	76.9	15	S
Fleurette—Robert W. Service	405	69.1	392	82.2	797	75.7	33	S
Floorless Room, The—Gelett Burgess	423	52.9	456	56.5	879	54.7	16	R

PUPILS' READING INTERESTS: GRADES 7-9
Ts and Ss = Teachers and Schools   S = Studied in Class
IR = Independent Reading   R = Read in Class

SELECTION—AUTHOR	Boys		Girls		Total		Ts & Ss	
	No.	%	No.	%	No.	Av. %		
Florence Nightingale—Jeanette C. Nolan	119	55.5	771	78.1	890	66.8		
Flounder, The—Arthur Guiterman	502	52.1	460	64.6	962	58.4	9	R
Flower Factory, The—Florence W. Evans	280	41.1	341	62.0	621	51.6	14	S
Flower in the Crannied Wall—Alfred Tennyson	1155	35.5	1232	48.2	2387	41.9	61	R
Flower of Liberty, The—Oliver W. Holmes	418	69.4	394	78.3	812	73.9	9	R
Flow Gently Sweet Afton—Robert Burns	395	44.9	403	60.7	798	52.8	17	R
Fly and a Flea, A—Unknown	309	75.2	321	84.4	630	79.8	14	R
Flying Saucers—Donald E. Keyhoe	250	78.8	43					
Flying with a Test Pilot—Edwin M. Teale	297	83.0	331	56.6	628	69.8	13	R
Flynn of Virginia—Bret Harte	400	62.4	411	66.4	811	64.4	18	R
Fog—Carl Sandburg	420	41.3	547	47.5	967	44.4	29	S
Fog and the Chisima—Anne Lindbergh	311	66.4	330	61.8	641	64.1	13	R
Fooling the People—Abraham Lincoln	1253	85.2	1245	87.8	2498	86.5	51	R
Fool's Prayer, The—Edwin R. Sill	516	64.1	512	73.0	1028	68.6	50	S
Fools Walk In—Howard M. Brier	417	95.2	378	92.3	795	93.8	13	R
Footpath to Peace, The—Henry Van Dyke	211	64.0	195	71.0	406	67.5	19	S
Forbearance—Ralph W. Emerson	723	27.4	701	32.0	1424	29.7	26	R
Forest Fires—Overton W. Price	166	83.1	152	61.5	318	72.3	17	S
For Sale—Dragon's Breath—Elizabeth Lewis	358	64.8	389	66.7	747	65.8	21	S
For the Supremacy of the Trail— Esther B. Darling	233	82.0	229	73.4	462	77.7	43	S

PUPILS' READING INTERESTS: GRADES 7-9
Ts and Ss = Teachers and Schools   S = Studied in Class
IR = Independent Reading   R = Read in Class

SELECTION—AUTHOR	Boys		Girls		Total		Ts & Ss	
	No.	%	No.	%	No.	Av. %		
For Those Who Fail—Joaquin Miller	395	57.8	427	63.1	822	60.5	15	R
Forty Singing Seamen—Alfred Noyes	391	57.7	415	52.7	806	55.2	30	S
For Want of a Nail—Mother Goose	300	84.7	261	85.8	561	85.3	13	R
Fountain, The—James R. Lowell	601	52.2	623	69.7	1224	61.0	60	S
Four-Footed Police of the Dog Patrol, The—Irving Crump	320	92.0	323	81.0	643	86.5	20	S
Four-Leaf Clovers—Ella Higginson	366	61.7	379	80.1	745	70.9	13	R
Four Little Foxes—Lew Sarett	394	56.5	406	58.7	800	57.6	20	S
Four Minute Mile, The—Roger Bannister	308	80.0	157	53.5	465	66.8		
Four Things—Henry Van Dyke	300	71.8	262	81.3	562	76.6	13	R
Fourth of July Celebration, A—Thomas B. Aldrich	315	90.2	295	88.1	610	89.2	22	S
Fox and the Goat, The—Aesop	277	42.6	275	51.1	552	46.9	16	R
Francis Drake—Hermann Hagedorn	283	79.2	207	67.9	490	73.6	85	IR
Frank Crane's Ten Rules	299	62.9	262	62.4	561	62.7	13	R
Franklin D. Roosevelt—Alden Hatch	225	70.7	171	75.4	396	73.1		
Franklin's Rules—Benjamin Franklin	267	36.3	264	45.6	531	41.0	14	R
Freckles—Gene S. Porter	331	74.0	618	83.3	949	78.7	154	IR
Freckles and His Friends (Comic Strip)	339	74.0	471	78.9	810	76.5	25	IR
French Tar-Baby, A—Joel C. Harris	288	67.7	303	67.1	591	67.4	33	S
Freshman Fullback, The—Ralph D. Paine	2495	86.9	2545	77.6	5040	82.3	171	S
Friends—Myra Kelly	375	61.9	419	83.8	794	72.9	16	S

PUPILS' READING INTERESTS: GRADES 7-9

Ts and Ss = Teachers and Schools   S = Studied in Class
IR = Independent Reading   R = Read in Class

SELECTION—AUTHOR	Boys		Girls		Total		Ts & Ss	
	No.	%	No.	%	No.	Av. %		
Friends in San Rosario— O. Henry	186	75.3	173	72.8	359	74.1	15	S
Frogs in the Marsh, The—Abraham Lincoln	312	61.9	320	54.7	632	58.3	13	R
From "Byron"—Joaquin Miller	402	43.8	417	49.8	819	46.8	15	R
From Here to Eternity— James Jones	267	79.6	361	83.8	628	81.7		
Frost Tonight—Edith M. Thomas	292	54.6	149	64.4	441	59.5	20	S
Fun! Fun! Fun!—Phyllis Fenner	130	48.5	178	58.2	308	53.4		
Funny Business (Comic Strip)	220	69.8	282	68.3	502	69.1	81	IR
Fun with Mathematics— Jerome S. Meyer	144	55.2	139	56.1	283	55.7		
Fuzzy-Wuzzy—Rudyard Kipling	265	68.3	297	63.6	562	66.0	21	R
Gallegher—Richard H. Davis	916	90.0	914	85.3	1830	87.7	96	S
Game, The—Grantland Rice	248	47.2	239	54.4	487	50.8	13	R
Gasoline Alley (Comic Strip)	464	67.2	596	75.1	1060	71.2	23	IR
Gaunt Gray Wolf, The— Hamlin Garland	449	60.1	450	52.9	899	56.5	19	R
Gay Goss-Hawk, The (British Ballad)	215	46.5	385	61.8	600	54.2	15	S
Gay-Neck—Dhan G. Mukerji	253	68.2	322	60.9	575	64.6	183	IR
Genuine Mexican Plug, A—Mark Twain	902	82.5	859	79.5	1761	81.0	36	R
Geographical Readers— Frank G. Carpenter	179	76.0	219	65.7	398	70.9	108	IR
George Washington— Rosemary C. and Stephen V. Benét	308	64.4	330	74.8	638	69.6	12	R
George Washington— Hermann Hagedorn	524	89.2	420	85.5	944	87.4	107	IR

PUPILS' READING INTERESTS: GRADES 7-9
Ts and Ss = Teachers and Schools   S = Studied in Class
IR = Independent Reading   R = Read in Class

SELECTION—AUTHOR	Boys		Girls		Total		Ts & Ss	
	No.	%	No.	%	No.	Av. %		
George Washington— William F. Kirk	514	89.8	512	91.8	1026	90.8	17	R
George Washington's Boyhood—Horace E. Scudder	362	73.9	384	85.5	746	79.7	11	R
Get Out or Get in Line —Elbert Hubbard	333	51.1	303	50.3	636	50.7	13	R
Gettysburg Address, The —Abraham Lincoln	393	91.1	431	93.7	824	92.4	14	R
Get Up and Bar the Door (British Ballad)	258	73.3	243	81.1	501	77.2	15	S
Ghitza—Konrad Bercovici	311	88.7	326	86.7	637	87.7	14	S
Ghost Dog of Sunnybank, The—Albert P. Terhune	306	60.3	301	65.3	607	62.8	20	R
Ghosts, Ghosts, Ghosts— Phyllis Fenner	519	69.1	538	70.5	1057	69.8		
Giants in the Sky—Alida Hurtebise	397	70.3	452	68.5	849	69.4	19	R
Gideon—The Bible	449	45.5	461	46.2	910	45.9	17	R
Gift of the Magi, The— O. Henry	2033	62.5	2069	82.5	4102	72.5	137	S
Gingerbread Boy, The— Eunice Tietjens	218	62.6	402	66.2	620	64.4	24	IR
Ginger Pye—Eleanor Estes	10		189	56.1				
Girl Can Dream, A— Betty Cavanna	7		516	80.5				
Girl in White Armor, The—Albert B. Paine	49		185	73.0				
Girl of the Limberlost, The—Gene S. Porter	28		429	92.7			127	IR
Girl Trouble—James L. Summers	58		615	78.8				
Give Your All—Elbert Hubbard	638	46.6	593	49.1	1231	47.9	22	R
Glad Young Chamois, The—Burges Johnson	308	58.3	330	58.3	638	58.3	14	R
Glenlogie (British Ballad)	480	49.3	523	69.3	1003	59.3	21	R

PUPILS' READING INTERESTS: GRADES 7-9
Ts and Ss = Teachers and Schools   S = Studied in Class
IR = Independent Reading   R = Read in Class

SELECTION—AUTHOR	Boys		Girls		Total		Ts & Ss	
	No.	%	No.	%	No.	Av. %		
Glorious Adventure, The —Richard Halliburton	148	76.4	185	73.2	333	74.8	77	IR
Glory of Ships, The— Henry Van Dyke	691	50.8	672	54.1	1363	52.5	27	R
Glory Trail, The—Badger Clark	399	63.4	404	56.7	803	60.1	22	R
Glove and the Lions, The—Leigh Hunt	748	69.8	733	75.7	1481	72.8	32	R
Godfrey Gordon Gustavus Gore— William B. Rands	459	71.6	482	78.4	941	75.0	22	S
God Is at the Anvil— Lew Sarett	285	54.7	302	68.9	587	61.8	19	S
God Is My Co-Pilot— Robert L. Scott	659	93.9	349	92.0	1008	93.0	129	IR
God's Gift—Alfred Noyes	312	64.7	133	71.4	445	68.1	17	S
Goethals: the Prophet Engineer—Percy Mackaye	490	62.9	465	52.7	955	57.8	74	S
Going Down Hill on a Bicycle— Henry C. Beeching	285	35.1	283	48.1	568	41.6	17	R
Going on Sixteen—Betty Cavanna	35		791	82.0				
Going Steady—Anne Emery	101	70.8	1283	83.8	1384	77.3		
Going to School in Iowa in 1871— Hamlin Garland	241	68.5	266	72.6	507	70.6	17	R
Going to Shout All Over God's Heaven (Negro Spiritual)	419	48.0	415	58.6	834	53.3	15	R
Gol-Darned Wheel, The (Cowboy Ballad)	331	87.8	323	86.2	654	87.0	21	S
Gold Brick, The—Brand Whitlock	197	67.8	201	69.4	398	68.6	16	S
Gold Bug, The—Edgar A. Poe	2329	84.2	2302	76.1	4631	80.2	209	S
Golden City of St. Mary, The—John Masefield	367	38.4	365	59.3	732	48.9	16	R

PUPILS' READING INTERESTS: GRADES 7-9
Ts and Ss = Teachers and Schools   S = Studied in Class
IR = Independent Reading   R = Read in Class

SELECTION—AUTHOR	Boys		Girls		Total		Ts & Ss	
	No.	%	No.	%	No.	Av. %		
Golden Touch, The—Nathaniel Hawthorne	323	74.9	325	81.2	648	78.1	15	R
Gold Seekers of '49, The—Edwin L. Sabin	211	77.0	100	71.0	311	74.0	140	IR
Gone With the Wind—Margaret Mitchell	291	78.0	519	91.9	810	85.0	74	IR
Goodbye, Mr. Chips—James Hilton	182	67.9	399	71.6	581	69.8		
Good Bye, My Lady—James Street	41		225	77.6				
Good Earth, The—Pearl Buck	93	74.2	181	81.8	274	78.0		
Good Fight, The—William C. Bryant	338	38.3	317	34.5	655	36.4	13	R
Good Hours—Robert Frost	267	53.6	299	68.2	566	60.9	17	S
Good Master, The—Kate Seredy	29		139	85.3				
Good Wits Jump—Sheila Kaye-Smith	305	75.1	305	92.0	610	83.6	15	R
Gorgon's Head, The (Greek Myth)	147	70.7	127	68.5	274	69.6		
Gospel Train, The (Negro Spiritual)	434	42.1	481	50.0	915	46.1	17	R
Go Team, Go—John R. Tunis	337	67.7	106	63.2	443	65.5		
Gradatim—Josiah G. Holland	248	45.2	300	53.0	548	49.1	25	S
Grand Cham's Diamond, The—Allan N. Monkhouse	321	83.6	341	87.8	662	85.7	23	S
Grandmother's Story of Bunker Hill— Oliver W. Holmes	711	82.0	733	82.9	1444	82.5	72	S
Grape Vine Swing, The—Samuel M. Peck	368	54.2	273	69.4	641	61.8	28	R
Grasshopper, The—Vachel Lindsay	254	36.4	216	51.4	470	43.9	14	R
Gray Champion, The—Nathaniel Hawthorne	675	47.9	685	40.6	1360	44.3	62	S

PUPILS' READING INTERESTS: GRADES 7-9
Ts and Ss = Teachers and Schools   S = Studied in Class
IR = Independent Reading   R = Read in Class

SELECTION—AUTHOR	Boys		Girls		Total		Ts & Ss	
	No.	%	No.	%	No.	Av. %		
Gray Horse Troop, The—Robert W. Chambers	276	82.1	275	81.6	551	81.9	13	R
Great Blizzard, The—Hamlin Garland	324	76.5	283	75.8	607	76.2	35	S
Great Guest Comes, The —Edwin Markham	361	66.9	414	76.9	775	71.9	19	S
Great Inventors—Frank P. Bachman	221	71.9	61					
Great Nickel Adventure, The—Joyce Kilmer	257	51.6	266	50.6	523	51.1	17	R
Great Possessions—David Grayson	364	54.5	369	64.6	733	59.6	24	S
Great Race, The—Clarence Hawkes	301	93.9	271	83.2	572	88.6	12	R
Great Stone Face, The—Nathaniel Hawthorne	1195	62.4	1574	72.1	2769	67.3	121	S
Green Grass of Wyoming, The—Mary O'Hara	110	73.6	197	81.0	307	77.3		
Green Mountain Boys, The—D. P. Thompson	417	73.5	168	64.6	585	69.1		
Grettir the Strong—Allen French	319	91.5	334	82.9	653	87.2	12	R
Gridiron Challenge—Jackson Scholz	152	78.0	12					
Grizzly Mother, The—Enos A. Mills	316	92.4	323	92.3	639	92.4	12	R
Grizzly King, The—James O. Curwood	388	90.6	388	79.9	776	85.3		
Growing Up—Gouverneur Morris	456	88.6	466	89.8	922	89.2	16	R
Guadalcanal Diary—Richard Tregaskis	585	98.0	376	89.9	961	94.0	62	IR
Gulliver Among the Giants—Jonathan Swift	357	90.6	364	90.0	721	90.3	20	R
Gulliver's Travels—Jonathan Swift	1371	82.9	1422	79.8	2793	81.4	92	IR
Gulliver the Great—Walter A. Dyer	908	87.9	831	86.3	1739	87.1	66	S

PUPILS' READING INTERESTS: GRADES 7-9
Ts and Ss = Teachers and Schools   S = Studied in Class
IR = Independent Reading   R = Read in Class

SELECTION—AUTHOR	Boys		Girls		Total		Ts & Ss	
	No.	%	No.	%	No.	Av. %		
Gulls, The—Clinton Scollard	184	54.6	183	51.9	367	53.3	17	S
Gunga Din—Rudyard Kipling	200	78.0	249	74.1	449	76.1	17	R
Guns of Bull Run, The— Joseph Altsheler	285	80.7	55					
Half Magic—Edward Eager	38		151	77.2				
Hammering of Storms, The—Edwin E. Slosson	366	37.2	327	33.0	693	35.1	9	R
Hanging a Picture— Jerome K. Jerome	526	84.0	486	88.6	1012	86.3	39	S
Hannibal—Hermann Hagedorn	337	77.2	172	70.5	509	73.9		
Hans Brinker—Mary M. Dodge	185	79.2	200	92.5	385	85.9	22	S
Hansel and Gretel— Grimm Brothers	376	66.2	602	78.9	978	72.6	25	IR
Happiness—Robert Burns	213	39.0	266	54.1	479	46.6	17	R
Happy Hollisters, The— Jerry West	37		232	60.6				
Happy Prince, The— Oscar Wilde	253	89.9	282	92.6	535	91.3	17	R
Happy Warrior, The— John G. Whittier	339	23.9	327	30.7	666	27.3	13	R
Hardy Boys (Stories)— Franklin W. Dixon	369	77.9	204	71.6	573	74.8		
Hare and the Hounds, The—Aesop	1196	71.9	1228	68.8	2424	70.4	49	R
Hark! Hark! the Lark— William Shakespeare	4340	41.1	4371	55.7	8711	48.4	199	R
Harvest, The— Aristophanes	298	43.6	262	54.0	560	48.8	13	R
Hate—James Stephens	309	61.7	339	66.7	648	64.2	14	R
Haunted and the Haunters, The— Edward Bulwer—Lytton	1014	77.4	1130	77.7	2144	77.6	84	S
Heart of Little Shikara, The—Edison Marshall	367	81.9	289	77.5	656	79.7	13	S

PUPILS' READING INTERESTS: GRADES 7-9

Ts and Ss = Teachers and Schools   S = Studied in Class

IR = Independent Reading   R = Read in Class

SELECTION—AUTHOR	Boys		Girls		Total		Ts & Ss	
	No.	%	No.	%	No.	Av. %		
Heave Away (Sea Chantey)	274	50.4	279	50.0	553	50.2	17	S
Heavens Declare the Glory of God, The— The Bible	296	52.2	323	67.0	619	59.6	13	R
Heaven to Betsy—Maud H. Lovelace	9		185	66.8				
Heidi—Johanna Spyri	943	73.3	1941	93.2	2884	83.3	107	IR
Height of the Ridiculous, The—Oliver W. Holmes	437	79.9	387	84.6	824	82.3	33	S
He Knew Lincoln—Ida M. Tarbell	193	64.5	214	69.6	407	67.1	14	S
Helen Keller Story, The —Catherine O. Peare	93	78.8	386	92.9	479	85.9		
Hell-gate of Soissons, The —Herbert Kaufman	375	74.0	412	61.0	787	67.5	25	S
Hem and Haw—Bliss Carman	375	47.6	358	51.1	733	49.4	10	R
He Never Knew—James Collins	306	75.5	305	76.9	611	76.2	10	R
Henry (Comic Strip)	1025	79.3	1044	75.2	2069	77.3	77	IR
Hens, The—Elizabeth M. Roberts	385	55.5	392	63.0	777	59.3	15	R
Hercules—Frances E. Sabin	237	89.0	395	80.1	632	84.6	14	S
Here Comes the King— Timothy Fuller	277	79.8	304	82.1	581	81.0	11	R
Here's a Health to King Charles—Walter Scott	10654	40.2	10699	45.0	21353	42.6	422	R
Heritage, The—James R. Lowell	409	58.4	446	67.4	855	62.9	45	S
Her Letter—Bret Harte	312	42.8	323	65.8	635	54.3	20	R
Hero of the South Pole— Irma Taylor	305	94.4	337	91.6	642	93.0	19	R
Hervé Riel—Robert Browning	1405	69.9	1442	62.5	2847	66.2	127	S
Hiawatha—Henry W. Longfellow	887	74.0	918	78.1	1805	76.1	85	S

PUPILS' READING INTERESTS: GRADES 7-9
Ts and Ss = Teachers and Schools   S = Studied in Class
IR = Independent Reading   R = Read in Class

SELECTION—AUTHOR	Boys		Girls		Total		Ts & Ss	
	No.	%	No.	%	No.	Av. %		
Highest and Lowest Air Temperatures, The— Edwin E. Slosson	398	46.6	428	44.2	826	45.4	14	R
High Tide—Jean S. Untermeyer	408	49.4	459	54.7	867	52.1	24	S
High Tide on the Coast of Lincolnshire— Jean Ingelow	398	27.6	393	28.2	791	27.9	15	R
Highwayman, The— Alfred Noyes	1931	81.7	1538	82.2	3469	82.0	140	S
Hills—Arthur Guiterman	203	55.4	218	72.7	421	64.1	14	S
Hindoo Legend, A— George Birdseye	455	61.0	428	73.4	883	67.2	18	R
His Clothes—Unknown	294	55.4	326	65.3	620	60.4	14	R
Hitty; Her First Hundred Years— Rachel L. Field	25		367	74.9			108	IR
Hohenlinden—Thomas Campbell	228	41.2	210	35.5	438	38.4	14	R
Homer Price—Robert McCloskey	469	78.8	609	77.3	1078	78.1		
Home Song, A—Henry Van Dyke	453	47.4	445	65.5	898	56.5	19	R
Home Sweet Home— John H. Payne	424	67.0	442	75.0	866	71.0	34	S
Home Thoughts from Abroad—Robert Browning	493	51.5	472	62.2	965	56.9	35	S
Home Thoughts from Europe—Henry Van Dyke	318	66.5	171	79.5	489	73.0	19	S
Homing Pigeons— Marshall Saunders	308	62.7	289	48.4	597	55.6	15	R
Hoosier Schoolboy, The —Edward Eggleston	224	80.1	297	76.8	521	78.5	108	IR
Hoosier Schoolmaster, The—Edward Eggleston	200	77.5	197	76.1	397	76.8	96	IR
Horace Greeley's Ride— Artemus Ward	239	82.6	261	87.2	500	84.9	18	R
Horatius at the Bridge— Thomas B. Macaulay	1153	79.6	1159	62.3	2312	71.0	121	S

PUPILS' READING INTERESTS: GRADES 7-9
Ts and Ss = Teachers and Schools   S = Studied in Class
IR = Independent Reading   R = Read in Class

SELECTION—AUTHOR	Boys No.	Boys %	Girls No.	Girls %	Total No.	Total Av. %	Ts & Ss	
Horse, The—Peter Parley	251	60.0	233	57.9	484	59.0	15	R
Horse, The—James Stephens	417	50.6	443	54.4	860	52.5	17	R
Horse Magic—Ralph Stock	271	72.9	236	57.4	507	65.2	13	R
Horsemen of the Plains—Joseph A. Altsheler	203	70.9	101	69.8	304	70.4		
Horseshoe Captures Five Prisoners— John P. Kennedy	299	86.8	296	74.8	595	80.8	30	R
Horse Who Lived Upstairs, The—Phyllis McGinley	61		158	67.1				
Horton Hatches the Egg—Dr. Seuss	242	55.6	298	64.6	540	60.1		
Hot Rod (Book)—Henry G. Felsen	415	81.7	110	73.6	525	77.7		
Hound of the Baskervilles, The— A. Conan Doyle	252	92.9	106	88.7	358	90.8	94	IR
Hound on the Church Porch, The— Robert P. T. Coffin	309	50.5	323	53.9	632	52.2	12	R
House by the Side of the Road, The— Sam W. Foss	904	63.7	857	80.5	1761	72.1	70	S
House on the Hill, The—Edwin A. Robinson	348	50.9	360	61.8	708	56.4	16	R
House with Nobody in It, The—Joyce Kilmer	339	74.2	403	90.2	742	82.2	28	S
How Abe Lincoln Paid for His Stockings—Edward Eggleston	304	90.5	270	96.3	574	93.4	13	R
How a Fisherman Corked His Foe in a Jar — Guy W. Carryl	233	68.9	292	67.7	525	68.3	16	R
How Air Is Put to Work—Alida Hurtebise	427	68.0	467	49.0	894	58.5	14	R
How Alexander Won His War Steed—Plutarch	638	70.9	621	65.0	1259	68.0	26	R

PUPILS' READING INTERESTS: GRADES 7-9
Ts and Ss = Teachers and Schools   S = Studied in Class
IR = Independent Reading   R = Read in Class

SELECTION—AUTHOR	Boys		Girls		Total		Ts & Ss	
	No.	%	No.	%	No.	Av. %		
How Arrowheads Are Made—Edwin E. Slosson	448	66.1	415	51.7	863	58.9	14	R
How Balto Brought the Serum to Nome— Gunnar Kasson	353	80.2	317	68.6	670	74.4	13	R
How Brer Tarrypin Learned to Fly— Joel C. Harris	270	77.8	270	76.3	540	77.1	18	R
How David Was Kidnapped—Robert L. Stevenson	357	54.1	365	47.8	722	51.0	12	R
How Did You Die?— Edmund V. Cooke	593	52.4	624	64.3	1217	58.4	26	R
How Do I Love Thee?— Elizabeth B. Browning	310	27.6	331	42.8	641	35.2	17	R
How I Found America— Anzia Yezierska	272	66.9	295	82.0	567	74.5	14	R
How I Killed a Bear— Charles D. Warner	765	78.6	772	74.8	1537	76.7	82	S
How Man Got His Shoe —Edwin E. Slosson	386	61.8	403	63.2	789	62.5	14	R
How Man Learned to Strike a Light— W. A. and A. M. Mowry	405	60.1	432	52.9	837	56.5	17	R
How Potts Saved the Night Express—Ray S. Baker	247	90.5	207	85.3	454	87.9	22	S
How Primitive Woman Provided for Her Family — Otis T. Mason	356	51.0	375	54.1	731	52.6	14	R
How the Beavers Saved Their Homes— Enos A. Mills	471	75.7	408	57.8	879	66.8	15	R
How the Bulldog Got His Jaw—Edwin E. Slosson	404	50.2	357	51.1	761	50.7	10	R
How the Cat Came to Have Nine Lives— John C. Branner	418	61.1	400	76.3	818	68.7	17	R
How the Old Horse Won the Bet— Oliver W. Holmes	1391	85.8	1417	80.4	2808	83.1	135	S

PUPILS' READING INTERESTS: GRADES 7-9

Ts and Ss = Teachers and Schools   S = Studied in Class

IR = Independent Reading   R = Read in Class

SELECTION—AUTHOR	Boys		Girls		Total		Ts & Ss	
	No.	%	No.	%	No.	Av. %		
How Theseus Slew the Minotaur—Charles Kinglsey	303	57.4	343	54.2	646	55.8	10	R
How the Ships Talk— Jackson and Evans	310	71.6	326	45.1	636	58.4	14	R
How They Brought the Good News from Ghent to Aix—Robert Browning	385	68.1	319	63.8	704	66.0	38	S
How Thor Found His Hammer—Hamilton W. Mabie	480	80.2	510	82.1	990	81.2	24	R
How to Be a Champion —Grantland Rice	359	70.8	323	69.3	682	70.1	17	R
How to Catch a Bird— Leland B. Jacobs	231	72.7	235	79.8	466	76.3	18	S
How to Make Friends with the Wild Animals— Charles A. Eastman	254	63.8	224	53.3	478	58.6	17	R
How Tom Sawyer Whitewashed the Fence — Mark Twain	297	89.2	790	89.9	1087	89.6	34	R
Huck Finn in Disguise— Mark Twain	422	95.3	414	92.9	836	94.1	20	R
Huckleberry Finn—Mark Twain	492	94.0	379	93.2	871	93.6	67	S
Human Comedy, The— William Saroyan	147	80.6	384	78.2	531	79.4	114	IR
Hunchback of Notre Dame, The—Victor Hugo	679	79.0	419	80.9	1098	80.0	129	IR
Hymn—Paul L. Dunbar	458	46.7	472	60.2	930	53.5	21	R
Hymn to the Night— Henry W. Longfellow	340	43.2	321	60.9	661	52.1	13	R
Hypnotizing Insects— Edwin E. Slosson	382	49.2	343	53.2	725	51.2	10	R
I Am an American—Elias Lieberman	279	72.8	315	72.1	594	72.5	21	R
Icarus Flies Too High (Greek Myth)	199	64.3	140	59.6	339	62.0		

PUPILS' READING INTERESTS: GRADES 7-9
Ts and Ss = Teachers and Schools   S = Studied in Class
IR = Independent Reading   R = Read in Class

SELECTION—AUTHOR	Boys		Girls		Total		Ts & Ss	
	No.	%	No.	%	No.	Av. %		
Ice Cart, The—Wilfred W. Gibson	361	53.9	256	50.0	617	52.0	22	S
If—Rudyard Kipling	778	71.7	491	76.5	1269	74.1	34	S
If I Can Stop One Heart from Breaking— Emily Dickinson	301	60.1	263	72.6	564	66.4	13	
If I Ran the Circus—Dr. Seuss	192	59.4	244	62.7	436	61.1		
If I Ran the Zoo—Dr. Seuss	182	60.2	183	63.4	365	61.8		
I Get a Colt to Break In —Lincoln Steffens	558	92.1	521	95.1	1079	93.6	17	R
I Have a Rendezvous with Death—Allan Seeger	289	61.0	197	54.8	486	57.9	26	S
I Hear America Singing —Walt Whitman	430	55.5	363	63.5	793	59.5	35	S
I Knew a Black Beetle— Christopher Morley	385	76.2	437	83.3	822	79.8	17	R
Ile—Eugene O'Neill	156	67.0	183	66.7	339	66.9	53	IR
Iliad, The—Homer	187	73.3	215	72.1	402	72.7	66	IR
I Married Adventure— Osa Johnson	336	83.5	420	85.4	756	84.5	175	IR
I. M. Margaritae Sorori— William E. Henley	259	37.5	292	45.5	551	41.5	16	S
In a Station of the Metro —Ezra Pound	569	13.9	577	19.3	1146	16.6	21	R
Inchcape Rock, The— Robert Southey	676	77.3	627	75.1	1303	76.2	38	R
Incident of the French Camp, An— Robert Browning	1964	78.8	1953	71.6	3917	75.2	132	S
Incorrigible—Burges Johnson	323	64.6	273	76.2	596	70.4	11	R
In Defense of Children— Arthur Guiterman	614	68.5	678	84.2	1292	76.4	23	R
Indian Boy's Training, An—Charles A. Eastman	1140	78.3	1021	74.7	2161	76.5	32	R
Indian Captive, The— Lois Lenski	96	76.8	266	81.6	362	79.2		

PUPILS' READING INTERESTS: GRADES 7-9

Ts and Ss = Teachers and Schools S = Studied in Class
IR = Independent Reading R = Read in Class

SELECTION—AUTHOR	Boys		Girls		Total		Ts & Ss	
	No.	%	No.	%	No.	Av. %		
Indian Summer—Emily Dickinson	245	41.8	265	53.9	510	47.9	16	R
Indian Woman, The— Walt Whitman	687	46.7	656	61.9	1343	54.3	34	R
In Explanation—Walter Learned	366	63.1	343	71.7	709	67.4	16	R
In Flanders Fields—John McCrae	1930	79.3	1772	82.8	3702	81.1	150	S
Information, Please	229	72.1	234	69.7	463	70.9		
In Hardin County, 1809 —Lulu E. Thompson	513	76.6	549	83.9	1062	80.3	19	R
Initiative—Elbert Hubbard	378	64.3	377	67.5	755	65.9	17	R
In March—Max Eastman	303	40.4	311	54.5	614	47.5	21	S
In Quebec—Rudyard Kipling	1121	74.0	1442	82.0	2563	78.0	54	R
In School Days—John G. Whittier	473	65.5	415	84.6	888	75.1	35	S
Inscribed on the Collar of a Dog— Alexander Pope	565	53.6	517	67.6	1082	60.6	18	R
Inside the F.B.I.—John J. Floherty	205	85.1	32					
Inside the U.S.A.—John Gunther	221	73.8	116	73.7	337	73.8		
Interlopers, The—H. H. Munro	335	83.0	314	83.3	649	83.2	11	R
Intervention of Peter, The—Paul L. Dunbar	425	76.9	412	80.8	837	78.9	19	R
In the Cool of the Evening—Alfred Noyes	419	38.7	394	53.3	813	46.0	10	R
In the Dark—A. A. Milne	608	45.4	585	64.7	1193	55.1	30	R
In the Fields—Elizabeth B. Browning	382	47.3	377	66.8	759	57.1	13	R
In the Light of Myth— Rannie B. Baker	186	50.0	573	64.0	759	57.0	16	S
In the Wilderness— Charles D. Warner	268	80.0	230	67.8	498	73.9	115	S
Invictus—William E. Henley	342	55.0	245	53.3	587	54.2	20	R

PUPILS' READING INTERESTS: GRADES 7-9

Ts and Ss = Teachers and Schools   S = Studied in Class

IR = Independent Reading   R = Read in Class

SELECTION—AUTHOR	Boys		Girls		Total		Ts & Ss	
	No.	%	No.	%	No.	Av. %		
Invincible Louisa— Cornelia Meigs	29		438	82.0			213	IR
I Remember, I Remember—Thomas Hood	554	49.1	550	69.2	1104	59.2	22	R
Irish Red—Jim Kjelgaard	157	77.1	231	77.3	388	77.2		
Irish Witch Story, An— Lady Wilde	242	81.8	263	86.9	505	84.4	13	R
Iron Duke, The—John R. Tunis	205	76.6	43					
Irradiations X—John G. Fletcher	289	27.0	322	29.8	611	28.4	13	R
Irreverent Brahmin, The —Arthur Guiterman	252	45.4	252	52.4	504	48.9	13	R
Israel Drake—Katherine Mayo	480	91.8	431	86.2	911	89.0	20	R
It Couldn't Be Done— Edgar A. Guest	370	73.0	353	84.1	723	78.6	20	S
It's-Me, O Lord (Negro Spiritual)	336	29.3	337	42.0	673	35.7	13	R
Ivanhoe—Walter Scott	3350	77.4	3371	72.4	6721	74.9	190	S
I Was a Teen-Age Dwarf (Book)—Max Shulman	105	81.4	218	83.7	323	82.6		
I Whistle—David Grayson	309	70.1	296	69.6	605	69.9	15	R
Jabberwocky—Lewis Carroll	329	35.4	304	39.0	633	37.2	20	R
Jack and the Beanstalk (English Fairy Tale)	458	66.7	622	68.9	1080	67.8	25	IR
Jack-in-the-Pulpit— Rupert S. Holland	262	61.6	248	68.5	510	65.1	17	S
Jack the Giant Killer (English Fairy Tale)	294	72.3	420	67.1	714	69.7	25	IR
Jaffar—Leigh Hunt	341	36.8	374	37.0	715	36.9	19	R
Jamestown Homeward Bound, The (Sea Chantey)	259	59.1	257	65.4	516	62.3	15	S
Jane Jones—Ben King	561	49.1	585	57.5	1146	53.3	24	R
Janitor's Boy, The— Nathalia Crane	383	79.0	455	89.9	838	84.5	30	S

PUPILS' READING INTERESTS: GRADES 7-9

Ts and Ss = Teachers and Schools S = Studied in Class

IR = Independent Reading R = Read in Class

SELECTION—AUTHOR	Boys		Girls		Total		Ts & Ss	
	No.	%	No.	%	No.	Av. %		
Jason and the Argonauts —Frances E. Sabin	291	67.0	319	74.5	610	70.8	14	R
Jazz Fantasia—Carl Sandburg	209	49.3	277	50.0	486	49.7	13	S
Jean and Johnny— Beverly Cleary	5		253	84.6				
Jean Desprez—Robert W. Service	240	90.4	247	86.2	487	88.3	14	R
Jefferson's Rules— Thomas Jefferson	268	46.8	269	49.6	537	48.2	15	R
Jesse James (American Ballad)	657	79.9	701	77.2	1358	78.6	27	R
Jest 'Fore Christmas— Eugene Field	394	85.0	353	93.3	747	89.2	18	R
Jim—Hilaire Belloc	271	72.9	298	80.5	569	76.7	19	R
Jim Bludso—John Hay	301	86.2	289	87.5	590	86.9	18	R
Jim Davis—John Masefield	259	80.7	171	78.4	430	79.6	87	IR
Jimsy—Dana Burnet	253	77.3	268	91.4	521	84.4	19	S
Jinx Ship, The—Howard Pease	206	69.9	108	61.1	314	65.5		
Joan of Arc—Hermann Hagedorn	153	77.1	226	82.7	379	79.9	47	IR
Jock o' Hazeldean— Walter Scott	496	43.2	759	61.7	1255	52.5	22	R
Joe Palooka (Comic Strip)	1136	77.9	1053	64.0	2189	71.0	77	IR
John Anderson, My Jo— Robert Burns	725	61.8	711	74.9	1436	68.4	32	R
John Gilpin's Ride— William Cowper	596	70.0	523	68.9	1119	69.5	45	S
John Henry and His Hammer—Harold W. Felton	302	75.3	105	63.3	407	69.3		
Johnie Armstrong (British Ballad)	361	65.4	463	53.1	824	59.3	22	R
Johnnie's First Moose— William H. Drummond	599	72.5	666	72.7	1265	72.6	26	R
Johnny Reb—Merritt P. Allen	298	77.0	148	69.9	446	73.5		

PUPILS' READING INTERESTS: GRADES 7-9
Ts and Ss = Teachers and Schools   S = Studied in Class
IR = Independent Reading   R = Read in Class

SELECTION—AUTHOR	Boys		Girls		Total		Ts & Ss	
	No.	%	No.	%	No.	Av. %		
Johnny Tremain—Esther Forbes	160	75.9	176	81.5	336	78.7	109	IR
Joseph and His Brethren —The Bible	309	78.0	418	86.6	727	82.3	19	R
Joys of the Road, The— Bliss Carman	362	53.9	364	64.0	726	59.0	17	R
Judas Goose, The— Winifred Van Etten	398	92.7	404	93.1	802	92.9	11	R
Juggler, The—Bliss Carman	284	54.3	301	68.1	585	61.2	17	R
Juggler of Notre Dame, The—Anatole France	513	61.4	458	66.2	971	63.8	26	R
Julius Caesar—William Shakespeare	263	66.0	408	66.8	671	66.4	33	S
Jumblies, The—Edward Lear	336	51.3	324	61.0	660	56.2	19	R
Jungle Beach, A— William Beebe	258	26.2	245	23.5	503	24.9	13	R
Jungle Books, The— Rudyard Kipling	1580	90.8	1333	86.7	2913	88.8	148	IR
Jungle Camp—Frank Buck	354	88.1	294	73.7	648	80.9	101	IR
Jungle River—Howard Pease	165	75.2	63					
Jungle War—Tom Gill	351	89.2	342	81.3	693	85.3	13	R
Junior Miss—Sally Benson	123	63.0	1756	87.1	1879	75.1	134	IR
Justice—John Galsworthy	388	44.5	380	40.3	768	42.4	15	R
Justin Morgan Had a Horse—Marguerite Henry	120	61.3	308	69.6	428	65.5		
Just Patty—Jean Webster	8		371	82.7			103	IR
Just Short of Eternity— Victor Heiser	436	91.2	438	90.8	874	91.0	12	R
Just So Stories—Rudyard Kipling	419	74.1	673	73.7	1092	73.9	86	IR
Kate Shelley, the Girl Who Saved the Midnight Express—John W. Davis	330	81.4	382	86.8	712	84.1	15	R

PUPILS' READING INTERESTS: GRADES 7-9
Ts and Ss = Teachers and Schools   S = Studied in Class
IR = Independent Reading   R = Read in Class

SELECTION—AUTHOR	Boys		Girls		Total		Ts & Ss	
	No.	%	No.	%	No.	Av. %		
Katherine Jaffray (British Ballad)	237	44.9	249	65.5	486	55.2	18	R
Kazan—Oliver Curwood	256	90.2	122	83.2	378	86.7	140	IR
Kelly Kid, The— Kathleen Norris and Dan Totheroh	390	89.0	424	96.5	814	92.8	16	R
Kentucky Babe—Richard H. Buck	926	64.2	922	76.8	1848	70.5	37	R
Kerry Drake (Comic Strip)	235	72.1	267	74.2	502	73.2	45	IR
Keys of the Kingdom, The—A. J. Cronin	186	83.6	344	83.7	530	83.7	69	IR
Kid Comes Back, The— John R. Tunis	177	75.1	39					
Kid from Tompkinsville, The—John R. Tunis	415	89.0	102	77.4	517	83.2	119	IR
Kidnapped—Robert L. Stevenson	181	76.7	172	75.0	353	75.9	52	IR
Kids Say the Darndest Things—Art Linkletter	529	88.1	924	91.2	1453	89.7		
Kilkenny Cats, The— Mother Goose	372	41.3	469	53.5	841	47.4	23	R
Kilmeny—Alfred Noyes	591	61.8	471	60.2	1062	61.0	43	S
Kim—Rudyard Kipling	310	70.6	340	65.0	650	67.8		
King Albert of Belgium —Chester M. Sanford and Grace A. Owen	458	92.6	439	92.3	897	92.5	13	R
King Arthur Stories— Thomas Malory	180	74.2	155	69.4	335	71.8	22	S
King Bruce and the Spider—Eliza Cook	295	64.1	320	68.3	615	66.2	11	R
King John and the Abbot of Canterbury (British Ballad)	127	75.6	326	65.6	453	70.6	14	S
King Midas (Greek Myth)	329	60.9	485	62.3	814	61.6		
King of the Golden River, The—John Ruskin	189	85.2	191	86.4	380	85.8	16	S
King of the Wind— Marguerite Henry	100	73.8	265	84.8	365	79.3		

PUPILS' READING INTERESTS: GRADES 7-9
Ts and Ss = Teachers and Schools   S = Studied in Class
IR = Independent Reading   R = Read in Class

SELECTION—AUTHOR	Boys		Girls		Total		Ts & Ss	
	No.	%	No.	%	No.	Av. %		
King of Yellow Butterflies, The—Vachel Lindsay	324	36.4	310	51.1	634	43.8	13	R
King Robert of Sicily— Henry W. Longfellow	747	66.4	1121	71.3	1868	68.9	86	S
King's English, The— Herbert Bates	350	86.7	401	88.4	751	87.6	31	S
King's Great Toe, The— Alice C. D. Riley	384	81.0	412	81.6	796	81.3	13	R
King Solomon and the Bees—John G. Saxe	614	45.8	606	49.3	1220	47.6	21	R
King Solomon's Mines—H. Rider Haggard	376	82.2	167	73.7	543	78.0		
King's Stilts, The—Dr. Seuss	102		164	64.0				
Kiskies, The—May Vontver	264	84.5	296	91.0	560	87.8	13	R
Kit Carson—Stanley Vestal	1124	85.9	420	74.0	1544	80.0	129	IR
Kit Carson's Ride— Joaquin Miller	446	62.8	445	63.7	891	63.3	15	R
Kit Carson, Trail Blazer and Scout— Doris S. Garst	1023	69.6	476	60.7	1499	65.2		
Knave of Hearts, The— Louise Saunders	444	72.2	420	84.9	864	78.6	27	S
Knights of the Silver Shield—Raymond M. Alden	437	92.1	454	92.3	891	92.2	23	R
Knight Whose Armor Didn't Squeak, The— A. A. Milne	522	58.4	427	47.5	949	53.0	21	R
Knowing People—June Etta Downey	302	61.7	299	63.4	601	62.6	19	S
Knute Rockne, All American—Harry A. Stuhldreher	200	94.8	36				88	IR
Kon-Tiki—Thor Heyerdahl	483	87.3	299	75.3	782	81.3		

PUPILS' READING INTERESTS: GRADES 7-9
Ts and Ss = Teachers and Schools   S = Studied in Class
IR = Independent Reading   R = Read in Class

SELECTION—AUTHOR	Boys		Girls		Total		Ts & Ss	
	No.	%	No.	%	No.	Av. %		
Korosta Katzina Song (Indian Lyric)	260	30.2	258	39.1	518	34.7	15	S
Koyo the Singer— Kenneth Gilbert	187	77.5	158	85.4	345	81.5	17	S
Labrador Doctor— Wilfred T. Grenfell	160	81.3	181	78.7	341	80.0	63	IR
Lad, a Dog—Albert P. Terhune	185	91.4	173	89.9	358	90.7	27	S
Laddie—Gene S. Porter	203	87.2	340	91.5	543	89.4	57	IR
Lady Cat Goes on a Journey, A—Irvin S. Cobb	386	57.5	373	56.8	759	57.2	24	R
Lady Clara Vere de Vere —Alfred Tennyson	285	59.6	313	76.2	598	67.9	16	S
Lady Clare—Alfred Tennyson	288	48.1	370	79.3	658	63.7	20	S
Lady in Distress, A— Harry Lee Marriner	382	61.9	421	78.9	803	70.4	23	S
Lady New Luck— Clinton Dangerfield	333	86.2	341	85.0	674	85.6	18	S
Lady of Antigua—Cosmo Monkhouse	315	68.1	347	86.2	662	77.2	14	R
Lady of Shalott, The— Alfred Tennyson	1196	55.9	1296	79.6	2492	67.8	102	S
Lady of the Lake, The— Walter Scott	735	63.1	849	70.9	1584	67.0	59	S
Lady or the Tiger, The— Frank R. Stockton	2033	69.3	2030	77.5	4063	73.4	158	S
Lame Duck, The— Thomas A. Curry	345	95.7	383	96.3	728	96.0	13	R
Lamplighter, The—Maria S. Cummins	59		154	70.5				
Lamp Posts—Helen Hoyt	272	42.1	295	48.3	567	45.2	14	R
Lamps of Bracken Town, The—Lew Sarett	318	34.8	370	44.6	688	39.7	18	R
Lance of Kanana, The— Harry W. French	231	91.1	260	81.0	491	86.1	20	R
Land Beyond, The— Robert Murphy	399	78.2	372	81.5	771	79.9	12	R

PUPILS' READING INTERESTS: GRADES 7-9
Ts and Ss = Teachers and Schools   S = Studied in Class
IR = Independent Reading   R = Read in Class

SELECTION—AUTHOR	Boys		Girls		Total		Ts & Ss	
	No.	%	No.	%	No.	Av. %		
Landing of the Pilgrim Fathers, The— Felicia D. Hemans	200	63.5	188	77.9	388	70.7	19	S
Lasca—Frank Desprez	274	71.7	282	72.0	556	71.9	17	R
Lassie Come Home— Eric Knight	791	93.1	975	96.5	1766	94.8	71	IR
Last Adventure, The— Albert P. Terhune	989	85.5	861	88.1	1850	86.8	56	S
Last Arrow, The— Joaquin Miller	311	65.8	248	59.5	559	62.7	22	S
Last Bull—Charles G. D. Roberts	311	78.1	288	59.5	599	68.8	19	R
Last Leaf, The—Oliver W. Holmes	470	58.4	492	72.6	962	65.5	43	S
Last Lesson, The— Alphonse Daudet	413	81.7	423	89.4	836	85.6	17	R
Last March, The—Robert F. Scott	352	77.8	380	62.8	732	70.3	17	R
Last of the Cowboys, The—Mary C. Davies	312	45.2	277	43.9	589	44.6	20	R
Last of the Irish Wolves, The—Ernest T. Seton	279	84.4	287	69.5	566	77.0	11	R
Last of the Mohicans, The—James F. Cooper	352	86.4	215	69.8	567	78.1	69	IR
Law of Club and Fang, The—Jack London	215	84.9	235	70.0	450	77.5	14	S
Lawrence of Arabia— Hermann Hagedorn	220	80.2	160	63.1	380	71.7	49	IR
Law West of the Pecos, The—Lloyd E. Naylor	210	68.8	81					
Leader of the Herd, The —Courtney R. Cooper	334	87.0	360	86.8	694	86.9	10	R
Leak in the Dike, The— Phoebe Cary	685	83.0	589	89.3	1274	86.2	40	S
Leap of the Roushan Beg, The—Henry W. Longfellow	317	70.7	379	59.2	696	65.0	26	S
Leetla Georgio Washeenton—Thomas A. Daly	310	86.8	304	94.9	614	90.9	17	S

PUPILS' READING INTERESTS: GRADES 7-9

Ts and Ss = Teachers and Schools   S = Studied in Class
R = Independent Reading   R = Read in Class

SELECTION—AUTHOR	Boys		Girls		Total		Ts & Ss	
	No.	%	No.	%	No.	Av. %		
Leetla Guiseppina—Thomas A. Daly	409	69.2	387	86.3	796	77.8	17	S
Leetla Humpy Jeem—Thomas A. Daly	291	67.2	276	74.3	567	70.8	17	R
Legend Beautiful, The—Henry W. Longfellow	238	62.6	310	66.8	548	64.7	15	R
Legend of Bishop Hatto, The—Robert Southey	261	75.3	244	79.5	505	77.4	15	R
Legend of Sleepy Hollow, The—Washington Irving	2239	82.6	2188	83.7	4427	83.2	222	S
Legend of the Moor's Legacy, The—Washington Irving	241	79.0	275	82.5	516	80.8	16	R
Leisure—William H. Davies	201	48.5	237	61.4	438	55.0	15	R
L'Envoi—Rudyard Kipling	392	60.1	189	72.7	581	66.4	22	S
Leonidas the Spartan—Herodotus	293	70.6	260	60.4	553	65.5	24	S
Lesbia Railing—Caius V. Catullus	272	43.9	295	68.2	567	56.1	12	R
Les Miserables—Victor Hugo	157	72.9	198	69.4	355	71.2		
Letter from Home, A—Wallace Irwin	390	71.4	344	81.1	734	76.3	15	R
Letter from Lewis Carroll to Gertrude Chataway, A	433	32.8	393	52.5	826	42.7	18	R
Letters of R. L. Stevenson—Robert L. Stevenson	357	54.9	324	63.3	681	59.1	25	S
Letter to Governor Clinton—George Washington	259	63.3	243	64.2	502	63.8	20	S
Letter to His Wife—George Washington	263	56.5	246	64.4	509	60.5	20	S
Letter to Mrs. Bixby—Abraham Lincoln	597	71.0	580	76.3	1177	73.7	45	R

PUPILS' READING INTERESTS: GRADES 7-9
Ts and Ss = Teachers and Schools   S = Studied in Class
IR = Independent Reading   R = Read in Class

SELECTION—AUTHOR	Boys		Girls		Total		Ts & Ss	
	No.	%	No.	%	No	Av. %		
Letter to Tacitus—Pliny the Younger	814	64.8	760	64.5	1574	64.7	19	R
Letter to the President in 1956— Franklin D. Roosevelt	365	63.6	379	65.2	744	64.4	16	R
Let the Hurricane Roar —Rose W. Lane	188	81.7	364	88.3	552	85.0	113	IR
Let Us Have Faith— Abraham Lincoln	962	58.9	996	61.2	1958	60.1	38	R
Liberty or Death— Patrick Henry	387	81.8	429	76.8	816	79.3	14	R
Life of a Prairie Lad, The—Hamlin Garland	211	71.8	221	74.7	432	73.3	28	S
Life of Robert E. Lee, The— Joseph and Mary Hamilton	315	73.7	150	65.7	465	69.7		
Life's Picture History	144	86.1	61					
Life with Father— Clarence Day	332	73.0	841	86.4	1173	79.7	199	IR
L'il Abner (Comic Strip)	458	74.8	555	70.1	1013	72.5	26	IR
Lilacs—Amy Lowell	253	51.8	263	74.9	516	63.4	19	S
Limeratomy—Anthony Euwer	556	70.5	592	73.1	1148	71.8	22	R
Lincoln—Vachel Lindsay	374	55.6	382	58.6	756	57.1	24	R
Lincoln—James R. Lowell	383	67.1	375	69.1	758	68.1	13	R
Lincoln and the Old Indian—Hezikiah Butterworth	595	83.8	532	84.3	1127	84.1	17	R
Lincoln, the Lawyer— Ida M. Tarbell	217	82.0	218	82.3	435	82.2	17	S
Lincoln, the Man of the People—Edwin Markham	393	78.0	305	69.3	698	73.7	33	S
Lindbergh—Hermann Hagedorn	472	92.4	420	90.1	892	91.3	32	R
Lindbergh Flies Alone— H. M. Anderson	322	64.9	325	61.7	647	63.3	30	S
Lindbergh Letter, A	301	49.7	229	52.6	530	51.2	14	R

PUPILS' READING INTERESTS: GRADES 7-9

Ts and Ss = Teachers and Schools S = Studied in Class
IR = Independent Reading   R = Read in Class

SELECTION—AUTHOR	Boys		Girls		Total		Ts & Ss	
	No.	%	No.	%	No.	Av. %		
Lion, The—Hilaire Belloc	304	61.0	337	61.1	641	61.1	14	R
Little Bateese—William H. Drummond	765	75.5	567	84.0	1332	79.8	42	S
Little Bells of Sevilla— Dora S. Shorter	453	35.0	471	53.4	924	44.2	19	R
Little Billee—William M. Thackeray	417	77.3	461	79.0	878	78.2	19	R
Little Black Hen, The— A. A. Milne	368	57.3	357	62.0	725	59.7	19	R
Little Breeches—John Hay	252	75.2	228	84.9	480	80.1	13	R
Little Britches—Ralph Moody	400	74.6	558	76.0	958	75.3		
Little Brown Hen, The— Clinton Scollard	374	72.5	378	82.5	752	77.5	31	S
Little Giffen of Tennessee— Francis O. Ticknor	384	73.7	370	77.0	754	75.4	29	S
Little Home in the Mountains, The— Arthur Guiterman	471	39.7	483	54.1	954	46.9	17	R
Little House, A—Abigail C. Davis	322	48.9	337	62.6	659	55.8	14	R
Little House in the Big Woods, The— Laura Wilder	32		391	64.5				
Little Lame Prince, The —Dinah M. Mulock	711	72.2	1345	85.0	2056	78.6	83	IR
Little Lord Fauntleroy— Frances H. Burnett	126	57.5	294	75.3	420	66.4	54	IR
Little Lost Pup, The— Arthur Guiterman	344	75.3	358	82.0	702	78.7	22	R
Little Lulu (Comic Strip)	346	74.0	492	81.8	838	77.9	23	IR
Little Men—Louisa M. Alcott	328	74.2	722	86.1	1050	80.2	93	IR
Little Orphan Annie (Comic Strip)	976	50.0	1111	55.4	2087	52.7	60	IR
Little Orphan Annie— James W. Riley	284	70.1	272	88.6	556	79.4	19	S

PUPILS' READING INTERESTS: GRADES 7-9

Ts and Ss = Teachers and Schools   S = Studied in Class
IR = Independent Reading   R = Read in Class

SELECTION—AUTHOR	Boys		Girls		Total		Ts & Ss	
	No.	%	No.	%	No.	Av. %		
Little Orvie's New Dog Ralph— Booth Tarkington	295	87.1	315	92.7	610	89.9	13	R
Little Peach, The— Eugene Field	365	61.5	364	74.2	729	67.9	22	R
Little Prince, The— Antoine de Saint Exupéry	50		233	73.0			86	IR
Little Princesses, The— Marion Crawford	15		247	75.7				
Little Road, The—Nancy B. Turner	250	45.4	273	68.5	523	57.0	13	R
Little Scouts, The (Comic Strip)	307	82.4	247	80.2	554	81.3	47	IR
Little Shepherd of Kingdom Come, The— John Fox, Jr.	131	83.4	342	80.8	473	82.1	166	IR
Little Turtle, The— Vachel Lindsay	437	80.7	395	87.1	832	83.9	14	R
Little Women—Louisa M. Alcott	122	62.8	606	96.5	728	79.7	81	IR
Lives of a Bengal Lancer (Book)—F. Yates-Brown	153	73.2	39					
Lives of a Bengal Lancer (Movie)	324	80.2	129	71.7	453	76.0		
Lobo, King of Currumpaw—Ernest T. Seton	309	88.5	308	69.8	617	79.2	17	R
Lochinvar—Walter Scott	1136	66.5	1704	80.6	2840	73.6	73	S
Log of a Cowboy, The— Andy Adams	350	80.9	346	63.3	696	72.1	26	R
London Idyll, A—John Presland	315	53.8	344	73.0	659	63.4	14	R
Lone Cowboy—Will James	258	83.1	131	78.2	389	80.7	169	IR
Lone Ranger (Comic Strip)	436	71.1	482	58.9	918	65.0	24	IR
Lone Wolf—Charles G. D. Roberts	338	92.9	343	89.1	681	91.0	21	R

PUPILS' READING INTERESTS: GRADES 7-9

Ts and Ss = Teachers and Schools   S = Studied in Class

IR = Independent Reading   R = Read in Class

SELECTION—AUTHOR	Boys		Girls		Total		Ts & Ss	
	No.	%	No.	%	No.	Av. %		
Long Pants—Irvin S. Cobb	299	81.4	302	78.5	601	80.0	16	R
Long Time Ago— Elizabeth P. Prentiss	384	74.3	381	82.3	765	78.3	13	R
Lord Chancellor's Song, The— William S. Gilbert	473	72.0	536	80.1	1009	76.1	23	R
Lord Lovel (British Ballad)	120	21.7	523	64.6	643	43.2	13	R
Lord Randal (British Ballad)	556	47.8	768	59.4	1324	53.6	38	S
Lord Ullin's Daughter— Thomas Campbell	216	44.0	644	65.1	860	54.6	21	S
Lorna Doone—Richard Blackmore	227	82.6	344	85.2	571	83.9	109	IR
Lost and Found— Octavus R. Cohen	220	83.9	238	96.0	458	90.0	14	R
Lost Horizon—James Hilton	227	79.5	278	77.7	505	78.6		
Lost Puppy, The—Henry Wood	392	52.0	425	71.2	817	61.6	14	R
Lost Worlds—Anne T. White	247	82.0	85	74.7	332	78.4		
Lou Gehrig, a Quiet Hero—Frank P. Graham	919	92.3	271	87.1	1190	89.7	196	IR
Lou Gehrig, Boy of the Sandlots— Guernsey Van Riper	229	83.2	19					
Louisa May Alcott's Journal— Louisa M. Alcott	237	48.9	273	78.4	510	63.7	20	S
Love Letters of Smith, The—H. C. Bunner	373	72.5	279	92.1	652	82.3	15	R
Lovers, The—Phoebe Cary	309	61.3	290	75.9	599	68.6	14	R
Low-Backed Car, The— Samuel Lover	238	78.6	271	86.3	509	82.5	21	R
Luck of Roaring Camp, The—Bret Harte	276	79.9	248	78.8	524	79.4	17	R
Lucky to be a Yankee— Joe DiMaggio	723	86.4	175	84.0	898	85.2	126	IR

PUPILS' READING INTERESTS: GRADES 7-9
Ts and Ss = Teachers and Schools   S = Studied in Class
IR = Independent Reading   R = Read in Class

SELECTION—AUTHOR	Boys No.	Boys %	Girls No.	Girls %	Total No.	Total Av. %	Ts & Ss	
Lucy Gray—William Wordsworth	369	53.8	388	74.4	757	64.1	21	R
Lullaby—Paul L. Dunbar	441	56.7	467	73.8	908	65.3	24	R
Mad Tea Party, The—Lewis Carroll	882	43.8	868	60.0	1750	51.9	24	R
Magic—Irene R. McLeod	420	35.7	391	51.4	811	43.6	11	R
Magical Melons—Carol R. Brink	23		203	75.6			106	IR
Magic Garden, The—Gene S. Porter	113	74.3	257	88.9	370	81.6	116	IR
Magic Touch, The—Ariadne Gilbert	286	62.6	239	68.0	525	65.3	20	S
Maid Freed from the Gallows, The (British Ballad)	456	51.6	411	69.6	867	60.6	23	S
Maker of Dreams, The—Oliphant Down	238	48.9	261	79.9	499	64.4	13	R
Makers of the Flag—Franklin K. Lane	233	57.9	246	67.5	479	62.7	21	S
Making the Incandescent Light— Thomas A. Edison	284	61.6	242	49.8	526	55.7	28	R
Mama's Bank Account—Kathryn Forbes	200	75.3	847	91.0	1047	83.2	120	IR
Man and the Lion, The—Aesop	782	68.4	785	65.2	1567	66.8	29	R
Mandalay—Rudyard Kipling	303	71.8	284	75.0	587	73.4	19	R
Mandrake the Magician (Comic Strip)	789	72.5	645	66.5	1434	69.5	75	IR
Man-Eaters of Kumaon, The—James E. Corbett	226	70.1	85	59.4	311	64.8		
Man in the House, A—Elsie Singmaster	417	74.3	415	83.7	832	79.0	10	R
Man of Words, A—Mother Goose	418	57.3	443	74.8	861	66.1	17	R
Man on the Moon—Robert A. Heinlein	163	70.6	42					
Man's a Man for a' That, A—Robert Burns	412	49.9	417	57.2	829	53.6	27	R

PUPILS' READING INTERESTS: GRADES 7-9
Ts and Ss = Teachers and Schools   S = Studied in Class
IR = Independent Reading   R = Read in Class

SELECTION—AUTHOR	Boys		Girls		Total		Ts & Ss	
	No.	%	No.	%	No.	Av. %		
Man's Highest Trip into the Air— Irma Taylor	353	96.0	339	91.0	692	93.5	13	R
Mansion, The—Henry Van Dyke	195	61.5	178	71.9	373	66.7	28	S
Man Who Cursed the Lilies, The— Charles T. Jackson	350	69.6	317	52.7	667	61.2	11	R
Man Who Was, The— Rudyard Kipling	574	52.0	593	36.8	1167	44.4	47	S
Man Without a Country, The—Edward E. Hale	2972	81.7	2948	76.1	5920	78.9	245	S
Man with the Good Face, The—Frank L. Mott	281	56.8	370	68.8	651	62.8	24	S
Man with the Hoe, The —Edwin Markham	558	57.9	420	61.7	978	59.8	40	S
Many Loves of Dobie Gillis, The— Max Shulman	379	74.4	547	78.2	926	76.3		
Marble Top—E. B. White	469	40.8	483	52.7	952	46.8	17	R
March—Lucy Larcom	401	60.2	429	69.6	830	64.9	20	R
Marie Sklodowski Curie —Chester M. Sanford and Grace A. Owen	425	71.1	433	75.1	858	73.1	21	R
Marjorie Daw—Thomas B. Aldrich	460	63.3	627	81.3	1087	72.3	65	S
Markheim—Robert L. Stevenson	1105	55.4	1224	52.9	2329	54.2	78	S
Mark Twain—Cornelia Meigs	407	85.5	366	82.5	773	84.0	15	R
Mark Twain's Autobiography	224	75.0	254	75.4	478	75.2	57	IR
Mark Twain's School Days—Albert B. Paine	343	77.7	333	82.4	676	80.1	12	R
Marse Chan—Thomas N. Page	153	66.7	155	69.4	308	68.1	23	S
Marvelous Legend of Tom Connor's Cat— Samuel Lover	166	72.3	135	81.4	301	76.9	20	R

PUPILS' READING INTERESTS: GRADES 7-9

Ts and Ss = Teachers and Schools   S = Studied in Class

IR = Independent Reading   R = Read in Class

SELECTION—AUTHOR	Boys		Girls		Total		Ts & Ss	
	No.	%	No.	%	No.	Av. %		
Marvelous Migrations of the Eel, The— Edwin E. Slosson	374	52.8	346	49.7	720	51.3	9	R
Maryland Yellow-Throat, The—Henry Van Dyke	226	57.1	274	70.3	500	63.7	22	S
Mary Poppins—Pamela L. Travers	299	68.1	1369	71.7	1668	69.9	127	IR
Mary White—William A. White	171	74.9	223	89.2	394	82.1	20	S
Mascot, A—Arthur Guiterman	179	67.6	176	77.0	355	72.3	15	R
Masque of the Red Death, The—Edgar A. Poe	390	70.6	393	65.5	783	68.1	34	S
Massa's in de Cold, Cold Ground— Stephen C. Foster	273	55.5	287	67.1	560	61.3	11	R
Matchlock Gun, The— Walter D. Edmonds	399	71.2	288	77.3	687	74.3	106	IR
Matilda—Hilaire Belloc	618	66.7	612	84.6	1230	75.7	27	R
Maud Muller—John G. Whittier	303	51.2	377	80.4	680	65.8	22	S
May Day—Sara Teasdale	328	51.1	355	68.2	683	59.7	19	S
May Is Building Her House— Richard Le Gallienne	413	42.3	413	61.9	826	52.1	23	R
Meaning of a Fragment, The—John C. Merriam	287	74.9	287	65.5	574	70.2	17	S
Measure Me, Sky— Leonora Speyer	492	32.5	532	40.5	1024	36.5	20	R
Measuring the Ocean's Depth—Edwin E. Slosson	474	56.3	500	41.4	974	48.9	24	R
Meddlesome Matty—Ann Taylor	290	53.1	326	81.0	616	67.1	14	R
Meet the Malones— Lenora M. Weber	19		333	77.2				
Meg Merrilies—John Keats	297	45.0	305	61.0	602	53.0	12	R
Men Against the Sea— Nordhoff and Hall	147	85.3	19					

PUPILS' READING INTERESTS: GRADES 7-9
Ts and Ss = Teachers and Schools   S = Studied in Class
IR = Independent Reading   R = Read in Class

SELECTION—AUTHOR	Boys		Girls		Total		Ts & Ss	
	No.	%	No.	%	No.	Av. %		
Mending the Clock— James M. Barrie	432	75.7	452	81.2	884	78.5	19	R
Mending Wall—Robert Frost	282	56.0	263	66.3	545	61.2	18	S
Men Longed to Fly— Maud and Miska Petersham	325	64.9	346	63.0	671	64.0	12	R
Men of Iron—Howard Pyle	668	86.7	385	81.3	1053	84.0	42	S
Men on Bataan—John Hersey	225	89.1	26					
Merchant of Venice, The —William Shakespeare	160	73.7	152	78.6	312	76.2	23	S
Merry Adventures of Robin Hood (Radio Play) — C. B. Co.	315	92.2	341	87.5	656	89.9	11	R
Merry Adventures of Robin Hood, The— Howard Pyle	943	91.4	734	81.5	1677	86.5	74	S
Message to Garcia, A— Elbert Hubbard	575	64.6	605	58.8	1180	61.7	36	S
Messenger, A—Mary R. S. Andrews	180	70.8	178	63.8	358	67.3	20	S
Messer Marco Polo— Donn Byrne	183	72.4	134	69.8	317	71.1	111	IR
Mia Carlotta—Thomas A. Daly	705	77.8	717	88.7	1422	83.3	55	S
Mickey Mouse (Comic Strip)	872	80.8	886	73.9	1758	77.4	70	IR
Midsummer Night's Dream, A—Charles Lamb	300	57.2	272	74.8	572	66.0	15	R
Midsummer Night's Dream, A— William Shakespeare	1108	49.3	1256	76.8	2364	63.1	68	S
Midwinter—John T. Trowbridge	377	43.2	358	55.2	735	49.2	10	R
Mildred Babe Didrikson —Leroy Atkinson and Austen Lake	321	67.0	352	72.2	673	69.6	21	S

PUPILS' READING INTERESTS: GRADES 7-9
Ts and Ss = Teachers and Schools   S = Studied in Class
IR = Independent Reading   R = Read in Class

SELECTION—AUTHOR	Boys		Girls		Total		Ts & Ss	
	No.	%	No.	%	No.	Av. %		
Mile with Me, A—Henry Van Dyke	177	56.5	229	67.9	406	62.2	15	R
Milk Pitcher, The— Howard Brubaker	394	80.7	389	78.1	783	79.4	18	S
Milky Way, The— William M. Reed	284	54.6	289	42.7	573	48.7	16	S
Miller, His Son and His Donkey, The— Aesop	331	74.0	341	75.1	672	74.6	17	R
Miller of the Dee, The— Charles Mackay	810	71.9	781	79.6	1591	75.8	29	R
Miniver Cheevy—Edwin A. Robinson	380	53.7	453	57.5	833	55.6	27	R
Minstrel Boy, The— Thomas Moore	444	46.1	452	49.1	896	47.6	25	R
Minuet, The—Mary Mapes Dodge	309	51.6	315	85.4	624	68.5	20	S
Miracles on Maple Hill— Virginia Sorenson	13		159	62.9				
Mischievous Morning Glory, The—Mary Fenollosa	237	52.8	252	70.8	489	61.8	15	R
Miss Hickory—Carolyn S. Bailey	42		229	59.6				
Miss Letitia's Profession —Lupton A. Wilkinson	285	74.4	338	79.0	623	76.7	19	R
Miss T—Walter de la Mare	304	41.8	327	51.2	631	46.5	14	R
Misty of Chincoteague— Marguerite Henry	58		279	81.9				
Moby Dick—Herman Melville	387	75.5	273	64.1	660	69.8	72	IR
Mocking Bird, The—Paul H. Hayne	363	54.1	358	53.5	721	53.8	26	S
Modern Hiawatha— George A. Strong	603	67.7	588	77.0	1191	72.4	29	R
Modern Theory of Earthquakes, The— Edwin E. Slosson	362	47.9	323	43.2	685	45.6	9	R
Moffats, The—Eleanor Estes	56		342	71.5				

PUPILS' READING INTERESTS: GRADES 7-9

Ts and Ss = Teachers and Schools   S = Studied in Class
IR = Independent Reading   R = Read in Class

SELECTION—AUTHOR	Boys		Girls		Total		Ts & Ss	
	No.	%	No.	%	No.	Av. %		
Molly McGuire, Fourteen —Frederick S. Greene	328	71.5	348	65.2	676	68.4	21	S
Moni, the Goat Boy— Johanna Spyri	190	71.1	264	77.8	454	74.5	70	IR
Monkey's Paw, The— William W. Jacobs	173	80.4	146	83.6	319	82.0	60	S
Monument Mountain— William C. Bryant	301	26.4	275	33.3	576	29.9	11	R
More Roses—George Eliot	399	28.6	436	39.9	835	34.3	23	R
Moses Sells the Colt— Oliver Goldsmith	707	61.6	717	64.6	1424	63.1	25	R
Moss, the Dentist— Carolyn Wells	342	69.3	387	86.6	729	78.0	17	R
Most Dangerous Game, The—Richard Connell	519	93.3	455	81.2	974	87.3	31	S
Mother Goose	190	48.4	291	55.3	481	51.9		
Moti Guj—Mutineer— Rudyard Kipling	705	79.3	678	72.9	1383	76.1	85	S
Mountain Girl— Genevieve Fox	40		313	71.7				
Mountains Are a Lonely Folk, The— Hamlin Garland	321	28.7	297	38.7	618	33.7	13	S
Mountain Stallion, The— Logan Forster	55		175	78.6				
Mr. Dickens' Little Boy —Sarah Addington	191	55.8	233	77.9	424	66.9	14	S
Mr. Hail Colomb— Thomas A. Daly	653	75.7	641	81.4	1294	78.6	26	R
Mr. Popper's Penguins— Richard and Florence Atwater	492	71.4	796	73.1	1288	72.3		
Mrs. 'Arris Goes to Paris —Paul Gallico	78	64.1	318	75.2	396	69.7		
Mrs. Lismore and Charles—McGuffey Reader	285	20.9	326	27.4	611	24.2	14	R
Mrs. McWilliams and the Lightning—Mark Twain	215	74.9	227	80.8	442	77.9	15	S

PUPILS' READING INTERESTS: GRADES 7-9
Ts and Ss = Teachers and Schools   S = Studied in Class
IR = Independent Reading   R = Read in Class

SELECTION—AUTHOR	Boys		Girls		Total		Ts & Ss	
	No.	%	No.	%	No.	Av. %		
Mrs. Mike—Benedict and Nancy Freedman	21		195	86.9				
Mrs. Piggle Wiggle— Betty MacDonald	118	58.9	490	62.3	608	60.6		
Mrs. Wiggs of the Cabbage Patch— Alice H. Rice	168	67.9	466	80.3	634	74.1	51	IR
Mumps—Arthur Guiterman	398	52.5	442	62.7	840	57.6	19	R
Music—Ralph W. Emerson	234	36.1	289	54.5	523	45.3	16	R
Music—Any Lowell	379	49.9	441	66.2	820	58.1	31	S
Music Comes—Freeman	445	31.7	515	40.0	960	35.9	25	R
Mutineers, The—Charles B. Hawes	173	79.2	34					
Mutiny on the Bounty— Nordhoff and Hall	348	85.9	254	82.5	602	84.2	113	IR
My Boyhood—John Burroughs	574	50.0	537	45.8	1111	47.9	17	R
My Cats—Jean Henri Fabre	673	68.2	653	79.6	1326	73.9	37	S
My Creed—Howard A. Walter	549	61.3	539	70.7	1088	66.0	50	S
My Dog—John K. Bangs	409	71.9	427	83.1	836	77.5	23	R
My Double and How He Undid Me— Edward E. Hale	764	60.7	777	63.9	1541	62.3	94	S
My Fair Lady—Alan J. Lerner	59		176	83.8				
My Financial Career— Stephen Leacock	470	79.7	435	89.5	905	84.6	24	R
My Friend Flicka—Mary O'Hara	266	96.2	389	94.2	655	95.2	25	IR
My Garden—Thomas Brown	256	51.4	298	66.4	554	58.9	21	R
My Heart Leaps Up— William Wordsworth	692	34.2	683	43.8	1375	39.0	26	R
My Lady's Dress— Edward Knoblock	213	63.4	240	84.8	453	74.1	20	S
My Life Story—Joe Louis	548	86.6	190	80.8	738	83.7	123	IR

PUPILS' READING INTERESTS: GRADES 7-9
Ts and Ss = Teachers and Schools   S = Studied in Class
IR = Independent Reading   R = Read in Class

SELECTION—AUTHOR	Boys		Girls		Total		Ts & Ss	
	No.	%	No.	%	No.	Av. %		
My Lost Youth—Henry W. Longfellow	445	51.9	456	63.0	901	57.5	49	S
My Luve Is Like a Red, Red Rose— Robert Burns	755	44.6	748	62.6	1503	53.6	33	R
My Native Land—Walter Scott	1213	66.3	1203	73.6	2416	70.0	96	S
My Poplars—Theodosia Garrison	312	44.1	391	45.7	703	44.9	30	S
My Sister Eileen—Ruth McKenney	47		383	79.1				
Mysterious Island—Jules Verne	252	89.7	266	85.3	518	87.5	169	IR
Mystery in Four-and-One-Half Street, The— Donald and Louise Peattie	408	93.8	416	93.8	824	93.8	20	R
Mystery of Paul Redfern, The—Irma Taylor	528	96.6	462	93.8	990	95.2	14	R
Mystery Over the Brick Wall—Helen F. Orton	68		162	79.3				
Myths and Their Meaning—Max J. Herzberg	324	51.4	351	60.8	675	56.1	30	S
My Visit to Niagara— Nathaniel Hawthorne	182	56.0	222	55.9	404	56.0	20	S
My White Mouse—G. E. Teter	310	60.0	356	74.0	666	67.0	15	R
Name of Old Glory, The —James W. Riley	279	68.8	277	66.1	556	67.5	25	S
Nancy Drew (Stories)— Caroline Keene	41		506	83.7				
Napoleon and Uncle Elby (Comic Strip)	290	63.3	238	51.3	528	57.3	47	IR
Nathan Hale—Francis M. Finch	449	67.6	469	77.9	918	72.8	17	R
Nathan Hale—Clyde Fitch	198	89.9	217	93.3	415	91.6	15	R
National Velvet (Book)— Enid Bagnold	112	77.2	528	93.3	640	85.3	117	IR
National Velvet (Movie)	623	85.4	1030	96.2	1653	90.8	128	

PUPILS' READING INTERESTS: GRADES 7-9

Ts and Ss = Teachers and Schools   S = Studied in Class
IR = Independent Reading   R = Read in Class

SELECTION—AUTHOR	Boys		Girls		Total		Ts & Ss	
	No.	%	No.	%	No.	Av. %		
Nation's Prayer, The— Josiah G. Holland	349	55.9	364	60.7	713	58.3	23	S
Nautical Extravaganza, A —Wallace Irwin	280	74.8	312	80.3	592	77.6	21	S
Navajo Prayer—Edward S. Yeomans	223	36.5	233	36.3	456	36.4	14	R
Nebuchadnezzar—Irwin Russell	310	65.6	303	71.8	613	68.7	16	R
Necklace, The—Guy de Maupassant	2117	63.0	2243	84.1	4360	73.6	133	S
Neighbors—Edwin A. Robinson	249	63.3	257	72.0	506	67.7	12	R
Neighbors, The (Comic Strip)	304	68.3	417	69.4	721	68.9	48	IR
Nelly's Silver Mine— Helen H. Jackson	53		318	79.9			132	IR
Ne Sit Ancillae Tibi Amor Pudori— Robert L. Stevenson	256	54.3	223	70.6	479	62.5	20	S
Nevertheless—Stuart Walker	212	83.0	276	87.9	488	85.5	20	R
New England Nun, A—Mary E. W. Freeman	286	46.1	311	78.7	597	62.4	15	S
New England Weather— Mark Twain	348	65.9	355	62.1	703	64.0	17	S
New Every Morning— Susan Coolidge	304	50.5	318	71.1	622	60.8	25	S
New International Encyclopedia, The	131	83.6	198	81.6	329	82.6	91	IR
New York to Paris— Charles A. Lindbergh	211	88.4	190	66.1	401	77.3	18	S
Nice Lion—Martin Johnson	361	86.4	329	78.7	690	82.6	13	R
Night at an Inn, A— Edward Dunsany	354	81.4	414	72.5	768	77.0	17	S
Night Clouds—Amy Lowell	433	31.4	508	35.9	941	33.7	25	R
Night Flyers, The— Frank M. Chapman	297	45.8	290	38.1	587	42.0	14	R

PUPILS' READING INTERESTS: GRADES 7-9
Ts and Ss = Teachers and Schools   S = Studied in Class
IR = Independent Reading   R = Read in Class

SELECTION—AUTHOR	Boys		Girls		Total		Ts & Ss	
	No.	%	No.	%	No.	Av. %		
Night of the Storm, The —Zona Gale	309	90.3	359	97.4	668	93.9	15	S
Night Ride in a Prairie Schooner, A— Hamlin Garland	361	80.1	313	75.7	674	77.9	17	R
Night to Remember, A— Walter Lord	409	90.2	388	87.5	797	88.9		
Night with Ruff Grouse, A—Clarence Hawkes	183	77.9	162	73.1	345	75.5	16	S
1984—George Orwell	200	85.3	86	82.6	286	84.0		
Nobility—Alice Cary	247	55.7	259	68.1	506	61.9	27	S
Nobody's Girl—Hector Malot	24		297	85.9			93	IR
Noiseless Patient Spider, A—Walt Whitman	378	32.5	377	31.7	755	32.1	23	R
No Other White Men— Julia Davis	173	78.0	95				80	IR
Northwest Passage— Kenneth Roberts	300	91.2	144	76.4	444	83.8	71	IR
No Time for Sergeants— Mac Hyman	587	89.8	533	85.6	1120	87.7		
Not Quite Such a Goose —Zona Gale	340	82.9	359	94.8	699	88.9	19	S
November—Thomas Hood	324	43.7	375	51.6	699	47.7	18	R
Nun's Story, The— Kathryn Hulme	129	79.8	578	92.7	707	86.3		
Nuvat the Brave—Radko Doone	199	68.1	171	58.2	370	63.2	78	IR
O Beautiful! My Country—James R. Lowell	869	60.3	903	69.2	1772	64.8	85	S
O Bury Me Not on the Lone Prairie (Cowboy Ballad)	270	71.9	224	69.9	494	70.9	17	R
O Captain! My Captain! —Walt Whitman	1109	77.8	1205	81.6	2314	79.7	105	S
Ocean, The—George G. Byron	384	40.0	367	38.4	751	39.2	20	R

PUPILS' READING INTERESTS: GRADES 7-9
Ts and Ss = Teachers and Schools   S = Studied in Class
IR = Independent Reading   R = Read in Class

SELECTION—AUTHOR	Boys		Girls		Total		Ts & Ss	
	No.	%	No.	%	No.	Av. %		
October's Bright Blue Weather— Helen H. Jackson	397	55.4	372	66.8	769	61.1	12	R
Ode (The Poets)—Arthur O'Shaughnessy	254	50.4	231	58.0	485	54.2	13	S
Odyssey, The—Homer	2781	70.2	3304	63.2	6085	66.7	199	S
Odyssey of K's, An— Wilbur D. Nesbit	398	58.7	415	65.7	813	62.2	19	R
Of Riches—Francis Bacon	10743	22.5	10690	25.7	21433	24.1	422	R
Of Studies—Francis Bacon	10712	39.4	10686	45.7	21398	42.6	419	R
Old Chisholm Trail, The (Cowboy Ballad)	546	78.3	576	78.9	1122	78.6	24	R
Old Elizabeth—Hugh Walpole	365	76.2	365	91.5	730	83.9	12	R
Old-Fashioned Girl, An— Louisa M. Alcott	17		479	84.6			84	IR
Old Folks at Home— Stephen Foster	395	61.8	371	74.0	766	67.9	20	R
Old Gray Squirrel, The— Alfred Noyes	432	50.5	181	48.9	613	49.7	15	R
Old Ironsides—Oliver W. Holmes	2097	84.4	2098	82.0	4195	83.2	195	S
Old Man and the Sea, The—Ernest Hemingway	502	77.8	347	76.1	849	77.0		
Old Oaken Bucket, The —Samuel Woodworth	202	66.3	185	68.6	387	67.5	15	R
Old Pipes and the Dryad —Frank R. Stockton	195	81.3	189	87.3	384	84.3	44	IR
Old Rattler and the King Snake—David S. Jordan	285	90.7	281	72.8	566	81.8	11	R
Old Sailor, The—A. A. Milne	483	65.8	458	64.4	941	65.1	21	R
Old Santa Fe Trail, The —Stanley Vestal	243	80.5	122	71.7	365	76.1	91	IR
Old Susan—Walter de la Mare	399	54.0	308	75.3	707	64.7	24	S
Old Swimmin' Hole, The —James W. Riley	532	82.5	479	81.6	1011	82.1	38	S

PUPILS' READING INTERESTS: GRADES 7-9

Ts and Ss = Teachers and Schools   S = Studied in Class
IR = Independent Reading   R = Read in Class

SELECTION—AUTHOR	Boys		Girls		Total		Ts & Ss	
	No.	%	No.	%	No.	Av. %		
Old Testament Stories	132	78.8	175	80.9	307	79.9	55	IR
Old Watchdog to His Son, The—Edward Anthony	402	68.8	401	70.2	803	69.5	15	R
Old Yeller—Fred Gipson	1338	86.7	1419	87.0	2757	86.9		
Oliver Twist—Charles Dickens	376	83.9	468	91.2	844	87.6	24	S
On Cats and Dogs— Jerome K. Jerome	330	83.0	308	89.9	638	86.5	12	R
On Digital Extremities— Gelett Burgess	416	59.3	423	74.8	839	67.1	17	R
One Ship Drives East— Ella W. Wilcox	316	52.7	338	62.3	654	57.5	19	S
One, Two, Three—H. C. Bunner	289	59.7	304	82.2	593	71.0	15	R
On His Blindness—John Milton	386	51.8	375	58.8	761	55.3	13	R
Onion John—Joseph E. Krumgold	87	55.2	162	58.0	249	56.6		
On Pixie Hill—Richmial Crompton	327	80.1	381	85.7	708	82.9	15	R
On the Beach—Nevil Shute	347	86.0	337	85.2	684	85.6		
On the Grasshopper and the Cricket— John Keats	474	31.6	475	35.3	949	33.5	25	R
On the Stairs—Arthur Morrison	649	35.5	704	55.3	1353	45.4	49	S
On to Oregon—Honoré W. Morrow	211	81.3	187	84.5	398	82.9	183	IR
On Trial for His Life— John Fox, Jr.	361	87.8	323	83.0	684	85.4	50	S
Opening of the Piano, The—Oliver W. Holmes	510	40.7	508	62.2	1018	51.5	23	R
Opportunity—Berton Braley	362	67.5	368	83.7	730	75.6	15	R
Opportunity—John J. Ingalis	1269	33.6	1218	41.3	2487	37.5	30	R
Opportunity—Walter Malone	183	57.7	173	63.3	356	60.5	19	S

PUPILS' READING INTERESTS: GRADES 7-9
Ts and Ss = Teachers and Schools   S = Studied in Class
IR = Independent Reading   R = Read in Class

SELECTION—AUTHOR	Boys		Girls		Total		Ts & Ss	
	No.	%	No.	%	No.	Av. %		
Opportunity—Edwin Markham	552	63.0	497	76.0	1049	69.5	21	R
Opportunity—Edward R. Sill	387	73.8	434	62.1	821	68.0	14	R
Oregon Trail, The— Arthur Guiterman	290	82.1	271	81.9	561	82.0	24	S
Oregon Trail, The— Francis Parkman	164	66.2	84	66.7	248	66.5		
Orphans, The—Wilfred W. Gibson	568	51.4	531	60.0	1099	55.7	22	R
Orpheus—Rannie B. Baker	349	48.3	321	60.7	670	54.5	43	IR
Orpheus—Frances E. Sabin	290	58.6	316	73.9	606	66.3	14	R
O, the Fierce Delight— Hamlin Garland	372	30.2	388	32.9	760	31.6	15	R
Other Wise Man, The—Henry Van Dyke	673	71.9	745	77.2	1418	74.6	67	S
Otto of the Silver Hand —Howard Pyle	175	81.4	211	73.7	386	77.6	146	IR
Ould Apple Woman, The —Thomas A. Daly	942	45.2	850	61.4	1792	53.3	21	R
Our Aromatic Uncle—H. C. Bunner	231	59.5	256	68.8	487	64.2	24	S
Our G Men—Irving Crump	331	79.0	45					
Our Guides in Genoa— Mark Twain	350	80.0	370	80.3	720	80.2	20	R
Our Responsibilities as a Nation— Theodore Roosevelt	170	62.9	175	56.9	345	59.9	20	S
Our Space Age Jets— Carroll B. Colby	169	76.6	10					
Outcasts of Poker Flat, The—Bret Harte	518	64.6	548	58.2	1066	61.4	28	S
Out Our Way (Comic Strip)	294	63.3	365	63.0	659	63.2	23	IR
Out to Old Aunt Mary's —James W. Riley	272	70.6	281	80.6	553	75.6	22	S

PUPILS' READING INTERESTS: GRADES 7-9

Ts and Ss = Teachers and Schools   S = Studied in Class

IR = Independent Reading   R = Read in Class

SELECTION—AUTHOR	Boys		Girls		Total		Ts & Ss	
	No.	%	No.	%	No.	Av. %		
Out Where the West Begins—Arthur Chapman	887	50.5	919	62.5	1806	56.5	37	R
Overcoming Handicaps— Lane	300	70.7	262	68.7	562	69.7	13	R
Overland—Unknown	292	41.3	320	44.1	612	42.7	16	R
Over the Land Is April—Robert L. Stevenson	304	50.5	350	62.4	654	56.5	23	S
Ovis Poli, The Great Horned Sheep— Theodore Roosevelt, Jr.	167	69.2	161	55.0	328	62.1	17	S
Owl and the Pussy Cat, The—Edward Lear	250	70.0	279	87.3	529	78.7	12	S
Owl Critic, The—James T. Fields	318	77.4	340	79.9	658	78.7	19	R
Owning the Earth— Earle Looker	294	73.5	309	73.8	603	73.7	11	R
Ox-Bow Incident, The—Walter Van T. Clark	187	74.6	41					
Ozymandias—Percy B. Shelley	202	31.7	238	29.2	440	30.5	15	R
Pandora—Rannie B. Baker	387	43.9	344	54.8	731	49.4	17	R
Pandora's Box— Nathaniel Hawthorne	407	52.8	859	66.9	1266	59.9	127	IR
Partners in Pluck— Ariadne Gilbert	362	47.5	333	65.8	695	56.7	15	R
Passing of the Flock, The —William Beebe	183	53.3	194	49.0	377	51.2	17	S
Pass of Thermopylae, The—Charlotte M. Yonge	330	80.8	322	68.8	652	74.8	12	R
Patchwork Quilt, The— Rachel Field	264	64.5	297	85.5	561	75.0	13	S
Pathway to Truth, The— Stephen Crane	279	38.4	287	44.9	566	41.7	12	R
Paul Bunyan—Esther Shephard	283	73.7	213	76.3	496	75.0	114	IR

PUPILS' READING INTERESTS: GRADES 7-9

Ts and Ss = Teachers and Schools   S = Studied in Class

IR = Independent Reading   R = Read in Class

SELECTION—AUTHOR	Boys		Girls		Total		Ts & Ss	
	No.	%	No.	%	No.	Av. %		
Paul Bunyan and His Great Blue Ox— Wallace Wadsworth	331	84.4	291	79.6	622	82.0	29	S
Paul Bunyan of the Great North Woods— Wallace Wadsworth	492	88.0	501	81.3	993	84.7	31	R
Paul Bunyan's Great Flapjack Griddle— Wallace Wadsworth	260	87.5	173	79.2	433	83.4	189	IR
Paul Bunyan Stories (Various authors)	1687	78.7	1620	74.0	3307	76.4	145	IR
Paul Jones—Molly E. Seawell	420	74.9	154	62.3	574	68.6		
Paul Revere's Ride— Henry W. Longfellow	1047	85.9	1045	82.9	2092	84.4	87	S
Pearl Diver, The—Victor Berge and Henry W. Lanier	153	83.3	69				98	IR
Pearl Lagoon, The— Charles B. Nordhoff	163	82.5	67				88	IR
Pear Tree, The—Edna St. V. Millay	273	39.6	324	59.3	597	49.5	17	R
Pecos Bill, Texas Cowpuncher—Harold W. Felton	211	61.4	120	55.8	331	58.6		
Pecos Bill, the Greatest Cowboy— James C. Bowman	1056	77.7	732	72.1	1788	74.9	133	IR
Pedigree—Emily Dickinson	292	52.2	295	64.6	587	58.4	16	S
Peek-a-Boo—William F. Kirk	381	52.5	377	69.5	758	61.0	17	R
Pegasus, the Winged Horse—Nathaniel Hawthorne	252	78.6	276	76.6	528	77.6	201	R
Peggy Covers the News—Emma Bugbee	20		184	66.6				
Penny Marsh (Books)— Dorothy Deming	22		385	77.0				

PUPILS' READING INTERESTS: GRADES 7-9
Ts and Ss = Teachers and Schools   S = Studied in Class
IR = Independent Reading   R = Read in Class

SELECTION—AUTHOR	Boys No.	Boys %	Girls No.	Girls %	Total No.	Total Av. %	Ts & Ss	
Penny Marsh, Public Health Nurse—Dorothy Deming	11		348	75.9				
Penrod—Booth Tarkington	461	84.3	433	85.8	894	85.1	42	S
Penrod and Sam—Booth Tarkington	471	88.7	476	88.7	947	88.7	85	S
Penrod's Busy Day—Booth Tarkington	1713	81.8	1772	90.2	3485	86.0	110	S
Perfect Tribute, The—Mary R. S. Andrews	877	81.9	881	82.0	1758	82.0	104	S
Perils of Thinking, The—Unknown	489	62.6	472	72.6	961	67.6	23	R
Persephone—Rannie B. Baker	280	58.0	290	68.8	570	63.4	14	S
Perseus—Frances E. Sabin	288	69.4	273	83.7	561	76.6	13	S
Pershing at the Front—Arthur Guiterman	531	91.1	574	89.6	1105	90.4	20	R
Pete of the Steel Mills—Herschel S. Hall	384	90.8	395	90.1	779	90.5	23	S
Peter and Wendy—James M. Barrie	149	63.8	317	76.7	466	70.3	41	R
Peterkin Papers, The—Lucretia Hale	105	66.2	331	72.7	436	69.5	153	IR
Peter Rabbit (Comic Strip)	645	66.8	739	63.3	1384	65.1	65	IR
Philosopher, A—John K. Bangs	473	47.0	472	53.4	945	50.2	19	R
Piece of Red Calico, A—Frank R. Stockton	204	75.7	242	86.8	446	81.3	22	S
Pied Piper of Hamlin, The—Robert Browning	696	71.3	717	75.5	1413	73.4	48	S
Pigs Is Pigs—Ellis P. Butler	313	91.9	307	86.3	620	89.1	11	R
Pine at Timerline, The—Harriet Monroe	472	42.4	418	44.5	890	43.5	24	R
Pine Tree Shillings, The—Nathaniel Hawthorne	558	69.1	593	74.5	1151	71.8	34	S

PUPILS' READING INTERESTS: GRADES 7-9
Ts and Ss = Teachers and Schools   S = Studied in Class
IR = Independent Reading   R = Read in Class

SELECTION—AUTHOR	Boys		Girls		Total		Ts & Ss	
	No.	%	No.	%	No.	Av. %		
Pink Dress, The—Anne Alexander	4		190	78.7				
Pinocchio—Carlo Lorenzini	1557	82.9	1858	84.8	3415	83.9	85	IR
Pioneer, The—Arthur Guiterman	232	60.3	265	58.0	497	59.2	17	R
Pioneer Boyhood in Indiana, A— Carl Sandburg	158	77.2	186	78.5	344	77.9	16	R
Pioneers! O Pioneers!— Walt Whitman	309	64.7	309	59.9	618	62.3	27	S
Pipes at Lucknow, The— John G. Whittier	1002	56.3	973	58.5	1975	57.4	47	S
Pippa's Song—Robert Browning	1266	37.0	1231	52.0	2497	44.5	49	R
Pippi Longstocking— Astrid Lindgren	65		499	72.0				
Pit and the Pendulum, The—Edgar A. Poe	973	77.4	769	69.6	1742	73.5	57	S
Plain Language from Truthful James— Bret Harte	279	69.4	341	65.1	620	67.3	29	S
Plaint of the Camel, The —Guy W. Carryl	234	68.6	208	78.1	442	73.4	15	R
Plantation Ditty, A— Frank L. Stanton	279	49.5	271	53.3	550	51.4	16	R
Plantation Memories— Irwin Russell	346	76.6	370	83.5	716	80.1	18	R
Please Don't Eat the Daisies—Jean Kerr	153	76.1	338	84.3	491	80.2		
Pledge of Allegiance, The	679	81.1	677	81.8	1356	81.5	26	R
Pobble Who Has No Toes, The—Edward Lear	863	67.8	815	77.8	1678	72.8	26	R
Pollyanna—Eleanor H. Porter	79		756	86.3			146	IR
Polonius' Advice— William Shakespeare	393	45.0	384	45.6	777	45.3	13	R
Pony Express, The— Arthur Chapman	1004	79.3	735	69.2	1739	74.3	127	IR

PUPILS' READING INTERESTS: GRADES 7-9
Ts and Ss = Teachers and Schools   S = Studied in Class
IR = Independent Reading   R = Read in Class

SELECTION—AUTHOR	Boys		Girls		Total		Ts & Ss	
	No.	%	No.	%	No.	Av. %		
Pony Express, The— Mark Twain	328	79.0	342	63.9	670	71.5	18	R
Pony Express Goes Through, The—Howard R. Driggs	446	70.4	221	58.8	667	64.6		
Pony Express Rider, The —Joseph Walker	388	88.1	417	73.3	805	80.7	14	R
Poor Benighted Hindoo, The—Cosmo Monkhouse	319	74.1	347	85.2	666	79.7	15	R
Poor Richard's Epigrams —Benjamin Franklin	297	83.5	261	85.2	558	84.4	14	R
Poor Voter on Election Day, The— John G. Whittier	517	48.1	564	50.7	1081	49.4	21	R
Popeye (Comic Strip)	1135	74.5	1091	62.1	2226	68.3	76	IR
Portrait by a Neighbor— Edna St. V. Millay	371	45.1	306	70.4	677	57.8	12	R
Portrait of a Boy— Stephen Vincent Benét	195	62.6	221	67.0	416	64.8	16	S
Powerful Eyes o' Jeremy Tait, The— Wallace Irwin	322	73.1	321	71.3	643	72.2	14	R
Power Plant, The— Berton Braley	283	42.9	299	44.8	582	43.9	13	R
Practically 17— Rosamond Du Jardin	11		422	82.8				
Prairie Schooner, The— Edwin F. Piper	392	37.6	408	37.5	800	37.6	22	R
Prayer, A—Edwin Markham	271	64.2	316	75.9	587	70.1	17	S
Prayer—Louis Untermeyer	297	57.6	340	76.2	637	66.9	17	S
Prayer for a Boy— Dorothy Plowman	287	55.2	268	68.8	555	62.0	12	R
Prayer for Rain (Indian Poem)	261	39.8	259	46.3	520	43.1	15	S
Prayer of Cyrus Brown, The—Sam W. Foss	477	74.3	468	86.9	945	80.6	19	R
Prayers of Steel—Carl Sandburg	237	47.3	296	46.8	533	47.1	15	R

PUPILS' READING INTERESTS: GRADES 7-9
Ts and Ss = Teachers and Schools   S = Studied in Class
IR = Independent Reading   R = Read in Class

SELECTION—AUTHOR	Boys		Girls		Total		Ts & Ss	
	No.	%	No.	%	No.	Av. %		
Preamble to the Constitution, The	676	68.9	690	63.6	1366	66.3	26	R
Preparedness—Edwin Markham	395	55.4	428	66.6	823	61.0	27	S
Pretty Words—Elinor Wylie	286	34.1	330	52.9	616	43.5	17	R
Prince and the Pauper, The—Mark Twain	357	79.8	422	83.8	779	81.8	50	S
Profiles in Courage—John F. Kennedy	189	71.2	191	74.9	380	73.1		
Prom Trouble—James L. Summers	8		231	75.1				
Psalm Nineteen—The Bible	421	74.5	395	85.1	816	79.8	11	R
Psalm of Life, A—Henry W. Longfellow	213	68.8	213	75.6	426	72.2	17	S
PT109: John F. Kennedy in World War II—Robert J. Donovan	207	84.3	42					
Punch, Brothers, Punch —Mark Twain	230	75.9	226	84.1	456	80.0	24	S
Pup Dog, The—Robert P. Utter	169	68.3	167	69.5	336	68.9	20	R
Puritan's Ballad, The—Elinor Wylie	369	49.6	399	56.9	768	53.3	19	R
Purloined Letter, The—Edgar A. Poe	931	63.9	962	65.2	1893	64.6	61	S
Purple Cow, The—Gelett Burgess	413	49.0	427	64.5	840	56.8	17	R
Pygmalion—Rannie B. Baker	340	64.4	308	80.4	648	72.4	14	R
Pyramus and Thisbe—John G. Saxe	266	72.9	257	86.4	523	79.7	15	R
Pyramus and Thisbe—William Shakespeare	216	71.8	238	76.9	454	74.4	13	R
Quality—John Galsworthy	318	65.7	364	73.2	682	69.5	32	S
Quality of Mercy, The—William Shakespeare	258	35.1	302	40.9	560	38.0	14	R

PUPILS' READING INTERESTS: GRADES 7-9

Ts and Ss = Teachers and Schools   S = Studied in Class

IR = Independent Reading   R = Read in Class

SELECTION—AUTHOR	Boys		Girls		Total		Ts & Ss	
	No.	%	No.	%	No.	Av. %		
Quest, The—John G. Whittier	366	59.0	343	79.3	709	69.2	24	S
Quintus Getting Well— Naomi Mitchinson	262	86.6	244	85.9	506	86.3	18	S
Rab and His Friends— John Brown	263	49.8	264	53.4	527	51.6	14	S
Rabbi Ben Ezra—Robert Browning	257	38.9	348	45.7	605	42.3	17	R
Rabbit, The—Elizabeth M. Roberts	313	65.0	347	72.5	660	68.8	17	R
Rabbit Hill—Robert Lawson	152	61.2	213	54.2	365	57.7		
Rabbit Roads—Dallas L. Sharp	222	86.0	225	73.8	447	79.9	14	R
Race for the Silver Skates, The— Mary M. Dodge	331	66.9	344	81.1	675	74.0	16	R
Raddisson—Agnes C. Laut	313	91.7	346	79.6	659	85.7	18	R
Raft, The—Robert Trumbull	252	87.1	109	80.3	361	83.7	137	IR
Raggedy Man, The— James W. Riley	488	75.0	540	87.4	1028	81.2	25	R
Raid on the Oyster Pirates, A—Jack London	256	88.9	327	73.5	583	81.2	13	S
Railroad Corral, The (Cowboy Ballad)	279	76.7	289	74.0	568	75.4	19	S
Railway Train, The— Emily Dickinson	437	52.5	358	54.3	795	53.4	21	R
Rain in Summer—Henry W. Longfellow	393	56.6	381	64.7	774	60.7	13	R
Rain or Shine (Negro Folk Song)	274	50.7	284	62.3	558	56.5	17	S
Rain Song, The—Robert Loveman	225	52.7	268	79.7	493	66.2	16	R
Rainy Day, The—Henry W. Longfellow	343	40.7	364	58.1	707	49.4	15	R
Raleigh and Elizabeth— Walter Scott	437	59.2	476	73.4	913	66.3	13	R

PUPILS' READING INTERESTS: GRADES 7-9
Ts and Ss = Teachers and Schools   S = Studied in Class
IR = Independent Reading   R = Read in Class

SELECTION—AUTHOR	Boys		Girls		Total		Ts & Ss	
	No.	%	No.	%	No.	Av. %		
Ramona—Helen H. Jackson	48		285	83.0			146	IR
Ranchman's Ride, The—Larry Chittenden	308	74.2	283	74.6	591	74.4	10	R
Ransom of Red Chief, The—O. Henry	2596	89.3	2642	85.7	5238	87.5	192	S
Rat That Could Speak, The—Charles Dickens	317	78.1	340	78.4	657	78.3	11	R
Raven, The—Edgar A. Poe	407	58.4	531	64.9	938	61.7	39	S
Real Book About Space Travel, The— Harold L. Goodwin	209	69.9	33					
Real Book of Submarines, The—Epstein and Williams	280	70.4	21					
Real Book About the Stars, The—Harold L. Goodwin	299	64.0	122	59.8	421	61.9		
Real Book of Jokes, The —Margaret Gossett	363	70.9	301	71.9	664	71.4		
Real Cowpuncher, The—Francis R. Wheeler	318	73.9	278	60.3	596	67.1	20	R
Real David Copperfield, The—Robert Graves	280	82.7	298	88.3	578	85.5	59	IR
Real Story of Lucille Ball, The—Eleanor Harris	111	69.8	270	77.4	381	73.6		
Real Thrill, The—Berton Braley	359	60.7	342	57.0	701	58.9	20	R
Rebecca—Daphne du Maurier	16		199	83.7				
Rebecca of Sunnybrook Farm—Kate D. Wiggin	362	64.4	1096	87.6	1458	76.0	84	IR
Recessional—Rudyard Kipling	589	57.9	421	64.3	1010	61.1	47	S
Recruit, The—Robert W. Chambers	187	72.7	231	71.2	418	72.0	15	R
Red-Headed League, The—A. Conan Doyle	269	79.0	267	75.5	536	77.3	26	S

PUPILS' READING INTERESTS: GRADES 7-9

Ts and Ss = Teachers and Schools   S = Studied in Class
IR = Independent Reading   R = Read in Class

SELECTION—AUTHOR	Boys		Girls		Total		Ts & Ss	
	No.	%	No.	%	No.	Av. %		
Red Horse Hill—Stephen W. Meader	93	71.5	207	72.9	300	72.2		
Red Planet, The—Robert A. Heinlein	385	77.4	128	73.8	513	75.6		
Red Pony, The—John Steinbeck	321	79.1	504	83.6	825	81.4	124	IR
Red Ryder (Comic Strip)	398	72.0	407	55.0	805	63.5	23	IR
Red Slippers—Amy Lowell	236	26.5	277	44.4	513	35.5	12	R
Red Sorcery—A. Malkus	195	66.4	169	75.1	364	70.8	17	S
Red Thread of Honor, The—Francis H. Doyle	344	62.4	394	55.2	738	58.8	11	R
Remarkable Wreck of the *Thomas Hyke*, The— Frank R. Stockton	237	92.2	221	85.1	458	88.7	13	R
Requiem—Robert L. Stevenson	367	52.3	556	73.9	923	63.1	36	S
Results and Roses— Edgar Guest	220	45.0	292	66.3	512	55.7	13	R
Retrieved Reformation, A—O. Henry	301	89.5	259	90.0	560	89.8	24	S
Return, The—David Grayson	154	74.7	174	72.7	328	73.7	25	S
Return to Constancy, A —Mary E. Chase	220	77.3	245	86.9	465	82.1	13	R
Revenge, The—Alfred Tennyson	287	76.8	288	63.5	575	70.2	37	S
Revenge of the Trees, The—Joseph Gaer	436	42.3	438	41.7	874	42.0	12	R
Revolt of Mother, The— Mary E. W. Freeman	1518	74.0	1587	89.6	3105	81.8	150	S
Reward of Merit, A— Booth Tarkington	219	85.8	263	87.8	482	86.8	28	S
Rhodora, The—Ralph W. Emerson	238	47.7	277	61.2	515	54.5	24	S
Rhoecus—James R. Lowell	135	48.1	199	60.1	334	54.1	22	S
Rhyme of the Chivalrous Shark, The— Wallace Irwin	396	79.4	439	80.4	835	79.9	22	S

PUPILS' READING INTERESTS: GRADES 7-9
Ts and Ss = Teachers and Schools   S = Studied in Class
IR = Independent Reading   R = Read in Class

SELECTION—AUTHOR	Boys		Girls		Total		Ts & Ss	
	No.	%	No.	%	No.	Av. %		
Rich Man, The—Franklin P. Adams	460	59.6	435	70.8	895	65.2	22	S
Rider of Loma Escondida, The— J. Frank Dobie	338	90.5	279	82.4	617	86.5	10	R
Riders of the Purple Sage—Zane Grey	335	81.9	298	79.4	633	80.7	121	IR
Riding Song—Unknown	516	45.8	549	55.8	1065	50.8	21	R
Rifles for Watie—Harold Keith	206	72.1	86	76.7	292	74.4		
Right Way to Read, The —Elizabeth B. Browning	202	37.1	239	40.6	441	38.9	15	R
Rikki-Tikki-Tavi— Rudyard Kipling	267	84.8	186	85.8	453	85.3	60	S
Ring of the Nibelungs, The—Rannie B. Baker	298	53.2	263	58.4	561	55.8	13	R
Rip Van Winkle— Washington Irving	1226	80.2	1216	81.3	2442	80.8	108	S
Rising in 1776, The— Thomas B. Read	345	42.5	365	44.0	710	43.3	10	R
Rising of the Moon, The —Augusta Gregory	305	72.0	336	70.0	641	71.0	14	S
Riverman, The—Stewart E. White	238	82.6	205	70.7	443	76.7	28	S
Road Race—Philip Harkins	207	81.4	24					
Road to the Pool, The— Grace H. Conkling	340	43.7	321	66.5	661	55.1	13	R
Road to Vagabondia, The —Dana Burnet	306	68.0	142	77.5	448	72.8	18	S
Roadways—John Masefield	338	48.1	270	60.2	608	54.2	14	R
Robert E. Lee—Bradley Gilman	258	75.2	245	71.2	503	73.2	160	IR
Robert E. Lee— Hermann Hagedorn	314	80.6	262	72.7	576	76.7	74	IR
Robert E. Peary— Hermann Hagedorn	230	83.7	239	78.0	469	80.9	41	IR
Robert Fulton—Alice C. Sutcliffe	281	76.7	218	71.1	499	73.9	206	IR

PUPILS' READING INTERESTS: GRADES 7-9

Ts and Ss = Teachers and Schools   S = Studied in Class

IR = Independent Reading   R = Read in Class

SELECTION—AUTHOR	Boys		Girls		Total		Ts & Ss
	No.	%	No.	%	No.	Av. %	
Robert Fulton, Boy Craftsman—Marguerite Henry	327	68.0	139	59.4	466	63.7	
Robert Lee's Boyhood—Bradley Gilman	191	79.3	180	80.8	371	80.1	15 S
Robert of Lincoln—William C. Bryant	307	63.8	341	81.1	648	72.5	25 S
Robert the Bruce—Walter Scott	261	75.9	241	71.0	502	73.5	22 S
Robina's Doll—Mary R. S. Andrews	326	54.4	368	83.6	694	69.0	23 R
Robin Hood—Amy Cruse	258	80.8	223	82.1	481	81.5	22 S
Robin Hood and Alan-a-Dale (British Ballad)	155	64.3	566	74.8	721	69.6	12 S
Robin Hood and Little John (British Ballad)	570	79.8	927	75.0	1497	77.4	34 S
Robin Hood and the Bishop (British Ballad)	168	92.3	265	78.5	433	85.4	42 IR
Robin Hood and the Butcher—Eva M. Tappan	300	89.8	303	89.1	603	89.5	11 R
Robin Hood and the Ranger (British Ballad)	383	82.2	371	68.9	754	75.6	13 R
Robin Hood Ballads, The (British Ballads)	637	90.7	406	79.3	1043	85.0	80 IR
Robin Hood, His Book—Eva M. Tappan	406	93.1	199	81.9	605	87.5	52 IR
Robin Hood Rescuing the Widow's Three Sons—(British Ballad)	161	78.3	340	76.8	501	77.6	13 S
Robin Hood's Birth (British Ballad)	125	90.8	438	75.7	563	83.3	34 IR
Robin Hood's Death and Burial (British Ballad)	382	79.6	705	78.1	1087	78.9	28 S
Robin Redbreast—William Allingham	463	46.0	395	56.7	858	51.4	23 R
Robinson Crusoe—Daniel Defoe	1939	89.7	1632	81.3	3571	85.5	125 S
Robinson Crusoe's Story—Charles E. Carryl	780	79.4	815	76.7	1595	78.1	57 S

PUPILS' READING INTERESTS: GRADES 7-9
Ts and Ss = Teachers and Schools   S = Studied in Class
IR = Independent Reading   R = Read in Class

SELECTION—AUTHOR	Boys		Girls		Total		Ts & Ss	
	No.	%	No.	%	No.	Av. %		
Rocket Ship Galileo, The —Robert A. Heinlein	176	70.5	43					
Roll a Rock Down— Henry H. Knibbs	457	67.8	473	58.1	930	63.0	21	R
Roller Skates—Ruth Sawyer	129	71.3	718	70.0	847	70.7	172	IR
Rolling Down to Old Maui (Sea Chantey)	276	48.9	274	57.1	550	53.0	17	S
Romance of a Busy Broker, The—O. Henry	344	65.6	420	76.7	764	71.2	31	S
Romancers, The— Edmond Rostand	392	63.6	473	87.0	865	75.3	24	S
Rondeau (Jenny Kissed Me)—Leigh Hunt	288	28.1	337	34.7	625	31.4	13	R
Roofs—Joyce Kilmer	216	50.0	225	71.6	441	60.8	19	S
Rose and the Gardener, The—Austin Dobson	360	60.6	347	80.0	707	70.3	39	S
Roses in the Subway— Dana Burnet	219	49.3	255	73.5	474	61.4	16	S
Round Trip into the Ocean's Depths, A— Irma Taylor	331	93.1	319	87.6	650	90.4	11	R
Rout of the White Hussars, The—Rudyard Kipling	401	78.3	361	67.3	762	72.8	10	R
Rudolph, The Headsman —Oliver W. Holmes	324	83.8	309	76.4	633	80.1	15	R
Rules for the Road— Edwin Markham	176	56.0	183	55.2	359	55.6	17	S
Runaway, The—Robert Frost	284	58.1	179	92.7	463	75.4	25	S
Runner in the Skies, A— James Oppenheim	296	16.2	324	30.6	620	23.4	13	R
Run Silent, Run Deep— Edward L. Beach	315	89.5	96	74.5	411	82.0		
Ruth—The Bible	253	31.8	472	64.6	725	48.2	14	R
Ruth—Thomas Hood	378	44.7	356	63.3	734	54.0	10	R
Sacrifice—Ralph W. Emerson	1326	41.6	1296	45.4	2622	43.5	56	R

PUPILS' READING INTERESTS: GRADES 7-9

Ts and Ss = Teachers and Schools   S = Studied in Class
IR = Independent Reading   R = Read in Class

SELECTION—AUTHOR	Boys		Girls		Total		Ts & Ss	
	No.	%	No.	%	No.	Av. %		
Sally in Our Alley—Henry Carey	285	67.2	301	86.5	586	76.9	19	R
Salute to the Trees—Henry Van Dyke	204	68.6	204	80.6	408	74.6	20	S
Same Train (Negro Folk Song)	291	40.2	298	43.5	589	41.9	19	S
Sand Creek—Stanley Vestal	398	74.5	386	78.4	784	76.5	11	R
Sandolphon—Henry W. Longfellow	212	57.8	201	67.4	413	62.6	14	S
Sandpiper, The—Celia Thaxter	469	52.8	468	63.5	937	58.2	41	S
Sands of Dee, The—Charles Kingsley	803	53.2	827	65.2	1630	59.2	30	R
Santa Fe Trail, The—Samuel Adams	279	64.9	104	63.0	383	64.0		
Santa Filomena—Henry W. Longfellow	288	67.4	329	74.9	617	71.2	26	S
Sapphire Signet, The—Augusta H. Seaman	66		316	90.2			83	IR
Sara Crew—Frances H. Burnett	64		417	87.2			122	IR
Satan the War Dog—Nora Baynes	361	86.8	304	79.6	665	83.2	24	S
Saturdays, The—Elizabeth Enright	41		298	72.0				
Sayings of Lincoln—Louise Lamprey	279	67.7	306	65.0	585	66.4	14	R
Science Selections (7)	958	45.6	972	42.3	1930	44.0	40	R
Science for the Young—Wallace Irwin	239	81.0	265	83.0	504	82.0	14	R
Scotty Bill—William H. Davies	537	56.1	621	55.0	1158	55.6	19	R
Scrub Quarterback, The—Jesse L. Williams	224	86.3	244	70.1	468	78.2	14	S
Sea, The—Eva L. Ogden	621	50.4	629	65.5	1250	58.0	22	R
Sea Around Us, The—Rachel Carson	157	72.0	77					
Sea Distances—Alfred Noyes	363	39.3	397	41.9	760	40.6	18	R

PUPILS' READING INTERESTS: GRADES 7-9
Ts and Ss = Teachers and Schools   S = Studied in Class
IR = Independent Reading   R = Read in Class

SELECTION—AUTHOR	Boys		Girls		Total		Ts & Ss	
	No.	%	No.	%	No.	Av. %		
Sea-Fever—John Masefield	1357	68.7	932	60.6	2289	64.7	71	S
Sea Gypsy, The—Richard Hovey	431	57.3	327	60.1	758	58.7	30	S
Sea Serpent Chantey, The—Vachel Lindsay	436	60.4	484	47.8	920	54.1	18	R
Sea Wolf, The—Jack London	525	83.3	113	70.8	638	77.1		
Secret Cargo—Howard Pease	237	69.8	148	67.9	385	68.9		
Secret Garden, The—Frances H. Burnett	324	77.6	467	94.8	791	86.2	31	S
Secret of the Machines, The—Rudyard Kipling	338	54.7	349	51.9	687	53.3	13	R
See Here, Private Hargrove—Marion Hargrove	227	85.0	180	82.2	407	83.6		
Seeing the Elephant—Dan Totheroh	401	80.2	370	92.7	771	86.5	15	R
Seein' Things—Eugene Field	201	71.6	236	82.0	437	76.8	21	S
Semaphore—Joseph Husband	326	63.7	345	52.2	671	58.0	12	R
Senior Prom—Rosamond Du Jardin	8		345	83.8				
Senior Year—Anne Emery	11		510	83.6				
September—Helen H. Jackson	333	57.5	390	76.4	723	67.0	19	R
September Gale—Oliver W. Holmes	400	73.5	411	82.6	811	78.1	20	R
Service, The—Burges Johnson	209	54.3	233	56.9	442	55.6	17	S
Seventeen—Booth Tarkington	126	74.2	457	84.8	583	79.5	76	IR
Seventeenth Summer—Maureen Daly	38		738	84.2				
Shaggy, the Horse from Wyoming—Russell G. Carter	160	83.8	263	88.2	423	86.0	87	IR

PUPILS' READING INTERESTS: GRADES 7-9
Ts and Ss = Teachers and Schools   S = Studied in Class
IR = Independent Reading   R = Read in Class

SELECTION—AUTHOR	Boys		Girls		Total		Ts & Ss
	No.	%	No.	%	No.	Av. %	
Shane—Jack Schaefer	292	82.5	175	75.7	467	79.1		
Shanty Boy—James Stevens	251	77.1	243	71.4	494	74.3	16	R
Shasta Daisy, The—Slusser, Williams, and Beeson	304	40.5	290	58.3	594	49.4	14	R
Shasta of the Wolves—Olaf Baker	187	87.4	139	83.1	326	85.3	112	IR
Sheener—Ben A. Williams	353	76.6	326	84.3	679	80.5	9	S
Shepherd of King Admetus, The— James R. Lowell	668	46.4	710	53.5	1378	50.0	67	S
Shepherd's Psalm, The— The Bible	683	81.0	825	82.2	1508	81.6	33	R
Sheridan's Ride—Thomas B. Read	378	79.0	418	69.3	796	74.2	26	R
Sheriff Roosevelt and the Thieves— Hermann Hagedorn	440	84.3	444	70.3	884	77.3	17	R
Shining Streets of London, The— Alfred Noyes	293	39.2	321	55.3	614	47.3	14	R
Shipment of Mute Fate, A—Martin Storm	326	91.0	324	87.2	650	89.1	13	R
Ship of State, The— Henry W. Longfellow	249	48.0	276	58.3	525	53.2	16	R
Ships in the Sky—Lucy Larcom	213	37.8	268	48.9	481	43.4	15	R
Side Glances (Comic Strip)	262	74.0	289	79.4	551	76.7	27	IR
Siege of Berlin, The— Alphonse Daudet	361	59.1	440	63.8	801	61.5	15	S
Silas Marner—George Eliot	153	76.1	167	92.5	320	84.3	20	S
Silent World, The— Cousteau and Dumas	218	81.7	66					
Silver—Walter de la Mare	218	45.4	253	65.2	471	55.3	13	R

PUPILS' READING INTERESTS: GRADES 7-9
Ts and Ss = Teachers and Schools   S = Studied in Class
IR = Independent Reading   R = Read in Class

SELECTION—AUTHOR	Boys		Girls		Total		Ts & Ss	
	No.	%	No.	%	No.	Av. %		
SilverBlaze—A. Conan Doyle	246	87.8	161	81.7	407	84.8	20	S
Silver Chief, Dog of the North—John S. O'Brien	617	93.0	470	90.1	1087	91.6	76	IR
Silver Lining, The— Constance D'Arcy Mackay	605	61.5	648	74.5	1253	68.0	17	R
Silver Mine, The—Selma Lagerlöf	227	63.2	390	64.5	617	63.9	17	R
Silver Pennies—Blanche Thompson	69		296	63.5			81	IR
Similies	428	54.3	446	61.8	874	58.1	20	R
Simon Legree—a Negro Sermon—Vachel Lindsay	752	77.2	795	72.4	1547	74.8	40	S
Sinbad the Sailor— Arabian Nights	280	78.6	314	73.7	594	76.2	25	R
Singing Leaves, The— James R. Lowell	1533	53.6	1545	78.2	3078	65.9	139	S
Sire de Malètroit's Door, The— Robert L. Stevenson	838	59.8	701	64.5	1539	62.2	60	S
Sir Galahad—Alfred Tennyson	438	72.9	453	71.7	891	72.3	37	S
Sir Patrick Spens (British Ballad)	564	54.8	1056	66.8	1620	60.8	37	S
Sis' Becky's Pickaninny— C. W. Chesnutt	247	59.1	235	69.4	482	64.3	14	S
Six Sorts of Smells— Edwin E. Slosson	399	31.6	364	39.7	763	35.7	9	R
Skaters, The—John G. Fletcher	406	31.3	424	37.9	830	34.6	15	R
Skeleton in Armor, The —Henry W. Longfellow	1529	71.0	1504	70.1	3033	70.6	143	S
Skiing Party, The—Cory Ford	312	75.0	305	75.7	617	75.4	11	R
Skipper—Norman Duncan	190	72.9	265	72.8	455	72.9	148	IR
Skipper Ireson's Ride— John G. Whittier	531	64.7	605	67.5	1136	66.1	34	S
Skippy (Comic Strip)	281	59.6	376	55.5	657	57.6	23	IR

PUPILS' READING INTERESTS: GRADES 7-9

Ts and Ss = Teachers and Schools   S = Studied in Class
IR = Independent Reading   R = Read in Class

SELECTION—AUTHOR	Boys		Girls		Total		Ts & Ss	
	No.	%	No.	%	No.	Av. %		
Sky-Born Music, A—Ralph W. Emerson	375	39.3	362	51.2	737	45.3	10	R
Sky Boy—Clara Lambert	332	35.5	318	29.6	650	32.6	13	R
Slave, The—James Oppenheim	253	48.2	259	50.8	512	49.5	15	R
Sleeping Outdoors—Frederick L. Allen	392	79.6	413	78.9	805	79.3	19	S
Sleet—Clara Lambert	347	55.8	329	72.6	676	64.2	15	R
Slom Season, The—Selma Lagerlöf	379	57.4	382	69.2	761	63.3	15	R
Smack in School, The—William P. Palmer	255	70.6	284	85.4	539	78.0	15	R
Smells (Junior)—Christopher Morley	344	55.8	364	70.9	708	63.4	24	R
Smilin' Jack (Comic Strip)	1198	81.6	1192	80.7	2390	81.2	77	IR
Smoky—Will James	378	87.8	273	83.3	651	85.6	68	IR
Snake, The—Stephen Crane	351	65.0	399	48.9	750	57.0	15	R
Snake, The—Emily Dickinson	327	45.8	464	56.0	791	50.9	21	S
Snakes—Herbert Zim	258	68.4	35					
Snark, The—Lewis Carroll	302	36.6	335	44.5	637	40.6	12	R
Sneezles—A. A. Milne	397	64.4	380	70.4	777	67.4	17	R
Snow, The—Emily Dickinson	274	52.2	326	62.9	600	57.6	16	S
Snow-Bound—John G. Whittier	1082	64.1	1148	72.9	2230	68.5	112	S
Snow Dog—Jim Kjelgaard	119	74.8	165	73.6	284	74.2		
Snow Song—Edith B. Price	423	36.6	443	54.6	866	45.6	24	R
Snow Storm, The—Ralph W. Emerson	1006	45.2	1032	47.5	2038	46.4	63	S
Snow-White and the Seven Dwarfs— Grimm Brothers	1092	52.2	1909	69.6	3001	60.9		

PUPILS' READING INTERESTS: GRADES 7-9
Ts and Ss = Teachers and Schools   S = Studied in Class
IR = Independent Reading   R = Read in Class

SELECTION—AUTHOR	Boys		Girls		Total		Ts & Ss	
	No.	%	No.	%	No.	Av. %		
Society upon the Stanislaus, The—Bret Harte	614	59.6	550	54.8	1164	57.2	20	R
So Handy (Sea Chantey)	274	51.1	277	50.5	551	50.8	17	S
Sohrab and Rustum—Matthew Arnold	437	64.9	495	60.8	932	62.9	19	S
Soldier, The—Rupert Brooke	438	64.8	362	64.4	800	64.6	37	S
Solitary Reaper, The—William Wordsworth	614	41.3	598	56.9	1212	49.1	20	R
Solitude—James Cox	280	48.2	258	60.7	538	54.5	12	R
Solitude—Harold Munro	180	50.0	176	58.2	356	54.1	16	S
Somebody's Mother—Unknown	314	81.5	327	94.3	641	87.9	14	R
Some Call Him Brave—S. Omar Barker	387	75.8	414	70.2	801	73.0	26	S
Some Snug Winter Beds—Dallas L. Sharp	335	43.6	343	42.0	678	42.8	13	R
Song—Rupert Brooke	478	37.1	475	53.2	953	45.2	22	R
Song Against Children—Aline Kilmer	343	64.4	313	81.0	656	72.7	17	R
Song for a Little House, A—Christopher Morley	341	47.1	376	74.5	717	60.8	22	S
Song in France, A—Walter Henry	587	85.3	622	83.4	1209	84.4	20	R
Song in the Songless, A—George Meredith	417	22.5	390	32.7	807	27.6	10	R
Song My Paddle Sings, The—Josephine Johnson	304	56.4	276	65.4	580	60.9	21	S
Song of Bernadette, The—Franz Werfel	182	82.7	490	92.7	672	87.7	71	IR
Song of Marion's Men, The—William C. Bryant	283	67.8	264	65.9	547	66.9	22	S
Song of Sherwood, A—Alfred Noyes	413	63.0	199	65.1	612	64.1	16	R
Song of Summer—Paul L. Dunbar	491	56.2	529	66.0	1020	61.1	30	R
Song of the Camp, The—Bayard Taylor	644	64.5	637	66.0	1281	65.3	56	S

PUPILS' READING INTERESTS: GRADES 7-9

Ts and Ss = Teachers and Schools   S = Studied in Class
IR = Independent Reading   R = Read in Class

SELECTION—AUTHOR	Boys		Girls		Total		Ts & Ss	
	No.	%	No.	%	No.	Av. %		
Song of the Chattahoochee, The— Sidney Lanier	701	45.2	696	53.2	1397	49.2	56	S
Song of the Western Men, The—R. S. Hawker	334	65.0	318	56.4	652	60.7	13	R
Songs for My Mother— Anna H. Branch	563	57.6	447	79.3	1010	68.5	34	S
Songs in the Garden of the House of God (Indian Poem)	256	37.5	257	51.2	513	44.4	15	S
Sonnets in a Lodging House—Christopher Morley	337	63.7	319	71.5	656	67.6	14	R
Sonny's Christenin'— Ruth McE. Stuart	221	67.2	269	68.0	490	67.6	22	S
Sorority Girl—Anne Emery	9		482	79.5				
Soul of Jeanne D'Arc, The— Theodosia Garrison	301	64.0	323	74.0	624	69.0	28	S
Souls—Fannie S. Davis	277	37.0	272	64.2	549	50.6	16	S
Space Cadet—Robert A. Heinlein	168	70.5	36					
" 'Spacially Jim"—Bessie Morgan	468	85.4	521	92.9	989	89.2	20	R
Spacious Firmament on High, The— Joseph Addison	325	35.5	339	53.5	664	44.5	15	S
Spanish Johnny—Willa Cather	490	50.4	507	53.2	997	51.8	24	R
Spanish Waters—John Masefield	217	76.0	170	69.1	387	72.6	19	S
Spark Neglected, A—Leo Tolstoy	886	87.2	763	88.9	1649	88.1	18	R
Spartacus to the Gladiators—Elijah Kellogg	397	63.1	405	53.2	802	58.2	23	R
Specter Bridegroom, The —Washington Irving	308	56.3	310	74.4	618	65.4	28	S

PUPILS' READING INTERESTS: GRADES 7-9
Ts and Ss = Teachers and Schools   S = Studied in Class
IR = Independent Reading   R = Read in Class

SELECTION—AUTHOR	Boys		Girls		Total		Ts & Ss	
	No.	%	No.	%	No.	Av. %		
Speed of Light, The— Richard T. Cox	249	36.8	288	24.3	537	30.6	14	R
Spelling Match, The— Ralph Connor	306	65.5	315	76.8	621	71.2	10	R
Spending a Day in an Igloo— Marie A. Peary	512	89.6	565	93.6	1077	91.6	19	R
Spider and the Fly, The —Mary Howitt	392	67.7	418	80.4	810	74.1	15	R
Spider Boy—Clara Lambert	329	41.2	317	35.6	646	38.4	13	R
Spires of Oxford, The— Winifred M. Letts	1049	66.7	984	78.8	2033	72.8	84	S
Spirit of St. Louis, The—Charles A. Lindbergh	733	80.9	329	75.2	1062	78.1		
Spirit of the Birch, The— Arthur Ketchum	304	43.1	309	63.8	613	53.5	21	S
Spot, the Dog That Broke the Rules— Carolyn S. Bailey	304	98.0	345	95.8	649	96.9	13	R
Spreading the News— Augusta Gregory	362	61.9	404	61.5	766	61.7	26	S
Spring—Henry Timrod	377	37.8	437	55.1	814	46.5	16	R
Spy, The—James F. Cooper	289	74.7	187	78.3	476	76.5	99	IR
Squirrels and Other Fur Bearers— John Burroughs	162	70.7	142	66.2	304	68.5	92	IR
Stairways and Gardens— Ella W. Wilcox	421	28.5	391	46.3	812	37.4	11	R
Stars—Sara Teasdale	515	40.1	555	60.9	1070	50.5	31	S
Star-Spangled Banner, The—Francis S. Key	621	78.6	595	85.8	1216	82.2	19	R
Steamer Child, The— Elsie Singmaster	273	66.3	230	83.5	503	74.9	12	R
Steam Shovel, The— Eunice Tietjens	330	48.3	381	36.5	711	42.4	19	R
Stethoscope Song, The— Oliver W. Holmes	265	64.5	278	71.6	543	68.1	14	R
Stickeen—John Muir	131	77.5	185	76.0	316	76.8	127	IR

PUPILS' READING INTERESTS: GRADES 7-9

Ts and Ss = Teachers and Schools   S = Studied in Class
IR = Independent Reading   R = Read in Class

SELECTION—AUTHOR	Boys		Girls		Total		Ts & Ss	
	No.	%	No.	%	No.	Av. %		
Stopping by Woods on a Snowy Evening— Robert Frost	243	50.8	265	55.7	508	53.3	13	R
Storekeeper, The— George Abbe	392	51.5	353	53.4	745	52.5	15	R
Stormalong—Alan J. Villiers	207	66.9	152	60.9	359	63.9		
Storming of Torquilstone, The— Mildred A. Butler	253	60.9	244	49.6	497	55.3	17	S
Story of a Bad Boy— Thomas B. Aldrich	254	80.9	325	76.2	579	78.6	72	IR
Story of Aboo Seer and Aboo Keer— Arabian Nights	172	81.7	184	80.2	356	81.0	44	IR
Story of a Stone, The— David S. Jordan	297	55.1	309	62.1	606	58.6	12	R
Story of a Thousand Year Pine—Enos A. Mills	371	71.8	361	62.1	732	67.0	13	R
Story of Captain Kidd, The—Henry Gilbert	371	87.7	416	75.5	787	81.6	22	R
Story of Clara Barton, The—Jeannette C. Nolan	35		221	78.7				
Story of Davy Crockett, The— Enid Meadowcroft	895	73.7	533	62.2	1428	68.0		
Story of D-Day, The— Bruce Blivin	479	87.5	90	75.0	569	81.3		
Story of Gareth, The— Thomas Malory	319	82.0	332	78.3	651	80.2	30	S
Story of Joan of Arc, The —Andrew Lang	364	76.8	448	85.2	812	81.0	44	R
Story of King Arthur and His Knights, The— Howard Pyle	850	85.2	572	74.7	1422	80.0	68	S
Story of Mankind— Hendrik W. Van Loon	201	75.6	200	69.3	401	72.5	275	IR
Story of My Life, The— Helen Keller	119	79.4	481	89.9	600	84.7	122	IR
Story of Raven, The (Indian Mythology)	289	51.7	294	50.7	583	51.2	13	S

PUPILS' READING INTERESTS: GRADES 7-9
Ts and Ss = Teachers and Schools   S = Studied in Class
IR = Independent Reading   R = Read in Class

SELECTION—AUTHOR	Boys		Girls		Total		Ts & Ss	
	No.	%	No.	%	No.	Av. %		
Story of the Salmon, The —Rex Beach	309	62.5	308	48.9	617	55.7	17	R
Story of the U.S. Marines, The—George P. Hunt	239	79.3	15					
Story of Thomas Alva Edison, The— Enid Meadowcroft	319	77.1	141	69.1	460	73.1		
Storyteller, The—H. H. Munro	428	52.7	513	68.7	941	60.7	63	R
Stowaway to the Mushroom Planet— Eleanor Cameron	239	72.2	201	70.1	440	71.2		
Stranger, The—Elizabeth M. Roberts	289	45.3	251	49.6	540	47.5	13	R
Strawberry Girl—Lois Lenski	59		892	77.2			130	IR
Street Lamps—Harry Kemp	445	28.4	515	47.4	960	37.9	23	R
Street Rod—Henry G. Felsen	279	86.0	49					
Strictly Germ Proof— Arthur Guiterman	458	75.9	426	80.5	884	78.2	26	S
Stuart Little—E. B. White	104	69.2	266	78.2	370	73.7		
Student Song—Robert L. Stevenson	269	47.2	237	57.2	506	52.2	20	S
Submarine—Edward L. Beach	175	80.0	13					
Sue Barton (Books)— Helen D. Boylston	49		675	93.2			58	IR
Suffering—Nathalia Crane	198	80.1	197	84.3	395	82.2	16	S
Summer Hail—Edith Wyatt	287	34.7	311	42.9	598	38.8	12	R
Sun, The—Emily Dickinson	378	54.2	357	74.2	735	64.2	10	R
Sunrise—Katherine Kosmak	349	34.1	377	58.5	726	46.3	16	R
Sunset—Gelett Burgess	845	44.4	873	55.2	1718	49.8	25	R

PUPILS' READING INTERESTS: GRADES 7-9
Ts and Ss = Teachers and Schools   S = Studied in Class
IR = Independent Reading   R = Read in Class

SELECTION—AUTHOR	Boys		Girls		Total		Ts & Ss	
	No.	%	No.	%	No.	Av. %		
Sunset—Emily Dickinson	468	43.1	496	56.1	964	49.6	20	S
Superman (Comic Strip)	975	75.5	824	72.2	1799	73.9	71	IR
Swamp Fox of the Revolution, The— Marion M. Brown	482	80.9	216	70.6	698	75.8		
Sweet Peas—John Keats	1054	27.8	1015	40.4	2069	34.1	46	R
Swimming with a Bear— Joaquin Miller	331	81.9	341	79.6	672	80.8	13	R
Swing Low, Sweet Chariot (Negro Spiritual)	281	55.2	288	61.3	569	58.3	14	R
Swiss Family Robinson, The—Johann D. Wyss	523	84.4	499	84.7	1022	84.6	51	IR
Switch in Lullabies, A— Grantland Rice	379	59.5	414	68.2	793	63.9	12	R
Sword of Robert E. Lee, The—Abram J. Ryan	278	64.7	317	64.2	595	64.5	19	S
Sympathy for Monday— Arthur Guiterman	281	39.0	286	66.1	567	52.6	13	R
Symphony Pathetique— Ruth Mitchell	286	33.2	308	45.6	594	39.4	15	R
Symptoms—Jerome K. Jerome	367	79.3	319	86.7	686	83.0	26	R
Tabby's Tablecloth— Louisa M. Alcott	243	86.0	250	94.0	493	90.0	14	R
Tad Lincoln's Father— Julia T. Bayne	300	82.7	293	91.0	593	86.9	14	R
Tale of Three Truants, A —Bret Harte	340	88.4	327	87.6	667	88.0	13	R
Tale of Two Cities, A— Charles Dickens	237	78.1	346	75.0	583	76.6	84	IR
Tale of Two Lumber Towns, A—Joseph Gaer	473	78.6	489	70.2	962	74.4	26	R
Tales—Edgar A. Poe	221	84.8	187	86.1	408	85.5		
Tales from Shakespeare —Charles and Mary Lamb	137	73.7	272	79.2	409	76.5	108	IR
Tales of a Wayside Inn— Henry W. Longfellow	198	67.7	229	78.4	427	73.1	17	S
Tamerlane—Bigelow Neale	292	84.8	291	67.7	583	76.3	18	R

PUPILS' READING INTERESTS: GRADES 7-9
Ts and Ss = Teachers and Schools   S = Studied in Class
IR = Independent Reading   R = Read in Class

SELECTION—AUTHOR	Boys		Girls		Total		Ts & Ss	
	No.	%	No.	%	No.	Av. %		
Taming of Animals, The —Peter C. Mitchell	347	58.1	360	42.0	707	50.1	15	R
Tam O'Shanter—Robert Burns	451	52.0	451	48.1	902	50.1	16	R
Tampa Robins—Sidney Lanier	192	54.2	186	57.0	378	55.6	23	S
Tanganyika Lions— Martin Johnson	322	90.4	243	76.5	565	83.5	24	S
Tanglewood Tales— Nathaniel Hawthorne	215	72.3	381	74.7	596	73.5	132	IR
Tarry Buccaneer, The— John Masefield	484	59.1	476	54.7	960	56.9	30	S
Tartary—Walter de la Mare	305	31.6	326	49.8	631	40.7	12	R
Tarzan (Book)—Edgar R. Burroughs	1419	86.8	789	81.9	2208	84.4	206	IR
Tarzan (Comic Strip)	1011	74.7	858	59.2	1869	67.0	78	IR
Tarzan (Movies)	2024	86.1	2013	81.3	4037	83.7	117	
Teahouse of the August Moon, The—John Patrick	56		146	78.8				
Tea Trader, The—Daniel Henderson	350	48.7	353	58.4	703	53.6	16	R
Ted Williams Story, The —Schoor and Gilfond	183	75.1	26					
Telling the Bees—John G. Whittier	286	48.4	295	68.8	581	58.6	26	S
Tempest, The—Charles Lamb	294	63.8	315	74.3	609	69.1	23	R
Tennessee's Partner— Bret Harte	1104	73.2	1049	61.2	2153	67.2	81	S
Ten Trails—Ernest T. Seton	505	62.0	462	51.9	967	57.0	9	R
Terry and the Pirates (Comic Strip)	422	79.0	495	79.6	917	79.3	23	IR
Test Pilot—James Collins	263	71.9	28					
Tewkesbury Road—John Masefield	410	57.8	303	64.5	713	61.2	24	S
Texas Cowboy, The— (Cowboy Ballad)	657	77.2	697	78.3	1354	77.8	27	R

PUPILS' READING INTERESTS: GRADES 7-9
Ts and Ss = Teachers and Schools   S = Studied in Class
IR = Independent Reading   R = Read in Class

SELECTION—AUTHOR	Boys		Girls		Total		Ts & Ss	
	No.	%	No.	%	No.	Av. %		
Texas Trains and Trails—Mary Austin	261	71.3	318	65.7	579	68.5	16	S
Thanatopsis—William C. Bryant	353	41.8	317	53.6	670	47.7	25	S
That Year at Lincoln High—Joseph Golcomb	204	91.9	171	92.1	375	92.0	19	S
Theodore Roosevelt—Hermann Hagedorn	206	84.7	128	81.3	334	83.0	67	IR
Theodore Roosevelt's Letters to His Children	360	55.3	413	62.2	773	58.8	30	IR
There Is a Tide—William Shakespeare	381	36.9	375	41.2	756	39.1	13	R
There Once Was a Packer of York—Unknown	447	71.7	438	80.1	885	75.9	23	R
There's a Sound of Drums and Trumpets—John Dos Passos	310	28.7	327	41.0	637	34.9	12	R
There She Blows (Sea Chantey)	273	67.8	280	57.5	553	62.7	17	S
There's Room at the Top—Lila T. Elder	492	55.2	504	55.2	996	55.2	23	R
There Was an Old Man in a Tree— Edward Lear	426	55.8	463	58.2	889	57.0	16	R
*There Was an Old Man of Blackheath—Unknown	430	80.2	441	87.4	871	83.8	19	R
There Was an Old Man of Calcutta— Edward Lear	861	65.3	888	75.7	1749	70.5	32	R
There Was an Old Man of Cape Horn— Edward Lear	425	50.8	457	46.6	882	48.7	16	R
There Was an Old Man of Coblenz— Edward Lear	306	67.3	307	76.4	613	71.9	10	R
There Was an Old Man of Peru—Edward Lear	445	77.4	448	85.0	893	81.2	19	R

*There is another limerick on Blackheath by Lear.

PUPILS' READING INTERESTS: GRADES 7-9
Ts and Ss = Teachers and Schools   S = Studied in Class
IR = Independent Reading   R = Read in Class

SELECTION—AUTHOR	Boys		Girls		Total		Ts & Ss	
	No.	%	No.	%	No.	Av. %		
There Was an Old Man of Tarentum— Edward Lear	419	69.1	422	82.8	841	76.0	17	R
There Was an Old Man of Thermopylae— Edward Lear	305	70.3	310	79.0	615	74.7	10	R
There Was an Old Man Who Said How— Edward Lear	965	43.1	1079	46.3	2044	44.7	35	R
There Was an Old Man With a Beard— Edward Lear	1518	76.3	1591	79.2	3109	77.8	65	R
There Was a Tall Russian —Harry A. Rothrock	274	71.2	307	85.2	581	78.2	19	R
There Was a Young Lady Named Perkins— Unknown	451	79.5	430	87.0	881	83.3	23	R
There Was a Young Lady of Butte—Edward Lear	305	67.5	312	79.8	617	73.7	10	R
There Was a Young Lady of Lynn—Unknown	456	75.5	462	85.7	918	80.6	18	R
There Was a Young Lady of Norway— Edward Lear	425	50.9	458	50.8	883	50.9	16	R
There Was a Young Lady Whose Eyes— Edward Lear	381	41.6	430	42.3	811	42.0	15	R
There Was a Young Man of Bengal— Unknown	409	74.4	431	86.0	840	80.2	17	R
These Happy Golden Years—Laura I. Wilder	8		265	81.3				
Theseus—Frances E. Sabin	338	69.5	334	73.2	672	71.4	15	R
They Bring Me Back Alive—Bierne Lay, Jr.	420	96.0	396	85.9	816	91.0	12	R
They Were Expendable —William L. White	599	92.6	361	82.6	960	87.6	130	IR
Thicker Than Water—R. H. Barbour and G. R. Osborne	271	78.4	310	89.0	581	83.7	14	R

PUPILS' READING INTERESTS: GRADES 7-9
Ts and Ss = Teachers and Schools   S = Studied in Class
IR = Independent Reading   R = Read in Class

SELECTION—AUTHOR	Boys		Girls		Total		Ts & Ss	
	No.	%	No.	%	No.	Av. %		
Thimble Summer—Elizabeth Enright	22		306	79.9			124	IR
Thing of Beauty, A—John Keats	420	29.3	397	42.6	817	36.0	10	R
Thinker, The—Berton Braley	731	75.4	374	63.5	1105	69.5	37	S
Thin Man, The—Dashiell Hammett	149	76.8	154	73.4	303	75.1		
Third Ingredient, The—O. Henry	714	66.0	863	89.0	1577	77.5	41	S
Thirty Seconds Over Tokyo—Ted W. Lawson	596	93.6	502	92.7	1098	93.2	71	IR
This Singing World—Louis Untermeyer	174	68.1	342	68.7	516	68.4	210	IR
Thomas A. Edison's First Workshop— Francis A. Jones	269	86.8	241	80.3	510	83.6	51	IR
Thomas Edison Himself —William H. Meadowcroft	237	64.1	211	61.1	448	62.6	18	S
Thomas the Rhymer (British Ballad)	293	45.9	433	60.2	726	53.1	21	S
Thomson Green and Harriet Hale— William S. Gilbert	241	69.9	237	81.6	478	75.8	13	R
Those Two Boys—Franklin P. Adams	321	85.4	294	89.1	615	87.3	15	R
Thoughts While Flying—Ruth Nichols	299	45.7	326	31.7	625	38.7	13	R
Three-Alarm Dogs—Paul W. Kearney	338	94.8	318	93.1	656	94.0	12	R
Three Fishers, The—Charles Kingsley	415	39.2	437	48.4	852	43.8	14	R
Three Musketeers, The—Alexandre Dumas	321	85.4	162	75.9	483	80.7	61	IR
Three Wishes, The—Constance D'Arcy Mackay	509	61.0	640	73.4	1149	67.2	24	R
Throstle, The—Alfred Tennyson	308	51.1	287	57.1	595	54.1	24	S

PUPILS' READING INTERESTS: GRADES 7-9
Ts and Ss = Teachers and Schools   S = Studied in Class
IR = Independent Reading   R = Read in Class

SELECTION—AUTHOR	Boys		Girls		Total		Ts & Ss	
	No.	%	No.	%	No.	Av. %		
Through the Heart of Africa—Irma Taylor	309	91.7	373	84.0	682	87.9	12	R
Through the Looking Glass—Lewis Carroll	174	60.3	418	71.3	592	65.8	76	IR
Thunderhead—Mary O'Hara	550	93.2	651	92.9	1201	93.1	65	IR
Thundering Herd, The—Clarence Hawkes	638	81.8	586	68.9	1224	75.4	42	S
Thunder Road—William C. Gault	143	84.5	30					
Ticket Agent, The—Edmund Leamy	511	42.9	491	50.7	1002	46.8	20	R
Tillie the Toiler (Comic Strip)	344	61.2	524	77.9	868	69.6	24	IR
Time Clock, The—Charles H. Towne	302	34.8	322	56.7	624	45.8	12	R
Time-Telling by Stone Icicles— Edwin E. Slosson	375	47.7	348	47.6	723	47.7	9	R
Timothy's Quest—Unknown	111	76.6	211	69.0	322	72.8	260	IR
Tired Tim—Walter de la Mare	599	61.9	563	70.8	1162	66.4	25	R
T-Model Tommy—Stephen Meader	420	82.6	223	74.9	643	78.8	222	IR
To a Blockhead—Alexander Pope	563	50.4	516	62.2	1079	56.3	18	R
To a Louse—Robert Burns	345	41.6	374	48.7	719	45.2	14	R
To a Locomotive in Winter—Walt Whitman	312	36.2	299	29.1	611	32.7	14	R
To a Mountain Daisy—Robert Burns	231	57.8	279	75.6	510	66.7	17	S
To a Mouse—Robert Burns	106	57.1	196	62.8	302	60.0	16	S
To a New World—C. W. Hodges	311	78.8	334	75.2	645	77.0	16	R
To a Pack Horse—Robert V. Carr	383	78.6	382	81.3	765	80.0	13	R

PUPILS' READING INTERESTS: GRADES 7-9
Ts and Ss = Teachers and Schools   S = Studied in Class
IR = Independent Reading   R = Read in Class

SELECTION—AUTHOR	Boys		Girls		Total		Ts & Ss	
	No.	%	No.	%	No.	Av. %		
To a Post Office Inkwell —Christopher Morley	308	58.1	280	74.5	588	66.3	16	R
To a Skylark—Percy B. Shelley	350	35.1	330	47.7	680	41.4	33	S
To a Skylark—William Wordsworth	906	38.4	916	48.3	1822	43.4	49	R
To a Telegraph Pole— Louis Untermeyer	293	47.3	326	49.8	619	48.6	14	R
To Autumn—John Keats	337	35.9	339	48.2	676	42.1	18	R
To a Waterfowl—William C. Bryant	737	44.3	736	54.8	1473	49.6	62	S
To Build a Fire—Jack London	368	88.5	389	77.6	757	83.1	22	R
Toby Tyler—James Otis	581	76.9	692	77.0	1273	77.0		
To Helen—Edgar A. Poe	521	36.1	506	51.6	1027	43.9	28	S
Tom Brown's School Days—Thomas Hughes	855	76.7	820	76.1	1675	76.4	87	S
Tom Cat, The—Don Marquis	545	63.6	515	65.5	1060	64.6	29	R
Tom Lincoln's Son— Nancy B. Turner	416	70.4	363	74.4	779	72.4	15	R
Tommy—Rudyard Kipling	265	80.0	279	86.0	544	83.0	19	R
Tom Sawyer—Mark Twain	928	95.3	860	93.9	1788	94.6	104	S
Tom Sawyer Abroad— Mark Twain	304	90.5	205	85.9	509	88.2	61	IR
Tom Swift (Books)— Victor Appleton	346	83.8	112	73.7	458	78.8	78	IR
Toomai of the Elephants —Rudyard Kipling	255	76.5	194	73.8	449	75.2	65	S
Too Much Horse—Ellis P. Butler	284	84.0	300	93.8	584	88.9	15	R
Torch of Life, The— Henry Newbolt	225	45.1	236	41.5	461	43.3	15	R
To Tell Your Love— Mary S. Stolz	11		177	65.5				
To the Cuckoo—William Wordsworth	229	50.4	251	60.2	480	55.3	13	S

PUPILS' READING INTERESTS: GRADES 7-9
Ts and Ss = Teachers and Schools   S = Studied in Class
IR = Independent Reading   R = Read in Class

SELECTION—AUTHOR	Boys		Girls		Total		Ts & Ss	
	No.	%	No.	%	No.	Av. %		
To the Dandelion—James R. Lowell	598	39.0	609	53.8	1207	46.4	53	S
To the Fringed Gentian—William C. Bryant	297	48.1	297	60.8	594	54.5	19	S
To the Moon—William H. Davies	411	37.2	455	46.4	866	41.8	16	R
To Think—Elizabeth J. Coatsworth	393	44.4	404	62.0	797	53.2	15	R
Tracks in the Snow—Ernest T. Seton	373	61.7	391	44.4	764	53.1	11	R
Tract for Autos, A—Arthur Guiterman	313	83.9	348	86.9	661	85.4	17	R
Trader Horn Hunts Leopards—A. Horn and E. Lewis	244	71.5	260	65.4	504	68.5	14	R
Trailing Arbutus, The—John G. Whittier	562	60.4	564	73.6	1126	67.0	39	S
Trail of the Sandhill Stag, The— Ernest T. Seton	434	84.0	356	76.3	790	80.2	28	S
Trail Signs and Indian Signals— Ernest T. Seton	436	75.2	389	58.7	825	67.0	10	R
Trap-Lines North—Stephen W. Meader	253	87.2	31				92	IR
Travel—Edna St. V. Millay	244	56.8	267	65.7	511	61.3	15	R
Travelling Around Home—Donald C. Peattie	270	50.9	290	46.2	560	48.6	14	R
Travelling Man, The—Isabella A. Gregory	362	86.9	324	91.4	686	89.2	13	R
Treasure Island—Robert L. Stevenson	3485	90.3	2840	77.8	6325	84.1	274	S
Treasurer's Report, The—Robert Benchley	321	62.0	330	68.7	651	65.4	17	R
Trees—Joyce Kilmer	1277	71.3	1137	85.1	2414	78.2	110	S
Trial in Tom Belcher's Store, The— Samuel A. Derieux	243	89.1	265	91.7	508	90.4	15	S
Triumph of Night, The—Edith Wharton	193	57.3	215	68.4	408	62.9	20	S

PUPILS' READING INTERESTS: GRADES 7-9

Ts and Ss = Teachers and Schools   S = Studied in Class
IR = Independent Reading   R = Read in Class

SELECTION—AUTHOR	Boys		Girls		Total		Ts & Ss	
	No.	%	No.	%	No.	Av. %		
Troop of the Guard, A—Hermann Hagedorn	336	54.2	316	55.2	652	54.7	13	R
Tropic Rain—Robert L. Stevenson	266	50.9	215	53.5	481	52.2	19	S
Trouble After School—Jerrold Beim	117	77.4	187	73.0	304	75.2		
Troy Unearthed—Marion F. Lansing	258	62.8	289	61.9	547	62.4	12	R
Try Again—William E. Hickson	535	53.8	512	65.9	1047	59.9	14	R
Trysting Place, The—Booth Tarkington	249	72.5	267	90.3	516	81.4	24	S
Tubby Hook—Arthur Guiterman	382	68.9	356	81.3	738	75.1	18	R
Tuft of Flowers, The—Robert Frost	224	40.8	251	60.8	475	50.8	17	S
Tulip Garden, A—Amy Lowell	204	44.6	213	67.1	417	55.9	17	S
Turkey Drive, The—Dallas L. Sharp	337	74.9	366	68.0	703	71.5	27	R
Turkey Red—Frances G. Wood	310	60.5	382	65.6	692	63.1	27	S
Turkish Legend, A—Thomas B. Aldrich	311	64.5	331	71.1	642	67.8	21	S
Turkish Trench Dog—Geoffrey Dearmer	516	56.7	518	56.8	1034	56.8	21	R
Turning the Grindstone—Benjamin Franklin	1158	80.3	1203	83.2	2361	81.8	49	R
Turquois Necklace, The—Alice C. D. Riley	335	68.7	338	85.8	673	77.3	12	R
Tutor, A—Carolyn Wells	440	66.9	444	79.3	884	73.1	22	R
Twa Corbies, The (British Ballad)	361	52.1	329	58.5	690	55.3	22	S
Twa Sisters (British Ballad)	371	34.9	350	55.9	721	45.4	26	S
Twenty-five Years of Flight—A. M. Jacobs	354	83.8	349	58.9	703	71.4	12	R
Twenty-one Balloons—William du Bois	172	74.7	267	68.2	439	71.5	111	IR

PUPILS' READING INTERESTS: GRADES 7-9
Ts and Ss = Teachers and Schools   S = Studied in Class
IR = Independent Reading   R = Read in Class

SELECTION—AUTHOR	Boys		Girls		Total		Ts & Ss	
	No.	%	No.	%	No.	Av. %		
Twenty Thousand Leagues Under the Sea— Jules Verne	520	88.0	155	77.1	675	82.6	189	IR
Twice-Told Tales— Nathaniel Hawthorne	139	71.2	227	69.2	366	70.2	92	IR
Twins, The—Henry S. Leigh	12237	87.8	12256	94.8	24493	91.3	477	R
'Twixt 12 and 20—Pat Boone	43		209	80.4				
Two Crooks and a Lady —Eugene Pillot	487	85.9	497	84.7	984	85.3	34	S
Two Little Confederates —Thomas N. Page	220	76.6	251	78.9	471	77.8	91	IR
Two Little Savages— Ernest T. Seton	185	79.7	177	75.7	362	77.7	218	IR
Two Opinions—Eugene Field	273	68.7	326	69.9	599	69.3	25	S
Two Sewing—Hazel Hall	297	23.4	276	37.1	573	30.3	16	R
Two Sparrows—Humbert Wolfe	250	51.6	237	63.8	487	57.7	13	R
Two Years Before the Mast—Richard H. Dana	617	76.8	483	49.0	1100	62.9	66	S
Ugly Wild Boy, The— Frank H. Cushing	290	66.7	306	75.5	596	71.1	11	R
Ulysses and Polyphemus —Charles Lamb	269	83.3	273	72.2	542	77.8	14	R
Uncle Remus—Joel C. Harris	221	67.9	314	69.1	535	68.5	105	IR
Uncle Reuben—Selma Lagerlöf	300	56.5	226	68.6	526	62.6	13	R
Uncle Tom's Cabin— Harriet B. Stowe	701	85.8	905	87.2	1606	86.5	108	IR
Understood Betsy— Dorothy C. Fisher	17		301	76.6			53	IR
Under the Barber's Knife —Stephen Leacock	311	67.8	281	65.1	592	66.5	12	R
Under the Lilacs—Louisa M. Alcott	31		460	78.6			57	IR
Under the Sea—John D. Craig	368	92.5	336	90.6	704	91.6	17	R

PUPILS' READING INTERESTS: GRADES 7-9

Ts and Ss = Teachers and Schools   S = Studied in Class

IR = Independent Reading   R = Read in Class

SELECTION—AUTHOR	Boys		Girls		Total		Ts & Ss	
	No.	%	No.	%	No.	Av. %		
Under Two Flags—Ouida	252	71.8	71	71.1	323	71.5		
Underwater Adventure—Willard deM. Price	398	81.0	98	72.4	496	76.7		
Union and Liberty—Oliver W. Holmes	249	68.9	252	70.6	501	69.8	29	S
Unrhymed Limerick, An—William S. Gilbert	862	62.5	880	62.1	1742	62.3	31	R
Untouchables, The—Ness and Fraley	333	92.3	150	83.0	483	87.7		
Up from Slavery—Booker T. Washington	205	70.5	188	77.9	393	74.2		
Up Front—Bill Mauldin	143	83.9	33					
Up Mount Everest—Marion F. Lansing	314	74.5	326	65.6	640	70.1	13	R
Upon Westminster Bridge—William Wordsworth	741	35.3	716	42.5	1457	38.9	28	R
Up the Trail from Texas—J. Frank Dobie	196	62.0	42					
Vagabond, The—Robert L. Stevenson	383	47.5	403	56.6	786	52.1	17	R
Vagabond Song, A—Bliss Carman	899	58.3	621	73.9	1520	66.1	64	S
Vain King, The—Henry Van Dyke	264	52.8	270	53.3	534	53.1	14	R
V-A-S-E, The—James J. Roche	320	46.7	370	60.8	690	53.8	16	R
Velvet Shoes—Elinor Wylie	520	29.5	525	43.2	1045	36.4	18	R
Vicar of Bray, The—Langford Reed	555	50.4	593	54.7	1148	52.6	23	R
Victory in Defeat—Edwin Markham	510	31.0	516	41.5	1026	36.3	24	R
Village Blacksmith, The—Henry W. Longfellow	333	71.5	275	78.0	608	74.8	23	S
Violet, Sweet Violet—James R. Lowell	169	50.9	171	70.8	340	60.9	15	R
Violin Maker of Cremona, The—François Coppée	267	69.9	249	81.3	516	75.6	19	S

PUPILS' READING INTERESTS: GRADES 7-9
Ts and Ss = Teachers and Schools   S = Studied in Class
IR = Independent Reading   R = Read in Class

SELECTION—AUTHOR	Boys		Girls		Total		Ts & Ss	
	No.	%	No.	%	No.	Av. %		
Virginian, The—Owen Wister	438	80.7	386	83.0	824	81.9	26	S
Virginia Reed, Midnight Heroine of the Plains— Kate D. Sweetser	235	86.2	209	91.4	434	88.8	16	R
Vision, A—Alfred Tennyson	395	46.3	375	52.8	770	49.6	16	R
Vision of Sir Launfal, The—James R. Lowell	1297	63.2	1457	66.2	2754	64.7	138	S
Visit from St. Nicholas, A —Clement C. Moore	493	60.5	462	72.3	955	66.4	9	R
Vive La France— Charlotte H. Crawford	354	64.1	281	72.6	635	68.4	20	R
Volcanoes—William M. Reed	238	65.3	281	59.8	519	62.6	13	R
Voyages of Dr. Dolittle, The—Hugh Lofting	247	84.6	267	74.3	514	79.5	43	IR
Vulture, The—Hilaire Belloc	663	58.8	630	65.2	1263	62.0	29	R
Waiting—John Burroughs	294	42.7	301	56.6	595	49.7	21	R
Waiting at the Window— A. A. Milne	399	55.5	379	67.3	778	61.4	17	R
Walking Man, The— Henry H. Knibbs	280	72.7	280	67.0	560	69.9	14	R
Walrus and the Carpenter, The—Lewis Carroll	166	68.4	218	58.0	384	63.2	15	S
Wanderer's Song, A— John Masefield	284	64.1	262	66.0	546	65.1	14	R
Wander Thirst—Gerald Gould	396	56.3	288	67.2	684	61.8	23	R
Wan Lee, the Pagan— Bret Harte	273	73.6	253	67.4	526	70.5	16	R
War of the Worlds—H. G. Wells	773	86.7	110	71.8	883	79.3		
Washington—James R. Lowell	868	49.4	811	50.1	1679	49.8	36	R
Washington on Horseback—Henry A. Ogden	195	73.8	141	69.1	336	71.5	41	IR

PUPILS' READING INTERESTS: GRADES 7-9

Ts and Ss = Teachers and Schools   S = Studied in Class
IR = Independent Reading   R = Read in Class

SELECTION—AUTHOR	Boys		Girls		Total		Ts & Ss	
	No.	%	No.	%	No.	Av. %		
Watcher in the Woods, A —Dallas L. Sharp	270	63.0	268	48.2	538	55.6	24	S
Watch Woman, The — Unknown	306	48.9	310	56.0	616	52.5	14	R
Water Clock, The— Frederick Kummer	324	80.1	309	84.0	633	82.1	14	R
Waterless Mountain— Laura Armer	76		212	68.0			101	IR
Ways of Chipmunks, The —Francis Harper	261	75.9	276	63.9	537	69.9	17	R
We—Charles A. Lindbergh	597	79.3	301	74.3	898	76.8	87	IR
Weapons—John R. Tunis	201	73.4	12					
Wear and Tear—Robert L. Stevenson	428	52.7	470	54.8	898	53.8	16	R
Weaver Maiden and the Herdsman, The (Chinese Myth)	357	51.3	357	67.5	714	59.4	18	S
We Capture Gorillas Alive—Martin Johnson	355	89.9	403	78.3	758	84.1	14	R
Wee Wee Man, The— Unknown	258	52.5	230	57.8	488	55.2	17	S
Wee Willie Winkie— Rudyard Kipling	1008	74.7	1111	81.9	2119	78.3	75	S
Well of St. Keyne, The— Robert Southey	581	62.6	602	72.9	1183	67.8	40	S
We Meet at Morn—H. D. Rawnsley	300	53.8	193	64.5	493	59.2	16	R
West Point Plebe— Russell P. Reeder	263	77.6	81	77.2	344	77.4		
West Point Story— Russell P. Reeder	385	79.2	101	78.2	486	78.7		
Westward Ho!—Charles Kingsley	279	78.7	176	69.6	455	74.2	64	IR
West Wind, The—John Masefield	509	61.5	275	75.8	784	68.7	34	S
What America Means to Me—Letta E. Thomas	171	69.6	187	77.8	358	73.7	15	S
What Brings Them Home?—John F. Vance	280	78.9	298	68.0	578	73.5	12	R

PUPILS' READING INTERESTS: GRADES 7-9

Ts and Ss = Teachers and Schools	S = Studied in Class
IR = Independent Reading	R = Read in Class

SELECTION—AUTHOR	Boys		Girls		Total		Ts & Ss	
	No.	%	No.	%	No.	Av. %		
What Constitutes a State?—William Jones	297	32.5	280	37.7	577	35.1	17	R
What Is Good?—John B. O'Reilly	11909	61.0	12066	75.8	23975	68.4	470	R
What Katy Did—Susan Coolidge	14		180	66.4				
What the Earliest Men Did for Us— William Burnham	324	67.6	327	62.2	651	64.9	26	R
What Was It?— Fitz-James O'Brien	375	75.3	341	78.4	716	76.9	31	S
What Will Power Did for Me—Unknown	428	77.9	397	80.5	825	79.2	26	S
When Icicles Hang by the Wall— William Shakespeare	717	52.1	725	61.5	1442	56.8	28	R
When Knighthood Was in Flower—Charles Major	169	55.0	154	64.0	323	59.5		
When Knights Were Bold—Eva M. Tappan	259	60.4	134	56.7	393	58.6		
When Malindy Sings— Paul L. Dunbar	300	77.0	285	88.1	585	82.6	18	S
When Nature Wants a Man—Angela Morgan	303	58.4	259	63.5	562	61.0	23	S
When One Loves Tensely—Don Marquis	388	58.0	441	62.9	829	60.5	19	R
When Patty Went to College—Jean Webster	5		355	85.1			83	IR
When the Frost Is on the Punkin—James W. Riley	367	68.3	391	73.8	758	71.1	15	R
When We Were Very Young—A. A. Milne	90	62.2	285	69.1	375	65.7	79	IR
Where But in America— Oscar M. Wolff	221	57.5	272	77.4	493	67.5	17	S
"Where Did You Go?" "Out." "What Did You Do?" "Nothing."—Robert P. Smith	146	79.8	251	75.7	397	77.8		

PUPILS' READING INTERESTS: GRADES 7-9
Ts and Ss = Teachers and Schools   S = Studied in Class
IR = Independent Reading   R = Read in Class

SELECTION—AUTHOR	Boys		Girls		Total		Ts & Ss	
	No.	%	No.	%	No.	Av. %		
Where Love Is, There God Is Also— Leo Tolstoy	344	78.1	330	87.3	674	82.7	21	R
Whipped by Eagles— Dallas L. Sharp	197	83.0	269	77.0	466	80.0	13	S
Whistle, The—Benjamin Franklin	582	50.9	596	57.1	1178	54.0	31	R
Whistling Stallion, The— Stephen Holt	149	74.5	173	78.3	322	76.4		
White Company, The— A. Conan Doyle	221	71.7	158	68.3	379	70.0	56	IR
White Fang—Jack London	419	93.2	201	82.8	620	88.0	124	IR
White-Footed Deer, The—William C. Bryant	427	77.0	403	82.8	830	79.9	16	R
White Horse Winter— Wilbur D. Steele	226	69.9	186	66.7	412	68.3	14	R
White House Gang, The —Earl Looker	230	78.7	239	80.8	469	79.8	56	IR
White Indian Boy, The— E. N. Wilson and H. R. Driggs	162	80.2	138	79.0	300	79.6	173	IR
White Mustang, The—S. Omar Barker	340	76.3	394	70.4	734	73.4	25	S
White Panther, The— Theodore J. Waldeck	170	84.7	114	72.4	284	78.6		
White Stag, The—Kate Seredy	239	81.6	265	84.2	504	82.9	133	IR
White Tiger, The— Samuel Scoville, Jr.	363	86.4	385	85.8	748	86.1	14	R
"Who Hath a Book"— Wilbur D. Nesbit	236	46.0	279	53.9	515	50.0	19	R
Who Is My Neighbor?— The Bible	296	82.9	263	86.1	559	84.5	13	R
Whoopee, Ti Yi Yo (Cowboy Ballad)	405	73.8	443	71.4	848	72.6	23	R
Who Owns the Mountains?—Henry Van Dyke	814	36.2	747	41.4	1561	38.8	26	R

PUPILS' READING INTERESTS: GRADES 7-9
Ts and Ss = Teachers and Schools   S = Studied in Class
IR = Independent Reading   R = Read in Class

SELECTION—AUTHOR	Boys		Girls		Total		Ts & Ss	
	No.	%	No.	%	No.	Av. %		
Why Bother with Ladders?—Lavina R. Davis	391	91.6	440	90.0	831	90.8	22	R
Why Tigers Can't Climb—Arthur Guiterman	229	70.3	221	70.8	450	70.6	15	S
Wide, Wide World, The —Susan Warner	164	63.4	155	56.8	319	60.1		
Wife of Usher's Well, The (British Ballad)	266	49.6	378	59.9	644	54.8	17	S
Wilbur and Orville Wright—Hermann Hagedorn	241	87.6	98	79.1	339	83.4	73	IR
Wild Animals I Have Known—Ernest T. Seton	256	79.3	155	71.9	411	75.6	137	R
Wild Bees, The—Henry Van Dyke	347	50.6	372	57.7	719	54.2	23	S
Wild Bill Hickok—Doris S. Garst	934	69.3	428	56.8	1362	63.1		
Wildfire—Zane Grey	260	87.1	137	81.0	397	84.1	98	IR
Wild Goat's Kid, The— Liam O'Flaherty	246	79.3	288	76.2	534	77.8	27	S
Wild Horse, The—Glenn Balch	158	72.2	226	81.4	384	76.8		
Wild Thoroughbred, The —Enos A. Mills	210	88.8	175	76.3	385	82.6	17	S
William Tell and the Apple—Friedrich von Schiller	221	68.6	215	66.5	436	67.6	17	R
Willow, Titwillow— William S. Gilbert	298	40.1	344	58.0	642	49.1	14	R
Will Rogers—Patrick J. O'Brien	678	84.4	491	84.7	1169	84.6	198	IR
Wind and the Window Flower, The— Robert Frost	562	33.9	519	48.5	1081	41.2	21	R
Wind Blew Shrill and Smart, The— Robert L. Stevenson	283	52.5	327	50.9	610	51.7	20	S

PUPILS' READING INTERESTS: GRADES 7-9
Ts and Ss = Teachers and Schools   S = Studied in Class
IR = Independent Reading   R = Read in Class

SELECTION—AUTHOR	Boys		Girls		Total		Ts & Ss	
	No.	%	No.	%	No.	Av. %		
Wind-in-the-Hair and Rain-in-the-Face— Arthur Guiterman	363	46.1	318	56.8	681	51.5	20	S
Wind in the Willows, The—Kenneth Grahame	172	66.9	431	70.6	603	68.8		
Windmill, The—Henry W. Longfellow	309	51.1	326	56.6	635	53.9	15	R
Window Pain, The— Gelett Burgess	426	42.5	468	51.0	894	46.8	16	R
Wings—Unknown	340	88.8	139	79.5	479	84.2	142	IR
Wings Rampant—Burr Layson	151	88.1	139				32	R
Winner Who Did Not Play, The— Merritt P. Allen	221	84.6	202	85.9	423	85.3	20	S
Winnie the Pooh—A. A. Milne	187	76.5	381	75.2	568	75.9	67	IR
Win or Lose—Bayard D. York	246	77.0	287	71.1	533	74.1	22	S
Winter Dusk—Sara Teasdale	263	53.8	238	68.1	501	61.0	18	S
Wish, A—Samuel Rogers	383	36.2	375	51.3	758	43.8	13	R
Witch of Blackbird Pond, The—Elizabeth G. Speare	30		172	84.0				
With the Photographer— Stephen Leacock	273	70.3	262	85.9	535	78.1	13	R
Wolfe's Victory and Death—Francis Parkman	287	73.7	302	56.0	589	64.9	14	R
Wolf, the Storm Leader —Frank Caldwell	262	90.5	163	80.1	425	85.3	140	IR
Woman's Will—Unknown	7515	62.8	7546	81.0	15061	71.9	278	R
Women, The— Aristophanes	263	52.7	301	74.1	564	63.4	12	R
Wonder Book, The— Nathaniel Hawthorne	157	75.8	229	76.1	386	76.0	107	IR
Wonderful Adventures of Nils, The— Selma Lagerlöf	126	73.1	195	69.2	321	71.2	321	IR

PUPILS' READING INTERESTS: GRADES 7-9
Ts and Ss = Teachers and Schools   S = Studied in Class
IR = Independent Reading   R = Read in Class

SELECTION—AUTHOR	Boys		Girls		Total		Ts & Ss	
	No.	%	No.	%	No.	Av. %		
Wonderful Tar Baby, The—Joel C. Harris	690	67.0	980	67.2	1670	67.1		
Wonderful Wizard of Oz, The—L. Frank Baum	749	74.4	972	81.7	1721	78.1	63	IR
Woodman, Spare That Tree—George P. Morris	417	58.5	421	66.2	838	62.4	24	R
Woodpeckers' Psychology, The—Edwin E. Slosson	373	39.5	325	43.7	698	41.6	9	R
Wood-Pile, The—Robert Frost	398	51.9	383	44.5	781	48.2	12	R
Work—Henry Van Dyke	466	70.0	239	65.5	705	67.8	25	S
Work: a Song of Triumph —Angela Morgan	350	60.1	95	61.6	445	60.9	17	S
Working Together in a Democracy— Theodore Roosevelt	218	54.8	236	47.2	454	51.0	15	S
World Almanac	496	75.9	390	71.5	886	73.7		
Wreck of the "Hesperus," The— Henry W. Longfellow	646	74.7	745	81.9	1391	78.3	52	S
Wreck of the "Julie Plante," The— William H. Drummond	259	72.8	259	80.1	518	76.5	22	S
Wright Brothers, The— Fred C. Kelly	178	73.9	99	61.6	277	67.8		
Wrights Fly, The— Mitchell V. Charnley	440	82.8	380	62.9	820	72.9	16	R
Written in March— William Wordsworth	4184	51.7	4145	60.1	8329	55.9	184	R
Wrong Road, The— Marquis James	321	78.8	332	66.7	653	72.3	17	R
Wuthless Dog, The— Franklin Holt	290	91.2	293	86.7	583	89.0	14	S
Wynken, Blynken, and Nod—Eugene Field	416	39.5	383	58.2	799	48.9	21	R
Yankee Doodle (Song)	896	78.0	1051	77.7	1947	77.9	77	IR

PUPILS' READING INTERESTS: GRADES 7-9
Ts and Ss = Teachers and Schools   S = Studied in Class
IR = Independent Reading   R = Read in Class

SELECTION—AUTHOR	Boys		Girls		Total		Ts & Ss	
	No.	%	No.	%	No.	Av. %		
Yarn of the "Nancy Bell," The— William S. Gilbert	543	76.2	940	75.2	1483	75.7	44	S
Yea!! Wildcats!—John R. Tunis	417	80.5	112	76.8	529	78.7	108	IR
Yearling, The—Marjorie K. Rawlings	539	75.1	645	79.5	1184	77.3		
Year the Yankees Lost the Pennant, The— Douglas Wallop	505	81.3	199	74.9	704	78.1		
Yellow Violet, The— William C. Bryant	376	35.8	424	51.1	800	43.5	25	S
Yim—William F. Kirk	342	63.3	363	74.7	705	69.0	16	R
You Are the Hope of the World—Hermann Hagedorn	569	59.1	547	58.4	1116	58.8	36	R
Young Beichan (British Ballad)	381	61.4	363	72.3	744	66.9	25	S
Young Englishwoman Named St. John, A— Unknown	366	38.3	387	42.0	753	40.2	15	R
Young Fellow, My Lad— Robert W. Service	294	89.1	339	93.2	633	91.2	15	R
Young Fu of the Upper Yangtze– Elizabeth F. Lewis	495	74.2	530	75.9	1025	75.1	112	IR
Young Hickory—Stanley Young	257	73.5	138	64.5	395	69.0		
Young Horseman, The— Lincoln Steffens	339	82.4	309	89.6	648	86.0	10	R
Young Lady of Niger, A —Cosmo Monkhouse	4089	80.3	4145	83.7	8234	82.0	179	R
Young Man in the City of Sioux, A— Unknown	376	59.6	391	67.3	767	63.5	14	R
Young Trailers, The— Joseph A. Altsheler	324	86.7	119	76.9	443	81.8	215	IR
Your Flag and My Flag— Wilbur D. Nesbit	254	63.7	245	74.5	499	69.1	13	R
Yussouf—James R. Lowell	466	63.9	468	62.6	934	63.3	32	S

PUPILS' READING INTERESTS: GRADES 7-9
Ts and Ss = Teachers and Schools   S = Studied in Class
IR = Independent Reading   R = Read in Class

SELECTION—AUTHOR	Boys		Girls		Total		Ts & Ss
	No.	%	No.	%	No.	Av. %	
Zebra Dun, The (Cowboy Ballad)	502	92.2	536	85.5	1038	88.9	19 R
Zenobia's Infidelity—H. C. Bunner	250	71.6	267	72.5	517	72.1	18 S

Appendix and Index

AUTHOR AND TITLE INDEX

Several hundred of the literary selections were tested in both the junior and senior high schools; they have two page references in the index. The first refers to the data for grades 10 to 12.

WILDE, Oscar
Happy Prince, 358
Importance of Being Earnest, 234
Requiescat, 280

WILDE, Percival
Confessional, 201
Finger of God, 218

WILDER, Laura I.
Little House in the Big Woods, 375
These Happy Golden Years, 416

WILDER, Thornton
Bridge of San Luis Rey, 193
Ides of March, 233
Our Town, 269
Skin of Our Teeth, 288

WILEY, Elinor
Pretty Words, 276

WILKINSON, Lupton A.
Miss Letitia's Profession, 256; 382

WILKINSON, Marguerite
Chant Out of Doors, 197

WILLIAMS and ABRASHKIN
Danny Dunn and His Homework Machine, 340

WILLIAMS, Ben A.
Sheener, 286; 405
They Grind Exceeding Small, 298

WILLIAMS, Jesse L.
Scrub Quarterback, 403

WILLSON, Meredith
Music Man, 258

WILMOT, J.
Epitaph on Charles II, 214

WILSON, E. N. and DRIGGS, H. R.
White Indian Boy, 427

WILSON, Sloan
Man in the Gray Flannel Suit, 251

WILSON, T. B. C.
In the City, 236

WILSON, Woodrow
Abraham Lincoln, 179; 316
New Freedom, 261

WIMBRIDGE, Eleanor R.
People of Moronia, 272

WINSLOW, Thyra S.
Birthday, 190

WINSOR, Kathleen
Forever Amber, 220

WISE, Winifred E.
Jane Addams of Hull House, 237

WISTER, Owen
Specimen Jones, 292
Virginian, 307; 424

WITHEROW , J. M.
Test, 297

WOLFE, Charles
Burial of Sir John Moore, 195; 331

WOLFE, Humbert
Two Sparrows, 422

WOLFE, Thomas
Look Homeward, Angel, 248

WOLFF, Oscar M.
Where But in America, 310; 426

WOOD, Frances G.
Turkey Red, 303; 421

WOOD, Henry
Lost Puppy, 377

WOODBRIDGE, Elizabeth
Searchings of Jonathan, 285

WOODWORTH, Samuel
Old Oaken Bucket, 265; 388

WOOLF, Virginia
Flush, 219

WOOLLCOTT, Alexander
Father Duffy, 217; 348

WORDSWORTH, William
Daffodils, 204; 339
It Is a Beauteous Evening, 237
Lines Composed a Few Miles above Tintern Abbey, 246
Lines Written in Early Spring, 246
London, 1802, 248
Lucy Gray, 250; 378
Michael, 255
My Heart Leaps Up, 259; 384
Ode on Intimations of Immortality, 263
She Dwelt Among the Untrodden Ways, 286
She Was a Phantom of Delight, 286
Solitary Reaper, 290; 408
Sonnets, 291
To the Cuckoo, 419

Wide Individual Reading Compared with the Traditional Plan of Studying Literature

THERE IS WIDESPREAD AGREEMENT THAT ONE OF THE CRUCIAL purposes of the teaching of literature is to promote a permanent reading habit based on a love of reading. That many of the literary selections commonly used in classrooms are not suited to promoting this habit is also well known, as the result of studies made by Abbott,[1] Burch,[2] Crow,[3] and many other investigators. Originally, no doubt, college-entrance requirements were responsible for the materials and indirectly, for the methods used in literature classes in high

George W. Norvell, New York State Education Department. Reprinted from *The School Review*, Vol. XLIX, No. 8, October, 1941.

[1]Allan Abbott, "Reading Tastes of High-School Pupils," *School Review*, (October, 1902), 585–600.
[2]Mary Crowell Burch, *Determination of a Content of the Course in Literature of Suitable Difficulty for Junior and Senior High School Students.* Genetic Psychology Monographs, Vol. IV, Nos. 2 and 3. Worcester, Massachusetts: Clark University, 1928.
[3]Charles Sumner Crow, *Evaluation of English Literature in the High School*, Teachers College Contributions to Education, No. 141. New York: Teachers College, Columbia University, 1924.

school. Yet the great revision of college-entrance requirements has not brought a corresponding change in secondary-school courses in literature. While tradition has, in part, been responsible, another powerful deterrent to the substitution of the wide reading of materials interesting to pupils for the intensive study of a few classics has been the general and deeply felt doubt whether the proposed plan would secure the other important ends of the study of literature even though it promoted the reading habit.

Plans with emphasis on reading have been tried in many schools and reported in educational periodicals. They have ranged from procedures that differed only slightly from the traditional line to procedures providing for reading so completely individualized that the classroom became a supervised reading-room, solely. In most instances evidence was not obtained to indicate the educational effectiveness of these plans. Questions that arose during the revision of the New York State *Syllabus in English for Secondary Schools*[1] pointed to the need for further investigation. As a result the study here reported was undertaken.

The writer was fortunate in securing the cooperation of teachers[2] in schools of all sizes and in communities of all types to be found in the state. In a number of instances teachers were chosen by department heads and were personally unknown to the writer. The returns of 10 teachers involving 24 classes that included 466 pupils were found to be usable.

PROCEDURES COMPARED

The more important procedures and conditions of the experiment are described in the following paragraphs.

Corresponding to each experimental class was a control class composed of pupils of equal capacity, as shown by the Thorndike-McCall Reading Scale for the Understanding of Sentences administered before the experimental procedures were undertaken. The paired classes were, in each instance, taught by the same teacher. The same amount of *class* time was devoted to the study of literature in corresponding control and experimental classes. A second form of the

---

[1] *Syllabus in English for Secondary Schools, Grades 7–12.* Albany, New York University of the State of New York Press, 1937.
[2] The following New York State teachers cooperated in the experiment described in this article: Elizabeth H. Buckley, Mary F. Burke, Marie D. Cox, Anna C. Fontanier, Jean Fraser, Lillian Gray, Florence S. Gottlieb, May M. Henry, Elizabeth von Kokerwitz, Elizabeth Law, Louise C. Maurer, Irene Meyers, Alice O'Connor, Cecelia O'Connor, Gertrude M. Pierce, Dorothy Pierman, Juliet B. Proulx, Marguerite Shephard, Isadore Simmons, Hazel Starr, and Earl C. Whitbeck.

Thorndike-McCall scale was given at the close of the experimental period, which lasted approximately one semester. Teachers kept records and made reports of methods and materials employed in both types of classes. All phases of the work, with the exception of literature, were taught by identical procedures in each pair of classes.

In the teaching of literature, each teacher used in his control class his customary methods and materials. While varying somewhat from teacher to teacher, these methods and materials were, in general, of the traditional type, with the following characteristics: (1) Selections for class study were uniform for all pupils. (2) Selections were few in number, were chosen largely from the classics, and were studied intensively. (3) The question-and-answer recitation was the outstanding classroom procedure though certain of the participating teachers encouraged considerable freedom in classroom discussion.

All the experimental classes were taught by a uniform procedure which will be briefly described. The *type* of literature (novel, drama, poetry, etc.) scheduled for the control class was taught also in the experimental class. The significant differences concerned both the particular literary selections used and the methods of presentation.

If poetry was to be taught, the typical control class used, for example, three or four of Milton's minor poems, selections from Browning or Tennyson, or some other traditional offering. The material was definitely limited in extent and was studied intensively by all pupils in the class. For the corresponding experimental class the instructions made markedly different provision. The teacher was asked to regard the period to be devoted to poetry as an opportunity to provide the pupil with an enjoyable and stimulating introduction to reading in the general field of poetry. In doing this, the instructor was reminded that a given high-school class is likely to have pupils with reading skills ranging from the fourth- or fifth-grade level to the college level and that individual tastes and interests are among the most formidable realities which must be met. From a list of short poems known through previous investigation to be well liked by nearly all pupils, the teacher was asked to choose one or more, as "The Highwayman" by Noyes or "O Captain! My Captain!" by Whitman, for reading and discussion by the class as a whole. The poems were not to be used to drill pupils in the technical aspects of poetics, to illustrate the peculiarities of a literary period, to provide a minute knowledge of background, or to point a moral lesson. They were to be read for enjoyment first and, second, for assisting pupils to overcome the very real difficulties of the neophyte in understanding what the poet says. Helping pupils to use their imaginations in dealing with condensed and figurative language, to expect and cope with the unusual in word order, to secure from rhythm the quickening that it can give, and to "read right over the capital letters" at the beginnings of lines are some of the ways in which teachers were asked to assist pupils to the formation of a profitable reading habit in the field of poetry. A key question in guiding the procedure was: "How can I be most helpful in preparing pupils for reading when their choices will be guided solely by their own purposes and interests?"

A few days at most were devoted to reading in common. Pupils were asked during the remaining weeks to follow individual tastes within very wide limits (set by the teacher) designed to exclude trashy materials. During this period pupils pursued personal reading interests both in and out of the classroom. From time to time a class period or a part of one was devoted to the free discussion characteristic of the literary club—discussion in which pupils frankly criticized what they had read, ranted about literary discoveries, argued heatedly over the challenging dicta of authors, and enjoyed the exhilaration of literary exploration. For pupils who desired to have a minimum assignment, the suggestion was made that not less than 150 pages of poetry be read during a period of three or four weeks. In the great majority of cases this minimum was greatly exceeded, as the records kept by teachers and pupils show. In the evaluation of the higher scores made by experimental classes, it should be noted that, while equal amounts of *class* time were devoted to the study of literature by the two groups, several times as many essays, poems, and other selections were read by pupils in experimental classes as by those in control classes. Further, the reports of pupils and teachers show that the experimental group voluntarily spent more time in out-of-class reading. That the greater pleasure and enthusiasm generated by reading materials of interest to them should lead these pupils by choice to spend more time, and that the time, unit for unit, should prove more productive than that employed in the required study of distasteful materials is in accordance with the psychology of learning.

RESULTS FOR ENTIRE GROUPS

Table 1 presents a summary of the evidence obtained. As mentioned earlier, 466 pupils were included in the 24 paired classes. Eighteen were eleventh- and twelfth-grades classes; six were tenth-grade. The average scores made in the first Thorndike-McCall test indicate the groups were equal at the start of the experiment. On the second form of the Thorndike-McCall test given at the close, the pupils in the control classes made an average gain of 1.03 points,

TABLE 1

MEAN SCORES ON THORNDIKE-MCCALL READING SCALE AND ON
REGENTS' EXAMINATION IN ENGLISH OBTAINED BY EXPERIMENTAL AND
CONTROL GROUPS

TEST	EXPER-MENTAL GROUP	CONTROL GROUP	DIFFER-ENCE	DIFF. P.E. diff.
Thorndike-McCall Reading Scale:				
Initial test	68.10	68.10		
Final test	70.58	69.13	1.45	3.53
Gain	2.48	1.03		
Regents' examination in English (141 pupils in each group)	77.24	75.51	1.73	2.90

while those in the experimental group made a gain of 2.48 points.

Corroborative evidence of the superiority of the experimental group is provided by results recorded by two of the teachers in their supplementary reports. One teacher gave the same examination on *Macbeth* to both classes. The control class had spent seventeen days on the play; the experimental class, five days. The median score for the control group was 84, and for the experimental group, 82. During the twelve days saved, the experimental group read several additional plays and thus added both to their reading skill and to their knowledge of literature; the control group apparently marked time. A second teacher reported that both classes studied *The Merchant of Venice*. "Although the control class took several days longer on the assignments, their tests at the end showed no better results in either knowledge or interpretation than did the tests of the experimental class." This evidence, so far as it goes, is in harmony with the results reported by Coryell.[1]

Fortunately it was possible to secure another check on results through the New York State Regents' examination in English. In this carefully supervised examination some of the questions are objective, some are semiobjective, and some are of the essay type. The papers are first rated by the local teacher in accordance with care-

[1]Nancy Gillmore Coryell, *An Evaluation of Extensive and Intensive Teaching of Literature*. Teachers College Contributions to Education, No. 275. New York: Teachers College, Columbia University, 1927.

fully prepared instructions and are then forwarded to the State Education Department, where they are re-rated by trained examiners.

So far as the present study is concerned, it is important to note that in any given pair of classes the same teacher rated the papers of both the experimental and the control groups. Further, these teachers did not know that the Regents' marks of their classes were to be compared. Any personal idiosyncrasies of the raters, therefore, presumably affected the results of the two sets of papers equally. The re-rating in Albany was done by examiners who were unaware that an experiment was in progress.

The Regents' examination was taken by 16 of the 24 classes and involved a total of 282 pupils. Table 1 shows that in this examination the experimental group had an average advantage of 1.73 points.

How significant, statistically, were the results of the examinations? Was the gain by the experimental group compared with the control group in the second Thorndike-McCall test sufficiently large to indicate a true difference in the results secured through the experimental procedure, or would further testing with other classes probably reduce or reverse the results? To answer this question the difference was divided by the probable error of the difference. Since pupils were paired in all classes, the formula used to find the probable error of the difference was the one appropriate when correlated means are available. The obtained difference between the average scores was 1.45, and the difference divided by the probable error of the difference between the average scores on the second form of the Thorndike-McCall scale was found to be 3.53. This quotient may be interpreted to mean that there are 99 chances in 100[1] that the difference in scores made in the second Thorndike-McCall test by the experimental group as compared with the control group is due to the use of the experimental materials and procedures.

Was the difference in Regents' scores made by the experimental group as compared with the control group sufficiently large to be significant? The quotient of the difference divided by the probable error of the difference (2.90) may be interpreted to mean that the chances are 97.5 in 100 that there is a true difference greater than zero. Put another way: the chances are 97.5 in 100 that the better scores secured by the experimental groups in the Regents' examination were due to the use of the experimental materials and methods.

[1]Henry E. Garrett, *Statistics in Psychology and Education*, Table 35, p. 214. New York: Longmans, Green & Co., 1937 (revised).

RESULTS FOR SUPERIOR AND WEAK PUPILS

Since the adaptation of the materials and methods of instruction to the needs of individual pupils is an outstanding problem in modern teaching, it seemed desirable to determine the relative effectiveness of the two techniques when differences in pupil capacities are considered. The control and the experimental groups, therefore, were each divided for purposes of record-keeping into two equal sections on the basis of ability as shown by the first Thorndike-McCall test. This grouping made it possible to note the progress made by superior pupils as compared with weak pupils, as revealed both by the second Thorndike-McCall test and by the Regents' examination. Table 2 presents the results.

On the Thorndike-McCall test the average scores for the superior pupils show a marked increase in progress by the superior pupils in the experimental classes as compared with the superior pupils of the control group. The quotient of the difference divided by the probable error of the difference (5.03) indicates that the chances are 99.94 in 100 that there was a true difference for which the experimental procedure was responsible. Put another way: there is a high probability that the better scores on the second Thorndike-McCall test made by superior pupils who followed the experimental procedure as compared with the scores of the corresponding pupils in the control group were due to the experimental procedure.

TABLE 2

AVERAGE SCORES ON FINAL TEST OF THORNDIKE-McCALL READING
SCALE AND ON REGENTS' EXAMINATION IN ENGLISH OBTAINED BY
SUPERIOR AND SLOW PUPILS

TEST	EXPERIMENTAL GROUP		CONTROL GROUP		DIFFER-ENCE IN SCORES	$\frac{\text{DIFF.}}{\text{P.E. diff.}}$
	NUMBER OF PUPILS	MEAN SCORE	NUMBER OF PUPILS	MEAN SCORE		
Thorndike-McCall Reading Scale:						
Superior pupils	116	73.7	116	70.9	2.8	5.03
Slow pupils	117	67.4	117	67.3	0.1	
Regents' examination in English:						
Superior pupils	70	80.7	70	78.0	2.7	3.11
Slow pupils	71	73.8	71	73.1	0.7	

The average scores for corresponding groups of slow pupils indicate that *weak* groups apparently progress equally under the two procedures.

The average score on the Regents' examination made by superior pupils in experimental classes compared with that made by superior pupils in the control group shows that the chances are 98 in 100 that there was a true difference for which the experimental procedure was responsible. As was the case with the Thorndike-McCall test, the difference in average scores for the two weak groups (0.7) seems to indicate that for weak pupils the two methods are of substantially equal value, though with some advantage shown for the experimental approach.

It is interesting to note that, while the results of the experimental procedure as shown both by the Thorndike-McCall test and by the Regents' examination are much more favorable for superior than for weak pupils, the results of these tests are consistent both for superior and for weak pupils.

Another question might be asked: Granted that, on the *average*, weak pupils may make as much progress under the experimental as under the traditional procedure, may not pupils as individuals be at a disadvantage? Evidence on this point is provided by the fact that experimental and control groups had an equal number of failures in the Regents' examination, while the number falling below the score of 60 in the second Thorndike-McCall test was within one of the same number for the two groups. It seems a fair conclusion that weak pupils, as individuals, progress as satisfactorily under the experimental plan as under the traditional procedure.

REACTIONS OF PUPILS AND TEACHERS

For the purpose of determining the reaction of pupils in the experimental classes to the experimental procedures, all (233) were asked to answer "Yes" or "No" to four questions. The results, expressed in percentages, are given in Table 3.

It is interesting to note that, by their answers to Questions 1 and 3, pupils strongly (nine to one) approve the outstanding features of the experimental procedure, and by a vote of six to one (Question 2) condemn the traditional intensive study of literature. In view of the advocacy in some quarters of placing pupil reading on a completely individualized basis, the overwhelming indorsement of group discussion as a class procedure (Question 4) is significant.

The views of the teachers who carried out the experiment were secured also by means of a questionnaire. The questions which were of a type permitting summary, together with the teachers' replies,

TABLE 3

PERCENTAGE OF AFFIRMATIVE AND NEGATIVE REPLIES MADE BY PUPILS
IN EXPERIMENTAL GROUP TO QUESTIONNAIRE CONCERNING
PROCEDURE OF TEACHING LITERATURE BY WIDE READING

QUESTION	YES	NO
1. Do you approve the plan of using part of the time for reading one or more selections by all pupils in common and part of the time in reading additional selections chosen by the pupil himself?	91.4	8.6
2. Would you prefer that most of the class time should be used in recitations based on one or two books of literature studied intensively by all pupils (the commonly used type of procedure)?	14.6	85.4
3. Do you approve the plan of using a part of the class time for rather free and informal class discussion of the various materials pupils have been reading according to the plan used this semester?	90.2	9.8
4. Would you prefer that all class time in literature should be spent by pupils in silent reading with no time given to class discussion of the selections read?	3.7	96.3

are given in Table 4. (It should be noted that occasionally a teacher omitted the answer to a question.)

The question may be asked, "Did not teachers, perhaps, put greater enthusiasm into the work with the experimental classes and thus unintentionally influence the results?" While a positive reply cannot be made, there are considerations which indicate that any influence from this source was fully offset. Chief among these is the fact that in every control class the teacher's own method, developed over a period of years, was on trial. It should be remembered, also, that the teacher's plan, representing years of experience and the gradual accumulation of useful aids and techniques, would be more skilfully presented than an untried procedure.

TABLE 4

NUMBER OF TEACHERS GIVING REPLIES TO QUESTIONNAIRE
CONCERNING PREFERABLE PROCEDURE OF TEACHING LITERATURE

QUESTION	EXPERI-MENTAL	CONTROL	EQUAL
1. Of the two approaches to teaching, which is the more enjoyable to you as a teacher?	9	0	
2. In which of the two classes did			

QUESTION	EXPERI-MENTAL	CONTROL	EQUAL
pupils develop greater interest and enthusiasm?	9	0	
3. Below are listed certain objectives of the teaching of English. Indicate in which of the two classes concerned in this study the particular objective was best obtained			
a) To develop skill in reading both in speed and in comprehension	10	0	
b) To form a permanent reading habit based on a love of reading	9	1	
c) To become acquainted with the reading field including both books and periodicals	9	1	
d) To develop skill in making discriminating choices of reading materials	8	2	
e) To develop skill in the use of the tools of reading: the library including the card catalogue, reference books, the dictionary, the book index and table of contents	9	0	1
f) To understand human life and character	5	2	1
g) To develop high ideals and worthy standards of conduct	6	2	1
h) To promote a broader and deeper knowledge of American and English literature	9	1	
4. Assuming that the necessary materials were provided, would the plan outlined for the experimental class be more difficult to use than the one used in your control class?	(Yes) 0	(No) 9	
5. In your opinion, can the average teacher use the experimental plan with success?	(Yes) 8	(No) 0	

CONCLUSIONS

(1) The experimental procedure featuring wide reading is superior to the control (traditional) procedure in teaching literature in high

school to groups of unselected pupils and to groups of superior pupils. (2) The experimental procedure is equal to or slightly superior to the control (traditional) procedure in teaching literature in high school to groups of weak pupils. (3) Both superior and weak pupils prefer the experimental procedure to the traditional one. (4) Both superior and weak pupils strongly approve informal class discussion as a technique of class method. (5) Teachers who have tested it agree that the experimental procedure is superior to the traditional plan in being of interest to their pupils and to themselves and in attaining eight enumerated objectives of teaching literature. (6) Teachers have found the experimental procedure as easy to carry out as the traditional procedure.

INDEX

Abbott, Allan, 20, 176
Adult adventure, 35
  detective story, 43, 61, 64, 66
  nonfiction. *See* Chapter XV
Adults, reading interests of, 59–60, 67, 145, 173
  studies of, 174–75
Adventure
  adult, 35
  change of interest in, 43, 44
  grim, 63–64
  grim vs. mild, 61, 63, 64
  without grimness, 61, 64
  and love, 43
  nonfiction, 43
  poems of, 64
  and sex differences, 68
  as a special interest factor, 43, 61, 68
  war, 7, 43, 68
Age
  as a factor in selecting reading materials, 6, 32–40, 41–46, 49
  as an influence in reading interests, 6, 49
  and intelligence, 26–31
  and literary types, 34, 35, 38, 43–46, 49
  major trends in the element of, 32
  other studies of, 35–40
  and particular reading materials, 32
  and sex differences, 47, 48
Anderson, Roxanna E., 35, 176
Animals, 43, 64
  domestic, 43, 61, 64, 85
  as a special interest factor, 64, 68
  wild, 43, 59, 61, 64, 68
Artistry in literature. *See* Chapter IX; also 29, 43
  of minor importance to students, 54, 64, 68, 69, 86
Atkinson, Dora, 77, 176

Bernoulli distribution, 25
Biography. *See* Chapter XVI
  approved for boys, grades 7–9, 121
  approved for boys, grades 10–12, 118–19
  approved for girls, grades 7–9, 122
  approved for girls, grades 10–12, 119
  approved for mixed classes, grades 7–9, 120–21
  approved for mixed classes, grades 10–12, 118
  interest in, 51, 116, 171
  interest in, determined by sex, 49, 51
Boys' reading interests. *See* Sex differences. *Also see* Subjects favorable and unfavorable, to boys

Cancellation of minor factors, 48, 50
Change in reading interests
  amount and direction of, 32, 34, 40
  and applicability of interest scores, 34
  junior high vs. senior high students, 33, 42
  other studies of, 35–40
  rate of, 40
Characters as a special interest factor, 43, 64–65, 68
  female, 43, 64–65, 68
  male, 43, 64–65, 68
Classics, 83, 170
Collecting the data, 10–14
Comic magazines and comic strips, 85, 168, 170, 173
Community, influence of, on young people's reactions, 16–18
Conclusions of this research study, 85–87
Content of books, influence of, on readers' reactions, 54, 61, 64

APPENDIX A—BIOGRAPHICAL SKETCH

GEORGE WHITEFIELD NORVELL

Throughout his career in education as principal, superintendent, supervisor, teacher, George Norvell planned programs *with* teachers and students, and often with parents—all working as members of the team: whether the subject were original writing or speaking; community research projects; journals of investigations; source books—or other.

He *listened* when young people advocated reading newspaper comic strips and cartoons.

He *believed in* paperback clubs of well-liked books with their invitation to read widely for pleasure.

He *viewed* with understanding the devotion of youth and adults to the mass media of communication.

He *cited* from his research that aside from television and radio, periodicals are for the vast majority the principal source of information about the world;

that following school days the mass media provide the most important means of lifetime education for American citizens;

that few adults have developed plans for the efficient reading of newspapers.

He *advocated* that periodicals be included in regular, carefully-planned classroom programs.

Frequently he *returned* to his theme that to increase reading skill, promote the reading habit, and produce a generation of book-lovers, there is no factor so powerful as *interest.*

He *questioned* when is it possible that enthusiasm for secondary aims has blinded educators to the *great objective:* enjoyment of literature with its priceless reward, a life-long reading habit based on a love of reading?"

PLACE OF BIRTH: Hartford, South Dakota
EDUCATION: Dakota Wesleyan U., Mitchell, S. Dakota
                   Rhodes Scholar—Queen's College 1907–1910 Jurisprudence
GRADUATE WORK: U. of Colorado and Columbia U.

TRAVEL: Wales, Belgium, Holland, Germany, Bohemia, Austria, Switzerland, Italy, France
The United States, Provinces of Canada

SPORTS: Track athletics: sprint, broad jump, hurdles
Oxford: O.U.A.C. Freshmen's Sports 1907, hundred yards, second
Queens College Sports 1909, hundred yards, first; 1910 hurdles

PROFESSIONAL LIFE: Teacher, principal, superintendent of schools, in Colorado, 1910–1915. County Superintendent of Schools, Moffat Co., Colo., 1915–1919; Superintendent of Schools, Craig, Colo., 1923–24; Head, Dept. Eng., Beaumont, Texas, 1925–26; Director, Secondary Education, Beaumont City Schools, Texas, 1927–28; State Supervisor of English Education, New York State, Albany, 1928–55. (Retired, 1955)

PUBLICATIONS: *Syllabus in English (Ed.)*, U. of State of N. Y. Press, 1935;
Experiments in Reading (with others), Harcourt Brace, 1935;
Hidden Treasures in Literature (with others), Harcourt Brace, 1935;
Reading in the Secondary School Program, U. of State of N. Y. Press, 1940;
English Handbook for Teachers in Elementary Schools (Ed.), U. of State of N. Y. Press, 1941;
Conquest in Reading and Literature (4 Vols.—with others), D. C. Heath, 1947;
The Reading Interests of Young People, D. C. Heath & Co., 1950;
English in the Senior High School, U. of the State of N. Y. Press, 1955;
What Boys and Girls Like to Read, Silver Burdett Co., 1958;
Various magazine articles